ETHNICITY IN THE UNITED STATES

THE WILEY SERIES IN URBAN RESEARCH

TERRY N. CLARK, Editor

ETHNICITY IN THE UNITED STATES:

A Preliminary Reconnaissance

ANDREW M. GREELEY

Center for the Study of American Pluralism
National Opinion Research Center

A WILEY-INTERSCIENCE PUBLICATION

JOHN WILEY & SONS, New York • London • Sydney • Toronto

Library of Congress Cataloging in Publication Data:

Greeley, Andrew M   1928–
   Ethnicity in the United States.

   (Wiley series in urban research)
   "A Wiley-Interscience publication."
   Bibliography: p.
   1. Minorities—United States.   I. Title.

E184.A1G827   301.45′0973   74-11483
ISBN 0-471-32465-5

Printed in the United States of America

10 9 8 7 6 5 4 3 2 1

For NORA MAEVE McCREADY

The Wiley Series in Urban Research

Cities, especially American cities, are attracting more public attention and scholarly concern than at perhaps any other time in history. Traditional structures have been seriously questioned and sweeping changes proposed; simultaneously, efforts are being made to penetrate the fundamental processes by which cities operate. This effort calls for marshaling knowledge from a number of substantive areas. Sociologists, political scientists, economists, geographers, planners, historians, anthropologists, and others have turned to urban questions; interdisciplinary projects involving scholars and activists are groping with fundamental issues.

The Wiley Series in Urban Research has been created to encourage the publication of works bearing on urban questions. It seeks to publish studies from different fields that help to illuminate urban processes. It is addressed to scholars as well as to planners, administrators, and others concerned with a more analytical understanding of things urban.

TERRY N. CLARK

Contents

INTRODUCTION

T HIS BOOK is devoted to a preliminary exploration of diversity in American
society, a diversity that I call "ethnic." For two reasons, special emphasis
will be placed on "ethnic" diversity in the narrow sense of the word, that is,
diversity among the descendants of the white immigrant groups who came
from western Europe in the eighteenth, nineteenth, and early twentieth
centuries. The reasons are that I am especially interested in the European-
American ethnic groups, and that American social science either has ignored
or written off as unimportant the existence of these European-American
groups.

However, one cannot speak of the European-American ethnics and ignore
the context of the total ethnic diversity in the United States. Hence the broader
concern of this book is with that diversity in American society that most social
researchers overlook—that is, diversity not based on sex, age, or social class.

Although a preliminary effort that is a long way from being a definitive
volume on American ethnic diversity, this book is far more advanced, I hope,
than my *Why Can't They Be Like Us?* My colleagues and I at the National
Opinion Research Center (NORC) have spent the last two years clearing the
ground for further research on ethnic diversity. In this book I intend to report
on that ground clearing. I am confident that five or more years of research are
needed before any definitive work on American ethnic diversity can be written.
I hope that this book raises more question than it answers, but I trust that it
will be noted that some questions will be answered here, questions that here-
tofore have never been answered with the support of empirical evidence.

There ought to be no need to justify the study of ethnic diversity. As Fredrik
Barth notes:

> Practically all anthropological reasoning rests on the premise that
> cultural variation is discontinuous: that there are aggregates of
> people who essentially share a common culture, and interconnected
> differences that distinguish each such discrete culture from all
> others. Since culture is nothing but a way to describe human beha-
> viour, it would follow that there are discrete groups of people, i.e.
> ethnic units, to correspond to each culture. . . .
>
> It is clear that boundaries persist despite a flow of personnel across
> them. In other words, categorical ethnic distinctions do not depend
> on an absence of mobility, contact and information, but do entail
> social processes of exclusion and incorporation whereby discrete
> categories are maintained *despite* changing participation and
> membership in the course of individual life histories. Secondly, one
> finds that stable, persisting, and often vitally important social rela-
> tions are maintained across such boundaries, and are frequently

2

based precisely on the dichotomized ethnic statuses. In other words, ethnic distinctions do not depend on an absence of social interaction and acceptance, but are quite to the contrary often the very foundations on which embracing social systems are built. Interaction in such a social system does not lead to its liquidation through change and acculturation; cultural differences can persist despite inter-ethnic contact and interdependence.[1]

Ethnic boundaries may be more permeable in the United States than in the less industrialized societies that are the principal concern of Barth and his colleagues. But at least the hypothesis that ethnicity may be one of the "very foundations on which embracing social systems are built" in the United States is testable. That ethnic diversity has not been studied seriously in the United States may be the result of dogmatic a priori assumptions, perhaps mixed with the unconscious guilt many social scientists may feel for having left behind their own ethnic groups. Available empirical evidence clearly shows that there are still ethnic concentrations in the United States. Nathan Kantrowitz, in his study of residential segregation in the New York Standard Metropolitan Area, found remarkably high indexes of residential segregation among white European-born foreign stock (either foreign born or the children of foreign born parents—that is, first and second generations).[2] In Table 1 (Kantrowitz's Table 2.9), one notes for example an index of residential segregation[3] of 45.8 between foreign stock Norwegians and foreign stock Swedes, and 48.0 index between foreign stock Irish and foreign stock Italian. The data further reveal that the index of segregation between Norwegians and Russians is 72.9; between Russians and blacks, it is 81.8. There is, then, almost as much segregation between Norwegians and Russians (presumably most of them Jewish) as there is between Russians and blacks. Furthermore, Kantrowitz argues that there is little evidence of decline in these indexes of segregation. He predicts that when the 1970 census data become available for analysis, the picture will not be much altered from that reported by the 1960 census. Even granting that Kantrowitz is dealing with foreign stock and not with third and fourth generation Americans, the persistence of residential segregation among immigrants and their children into the 1960s is one reason to suggest that ethnic diversity in the United States is worthy of further study.

In a useful theoretical study, William Newman makes the point that the assimilation and pluralist models can coexist in complex societies. The assumption that they are mutually exclusive concepts for understanding American society cannot be accepted, and in the first part of this book I attempt to provide sufficient reason for suspending judgment on the question of whether assimilation is eliminating ethnic diversity in the United States.

Table 1. Indexes of Residential Segregation Between Selected Ethnicities (Foreign Stock) and Race, New York SMSA, 1960

Ethnicity and Race	United Kingdom	Ireland (Eire)	Nor-way	Swe-den	Ger-many	Poland	Czech-oslova-kia	Austria	Hungary	U.S.S.R.	Italy	Black	Puerto Rican
United Kingdom	—												
Ireland (Eire)	28.1	—											
Norway	51.4	58.7	—										
Sweden	31.8	41.3	45.8	—									
Germany	25.6	33.3	56.4	38.2	—								
Poland	45.0	51.7	67.9	57.9	47.1	—							
Czechoslovakia	39.5	44.5	65.6	51.1	39.5	41.7	—						
Austria	40.2	47.1	68.0	54.2	40.4	20.3	39.9	—					
Hungary	39.1	44.2	68.3	52.9	38.7	31.3	33.9	24.7	—				
U.S.S.R.	50.2	57.1	72.9	62.2	52.1	20.0	49.0	19.0	32.7	—			
Italy	44.9	48.0	60.2	51.9	45.6	52.7	51.6	53.0	53.9	60.5	—		
Black	80.3	80.3	88.4	83.7	80.6	79.7	81.9	81.1	80.4	81.8	80.5	—	
Puerto Rican	79.8	76.5	88.2	83.9	79.7	75.5	78.6	76.6	76.3	78.1	77.8	63.8	—

Source: U.S. Census of Population, 1960, U.S. Bureau of the Census. From *Ethnic and Racial Segregation in the New York Metropolis: Residential Patterns Among White Ethnic Groups, Blacks, and Puerto Ricans*. © 1973 by Praeger Publishers, Inc., New York. Excerpted and reprinted by permission.

Newman writes:

> What may be said of the concepts of assimilation and pluralism?
> Do they remain useful theoretical constructs or have they become
> useless intellectual products? Both terms remain useful if so-
> ciologists are willing to refrain from predicting the ultimate out-
> come of group relationships and the larger social process that those
> relationships constitute. Milton Gordon's identification of the
> subprocesses of assimilation and group coalitions remains useful as
> long as it is remembered that not all groups become "American" in
> the same way. Some groups become less culturally assimilated than
> others. Different groups will express these choices in terms of very
> different kinds of structural arrangements. In principle, there is
> nothing to prevent the eventual disappearance in the future of those
> racial, religious, and ethnic differences that have been souces of di-
> vision among America's social groups in the past. While it seems
> more likely that these kinds of differences will not disappear, they
> may become less important for the social fabric of a society that re-
> volves around new kinds of differences—differences in social class,
> occupational status, and social ideology. In other words, it is not
> more theoretically defensible to rule out the reemergence of old plu-
> ralisms than to rule out the emergence of new ones.
>
> Pluralism and assimilation remain useful concepts if they are
> viewed, not as absolutes, but as reciprocal aspects of group rela-
> tionships. Like social change and social order, group conflict and
> group consensus, pluralism and assimilation may be viewed as twin
> aspects of the social structure. For just as any given instance of
> social conflict may split two groups farther apart, it may at the very
> same time drive other groups closer together. Even as groups at-
> tempt to assimilate into the social, political, and economic
> mainstream of a society, they must organize and develop a sense of
> their group distinctiveness in order to enter the social process.[4]

It ought to be relatively easy to study ethnic diversity in the United States,
but it turns out not to be easy at all.

Because there has been so little research on the subject we lack theories,
methods, and data. In the next chapter, I suggest some reasons why there has
been so little research. Much of the rest of the book is devoted to trying to
develop theories and methods, and to presenting some of the data that my
colleagues and I have collected during two years of reconnaissance in the field.

The agreement between the Ford Foundation and the Center for the Study
of American Pluralism at NORC was that the first two years of our work
would be devoted mostly to secondary analysis of existing data to clarify what

seemed to be the important ethnic issues in American society and to create a more solid ground for further primary research. This book is a record of those first two years.

The first chapter is a statement of the preliminary organizing impressions with which my colleagues and I began. In subsequent chapters we address ourselves to certain specific and relatively simple questions about American diversity. These questions are more easily asked than answered. In Chapter 11, we gather together both our data and our thinking in what might be considered the beginning of a theoretical perspective. The intervening chapters recount the journey from the impressions of Chapter 1 to the perspective of Chapter 11. Finally, we turn our attention to the social policy implications of the "new" ethnic consciousness in the United States. (It is not new, of course, merely newly legitimated.) There, we stress particularly the so-called white ethnic movement.

The questions we will ask about ethnic diversity are:

1.   Who and where are the ethnics, and how many of them are there? (Chapter 2.)

2.   To what extent does the ethnic group play the role suggested by Barth (quoted in the beginning of this introduction)? Are American ethnic groups really the bearers of culture? Do they keep alive cultural traditions of the Old World? (Chapter 3.)

3.   Is the "ethnic factor" simply another version of the "religious factor"? Are those differences that are apparently ethnic in fact merely religious? (Chapter 5.)

4.   Does ethnicity make any difference in human behavior? Is whatever difference that might be observable merely the result of social class difference? In other words, is ethnicity merely a social class phenomenon, or does it have predictive power of its own, independent of social class? (Chapters 6 and 8.)

5.   How are ethnic differences transmitted from generation to generation? Do differences in family structure persist even among relatively acculturated groups in American society? (Chapter 7.)

6.   Are the white ethnics racists, bigots, hawks, and hard hats? Is there a white ethnic backlash? (Chapters 9 and 10.)

I cannot help feeling somewhat apologetic about these questions. It is fashionable in social research today to ask far more complicated questions. However, I would submit that one can ask complicated questions only when one has first answered the simple ones. The state of research on ethnic diversity in the United States is such that even the simple questions have not been answered. Knowing that it is the fashion among social scientists to refuse to be surprised at anyone else's findings, I am prepared to have the answers to our simple questions written off as being something that everyone knew all along. I would merely like to suggest at the beginning that a substantial body of social science opinion in the United States would argue that the Irish are still members of the lower middle class, that most of the European cultural heritages have disappeared in American society, that religion is a more important predictor of attitudes and behavior than ethnicity, that Italians are disproportionately blue-collar workers, that social class is a much more important predictor of family structure than ethnicity, and that ethnics tend to be hardhats, racists, and hawks. That all of these propositions are false may surprise not a few people.

My colleagues at the Center for the Study of American Pluralism have been so much involved in the work that has led to this book that it is impossible for me to distinguish what is their thought from what is mine. All I can do is to acknowledge their help and support. I must simply say, then, that I am grateful to David Greenstone, William McCready, Kathleen McCourt, Ilona Fabian, Douglas Zeman, Barbara Currie, Shirley Saldanha, and Ellen Sewell for all their help. I am also grateful to the two directors of NORC during the time this research was done. Norman Bradburn and James Davis encouraged and supported our work when it was both unfashionable and risky to do so. Professor Norman Nie, a senior study director at NORC, has infected all of us with his contagious enthusiasm, as well as providing us with immense amounts of intellectual and methodolical insight—to say nothing of the indispensable SPSS computer system. The chapter that bears his name and Barbara Currie's is far more theirs than mine.

Virginia Reich and Julie Antelman agonized over the typing of various drafts and the interminable stack of tables. Paige Wickland and Susan Campbell were responsible for proofreading; Susan Campbell also prepared the index.

Finally, William McCready is the author of one chapter and the junior author of two others. His close collaboration on the entire book lends him co-responsibility for the volume—though it remains to be seen whether that will be an asset or a liability to his career. It is to his daughter that the volume is dedicated. She is a tough little ethnic who should have no trouble at all shouldering the weight of her own "hurtage," to use the term of a fellow Chicago ethnic, Martin Dooley.

NOTES

1. Fredrik Barth, ed. *Ethnic Groups and Boundaries: The Social Organization of Culture Difference*. Boston: Little, Brown and Company, 1969. A Little, Brown Series in Anthropology, originally published in Norway for Scandinavian University Books, Universitetsfor-

laget, Bergen, Oslo, Tromso, and in the United Kingdom by George Allen & Unwin, London, pp. 9–10.

2. Nathan Kantrowitz. *Ethnic and Racial Segregation in the New York Metropolis: Residential Patterns Among White Ethnic Groups, Blacks, and Puerto Ricans.* New York: Praeger Publishers, Inc., 1973.

3. The index of residential segregation indicates the proportion of the population that would have to be redistributed so that both groups would be evenly spread throughout the area being measured.

4. William M. Newman. *American Pluralism: A Study of Minority Groups and Social Theory.* New York: Harper & Row, 1973, paperback ed., p. 182.

1. THE REDISCOVERY OF DIVERSITY

FOR THOSE OF US who read serious newspapers, magazines, and books, the most important conflict that has divided man in the last quarter century has been ideological. The critical question for us is where one stands in relationship to Karl Marx. We ask whether a man is a capitalist or a socialist, a "citizen of the free world" or one who lives "behind the Iron Curtain." Is he on the side of the "imperialists" or of the "peoples' democracies"? But in fact the conflicts that have occupied most men over the past two or three decades, those that have led to the most appalling outpourings of blood, have had precious little to do with this ideological division. Most of us are unwilling to battle to the death over ideology, but practically all of us it seems are ready to kill each other over noticeable differences of color, language, religious faith, height, food habits, and facial configuration.

Millions have died tragically in what are purported to be ideological conflicts in Korea and Vietnam, but more millions, perhaps as many as 20 million, have died in conflicts that have to do with far more ancient divisions than those separating capitalists and socialists. One need only think of the Hindus and Moslems at the time of the partition of India, of Sudanese blacks and Arabs, of Tutsi and Hutu in Burundi, of Kurds in Iraq, of Nagas in India, of Karens and Kachins in Burma, of Khambas in Tibet, of Somalis in Kenya and Ethiopia, of Arabs in Zanzibar, of Berbers in Morocco and Algeria, of East Indians and blacks in Guiana, of Ibos in Nigeria, and, more recently, of Bengalis in East Pakistan to realize how pervasive is what might be broadly called "ethnic" conflict and how incredible the numbers of people who have died in such "irrational" battles. Two million died in India, 500,000 perished in the "unknown" war in the Sudan, 200,000 in the equally unknown war in Burundi. The dead may exceed a million in Biafra, half a million in Malaysia and Indonesia. As many as 100,000 may have died in Burma and Iraq.

Ethnic conflicts have not been so bloody in other parts of the world, but tens of thousands have died in the seemingly endless battle between those two very Semitic people, the Jews and the Arabs. The English and French glare hostilely at each other in Quebec, Christians and Moslems have renewed their ancient conflicts on the island of Mindanao, Turks and Greeks nervously grip their guns on Cyprus, and Celts and Saxons in Ulster have begun to imprison and kill one another with all the cumulative passion of a thousand years hostility.

Even when there is practically no violence, tension and conflict still persist,

This chapter is a compilation of two articles: "The Rediscovery of Diversity," which appeared in *The Antioch Review* (Fall 1971), and "The New Ethnicity and Blue Collars," *Dissent* (Winter 1972).

as the old nationalisms of Wales, Scotland, Brittany, Catalonia and Navarre, Flanders, and even the Isle of Man are reasserted. In the socialist world, Great Slav and Little Slav do not trust each other, and Slav and Oriental have renewed their ancient feuds. Moreover, the rulers of the Slavic socialist states are troubled by internal conflict. What, for example, are the Great Russians to do about the Little Russians, much less about the Volga Germans or the Kahsacks, to say nothing of the Crimean Tartars? The new masters of Czechoslovakia still struggle with the ancient conflict between Prague and Bratislava. Finally, the old partisan leader, Marshall Tito, spends his last years trying desperately to hold his polyglot peoples' democracy together.

In a world of nuclear energy, the jet engine, the computer, and the rationalized organization, the principal conflicts are not ideological but tribal. Those differences among men that were supposed to be swept away by science and technology and political revolution are as destructive as ever.

Indeed, if anything, the conflicts seem to be increasing rather than decreasing. Just as the collapse of the Austro-Hungarian empire increased tension in central Europe, so the collapse of the old colonial empires has opened a Pandora's box of tribal, linguistic, religious, and cultural conflicts. It may be also the "turning in on oneself" that follows the relinquishing of imperial power that has given rise to the new nationalisms in western Europe. Finally, it seems that the failure of both capitalism and socialism to deliver on their promises of economic prosperity for all are responsible for the tensions both in eastern Europe and between black and white in the United States. Men were promised affluence and dignity if they yielded their primordial ties. They now suspect that the promise was an empty one and are returning to those primordial ties with a vengeance.

The differences over which we kill each other are relatively minor. It is not those who are tremendously different from us that we slay or hate; it is rather those similar to us. Punjabi and Bengali share the same religion; they differ only in geography and to some extent in skin color. A Canadian would be hard put to tell the difference between an Ibo, a Hausa, a Fulani, and a Yoruba. The difference between a French and English Canadian would escape all but the most sophisticated Yoruba. A Kurd could not tell a Fleming from a Walloon on a street in Brussels. Most Africans would be struck by the similarity in everything but skin color between American blacks and American whites. An American black, in his turn, would find it very difficult to tell the difference between Catholic brogue and Protestant brogue in Ulster. An Indonesian would be properly horrified at the thought that he resembled a Filipino, but he would not understand how a Greek could distinguish another Greek from a Turk, or even how one could tell the difference between a Jew and an Arab.

I sometimes speculate that the incredible diversity of the human race is a great joke of a humorous God; He finds it hilarious, but we are not laughing.

What is the nature of this primal diversity over which we so eagerly do battle? The question is a difficult one. With characteristic elegance, Clifford Geertz observes:

> When we speak of "communalism" in India we refer to religious contrasts; when we speak of it in Malaya we are mainly concerned with racial ones, and in the Congo with tribal ones. But the grouping under a common grouping is not simply adventitious; the phenomena referred to are in some way similar. Regionalism has been the main theme in Indonesian disaffection, differences in custom in Moroccan. The Tamil minority in Ceylon is set off from the Sinhalese majority by religion, language, race, region, and social custom; the Shiite minority in Iraq is set off from the dominant Sunnis virtually by an intra-Islamic sectarian difference alone. Land-national movements in Africa are largely based on race, in Kurdistan on tribalism; in Laos, the Shan, and Thailand, on language. Yet all these phenomena, too, are in some sense of a piece. They form a definable field of investigation.
>
> That is they would, could we but define it.[1]

But Geertz at least attempts a definition. Leaning on a concept introduced by Edward Shils,[2] Geertz suggests that what we are dealing with are "primordial attachments."

> By a primordial attachment is meant one that stems from the "givens"—or more precisely, as culture is inevitably involved in such matters, the "assumed" givens—of social existence: immediate contiguity and kin connection mainly, but beyond them, the givenness that stems from being born into a particular religious community speaking a particular language, or even a dialect of language, and following particular social patterns. These congruities of blood, speech, custom, and so on, are seen to have an ineffable, and at times overpowering, coerciveness in and of themselves. One is bound to one's kinsman, one's neighbor, one's fellow believer, *ipso facto*, as a result not merely of one's personal affection, practical necessity, common interest, or incurred obligation, but at least in great part by the virtue of some unaccountable absolute import attributed to the very tie itself. The general strength of such primordial bonds, and the types of them that are important, differ from person to person, from society to society, and from time to time. But for virtually every person, in every society, at almost all times, some attachments seem to flow more from a sense of natural—some would say spiritual—affinity than from social interaction.[3]

It is the primordial tie, then, a "longing not to belong to any other group," according to Geertz, that is essential to what is broadly defined as "ethnic" behavior.

Following Geertz, Professor Harold Isaacs speaks of "basic group identity," which is not merely related to a need to be special or unique or different from others; it is fundamental to an individual's sense of *belongingness* and to the level of his *self-esteem*.

> In my own mind, I picture group identity as looking more like a cell of living matter with a sprawling, irregular shape. It is a part of a cluster of cells making up the ego identity, sharing elements and common membranes with that other elusive quarry, the "individual personality." In it, floating or darting about, are specks and flecks, bits and pieces, big shapes, little shapes, intersecting each other or hanging loose or clinging to one another, some out at the margins, some nearer the middle, some in wide orbits around the edges, some more narrowly moving deeper inside, but each one impinging upon, drawn to or repelled by a nuclear core that exerts gravity upon them all and fixes the shape and content of the messages that go out along the tiny meshes of the nervous system. The arrangement and mutual relationship of these elements differ from cell to cell, and the nature of the nuclear core differs not only from cell to cell but can change within any one cell, all of these interactions having a fluid character and subject to alteration under the pressure of conditions that come in upon them from the outside.
>
> I think, in the inwardness of group identity is where we can learn more than we know now about the interactions of the individual, his group, and the larger politics of his time and place, and more, therefore, about the nature of our own contemporary experience.[4]

Isaacs, Geertz, and I are deeply indebted to Edward Shils for his ideas of primordial ties. In his famous article in the 1957 *British Journal of Sociology*, Shils comments:

> Man is much more concerned with what is near at hand, with what is present and concrete than with what is remote and abstract. He is more responsive on the whole to persons, to the status of those who surround him, and the justice which he sees in his own situation than he is with the symbols of remote persons, with the total status system in the society and with the global system of judgment. Immediately present authorities engage his mind more than remote ones. . . . That is why the ideologist, be he prophet or revolutionary, is affronted by the ordinary man's attachment to his mates, to his home, to his pub, to his family, to his petty vanities and his

> job, to his vulgar gratifications, to his concern for the improvement
> of his conditions of life. That is also why the ideologist dislikes the
> politician, who aspires to do no more than to help keep things run-
> ning and to make piecemeal change, and of course, the busi-
> nessman, the manager, the technologist who brooks an ultimate
> affront . . . [5]

The striking thing about the comments of Isaacs, Geertz, and Shils is that
they all use a rhetoric that is uncommonly poetic for the social sciences. Part of
the poetry is no doubt the result of the fact that the three men are masters of
English style, but part of it too, I suspect, comes from the fact that they are
dealing with something so basic and so fundamental in the human condition
that academic prose is not altogether adequate to deal with it.

Since the primoridal tie has to do with something that is so basic in man's
life, it is not at all a mystery that he is willing, indeed almost eager, to die in
the defense of it. As Isaacs has pointed out, much of what is evil in the human
condition—as well as much of what is good—flows from a man's primal sense
of *belonging* to something that makes him a *somebody*.

When we consider all the evil that stems from ethnic diversity, we are
strongly tempted to conclude that such diversity should be done away with.
Peace and harmony will come to the world through rational, liberal, scientific,
democratic homogenization. There was a time when such optimistic liberal
faith did not seem naïve. It must be confessed that many illustrious Americans
still subscribe to the faith that "ethnicity" is part of man's primal, primitive,
and prerational (meaning, of course, "irrational") past, a past out of which he
is supposed to be evolving. With more faith in science, with more experience in
political democracy, with more of the advantages of economic progress, with
more replacement of the sacred by the secular, man will finally "come of age,"
to use Dietrich Bonhoeffer's phrase. He will not need tribal ties, and all the
paraphernalia of his old prerational, superstitious, unscientific past can safely
be cast off.

When Professor Harvey Cox wrote his now famous *Secular City*, such a
liberal optimistic faith seemed justified. But Professor Cox himself has made a
pilgrimage from the "Secular City" to "The Feast of Fools," a medieval feast
that takes place in a festive and fantastic Camelot. The mood of American
academia today is one of massive apostasy from liberal rationalism.

One need not swing quite so far from the dialectics of the rational to the irrational to recognize that man does not live by reason alone. Modernization
and the collapse of empires, which were supposed to bring liberal democracy
and rational secularism to the uttermost parts of the earth, have instead
produced a resurgence of the tribe and the clan. Under such circumstances,
every man must reconsider the possibility and the desirability of homogeniza-

tion. At a time when many in the American academy rigorously support what they take to be black separatism—and at times enforce such separatism on blacks who might not be inclined in that direction—it is hardly possible or logical to insist that everyone else be homogenized.

But we are dealing with far more than the abandonment of one fad for another or an overhasty apostasy of a naïvely held scientific faith. Serious scholars like Shils, Geertz, Isaacs, and Glazer have offered persuasive evidence of the persistence of diversity. The profound and ingenious work of Noam Chomsky in linguistics and Lévi-Strauss in anthropology suggests that diversity might be "structured" into the human experience. Differentiation may be the only way man can cope with the reality in which he finds himself, including the reality of his own relationship network. Such a view of things suggests that the hope of unity through homogenization was not just naïve and premature but also betrayed a profound misunderstanding of the human condition. Diversity may lead to hellish miseries in the world, but without the power to diversify and to locate himself somewhere in the midst of the diversity man may not be able to cope with the world at all.

To set the context for the discussion that concludes this introductory chapter, I would like to make three comments.

1.   Terry N. Clark, the extremely helpful and generous editor of this series, has suggested that to some extent I may be battling a straw man in my arguments with sociologists who reject the importance of ethnicity. He quite properly points out that there has been some political, psychiatric and medical, and delinquency research on ethnic diversity, so it is not altogether fair to say that we know practically nothing of the subject. Surely the extensive bibliography appended to this volume is evidence that some literature does exist. Yet one could go through the major sociological journals of the last 20 years and find virtually nothing written on the European immigrant ethnic groups in the United States. Part of the problem of this book is that so few national surveys over the last two decades have even bothered to ask an ethnic question. (Yet one of the advantages for the authors is that those who did ask the question never bothered to analyze the ethnic factor.)

Professor Clark is quite correct that no sociologist seriously concerned with ethnicity in the United States has argued the position that I have set up as the adversary one for this volume. But only a handful of sociologists (Milton Gordon, Nathan Glazer, Stanley Lieberson, and Daniel P. Moynihan) have bothered to look at ethnicity, and one could count on the fingers of two hands the political scientists who have done so (Wilson, Banfield, Parenti, and Wolfinger, for example). Professor Clark himself has discovered, somewhat through serendipity I think, that the proportion of Irish in the population of an American city seems to have a positive impact on public expenditure.[6]

The straw man with whom I argue does not exist as a specific social scientist, but he is real enough. Paul Metzger[7] documents quite convincingly the strong assimilationist biases of American sociology, and he provides an extensive bibliography to support his contentions. Metzger documents the existence of a collection of implicit assumptions and obiter dicta that become fundamental perspectives. We do not tilt against windmills but deal with a series of will o' the wisps that do not constitute a sociological school or tradition against which one might engage in direct combat or argument, but are instead amorphous assumptions that emerge in questions at professional meetings, dubious frowns when you explain your findings, skeptical smiles when you report what you are doing, and in mildly nasty comments that you are, after all, underwriting white racism. But for the sake of Professor Clark's peace of mind—as well as for the sake of scholarly precision—let me make it clear that I am arguing aginst a widespread implicit assumption about the importance of the ethnic factor, not against a specific sociologist who denies its importance. The reader who wishes to find that these assumptions are not altogether a product of my Celtic imagination is referred to the Metzger article.

2.   The present volume is an exercise in secondary analysis and suffers from all its weaknesses. None of the data used were designed explicitly for the purposes to which we have put them. I am convinced that such secondary analysis was a necessary preliminary to the designing of primary research on American ethnic diversity. Still, one must be cautious in the uses of secondary analysis, and I hereby note that however pontifical I may become in later chapters, I submit the findings of this book cautiously and tentatively.

Some of the data are better than other. In particular, the Verba-Nie political participation study and the 15 city University of Michigan civil disturbance study provide material of which I am reasonably confident. How far one can push the data in a secondary analysis is a matter of hunch and instinct, I suspect. If one had one's own primary material and a sufficient number of ethnic respondents, one would want to push analysis further than I have in some of the chapters of this book. The analysis of the civil disturbance data, for example, shows very impressive regional differences among American ethnic groups. One would want to go back to other chapters and introduce "the regional factor," but there are simply not enough ethnics in the other data sets to make this feasible. The civil disturbance study had a much higher proportion of ethnic respondents because it was limited to 15 cities. Because most ethnics live in cities, this limitation would necessarily produce a higher proportion than would a national sample survey.

I do not apologize for any of the decisions we have made about how far we can push the data in this book. I simply want to make clear to the reader beforehand that I am acutely aware of the limitations of what we have set out to do.

3. The same constraints that exist for the kind of analysis we are pursuing, plus the variable we are studying, make it necessary for us to say something about significance tests. I do not believe that the debate among statisticians about the utility of significance tests has been resolved satisfactorily. I realize that there is a tendency in survey research to take significance tests more seriously than we did in the past, and I am in sympathy with this tendency. However a number of problems arise in using significance tests on the material in this volume.

First of all, let it be said that all the analysis of variance tables presented in the book are statistically significant. In each case ethnicity is a "significant" factor, but given the size of the samples we have such a statement is little more than trivial observation. A more pertinent question is whether differences among specific ethnic groups are "significant." Are the Irish "significantly" different from the Jews? The Poles? One would need a 12 by 12 matrix (for such tables in which there are 12 ethnic groups). To comment on and analyze such a table would be a tedious and often unintelligible task. Worse still, it would I think be a pretense at scientific precision that an exploratory volume like this has no right to claim. When the intellectual question involves the comparison between pairs of groups, as it does in Chapter 3, we do indeed use signigicance tests. When the intellectual question has to do with tentative exploration of patterns of diversity among many different groups, as in the case of Chapter 4, we do not use significance tests even though ethnicity itself is always a significant predictor of political behavior. The differences among groups within the tables, however, we present to the reader as suggestive. The wise reader would be cautious even about the findings that are significant. The basic issues—the persistence and importance of ethnicity—is established with reasonable confidence. What is going on within the different ethnic groups should be considered material for further and far more elaborate research.

In America there is a profound distrust of diversity based on anything other than social class, which is the only "rational" diversity. American theory endorses cultural pluralism, but our behavior insists on as much assimilation as possible as quickly as possible. Most Americans feel ambivalent about the fact of diversity and also about their own particular location in ethnic geography. We are torn between pride in the heritage of our own group and resentment at being trapped in that heritage. This ambivalence is probably the result of the agonies of the acculturation experience in which an immigrant group alternately felt shame over the fact that it was different and unwanted and a defensive pride about its own excellence, which the rest of society seemed neither to appreciate nor understand. The superpatriot is the man who is proud of his uniqueness and yet simultaneously wants to be like everyone else, only more so.

The ambivalence about one's own specific contributions to diversity is clear in both the Irish and the Jewish novels written in America. Jewish authors, it has always seemed to me, achieve a far better balance of self-acceptance and self-rejection than do their Irish counterparts. One need only compare Farrell with Malamud and Saul Bellow with Tom McHale to discover that the Jewish writers are more at ease with who and what they are than are the Irish. (Or to take a more extreme case: Philip Roth is surely ambivalent about being Jewish; John O'Hara was not ambivalent about being Irish, he was ashamed of it.) Perhaps the centuries of persecution of Jews by Christians did not have nearly the impact on Jewish self-respect that the millennium of political oppression of the Irish by the English had on Irish self-respect.

The Anglo-Saxon Protestant may be free of this ambivalence, though if he is there are enough strains toward guilt in the American Protestant consciousness to even the score. But whatever is to be said of the WASP, those who came to this country after him were different and felt ambivalent about that difference. We praise the melting pot out of one side of our mouth and honor cultural pluralism out of the other.

A theoretical underpinning of the assumption that all diversity except that of social class ought to disappear is a basic model that, in either pop or sophisticated versions, permeates most of American social science. It is an evolutionary model that sees the human race moving from *Gemeinschaft* to *Gesellschaft*, from community to association, from the sacred to the profane, from the particularistic to the universalistic. The great men of protosociology—Tönnies, Tröelsch, Weber, Durkheim—all chronicled the end of a peasant, feudal era and the beginning of a modern, urban era. *Gemeinschaft* was dying, they thought, and the rationalized, formalized, bureaucratized city was replacing the tribal, ascriptive society of the peasant commune. Ties of blood, faith, land were becoming less important. What counted was one's place in the technostructure (though the name was yet to be invented). What was important was what one did, not who one was. The bureaucrat must treat all men evenhandedly because in the world of rationalized bureaucracy all men were interchangeable. Ties of common faith, common ancestry, common race were unimportant and could be expected to vanish quickly.

For men like Max Weber the disappearance of *Gemeinschaft* was not necessarily a cause for rejoicing. Weber, Tönnies, and others felt distinct nostalgia for the world that was disappearing and grave unease about the new one that was emerging. But many of their successors have taken the unidirectional evolutionary model not merely as description but as a norm. The irrational, that is, the sacred, the ascriptive, the particularistic, was not only going away, it *ought* to go away. Men not only were organizing themselves around the dimension of social class, this was the way they *ought* to organize themselves. Communities based on common kinship or common faith or common race or common historic experiences were "irrational" and hence immoral. They belonged to a past that the evolutionary process was inevitably leaving behind.

One can leave to existential philosophers like Gabriel Marcel and political critics like John Schaar the question of whether the bureaucratic model is an adequate one for human life. One can also assume that most sociologists are sophisticated enough to realize that *Gemeinschaft* has survived and is doing nicely, thank you. But the pop version of the *Gemeinschaft-Gesellschaft* model has become an accepted part of the official conventional wisdom. The sooner men stop defining themselves as Irish or Italian or Catholic or Missouri Synod Lutheran the sooner they will be better human beings, and the society in which they live will be better, too.

It is very difficult to deal with the assimilationist mentality, particularly because it is usually implicit. In addition, the assimilationist is often someone who himself is in the process of assimilation. Anyone who lectures even to scholarly audiences on the subject of ethnic diversity is almost certain to be asked whether, after all, the emphasis on diversity is not dangerous, since it stresses those things that separate men rather than those things that unite them. He is also likely to be cornered before he leaves the lecture hall by an eager questioner who wonders whether it isn't true that the Irish (for example) have really become "just like everyone else." What makes it even more difficult to cope with these questions is that those who ask them frequently bear names that indicate that they were born other than white Protestants. The last one who wants to hear that diversity is now a fit subject for research is he who has embarked, perhaps irrevocably, on the process of liquidating his own diversity.

A number of misconceptions flow from a conviction that irrational diversities ought to go away.

1. *In the last quarter-century there has been relatively little in the way of serious research on the subject, even though the later stages of the acculturation of the immigrant groups should have been considered a fascinating subject for social science.* One can look through the indexes of the various sociological and psychological journals for the last three decades and find practically nothing on the subject of American ethnic groups, a vacancy even more perplexing when one understands that there is a vast market for such research. (Nathan Glazer and Daniel Patrick Moynihan's *Beyond the Melting Pot* has sold over a half million copies.) Even today, the Gallup organization does not routinely ask about ethnicity, the United States Census cannot ask a religious question (an indicator of ethnicity), and probably a majority of survey questionnaires still contain no ethnic question. During the 1960s, those of us who were interested in the subject often had to explain to skeptical colleagues that what we were concerned about was a legitimate field of re-

search. The presumption seems to have been that there was nothing there to study, or if there was it was immoral to be concerned about it. Even today, there is a considerable residue of skepticism on the subject of ethnic diversity. (This skepticism, incidentally, coexists with an unending flow of anecdotes about it. Many conversations that begin with one social scientist politely but firmly suggesting that the ethnic researcher might be a charlatan end with nostalgic comments about respective ethnic childhoods.)

Recently, with the spur of national events and a popular recognition of the existence of "the ethnics," social science has begun to take an interest in ethnicity. But the lack of data has made research more difficult and conclusions more tentative as the number of generations since immigration increases.

2. *The demand for cultural pluralism is confused with a demand for separation, and since separation is bad, cultural pluralism is bad.* The blacks and the Spanish-speaking and the American Indians may force upon mainstream America the cultural pluralism that we have honored in theory and rarely accepted in practice. They may eventually even persuade mainstream America that cultural pluralism is not separatism. American blacks, for example, are not asking for separation from the rest of society, but for the right to pursue the development of their own culture and their own heritage within the society. Research done at the University of Michigan shows that large majorities of blacks are in favor of black studies, but only tiny minorities are seeking some kind of black nation. The Michigan research demonstrates that what we are dealing with in the black pride phenomenon even among the young is not a desire for isolation from the rest of American society but the right to have one's own particular heritage and culture respected as part of the society.

When that is recognized, mainstream America may begin to understand the gross injustices that it did to earlier minority groups, such as the destruction of German-American culture during and after World War I. The overwhelming majority of German-Americans were loyal citizens of this country. It was made perfectly clear to them, however, that they were either Americans or Germans; they couldn't be both. For the Germans, it is now too late. Their ethnic heritage has been strangled by assimilation. So, too, the Irish; but the blacks and the Spanish-speaking and the Indians may make it possible for the Italians and the Poles to protect their own cultural heritages and to keep alive in the larger American context something of the past.

The sociologist Paul Metzger has argued persuasively the case for cultural pluralism. He notes:

> Sociologists, by and large, have accepted the image of Horatio Alger
> in the Melting Pot as the ideal definition of American society. Al-

though they have repeatedly documented the discrepancy between social reality and cultural myth in America, they have also taken the view that the incorporation of America's ethnic and racial groups into the mainstream culture is virtually inevitable. . . . Successful assimilation, moreover, has been viewed as synonymous with equality of opportunity and upward mobility for the members of minority groups; "opportunity," in this system, is the opportunity to discard one's ethnicity and to partake fully in the "American Way of Life"; in this sense, assimilation is viewed as the embodiment of the democratic ethos.[8]

Metzger offers three conclusions:

1. The belief that racial assimilation constitutes the only democratic solution to the race problem in the United States should be relinquished by sociologists. Beyond committing them to a value premise which compromises their claim to value neutrality, the assimilationist strategy overlooks the functions which ethnic pluralism may perform in a democratic society. . . . The application of this perspective to the racial problem should result in the recognition that the black power and black nationalist movements, to the extent that they aim at the creation of a unified and coherent black community which generates a sense of common peoplehood and interest, are necessarily contrary neither to the experience of other American minorities nor to the interest of black people. The potential for racial divisiveness—and in the extreme case, revolutionary confrontation—which resides in such movements should also be recognized, but the source of this "pathological" potential should be seen as resting primarily within the racism of the wider society rather than in the "extremist" response to it on the part of the victimized minority.

2. To abandon the idea that ethnicity is a dysfunctional survival from a prior stage of social development will make it possible for sociologists to reaffirm that minority-majority relations are in fact group relations and not merely relations between prejudiced and victimized individuals. As such, they are implicated in the struggle for power and privilege in the society, and the theory of collective behavior and political sociology may be more pertinent to understanding them than the theory of social mobility and assimilation. Although general theories of minority-majority relations incorporating notions of power and conflict can be found in the writings of sociologists . . . it is only recently . . . that such perspectives have found their way into sociologists' analyses of the American racial situation.

3.   To abandon the notion that assimilation is a self-completing
process will make it possible to study the forces (especially at the
level of cultural and social structure) which facilitate or hinder
assimilation or, conversely, the forces which generate the sense of
ethnic and racial identity even within the homogenizing confines of
modern society. On the basis of an assessment of such forces, it is
certainly within the province of sociological analyses to point to the
possibilities of conscious intervention in the social process (by either
the majority or the minority group) to achieve given ends and to
weigh the costs and consequences of various policy alternatives.
These functions of sociological analysis, however, should be informed by an awareness that *any* form of intervention will take
place in a political context—that intervention itself is in fact a
political act—and that the likelihood of its success will be condi-
tioned by the configuration of political forces in the society at large.
Without this awareness—which is nothing more than an awareness
of the total societal context within which a given minority problem
has its meaning—sociological analysis runs a very real risk of spin-
ning surrealistic fantasies about a world which is tacitly believed to
be the best of all possible worlds. Whether the call of sociologists
for racial assimilation in American society as it is currently organized will fall victim to such a judgment remains to be seen.[9]

Metzger's conclusions seem eminently sane and reasonable. Of course
American society is complex and variegated, and the idea of assimilation and
homogenization is absurd. But the model of diversity and pluralism still seems
to fly in the face of many cherished assumptions that persistently find echos in
our political behavior.

3.   *Our adherence to the assimilationist model leads us to completely
misunderstand the political structure of American society.* Elite groups assume
that "issue politics" are the issues of social class. If we are to have a rational
politics, we must have one of social class in which men are divided into liberal
and conservative, depending on whether they take the positions of the rich or
the poor. (Of course, liberal academics naturally side with the poor.) The
black phenomenon can be fitted to this image of politics by assuming that all
blacks are poor and, hence, belong on the "liberal" side of the political game.
It is a little more difficult to figure out why most Jews are liberal; their social
class position would put them on the side of the conservatives. This problem is
solved by recourse to a complicated theory of minority groups identifying with
the cause of other minority groups—a theory that becomes increasingly difficult to defend as blacks and Jews find themselves engaged in political conflicts
within the large cities, New York especially.

In the implicit Marxism that is so powerful among Western intellectuals there is an assumption that the only meaningful differences among human groups are social class differences—even black militancy and women's liberation are justified as class movements. In such a perspective, differences of language, religion, or national background are either irrational and ought not to be taken seriously or are a disguised attempt of the oppressor class to justify continuing oppression. A society divided along class lines and along lines of essentially economic political issues is an acceptable society, but there is no room there for divisions on issues that are primordial, ethnic, particularistic, and personal. Such issues and divisions are "irrational."

There are implications here, too, for the lack of serious research on ethnic pluralism and diversity. Most of those who might do such research prefer their politics to be ideological. They place themselves on the liberal end of the ideological spectrum. As they perceive the rest of the world, those groups that are especially likely to be labeled "ethnic" not only reject ideological politics but in fact are opposed to precisely those liberal social changes that American scholars support.

As one intellectual on the staff of a government agency remarked to me, "I suppose those people have problems of their own. The only way I can think of them is as enemies to social progress." Such a view is reinforced by the fact that the geographical location of many of the ethnic communities puts them in immediate competition with blacks for jobs and housing. Hence, their reaction to black militancy is obvious grist for the mills of the mass media. The hardhat ethnic on the one hand and the militant black—plus his student supporters—on the other, represent for many American intellectuals the most obvious conflict in society, and the intellectual has no doubt as to which side he wants to be on—the side where all virtue is to be found.

The data to refute this myth are overwhelming, but the myth refuses to die. Survey after survey shows (as we will in later chapters) that the ethnics are more pro-integration and pro-peace (during the Vietnam War) than the American population in general. One can even point out that the Irish, in some ways the most hated of all the ethnics (they include George Meany and Richard Daley among their number), are second only to the Jews in their support for "liberal" political reforms. It does no good, however, to assert that the ethnics are still very much a part of the old liberal coalition, for they have been drummed out of it.

From the beginning, American politics were denominational and regional. It seems likely that the framers of the Constitution were already operating within the framework of a cultural consensus that revealed the necessity for recognizing that regional and religious diversity required toleration of pluralism. The political structure of the early years of the republic reinforced that consensus and made it official in the political world. However much the ideal of assimilation might be urged and however strong the pressure might be for immigrant groups to eliminate that which made them different, in practical politics it was nevertheless essential to recognize that in addition to social class issues there were also issues of race, religion, and nationality that had to be taken into account. American elites rail against these sorts of issues without realizing that ethnic politics is part of the fabric of American life. The attempt to impose the European left-right continuum on American political structure simply does not correspond to the multidimensional nature of the American political game. Worse, it fails to recognize one of the most important political accomplishments of American life: We have learned not only to harmonize social class diversity within some kind of civil and political unity—however tenuous it may be at times—we have also been able to harmonize, more or less well, regional, religious, ethnic, and racial diversity.

4. *An emphasis on the politics of "rational issues," that is, issues of social class, ignores the richness and the success of the American political enterprise.* The dogmatic conviction that only social class differences are rational is too sacred to question. Conflict between capital and labor about the division of the economic pie is rational and legitimate. Conflict between black and Pole or, in New York, between black and Jew over access to the land and services of the city is irrational and illegitimate. It is acceptable for society to develop mechanisms to deal with the former conflict in the political order, but it is somehow immoral for society to try to develop mechanisms for trying to deal with the latter problem—or, if mechanisms are to be developed, they must be based on the assumption that one side is moral and the other is not.

I have always been fascinated by the eagerness of such social scientists as Herbert Gans and Thomas Pettigrew to explain differences among American ethnic groups as differences in social class. By now the data (shown in later chapters) indicate rather conclusively that differences in values, attitudes, and family structures do exist even in third and fourth generation ethnics. But I have long since given up any hope of breaking through such dogmatic assumptions.

5. *Since it is assumed that most ethnic groups ought to vanish (exceptions will be made for Jews, blacks, Spanish-speaking, and American Indians), and since it is also assumed that most ethnic groups have no positive contribution to make to American society, it is therefore scarely worth learning anything about them.* Italians provide pizza, Poles provide sausage and jokes, and the Irish provide corrupt politicians. The Greeks, Latvians, Slovaks, Slovenes, Luxembourgers, Armenians? Well, they will all disappear. The blunt truth is that many members of that elite group of Americans who read the *New York Times, Washington Post, Commentary,* and *New York Review of Books* know more about Nigeria than they do about Queens or the northwest side of

Chicago. They have a better understanding of the issues facing Britain's entry into the Common Market than they do of the issues facing American Poles and Italians. The myths that hard hats supported the war and white ethnics are racist persist in the face of considerable statistical evidence to the contrary, in part because the opinion-makers and the intellectual and political elites of the national society know nothing about them and care little to learn.

Such ignorance can be useful. In a city like Newark the decision to base promotion in the school system on racial factors rather than on test scores benefited the blacks to the disadvantage of the Italians. In Newark, anything that is done to help blacks will certainly hurt Italians. The latter group may argue that nobody sought balance for them 30 or 40 years ago. When they have just begun to make it on their own efforts in American society, they wonder why they are punished for social injustice not of their making. If one knows something about Italian Americans—about their history and social structure and where they presently stand in American society—one will be troubled by a situation in which they are made to pay the price for the improvement of the condition of the blacks. It is a gross injustice. But why complicate things? No doubt the Italians are caught in the middle, but after all, as white ethnic racists who refuse to confess their guilt they deserve to pay the full price. They are immoral, they are superpatriots, they supported the war, and they don't like blacks, so we can with clear conscience take something away from them and give it to the blacks.

And that brings us full circle from ignorance and reluctance to study ethnicity on a theoretical level to ignorance and reluctance to learn about ethnics on all levels.

6. *Finally, interest in ethnicity is considered to be immoral.* When the subject of ethnicity is discussed, there is often a black person present who shakes his head and wonders why this interest seems to have come precisely at the time when American blacks are finally beginning to achieve some modicum of justice. It looks to him, he observes, as though the concern for ethnicity is simply one more form of white racism. His observations, while perhaps understandable, ignore the fact that the new consciousness of ethnicity is in part due to the efforts of blacks to legitimate cultural pluralism as it has never been legitimated before. Other Americans, seeing that now one can and should be proud of being black, wonder why one can not and should not be just as proud of being Italian or Polish. Perhaps more important, without some kind of fundamental consensus from (if not the active cooperation of) white ethnic Americans, the reasonable goals of American blacks will never be achieved. I shall leave aside for the moment the question of possible coalititons between white ethnics and blacks, except to note that one exists in Chicago. If positive cooperation is not possible, it still is true that in most American cities, black

goals will be achieved only with some kind of at least passive consent of substantial number of white ethnics. The response that white ethnics are so racist that even passive consent cannot be expected is not borne out by research evidence.

Another objection to concern about ethnicity comes from those mainstream American liberals who are still convinced that ethnic diversity is a "bad thing." A variant of this argument was proposed to me by Professor William Simon, who argued that life is so narrow, dull, provincial, and frustrating in white ethnic communities that the best thing we could do is to help the few sensitive, bright young people there break out of them. The fact that there is still considerable reluctance to admit interest in ethnicity as such is evidence of how powerful the official model of the conventional wisdom really is. I have been told that ethnicity is too sensitive an issue to approach directly. How ethnic groups can be sensitive and at the same time vanishing is a question I have never been able to answer.

I have a model of my own, and its broad outlines, I suppose, are implicit in my railings against the official model. What has happened with the urbanization and industrialization of society is not the replacement of *Gemeinschaft* by *Gesellschaft,* but rather a vast expansion of human relationships. Most of the new relationships—with the bus driver, the traffic policeman, the department store clerk, the government bureaucrat, the personnel officer at the factory—are in fact associative; but because whole new areas of relationships have been created, it does not follow that the old forms have been eliminated. It merely means that they no longer exhaust the totality of life.

In what Peter Rossi calls the "public sphere," the rational principles of the technostructure prevail. In the private sphere, men are still inclined to choose to be with "their own kind." There is, of course, considerable overlap. Real estate, construction contracting, law, medicine, the church, and politics are part of the public sphere, but they are still organized in many cities around ethnic, religious, and racial diversity. In other words, when it comes to choosing role relationships where either intimacy or trust are involved, there is still a strong tendency to choose people to whom we can say in effect, "Your mother knew my mother." The persistence of the *Gemeinschaft* in the midst of the *Gesellschaft* society has been amply demonstrated by the social research of the last three decades. William White's study of street gangs in Boston, the research of Paul Lazarsfeld and his colleagues on voting decisions and market choice, the famous Hawthorne experiement of Elton Mayo, the tradition of the sociology of religion beginning with Gerhard Lenski, the studies of various military establishments by Stauffer, Shils, and Janowitz all show not merely that informal and primary relationships survive in an industrial, contractual society but that they provide the very stuff out of which the society is created and the cement that keeps it from coming apart.

If there is to be *Gemeinschaft,* then who are one's partners to be? Obviously, one's own kind. The survival of religious and ethnic diversity in American society is motivated by a search for one's own kind, who will be preferential role opposites in one's intimate and trusting relationships. The ethnic groups did not come into being in the Old World; they are American creations. In the old country the immigrants were citizens of towns, not nations. They became ethnics in the United States partly because the larger society defined tham as ethnic and partly because it was in their own interest to become ethnics, both because of the political power that might accrue to them in ethnic cohesiveness and because of the social support the ethnic collectivity provided for, its members. It was good to be able to say to the personnel manager at the factory, "My mother knows your mother." It meant that he would be less cold and impersonal to you. And it meant that you were more likely to get the job.

In my model, then, ethnicity is one of the forms of *Gemeinschaft* that has survived in a rationalized, bureaucratized society. It is one of the tools we use to brush off the sharp edges of human relationships in a society run *sine ira* and *sine studio* and one of the criteria we have available for finding role opposites with whom we are able to relax. I am not suggesting that a sense of presumed common origin (Weber's definition of ethnicity) is the only criterion around which an intimate relationship might be established; I am suggesting merely that ethnic collectivities are one of the resources available to contemporary Americans for finding self-definition, social location, and preferential role opposites. Not everyone has to be an ethnic, and there are other collectivities that can be functional equivalents of ethnic groups. (I once suggested that intellectuals are an ethnic group and got into a lot of trouble.) My only point is that ethnicity is one of the available alternatives.

From the perspective of my model, then, ethnicity is far from being a divisive force in society. It can be viewed as a constructive one; at the least, it is an inevitable one. Men will necessarily differentiate themselves. What is important is whether the differentiations that take place can become socially constructive. Lévi-Strauss has pointed out that in primitive tribes the totemic clans are always made up of animals of the same class of beings. Thus one can have a tribe in which there is a bear totem, a lion totem, and a tiger totem; another tribe may have an eagle totem and a falcon totem; but one will never have in the same tribe eagles, lions, falcons, and bears (unless it is the National Football League). The reason for this, Lévi-Strauss says, is that the purpose of the totemic clans is to differentiate the tribe as a prelude to its reintegration. The tribe achieves structural integrity not by homogenization but by diversification. It may very well be that because they provide self-definition and also a substructure within the larger society, ethnic groups are a strong, positive social asset.

It is a sorry fact that in America some people seem incapable of even considering the possibility that something good has happened here. In fact, we Americans have learned how to integrate, more or less well, more or less justly, and in a rather brief period of time, an unheard of variety of racial, ethnic, and religious groups. If we have not made a perfect job of it, the fact that the society exists at all is amazing. We have developed an elaborate scheme of compromise, accomodation, protocols, and subterfuges for keeping all of the large subpopulations reasonably satisfied with what is going on, or at least satisfied enough so that they are unwilling to withdraw from the consensus. And then for some bizarre reason, we would like to be persuaded that our sucess has come not from learning how to deal with diversity but rather from having eliminated it. We ignore the wisdom by which this tenuous harmony has been created and substitute for it a conventional wisdom that says we don't have to consider it because diversity is going away. As a result, when we discover that some groups are considerably less satisfied with their portion in society than others, we are quite incapable of applying the wisdom of our own experiences to the newly discovered problems. We are a nation that has rediscovered the fact of human diversity, and we act as though we have encountered this fact for the first time with absolutely nothing in our past experience to help us understand how to cope with it.

How has a society of such diverse components as the United States survived? The country's richness of natural resources and its resultant economic prosperity have had something to do with the success of pluralism. People seem less inclined to go after their neighbors with a rock, club, or knife when they have just consumed a succulent steak from the backyard barbecue. It may well be that the ultimate answer to primordial conflict around the world is universal affluence.

But perhaps more than economics are involved. The immigrants of the nineteenth century were not affluent. The Irish, for example, were improverished and diseased fugitives from famine. Yet, while they were not particularly welcome and did not in their turn profess much affection for their hosts, the riots between the Irish and the Yankees were limited in number and extent.

My own hypothesis is that the cultural matrix that has made American diversity possible is denominational pluralism. The United States was a religiously pluralistic society even before it became a politically pluralistic one. The pluralism that was institutionalized in the Constitution antedated that document. It developed in the previous half-century, mostly because Virginia

Episcopalians and Massachusetts Congregationalists learned that they had to get along with one another despite their serious religious differences. The Congregationalists, the Quakers, the Episcopalians, and the Methodists all shared one English cultural tradition; but they shared it in diversified styles, styles that were shaped by their denominational affiliations. By 1789, such diversity was so obvious to the framers of the Constitution that they did not even have to advert explicitly to it. Denominational differences among the various states had to be respected.[10] The Constitution, then, specified for the political dimension of society a heterogeneity that was already taken for granted in the common culture.

This heterogeneity was broad enough to be able to absorb the later immigrant groups when they came ashore. Many native Americans may not have wanted the immigrants, and many assumed that the only appropriate behavior for the immigrants was for them to become native Americans as quickly as possible. Nevertheless, the pluralistic culture of the society was such that it would be a century before the country could bring itself to act against its own self-image of diversity and begin to systematically exclude certain kinds of immigrants. Without understanding how it had been accomplished, America had arrived at a political, cultural, and social style that had made it possible for a vast diversity of different groups to live together with at least some harmony and if not with justice, still at least with the conviction that justice was in order. By our own very high standards, there was still much injustice, but at least one question ought to be asked in defense of American pluralism: How come the standards are so high?

Shocking injustice has been done and is being done to American blacks. Considerable injustice was done to other American groups. The Japanese were locked in concentration camps. The Germans, only too willing to fight and die for the United States against their native land, were forced to yield much of their culture and language. In some American cities after World War I it was impossible even to play Beethoven's music. Those with Slavic and Italian names are still systematically excluded from important corporate offices. Jews are still subject to subtle social discrimination. There is only one Catholic president of any major American university. The Irish have become respectable—something they always desperately wanted—at the price of losing any sense of their own history or culture.

But despite all these injustices, three things must still be said. First, our multifarious society has survived. Second, minority groups are treated better in the United States than they are in any other large nation of the world, or in many of the small ones. (The American black, while a tragic victim of injustice, is still in far better political, economic, and social condition than is the Catholic in Ulster.)[11] Third, the ideology of cultural diversity to which most

Americans are more or less committed makes it impossible for us to be complacent at the continuation of injustice. In the three decades since Myrdal gave a name to the American dilemma, immense progress has been made. To point to the fact of progress is not to make an excuse from further effort. Progress might well be conceived of as a context for further efforts.

There has been a recent and dramatic increase of interest in America's cultural heterogeneity. We touched on one of the reasons for this earlier: The black pride movement has legitimated definitively the idea of cultural pluralism.

In addition, the loss of faith on the part of many younger Americans in the optimistic, liberal rationalist vision of their predecessors and teachers has reopened for these young people the question of self-identity. It has been my experience that many if not most of the graduate students who have suddenly appeared in faculty offices all over the country clutching proposals for ethnic research are motivated by highly personal reasons. In the process of doing their dissertations, they want to find out who they are.

Both on the college campuses, then, and in the bastions of middle America, the new, or at least the newly manifested, interest in diversity is part of a cultural identity crisis. That the question, "Who am I?" can arise after so many years of pretending that it is either unimportant or that it has already been solved is some evidence of how persistent and powerful the issue may be.

There are two major thrusts in the new interest in diversity. The first is the "rediscovery of middle America." The social, cultural, and intellectual elites of the country have discovered that there is a substantial segment of the population living somewhere between them and the poor and the nonwhites who view social reality from a different perspective. These people are still patriotic Americans and for some unaccountable reason they are afraid of crime and violence. Some of this rediscovery of middle America (or blue collar workers or white ethnics or whatever name one chooses to use) is faddist and patronizing; some of it is moralistic and self-righteous. But a good deal of it is honest and open and sympathetic. As this thrust is represented by such agencies as the Ford Foundation and the American Jewish Committee, it is a sensible and realistic comprehension that social reform and indeed social harmony in the United States is impossible if some groups are deliberately or undeliberately excluded from the consensus. Still, there is a tendency for some of the practitioners of this rediscovery of middle America to view middle Americans as a "problem," or at least as people with "problems." However, as empirical data begin to become available which indicate that the ethnic component of middle America is not all that hawkish or all that racist, this emphasis on problems is beginning to change.

The other major thrust in the concern about ethnic diversity is what I would call the "rediscovery of pluralism." It is, I suppose, more ordered toward thought and reflection than toward immediate ends, but it asks a fundamental question that ought to precede any action: What makes a society tick?

The cultural pluralist approach has a limited interest in immediate social action to alleviate problems, though it certainly applauds and supports such action and makes whatever contribution it can to it. It is more concerned about figuring out how cultural diversity persists along primordial lines in the United States and what contributions this persistence makes to the American social structure. It is an extraordinarily difficult task and one that has led to more failures than successes up to the present time. There is so little in the way of social history for the ethnic groups. There is quite an extensive literature on American Jews and a small but consistent literature on American Italians. But there is nothing in the way of social theory to provide a perspective for investigating ethnicity—no empirical data from past studies, no agreement among survey researchers as to how questions ought to be asked, and no clear indicators as to what research and analytic methodologies are pertinent.

There are, as I see it, three different approaches to the problem: the social class approach, the political approach, and the cultural approach. In the first, ethnic differences are equated with social class differences. Thus, Herbert Gans in his *Urban Villagers* explains the behavior of Italians in Boston threatened by urban renewal as a class rather than a cultural phenomenon. Second, Daniel Patrick Moynihan and Nathan Glazer in *Beyond the Melting Pot* argue that at least in New York City, the ethnic collectivities are essentially giant political interest groups without too much in the way of a cor-related cultural heritage. Finally, such observers as Edward Laumann and Peter Rossi argue that there is persuasive evidence that the ethnic collectivities do indeed act as bearers of differential cultural heritages. Rossi suggests that the heritage may have to do with subtle but important differences of expec-tation in one's most intimate personal relationships.

The burden of the evidence that we have been piling up at the National Opinion Research Center for the past several years strongly supports the third position. Indeed, data we now have on the differential personality constella-tions of eight American white ethnic groups seems to me to offer conclusive evidence that even when social class is held constant, immense differences of personalities have persisted among these groups.

But theoretical problems persist. Is everyone ethnic?[12] Does one have to be an ethnic whether one wants to or not? For example, are Appalachian whites an ethnic group? Are Texans? Are some basic "membership groups" in American society based on nationality, racial, or religious factors while others could be based on geographical or social class or organizational or professional factors? Are intellectuals, as I not altogether facetiously suggested, an ethnic group? What happens in an ethnically mixed marriage? Does one select one's basic membership group or does one absorb it from the parents of the same or opposite sex?

Indeed, to what extent is basic group membership a matter of choice? Does it matter whether you consciously identify with a group or not? For example, it seems reasonably clear that most of the American Irish know very little about their own Irish heritage and explicitly think of themselves as Irish only on rare occasions. Nevertheless, our data indicate very strong correlations between Irishness and patterns of attitudes and behavior. And once we have established such patterns, are they a part of the heritage that the group brought with it from the Old World or are they a function of its experiences when it arrived in American society, experiences which in turn were functions of the shape of American society at that time? Or, finally, are they the result of where the group is in American society at the present time?

These thorny questions place social scientists in an embarrassing position. The more we probe the question of primordial bonds the more obvious it becomes that they are pervasive in American society. Despite and perhaps because of our ambivalence about primordial bonds, we will never understand American society without first coping with the phenomenon of their existence. But at the present state of our knowledge we don't know quite what to do with them. Man may have traveled a long way indeed from one end of the continuum represented by Parson's pattern variables to the other, from the particularistic to the universalistic, from ascription to achievement, from the diffuse to the specific; but he still seems to have kept one foot on the particularistic, diffuse, and ascriptive end of the continuum, and not just in his family relationships. It will take some years to be able to understand just how this has occurred and perhaps additional years to be able to make intelligent suggestions to social policy-makers concerning what if anything they should do about the extraordinary survival of primordial diversity.

In the meantime, however, it has become possible for men and women to talk about it. We can recall our heritage and even enjoy it, if not altogether without guilt at least with the feeling that there are some others who will understand. It has even become possible for us to begin to understand and appreciate and enjoy the heritages of others, which may be the beginning of an evolutionary step of considerable moment.

Celts and Saxons are killing each other once again in Ulster, as they have for centuries. In the United States, however, Scotch-Irish Presbyterians and Celtic Irish Catholics get along with each other moderately well. They do not feel constrained to shoot at each other from behind the hedges or out of the windows of slums. Given the history of the two groups, that is not inconsiderable progress.

NOTES

1. Clifford Geertz. "The Integrated Revolution," in *Old Societies And New Societies,* Clifford Geertz, ed. Glencoe, Ill.: The Free Press, 1963, p. 109.

2. Edward Shils. "Primordial, Personal, Sacred, and Civil Ties." *British Journal of Sociology* (June 1957), pp. 130–145.

3. Clifford Geertz, *op. cit.,* pp. 109–110.

4. Harold Isaacs. "Group Identity and Political Change." *Bulletin of the International House of Japan* (April 1964), pp. 24–25.

5. Edward Shils, *op. cit.*, pp. 130–131.

6. See Terry N. Clark. "Constitutions and Catholics: Remarks on Professor Stigler, 'Altruism and Minimal Winning Coalitions.'" Unpublished paper, University of Chicago, August, 1973. Also "Citizens, Values, Power, and Policy Outputs: A Model of Decision-Making." *The Journal of Comparative Administration* (February 1973), pp. 385–427.

7. L. Paul Metzger. "American Sociology and Black Assimilation: Conflicting Perspectives." *American Journal of Sociology,* **76,** 4 (January 1971), pp. 643–644.

8. Ibid., pp. 628–629. Reprinted by permission.

9. Ibid., pp. 643–644. Reprinted by permission.

10. And of course the fact that the economies of these denominationally diverse states were also different reinforced the religious pluralism.

11. See Professor Richard Rose's comparison in *Governing Without Consensus.* Boston: Beacon Press, 1971.

12. *The Christian Century* has recently suggested that even WASPS are ethnic.

2. THE DEMOGRAPHY OF ETHNIC IDENTIFICATION

PART I: THE RELIGIO-ETHNIC COMPOSITION AND DISTRIBUTION OF THE AMERICAN POPULATION

W ITH THE RESURGENCE OF INTEREST in ethnic diversity in recent years, the lack of useful demographic information about ethnics in American society has become apparent. In the 1972 election year particularly, there was a frantic search for information on "ethnics" and very little information available in response to that search other than educated guesses. The dicennial census loses interest after the second generation of immigrants, and while the November 1969 Current Population Survey did indeed ask a question about "origin or descent," it was constrained to ask a religious question. Thus CPS ethnic tabulations combined Protestant and Catholic Irish, Protestant and Catholic and Jewish Germans, and Catholic and Jewish Poles. There is some reason to think that it is precisely the combination of religion and nationality that constitutes ethnic identification for a considerable number of Americans. As we shall see later in this chapter, Irish Catholics and Irish Protestants differ considerably from one another in their incomes, occupations, education, and geographic distribution. A cursory reading of history books would also suggest that the two groups have very different cultural backgrounds. Demographic data that does not permit Irish Catholics and Irish Protestants, for example, to be separated must be considered severely limited in its usefulness.

The data used in this chapter were taken from the composite of seven NORC surveys. Both religious and national background questions were asked in these surveys, which were done between 1963 and 1972 (Table 1). In a subsequent chapter we shall use the composite NORC data and an SRC composite sample to focus on the difference among religio-ethnic groups with regard to occupation, education, and income. It is necessary to specify at the very beginning the serious weaknesses under which these data labor.

1. It is not yet clear conceptually what an American ethnic group is. The tentative definition of an ethnic group as a "collectivity based on presumed common origin" is useful merely as a point of departure.[1] The somewhat arbitrary divisions of the American population used in this chapter involve race, religion, nationality, and language. The division was based both on the existence of a sufficient number of respondents to be able to provide meaningful information about the group, and on the intuitive impression that such a particular group did correspond to some reality in the American population. Other divisions and combinations are surely possible.

2. Even with a sample of 9593 respondents, there is an insufficient number in many American ethnic groups for any information to be provided about them. Furthermore, the categories that we use are frequently combinations of several groups. Thus "British" is composed of English, Scotch, and

For assistance in this chapter thanks are owed to Otis Dudley Duncan, Stanley Lieberson, William McCready, Norman Nie, John Petrocik, and Shirley Saldanha.

Table 1. NORC's Surveys with Ethnic Identification Questions

Study Number	Year of Study	Sample Size	Type of Sample	Ethnic Question
160	1963	1515	Block	53. What is your main nationality background? A. First, how about your *father's side?* B. What is your main nationality background on your *mother's side?*
630	1964	1500	Block	54. What country did most of your ancestors come from?
466	1965 (June)[a]	506	Block	33. A. What country would you say most of your ancestors are from? B. (If married currently) What country are most of your (husband's/wife's) ancestors from?

857	1965	Block	1469	61. (White respondents only) A. Please tell me what country most of your ancestors came from. B. (If married or widowed) What country did most of your (husband's/wife's) ancestors come from?
4100	1970	Block	1490	3. (If white) From what country did most of your ancestors come?
4119	1971	Block	1500	ZZ. (If white) From what country did most of your ancestors come?
4139	1972	Block	1613	6. From what countries or part of the world did your ancestors come? A. (If more than one country named) Which one of these countries do you feel closer to?

[a] Month used to distinguish from other NORC studies with the same number.

Welsh; "German" of Germans and Swiss; "Scandinavian" of Norwegians, Swedes, Danes, and Finns; "Slavic" includes all non-Polish eastern European Catholics, some of whom, such as the Hungarians and the Lithuanians, would not technically be considered Slavs; "French" includes Belgians; and "Spanish-speaking" includes Mexicans, Puerto Ricans, Cubans, and other Latin Americans as well as those respondents whose families came directly from Spain. Finally, in many tables the three Jewish groups—German, East European, and other—were combined.

3. Furthermore, even with such arbitrary combinations the composite sample of slightly under 10,000 respondents is not large enough to make possible the detailed cross tabulations of the sort that would be desirable. As will be seen later in this chapter, the number of cases in a given cell can become quite small even when a simple cross tabulation on 10-year age cohorts is attempted.

4. As the questions in Table 1 indicate, limitations on the time and space allowed for NORC's ethnic questions provide us with information more about ethnic identification than precise ethnic lineage. Usually the respondent was asked what country "most of his ancestors" came from. (When both father's and mother's ancestry were asked, father's ancestry was assigned for no better reason than that one had to choose one or the other.) With larger samples and more interview time, more details about ethnic background could be sought. It will be noted later in this chapter (see Tables 16 and 18) that in comparing NORC data with the Current Population Survey data, the different wording of the background question in the CPS produced a different distribution of responses, particularly for the English and German categories. NORC data, however, are simply not large enough to permit us to say anything meaningful about the ethnic "mixture."[2]

5. The seven NORC surveys in which an ethnic question was asked began in 1963 and ran until 1972 (Table 1). What we are reporting in this chapter is at best a description of the demography of American ethnic identification somewhere in the middle or late 1960s. Since there is some reason to believe that the Catholic ethnic groups in particular have gone through major social and economic change in the last two decades, our data may be even less adequate for them than it is for other groups.

6. All the NORC surveys were of the "block quota" variety; hence, we can be even less confident of the findings reported here than we would be if full probability sample techniques were used.

7. Respondents of mixed ethnic parentage were in effect forced by the NORC question to choose one heritage. Hence no distinction is made between those whose ethnic backgrounds are "pure" and those whose backgrounds are "mixed." In the 1972 survey, however, respondents were asked which coun-

tries their ancestors came from, and then which one they felt closest to, thus making the question even more strongly one of ethnic identification rather than ethnic origin. As Table 2 indicates, the majority of respondents listed one country only, and most of those who listed more than one had little trouble choosing one they felt closer to. Three-fifths of the respondents listed just one country, and more than 70 per cent of the German, Italian, and Polish Catholics and the German and Scandinavian Protestants listed only one identification.

Table 2. Response to Ethnic Question by Religio-ethnic Group in 1972 (Per Cent)

Religio-ethnic Group	Names One Country	Names Two Countries, Chooses One	Names Two Countries, Cannot Choose	Cannot Name Country
Protestants				
British (184)	66	34		
German (177)	75	25		
Scandinavian (76)	84	16		
Irish (81)	58	42		
Other (28)	21	11	36	33
Catholics				
Irish (67)	54	46		
German (46)	72	28		
Italian (67)	88	12		
Polish (53)	87	13		
Spanish-speaking (29)	93	7		
Other (130)	45	19	30	6
Jews (53)	51	15	34	
Blacks (242)	69		8	23
Other religion (23)	74	26		
No religion (72)	58	17	15	10
National average	59	19	12	10

Note: In this and subsequent tables we follow the convention of putting the base figures in parentheses; thus the percentages in the first row are based on 184 British respondents.

Subject to far more intensive research, it seems safe to say that a considerable number of Americans have little trouble stating what their primary ethnic identification is.

8. Finally, approximately one-quarter of the NORC composite sample falls into the two major residual categories of "Other Protestant" and "Other Catholic." While some information will be reported on these two residual categories in the course of this chapter, it should be kept in mind that they are residual categories, *not* ethnic groups. As Table 3 indicates, about 7 per cent of the "others" simply listed their ethnicity as "American," while 4 per cent did not know what their ethnicity was. The remaining 15 percent was made up either of people whose ethnic background was too complex for them to be able to describe it, or of people who did not fall into any of our major analytic categories—Italian Protestants and British Catholics, for example. Our analysis is necessarily limited to the three-quarters of the population that has little or no trouble giving a single ethnic identification and whose identification falls into one of our major analytic categories.

There is no point in trying to mimimize any of the above weaknesses. The principal reason for proceeding with description and analysis despite them is that for all the limitations on the data of the NORC composite sample, it still represents the only body of data on American ethnic identification currently available. At the conclusion of this chapter, we shall compare the NORC findings with those of the Current Population Survey to determine what sort of confidence can be placed in the NORC data. To anticipate our conclusion, it does not seem unreasonable to use these data until better data become available.

Table 4 is a summary table, providing information on education, age, occu-

Table 3. Distribution of "Other Protestants" and "Other Catholics" in NORC's Combined Sample (Percentages and Frequency)

Response	Protestants	Catholics	Total
"American"	6	1	7
	(597)	(90)	(687)
"Mixed"	11	4	15
	(928)	(207)	(1235)
"Don't know" ethnicity	3	1	4
	(260)	(90)	(350)
Total	20	6	26
	(1785)	(487)	(2172)

pation, number of children, and family income for the major religio-ethnic groups. It will be noted, first of all, that British Protestants are the largest single nonresidual group in the population, although if German Protestants and German Catholics are combined, there are slightly more Americans who identify as German than there are Americans who identify as British. Blacks appear slightly overrepresented in the NORC sample; Spanish-speaking Catholics appear considerably underrepresented.[3] It is also interesting to observe that there are more Irish Protestants than Irish Catholics.

Jews, Irish Catholics, and those with no religious affiliation have the highest mean years of education, with an average exceeding 12 years.[4] British Protestants are only one-tenth of a point beneath the mean score of 12 years of education. The lowest educational means in the sample are reported by blacks, and Spanish-speaking and Polish Catholics.

The Spanish-speaking Catholics have by far the youngest average age in the population, a function perhaps of immigration patterns. The German Jews and the British Protestants are the oldest groups of the population, with Catholic groups generally being younger than Protestant groups.

On the NORC Occupational Prestige Scale, Jews, Irish Catholics, and British Protestants have the highest occupational prestige. Among the white groups, the Polish, Spanish, and French Catholics and Irish Protestants have the lowest. So, despite the myth of the blue collar ethnic so prevalent in the press before the 1972 election, Irish and German Catholics are more likely to be white collar than the American average, while Italian and "Other" Catholics are at the national average. Polish, Slavic, and French Catholics are slightly below the national average of per cent white collar; but still approximately one-third of these groups are white collar workers.

As might be expected, the Catholic groups have a higher number of children per woman ever married than do the Protestants. The Germans with 3.1 children per woman ever married and the Poles with 2.9 are the most fertile groups in the white population, although the Poles have exactly the same number of children per woman ever married as do the blacks.

Finally, Jews and Irish Catholics have the highest average family income in the country, followed by those with no religion; all three groups have an average family income of over $9000 a year. Black and Spanish-speaking have the lowest family income, and the third lowest family income is that of the Irish Protestant. It is worth noting that Italian and Polish Catholics—the blue collar ethnics par excellence—rank just behind British Protestants in their average family income and ahead of all other Protestant groups.

One can observe in Table 4 how deceptive the combinations of Irish Catholics and Irish Protestants in the Current Population Survey can be. The former are high in education, occupational prestige, and income, while the latter are generally the lowest of the white English-speaking groups.

Table 4. Demographic Information on American Religio-ethnic Groups, Based on Seven NORC Surveys

Religio-ethnic Group	Years of Education	Average Age[a]	Occupation Prestige	Per Cent White Collar	Number of Children[b]	Family Income	Per Cent of Population
Protestants							
British (1303)	11.9	47.5	3.98	53	2.3	$8309	13.6
German (1205)	11.0	45.8	3.46	40	2.5	7858	12.6
Scandinavian (359)	11.3	45.1	3.38	42	2.7	7869	3.7
Irish (530)	10.6	46.2	3.17	38	2.7	7022	5.5
Other (1883)	10.5	45.5	3.33	41	2.6	7275	19.7
Catholics							
Irish (328)	12.2	44.5	4.27	49	2.8	9255	3.4
German (342)	11.3	44.4	3.88	45	3.1	8903	3.6
Italian (346)	10.7	44.6	3.48	39	2.8	7979	3.6
Polish (136)	10.0	45.1	2.69	34	2.9	7940	1.4
Slavic (237)	10.4	45.0	3.48	31	2.3	7693	2.5
French (156)	10.4	43.9	3.30	25	2.8	7478	1.6
Spanish-speaking (122)	9.3	38.2	3.10	24	3.1	6145	1.3
Other (609)	11.0	41.1	3.46	38	2.7	8105	6.4

Jews						
German (30)	12.9	48.0	5.36	57	2.3	9326	0.3
Eastern European (160)	13.3	45.0	4.77	79	1.7	11,114	1.7
Other (50)	13.3	43.6	4.38	73	2.0	11,218	0.5
Blacks (1285)	9.7	43.3	2.47	18	2.9	5425	13.4
Orientals (20)	11.6	42.0	2.60	35	2.6	7918	0.2
No religion[c] (304)	12.0	41.7	3.49	45	1.9	9046	3.2
Other (150)	11.2	45.2	3.72	44	2.3	7654	1.6
National average	10.9	44.8	3.42	39	2.6	7588	100 (9593)

[a] Adults over age 18.

[b] Per women ever married.

[c] The "no religion" category is composed of those who described their religious affiliation as "none," no matter what their ethnic background.

To summarize Table 4, the educational, occupational, and income elites of the American population seem to be the Jews and the Irish Catholics, closely followed by the British Protestants. Blacks and the Spanish-speaking are at the bottom of the educational, occupational, and income ladders, with Irish Protestants the lowest of the white English-speaking groups. The Catholic "ethnics," that is to say, the Italians and the Poles, seem somewhat higher on these measures than one might have expected, at least high enough to call into question many of the generalizations about the so-called blue collar ethnics.

Table 5 presents a distribution of the various groups by sex. Irish

Table 5. Sex and Ethnic Identification (Per Cent)

Religio-ethnic Group	Male	Female
Protestants		
British	50.6	49.4
German	52.0	48.0
Scandinavian	53.2	48.0
Irish	46.0	54.0
Other	43.8	56.2
Catholics		
Irish	54.1	45.9
German	49.6	50.4
Italian	48.4	51.6
Polish	50.4	49.6
Slavic	51.1	48.9
French	45.1	54.5
Spanish-speaking	56.6	43.4
Other	44.7	55.3
Jews		
German	38.7	61.3
Eastern European	50.0	50.0
Other	41.2	58.8
Blacks	46.9	53.1
Orientals	55.0	45.0
No religion	68.8	31.3
Other religion	50.3	49.7
National average	48.9	51.1

Protestants are more likely to be female, Irish Catholics more likely to be male, a phenomenon that may have as much to do with the tendency of men and women to chose an ethnic identification as with different sex ratios in the population. The high ratio of men among Spanish-speaking Catholics may well be a phenomenon of immigration patterns (perhaps also for the Orientals); and the high proportion of women among German Jews may be a matter of sampling variation, since there are only 30 German Jews in our sample. Finally, the very high proportion of males among those of no religion is in all likelihood a result of the fact that men are more likely to relinquish their early religious affiliations than are women.

Family status of individuals in the various ethnic identification groups is presented in Table 6. Those with no religion are the least likely to be married, perhaps partially because, as the next table shows, they are younger than the rest of the population, and partially because religious identification frequently seems to be renewed at the time of marriage. Among the three major religious bodies, the Jews (at least if they are East European and "Other") are rather surprisingly less likely to be married than the Catholics, and the Catholics are less likely to be married than the Protestants. Among the Gentile groups, those most likely to have never been married are the Slavs (11.4 per cent never married) and the Irish Catholics (9.8 per cent never married). The Irish Protestants, on the other hand, have the lowest rate of never married of all the Gentile groups (4.5 per cent), slightly behind the Spanish-speaking Catholics (4.9). The Spanish-speaking also have the highest percentage of separations and divorcees among white Gentile groups (6.6 per cent), while the Irish Catholics have the lowest (1.8 per cent). The black divorce rate (12.7 per cent) is the highest of the sample. The German Protestants have the highest proportion of those currently married (83.8 per cent), while among the white groups, the lowest proportion currently married are "Other" Jews (74.5) and the French and Polish Catholics (75.0 and 75.4 per cent respectively). These two groups and the Irish Protestants have the highest percentage of widowed. The Spanish-speaking Catholics have the lowest percentage of widowed (1.6 per cent). It would appear that the reluctance of the Irish in the Old Country to marry has not been transferred to the United States, though their reluctance to seek divorce and separation has persisted.

In Table 7 we turn to the age distribution of the various ethnic identification groups. Among the Gentile groups, the British Protestants are the oldest; Spanish-speaking Catholics, the youngest. Catholic groups are less likely than Protestants to be above the national average of those in their sixties and over, although most Catholic groups are slightly beneath the national average of those in their twenties, suggesting perhaps that population control became popular among Catholics between 20 and 30 years ago and not merely since

Table 6. Family Status and Ethnic Identification (Per Cent)

Religio-ethnic Group	Married	Widowed	Divorced, Separated	Never Married
Protestants				
British	79.1	9.3	4.6	7.1
German	83.8	7.0	4.1	5.1
Scandinavian	80.5	7.2	3.9	8.4
Irish	79.7	10.9	4.9	4.5
Other	80.9	9.2	4.3	5.6
Catholics				
Irish	80.8	7.6	1.8	9.8
German	85.1	5.2	3.2	6.4
Italian	81.8	8.1	2.0	8.1
Polish	75.4	10.9	4.3	9.4
Slavic	75.5	8.4	4.6	11.4
French	75.0	12.2	4.5	8.3
Spanish-speaking	86.9	1.6	6.6	4.9
Other	78.6	5.6	4.9	11.0
Jews				
German	80.6	12.9	3.2	3.2
Eastern European	78.8	5.6	4.4	11.3
Other	74.5	7.8	2.0	15.7
Blacks	66.8	10.2	12.7	10.2
Orientals	70.0	5.0	10.0	15.0
No religion	67.0	3.0	8.3	21.8
Other religion	69.5	11.9	3.3	15.2
National average	78.1	8.4	5.4	8.1

the Vatican Council. The Irish Catholics—those whose devotion to Catholic teaching might be thought to be most serious—are almost indistinguishable in their age distribution from the national average.

As the largest American denominations, the Baptists and the Methodists claim the highest proportion of church membership among Protestant ethnic groups. Approximately half the British-American group is either Baptist or Methodist (Table 8), and more than half the Irish Protestants belong to these two denominations. Over half the Scandinavians are Lutheran, as are about one-quarter of the Germans. One-fifth of the Irish and one-fifth of the

Table 7. Age and Ethnic Identification (Per Cent)

Religio-ethnic Group	Twenties and Under	Thirties	Forties	Fifties	Sixties and Over
Protestants					
British	15.1	19.3	19.1	17.9	28.7
German	19.6	19.9	19.0	14.8	26.7
Scandinavian	23.7	18.4	15.9	15.6	26.3
Irish	20.3	15.6	19.8	20.2	24.1
Other	19.8	20.6	19.4	14.2	25.9
Catholics					
Irish	22.4	20.2	18.7	16.3	22.4
German	19.4	22.6	22.0	16.1	19.9
Italian	17.7	22.9	22.9	18.0	18.6
Polish	14.5	20.3	26.1	20.3	18.8
Slavic	17.8	19.1	24.2	20.8	18.2
French	23.7	20.5	17.3	19.9	18.6
Spanish-speaking	36.9	23.0	21.3	8.2	10.7
Other	28.0	24.0	20.9	11.8	15.3
Jews					
German	10.0	20.0	23.3	13.3	33.3
Eastern European	17.1	22.2	22.8	20.3	17.7
Other	24.0	14.0	28.0	20.0	14.0
Blacks	24.1	21.3	21.3	12.2	21.1
Orientals	35.0	10.0	20.0	15.0	20.0
No religion	33.1	18.9	14.2	13.9	19.9
Other religion	21.2	18.5	18.5	17.9	23.8
National average	21.0	20.3	19.9	15.5	23.4

Germans belong to "Other" denominations—perhaps, at least in the Irish case, fundamentalist Protestant groups. It is interesting to note that while a substantial component of the Irish Protestant population must be thought to be the descendants of the Scotch-Irish Presbyterians who arrived in the United States before 1800, only 7 per cent of them are now Presbyterians.

In Table 9 we present data on the geographic distribution of American ethnic identification groups. The British Protestant population is distributed roughly in the same geographic proportion as is the total American popu-

Table 8. Protestant Denomination and Ethnic Identification (Per Cent)

Religio-ethnic Group	Baptist	Episcopalian	Lutheran	Methodist	Presbyterian	Congregational	United Church	Other	No Denomination
British	23.3	8.2	5.4	24.8	11.6	3.1	1.2	19.0	3.3
German	14.6	2.9	27.5	19.5	9.5	2.7	1.2	20.4	1.8
Scandinavian	5.1	2.4	54.8	12.9	6.3	1.5	0.3	15.3	1.5
Irish	37.5	3.0	5.6	20.0	7.6	1.8	0.6	20.6	3.4
Other	30.1	3.4	9.9	19.9	7.9	2.4	1.3	22.0	3.0

Table 9. Ethnic Identification by Region (Per Cent)

Religio-ethnic Group	Northeast	Middle Atlantic	East North Central	West North Central	South Atlantic	East South Central	West South Central	Mountain	Pacific	Total[a]
Protestants										
British	8	12	18	6	18	5	12	5	16	100
German	1	17	27	18	11	3	7	3	13	100
Scandinavian	2	8	16	39	4	1	5	10	16	100
Irish	2	6	17	7	20	9	25	2	12	100
Other	2	10	14	10	20	7	20	4	14	100

Catholics										
Irish	14	38	15	10	7	1	3	2	9	100
German	2	22	33	23	7	1	2	3	7	100
Italian	15	56	10	3	3	1	2	1	10	100
Polish	7	38	46	4	2	0	1	1	1	100
Slavic	5	43	32	7	4	1	2	2	4	100
French	24	11	15	10	3	0	24	2	10	100
Spanish-speaking	2	22	9	1	2	0	10	10	45	100
Other	15	27	18	10	4	1	9	5	11	100
Jews										
German	0	74	16	0	0	0	0	0	10	100
Eastern European	4	72	11	0	5	0	0	1	8	100
Other	4	55	20	0	8	0	2	2	10	100
Blacks	1	15	18	0	27	12	18	0	9	100
Orientals	10	10	5	0	10	5	0	0	60	100
No religion	4	14	22	9	9	4	4	4	29	100
Other	6	21	24	7	5	1	6	2	28	100
National average	5	19	19	10	14	4	12	3	13	100

[a] In some cases the actual total is 99 per cent or 101 per cent because of rounding error.

lation. German Protestants are concentrated in the north central region, as are Scandinavian Protestants. Irish Protestants are disproportionately in the South, and particularly in the west south central region, where fully one-quarter of them are to be found. One-fifth of them are also in the south Atlantic region. Forty-seven per cent of the Irish Protestants are in the three southern regions, as opposed to 28 per cent of the national population, suggesting, as we have said before, that large numbers of them may well be descendants of the pre-1800 immigrants, who settled mostly in the South.

Irish Catholics are heavily concentrated in the northeast and mid-Atlantic regions. More than half are found in these two regions, as opposed to 24 per cent of the total population. German Catholics, like German Protestants, are to be found in the north central region, but 71 per cent of the Italians are in the northeast and mid-Atlantic regions. Half the Poles are in the north central region, as are two-fifths of the other Slavic groups. The highest proportion of Spanish-speaking Catholics is in the Pacific area (45 per cent); and the French group is concentrated in the northeast and the west south central, the former obviously being recent immigrants from French Canada, and the latter being immigrants from French Canada in the distant past to southern Louisiana. Finally, as one might expect, Jews are concentrated in the mid-Atlantic region, though about one-tenth of them are to be found in the Pacific coast region.

With the exception of the French, the Catholics are clearly metropolitan dwellers, with the Italian and the Spanish-speaking the most likely (44 and 45 per cent respectively) to be in the great cities of over 2 million population (Table 10). (Presumably the Italians are especially likely to be found in New York and the Spanish-speaking in Los Angeles.) The most rural Gentile ethnic group is the French Catholic (32 per cent), followed by the Irish Protestant (29 per cent), the "other" Protestant (28 per cent), and the German Protestant (25 per cent). The Jews are the least rural of all—in fact, none of the 240 Jews in the NORC composite sample reported rural residence. The Spanish-speaking, Italian, Polish, and Irish Catholics also report less than 5 per cent of their population to have rural residence.

The Jews and those with no religion and "other" religions are the most likely to have attended graduate school (Table 11); among the Gentiles, the Irish Catholics are both the most likely to have attended graduate school (3 per cent) and the most likely to have gone to college at all (40 per cent as opposed to 37 per cent for the British Protestants). Among the English-speaking white Gentiles, the Polish are the least likely to have gone to college (15 per cent), followed by the Slavic group (16 per cent) and the Italians (17 per cent). The eastern and southern European Catholics, in other words, have not yet caught up to the national average in college attendance, though their German co-religionists are slightly ahead of the national average and their Irish co-religionists are substantially above it.

Table 10. Ethnic Identification by Size of Place (Per Cent)

Religio-ethnic Group	Metropolitan over 2,000,000	Metropolitan under 2,000,000	Urban County	Rural County	Total
Protestants					
British	17	43	18	22	100
German	18	35	22	25	100
Scandinavian	15	37	31	17	100
Irish	14	44	13	29	100
Other	14	40	17	29	100
Catholics					
Irish	36	43	16	5	100
German	28	34	22	16	100
Italian	44	44	9	3	100
Polish	30	50	16	4	100
Slavic	28	42	14	16	100
French	17	36	15	32	100
Spanish-speaking	45	51	3	1	100
Other	29	46	12	13	100
Jews					
German	81	16	3	0	100
Eastern European	81	17	2	0	100
Other	67	27	6	0	100
Blacks	27	51	7	15	100
Orientals	55	35	10	0	100
No religion	36	40	10	14	100
Other	33	40	11	16	100
National average	24	42	15	19	100

Italians have reached the national average in the percentage of those who have become managers or owners or professional or technical workers (26 per cent) (Table 12). The Poles and the other eastern European Catholics are still substantially beneath that average (17 and 19 per cent respectively). The Jewish groups are the most likely to be found in these two categories; blacks and Spanish-speaking the least likely. Among English-speaking white Gentiles, British Protestants have a miniscule advantage over Irish Catholics in the proportion in these two top categories (36.5 per cent as against 36.2 per

Table 11. Education and Ethnic Identification (Per Cent)

Religio-ethnic Group	Grammar School or Less	Some High School	High School Graduate	Some College	College Graduate	Graduate School
Protestants						
British	14.9	16.9	31.0	21.1	13.6	2.5
German	22.4	19.0	33.9	14.4	8.6	1.6
Scandinavian	20.3	16.4	32.6	18.1	11.4	1.1
Irish	24.3	24.5	28.7	15.7	5.8	0.9
Other	27.6	22.3	28.1	13.3	7.6	1.1
Catholics						
Irish	10.1	16.2	34.1	22.6	14.0	3.0
German	20.5	18.4	32.2	16.4	10.5	2.0
Italian	23.1	23.1	35.8	10.7	6.1	1.2
Polish	30.9	20.6	33.1	10.3	5.1	0.0
Slavic	27.0	19.0	38.4	10.5	5.1	0.0
French	28.2	22.4	28.8	13.5	5.8	1.3
Spanish-speaking	40.2	27.0	23.0	5.7	4.1	0.0
Other	19.9	22.8	33.2	16.1	6.7	1.3
Jews						
German	3.3	16.7	36.7	16.7	23.3	3.3
Eastern European	6.3	9.4	30.6	19.4	27.5	6.9
Other	6.0	10.0	26.0	28.0	26.0	4.0
Blacks	37.0	25.1	23.6	9.6	4.0	0.7
Orientals	30.0	5.0	20.0	20.0	20.0	5.0
No religion	20.7	12.5	24.7	19.1	14.1	8.9
Other religion	24.7	16.0	27.3	15.3	12.7	4.0
National average	23.9	20.3	30.0	15.0	9.0	1.8

cent). It is interesting to note that the occupational distribution of Irish Protestants virtually matches the national average. Germans and Scandinavians are the most likely to be farmers; Italians, Spanish-speaking, blacks, and Orientals to be service workers; Poles and Slavs to be skilled or craft workers; Spanish-speaking, blacks, and French to be operatives or unskilled factory workers (though the Poles are also disproportinately respresented in this group).

Jews, Orientals, and those with no religion are the most likely to be earning more than $15,000 a year (Table 13). Among white Gentiles, the Irish Catholics and the German Catholics (16 per cent and 12 per cent respectively) are the most likely to be in the $15,000 plus category, with the British Protestants (11 per cent) right behind them. The blacks (48 per cent) and the Spanish-speaking are the most likely to have incomes under $4000 a year. Among the white English-speaking groups, 30 per cent of the Irish Protestants earn less than $4000, as do approximately one-fifth of the Italian, Polish, Slavic, and French Catholics.

Before turning to more detailed analysis of the social class situation of the various religio-ethnic groups, there is one final descriptive question we shall ask: What do we know about the proportions of each group that are native born? Unfortunately the NORC composite sample does not contain data to answer this question. But a composite sample put together from the Survey Research Center (Michigan, 1960–1970) election studies during the 1960s does provide data (Table 14). More than nine-tenths of the English and Irish Protestants are native born of native parents, and approximately eight-tenths of the Germans (both Protestant and Catholic) and Irish Catholics are also native of native stock. Only about half the Scandinavians and about three-tenths of the Italian, Polish, and eastern European Catholics are in this category. Jews (23 per cent) are the least likely to be native born of native parents. Similarly, 22 per cent of the Slavs, 16 per cent of the Italians, 16 per cent of the Jews, and 9 per cent of the Poles were foreign born. No one will be particularly surprised by the data in Table 14; it is well known that most of the southern and eastern European immigrants came to this country at the end of the last century and the beginning of the present one. But because this fact is so obvious, it does not follow that it is an unimportant aspect of American society. For the groups at the bottom half of the table, the immigrant experience, which included the experience of being unwanted and despised, is still very much a part of recent family memory, if not of personal experience.

In summary, then, American society has bestowed economic, occupational, and educational success on its Jewish, British Protestant, and Irish Catholic populations. German and Scandinavian groups have done moderately well, the southern and eastern European Catholic groups less well, and the blacks and Spanish-speaking rather poorly. Surprisingly enough, the Irish Protestants are in last place among the white English-speaking groups on most measures, perhaps in part because of their heavy concentration in the South and in rural areas. It is the purpose of this chapter to report these phenomena; data are not available in this analysis to sort out the social, cultural, psychological, historical, and racial discrimination factors that may be responsible for these differences. We can, however, in a crude sort of way take into account differences

Table 12. Occupation of Head of Household and Ethnic Identification (Per Cent)

Religio-ethnic Group	Other Labor	Farm Workers	Service	Operative, Unskilled Factory	Crafts, Skilled	Sales	Clerical	Managers, Owners	Farmers	Profes- sional, Technical
Protestants										
British	3.6	0.7	5.7	12.3	19.2	7.4	8.6	17.3	6.2	19.2
German	4.0	0.7	5.9	15.9	22.2	6.2	6.4	13.1	11.7	13.9
Scandinavian	2.0	0.6	5.2	18.1	17.8	5.8	9.0	12.2	14.6	14.6
Irish	4.3	1.4	6.7	18.3	23.4	6.7	6.9	14.4	7.9	10.0
Other	5.5	1.5	6.8	17.9	20.6	5.5	7.5	14.2	9.4	11.2
Catholics										
Irish	2.0	0.3	5.3	15.5	25.3	6.6	5.9	16.8	3.0	19.4
German	4.3	0.0	4.6	14.2	22.6	5.6	7.1	15.8	9.6	16.1
Italian	2.8	0.0	13.5	19.7	24.5	4.4	8.2	11.6	0.6	14.7
Polish	2.4	0.0	7.1	27.0	28.6	5.6	11.9	7.1	0.8	9.5

Slavic	7.6	0.0	8.5	20.2	29.6	3.6	7.6	6.3	3.1	13.5
French	3.4	1.4	7.5	26.0	24.0	5.5	5.5	13.7	2.7	10.3
Spanish-speaking	9.4	6.0	12.8	29.1	17.9	3.4	8.5	6.0	0.9	6.0
Other	5.0	1.3	8.8	22.1	22.6	5.5	9.7	11.6	2.6	10.8
Jews										
German	3.3	0.0	3.3	10.0	6.7	13.3	13.3	20.0	0.0	0.0
Eastern European	0.7	0.0	3.4	6.9	10.3	13.1	15.2	21.4	0.0	29.0
Other	0.0	0.0	6.3	4.2	16.7	14.6	6.3	18.8	0.0	33.3
Blacks	16.0	1.6	19.7	28.1	13.5	1.1	7.2	2.9	2.6	7.2
Orientals	15.0	0.0	20.0	5.0	20.0	0.0	10.0	5.0	5.0	20.0
No religion	2.1	1.4	6.6	16.6	19.0	4.5	6.6	16.6	5.5	21.1
Other religion	2.8	0.7	12.7	16.2	19.0	7.0	4.9	12.0	2.1	22.5
National average	5.8	1.0	8.7	18.5	20.2	5.4	7.7	12.5	6.5	13.7

Table 13. Family Income and Ethnic Identification (Per Cent)

Religio-ethnic Group	Under $4000	$4000–$9999	$10,000–$14,999	$15,000 +
Protestants				
British	20.0	47.7	21.0	11.4
German	20.6	51.9	18.7	8.7
Scandinavian	21.6	49.1	21.3	8.0
Irish	30.2	46.7	15.7	7.5
Other	28.2	47.2	16.0	8.6
Catholics				
Irish	11.9	51.0	21.5	15.7
German	12.7	52.5	22.5	12.3
Italian	20.6	50.9	18.7	9.8
Polish	19.4	49.6	25.6	5.4
Slavic	20.2	54.3	18.4	7.2
French	24.2	50.3	18.1	7.4
Spanish-speaking	33.3	51.3	14.5	0.9
Other	20.1	49.7	20.4	9.9
Jews				
German	19.2	38.5	23.1	19.2
Eastern European	9.5	38.8	19.0	32.7
Other	16.3	27.9	18.6	37.2
Blacks	47.5	40.5	8.1	3.9
Orientals	16.7	66.7	0.0	16.7
No religion	22.0	37.9	20.9	19.1
Other religion	30.1	40.6	16.8	12.6
National average	25.8	47.3	17.4	9.5

of city size and region as they affect education and income, and shall do so in a subsequent chapter. Before attempting this exercise, however, it is necessary to ask how adequate the data from the NORC composite sample really are.

The first comparison is with a composite sample constructed from the Survey Research Center's election studies during the 1960s. (Election surveys from 1960, 1964, 1966, 1968, and 1970 are used. There was no ethnic question in the 1962 SRC election survey questionnaire.) Unfortunately, slight differences in the wording of questions make it impossible to combine the NORC and SRC samples into one massive composite. The principal difference also makes strict comparison between the two composites difficult; that is, in most surveys the SRC interviewer could accept the ethnic identification "American," while the NORC interviewer would press for a foreign nation of origin. Thus one would expect a higher level of foreign ethnic identification in the NORC composite sample. Table 15 demonstrates that this phenomenon has in fact occurred. The category "Other Protestant" (which is mostly "American") is 13 percentage points higher in the SRC sample, mostly at the cost of a reduction in German, English, and Irish Protestant responses. However, once this difference is taken into account, the remaining figures in the rows of Table 15 are quite similar. We can conclude that the SRC question is better suited for getting at "conscious" ethnic identification, while the NORC question more effectively taps ethnic background. Both types of questions get roughly the same distribution of answers from Catholics.

Table 14. Nativity of White American Religio-ethnic Groups (Per Cent)

Religio-ethnic Group	Foreign Born	Native, Two Foreign Born Parents	Native, One Foreign Born Parent	Native of Native Parents	Total
Protestants					
English	2	2	6	90	100
Irish	0	1	3	96	100
Scandinavian	8	16	31	55	100
German	3	7	8	82	100
Other	1	2	4	93	100
Catholics					
Irish	3	9	8	80	100
German	7	8	8	77	100
Polish	9	38	22	31	100
Slavic	22	30	18	30	100
Other	8	3	16	73	100
Jews	16	37	24	23	100
National average	6	8	9	77	100

Source: Survey Research Center, University of Michigan, election studies of 1960, 1964, 1966, 1968, 1970. A composite sample.

Table 15.　Distribution of Religio-ethnic Identification in NORC and SRC Composite Samples (Per Cent)

Religio-ethnic Group	NORC	SRC
Protestants		
English	14	11
	(1303)	(1889)
German	13	9
	(1205)	(838)
Scandinavian	4	3
	(359)	(223)
Irish	6	4
	(530)	(441)
Catholics		
Irish	3	3
	(328)	(243)
German	4	3
	(342)	(224)
Italian	4	3
	(346)	(217)
Polish	1	2
	(136)	(112)
Eastern European	3	3
Spanish-speaking	1	1
	(122)	(123)
Other	8	7
	(609)	
Jews	3	3
	(240)	(200)
Blacks	13	9
	(1285)	(640)
Other and none	5	6
	(454)	

It is also possible to compare the two composites with the findings reported by the Current Population Survey (Current Population Reports 1971). Since the CPS may not ask a religious question, the comparison must be made with the religious dimension removed from the SRC and NORC data. The CPS question is more like the SRC question, asking "origin or descent," while the NORC question usually asks, "What country did your ancestors come from?"

Hence the census distribution may be expected to be more like the SRC than the NORC distribution.

Table 16 indicates that this is indeed the case. The NORC question is more likely to elicit the name of a specific foreign country than either the census or SRC questions, with the principal losses being among the English, German, and Irish respondents. The Spanish-speaking are underrepresented in both NORC and SRC samples—we suspect because of their geographic concentrations. The Polish seem overrepresented in the census sample, but in all probability the reason for this is that Polish Jews are included in the census Polish category, and they are not included in the comparable SRC and NORC categories.

Since the ethnic question is asked differently in the NORC interview, we could not have expected a precise similarity in ethnic distributions between the NORC tabulations and those of the other two agencies. However, within the context set by the different questions, the distributions in the three samples are roughly comparable. We must ask, however, whether the different distributions lead to different socioeconomic findings among the various ethnic collectivities. Table 17 attempts an answer to that question by comparing the

Table 16. Distribution of Selected Ethnic Groups over 25 Years Old: A Comparison of NORC Composite Sample, SRC Composite Sample, and U.S. Census Survey[a] (Per Cent)

Ethnic Group	NORC	SRC	Census
English	18[b]	12	10
German	20	11	10
Irish	11	8	7
Italian	4	3	4
Polish	2	2	5
Spanish-speaking	2	1	5
Other	43	63	60
Total	100	100	100

Source: NORC (1963–1972); SRC (1960–1970); *Current Population Reports* (1971).

Note: In this table the comparison is of ethnic groups, not religio-ethnic groups, because the Current Population Survey, like all Census surveys, does not ask a religious question.

[a] Question: "What is ——'s origin or descent?"

[b] Combines Welsh, Scotch, and British Canadian.

Table 17. Occupation, Education, and Income for American Religio-ethnic Grou Compared in SRC Composite Sample and NORC Composite Sample

Religio-ethnic Group	Professional and Managerial (Per Cent)		College Attendance (Per Cent)		Mean Income (In Dollars)	
	SRC	NORC	SRC	NORC	SRC	NORC
Protestants						
British	37	37	37	37	8512	8309
Irish	25	24	24	22	7544	7022
German	21	27	27	24	8146	7808
Scandinavian	33	27	33	32	8963	7869
Catholics						
Irish	40	36	29	37	8907	9254
German	30	32	25	27	8615	8903
Italian	30	26	18	19	8945	7979
Polish	20	17	18	15	8317	7940
Spanish-speaking	15	12	18	10	6360	6145
Jews	48	50	50	45	10,940	11,100
Blacks	9	10	11	15	4860	5425
National average	28	26	24	26	7812	7588

percentage of professional and managerial, the percentage who attended college, and the mean income for the various religio-ethnic groups.

If we assume that a difference of 5 percentage points and $600 in annual income is worth commenting on, there are five notable differences in Table 17. In comparison with SRC, the NORC sample underestimates the percentage managerial for the Scandinavian Protestants, the percentage college attendance for Jews, and the income of the Italians. It overestimates the college attendance of the Irish Catholics and the income of the German Protestants. In all other groups there is a rough compatibility between the two composite samples.

If we then turn to a comparison of educational, occupational, and income data among the three samples (Table 18), one notes that in most cases where there are differences of two or more percentages points (9 out of 14) between SRC and CPS, the NORC figures are closer to the CPS figures. (The Polish percentages are not strictly comparable, because the CPS has included Polish Jews in its sample.)

Table 18. Education, Occupation, and Income of Selected Ethnic Groups over 25 Years Old Compared in NORC Composite Sample, SRC Composite Sample, and U.S. Census Survey (Per Cent)

Ethnic Group	College Graduates			More than $10,000			Managerial and Professional		
	SRC	NORC	CPS	SRC	NORC	CPS	SRC	NORC	CPS
English	20	16	14	31	34	35	38	34	34
German	11	12	11	27	29	37	30	28	30
Irish	12	11	10	27	31	34	21	29	30
Italian	10	7	7	28	29	37	27	30	28
Polish	2	9	9	19	36	38	18	22	29
Spanish-speaking	5	5	5	17	14	15	17	14	15

In summary, a comparison between the NORC composite sample and two other data sets would indicate that we can have sufficient confidence in the general accuracy of the NORC data to proceed to more detailed analysis.

NOTES

1. For further discussion on the nature of ethnicity, see Geertz (1968), Shils (1957), Weber (1961), Francis (1945), Isaacs (1968), and Greeley (1971).

2. Research underway at the American Council on Education on a sample of 400,000 college freshmen will permit comments on ethnic "mixture" at a future date.

3. This may well be a function of the fact that in most NORC surveys racial identification is done visually by the interviewer, and the ethnic question is asked only of "white" respondents. Many Spanish-speaking Americans with dark skins may have been coded as black.

4. Since apostasy is more likely to occur among college graduates than among other segments of the population, it may well be that the high educational mean of those who have no religion is less an indication that the nonreligious are more likely to have education than it is that those who have more education are more likely to be nonreligious.

REFERENCES

U.S. Government Census Bureau. *Current Population Reports,* nos. 220, 221. April 8 and April 20, 1971.

Francis, E. K. "The Nature of the Ethnic Group." *American Journal Of Sociology,* **52** (1945), pp. 393–400.

Geertz, Clifford. "The Concept of Culture and the Concept of Man." *Social Education,* **32,** 2 (February 1968).

Greeley, Andrew M. *Why Can't They Be Like Us?* New York: E. P. Dutton, 1971.

Isaacs, Harold. "Group Identity and Political Change." *Survey,* **00** (October 1968), pp. 000–000.

Shils, Edward. "Primordial, Personal, Sacred, and Civil Ties." *British Journal of Sociology,* **8** (June 1957), pp. 130–145.

Survey Research Center. *Election Studies 1952, 1956, 1958, 1960, 1964, 1966, 1968, 1970.* Ann Arbor: University of Michigan, 1952–1970.

Weber, Max. "The Ethnic Group." In *Theories of Society,* Vol. 1., Talcott Parsons, ed. Glencoe, Ill.: The Free Press, 1961.

3. THE DEMOGRAPHY OF ETHNIC IDENTIFICATION

PART II: EDUCATIONAL AND ECONOMIC
DIFFERENCES AMONG RELIGIO-ETHNIC
GROUPS

I N THE PREVIOUS CHAPTER we presented data on the religio-ethnic composition and distribution of the American population based on a composite
of seven NORC samples collected from the mid-1960s to the early 1970s. The
weaknesses of the data were acknowledged; but it was argued that since no
better data are available on the increasingly interesting question of American
ethnic groups, the tables from the NORC composite sample might be of some
use, particularly since they were reasonably consistent with an SRC composite
sample, and with Current Population Survey data that lack religious information.

Because of the size of the NORC composite sample (n = 9593) and the similarity between tables drawn from it and from the SRC and census materials,
it seems justified to place a moderate amount of confidence in the findings.
However, there has been in recent years considerable demand for information
about the educational and economic differences among the various white ethnic
groups and about whether these differences are diminishing as the more
recently arrived groups undergo "assimilation."

Since religion seems to be an essential component of ethnic identification—
as seen in Chapter 2, there are striking dissimilarities between Irish Catholics
and Irish Protestants, and between Polish Jews and Polish Catholics—and since
religious data are unavailable from the federal census, it is to be feared that for
the foreseeable future, analysis of the differences among the various
ethnic groups will have to rely on survey data. This chapter presents a
tentative analysis of the differences among such groups in education, and asks
whether such differences are a function of size of residential place and region.
It also explores whether differences in income are a function of differences in
education, size of place, and region. Finally, with the help of the SRC National Election composite sample, we attempt to determine whether there has
been cohort mobility among the various groups between the 1950s and the
1960s.

It should be clear to the reader that this is a very speculative enterprise, justified solely by the absence of better data. The first columns of Tables 1, 2, and
3 present in another way findings reported in Chapter 2, and thus enjoy the
same kind of confidence. The rest of the analysis in this chapter can be
considered suggestive at best, and perhaps as a spur to the undertaking of a
massive national survey. Note however that the analysis acquires marginally
greater plausibility because of the rough but fundamental similarities between
the conclusions drawn from the SRC and NORC materials.[1]

In Table 1 we present the "advantage" and "disadvantage" of the various
groups in educational attainment. The first column shows the deviation in years
from the national average of 10.9 years of education for each of the groups. The
second column shows the deviation with city size (metropolitan versus

Table 1. Deviation from Educational Mean among American Religio-ethnic Groups (Mean = 10.9 Years)

Religio-ethnic Group	Gross Deviation	Net Deviation[a]
Protestants		
British	1.0	1.0
German	0.1	0.1
Scandinavian	0.4	0.3
Irish	−0.3	0.0
Other	−0.4	−0.1
Catholics		
Irish	1.3	1.0
German	0.4	0.2
Italian	−0.2	−0.7
Polish	−0.9	−1.1
Slavic	−0.5	−0.7
French	−0.5	−0.4
Spanish-speaking	−1.6	−2.0
Other	−0.9	−0.8
Jews	2.4	1.8
Blacks	−1.2	−1.1

[a] Standardized for region (South versus non-South) and size of place (metropolitan versus nonmetropolitan).

nonmetropolitan) and region (South versus non-South) taken into account.[2] In the second column we asked what the differences in educational attainment would be if all the ethnic groups had the same regional and metropolitan distributions.

We note in the first column that the Jews, the British Protestants, and the Irish Catholics have the greatest educational advantage, while the blacks and the Spanish-speaking have the greatest educational disadvantage. The two German groups and the Scandinavian Protestants are virtually at the educational mean. Among the English-speaking white Gentile groups, the Poles are almost a year beneath the national average, and the Slavs and the French Catholics are almost a half-year beneath the national average. But the performance of the southern and eastern European Catholics may be even worse than appears in the first column, because these groups (though not the French) tend to be concentrated in large cities and in the North where there is more opportunity for education and educational achievement is higher. Hence we turn to column 2 to see how these groups do in a situation in which geographic and metropolitan distribution is held constant.

Standardization has little effect on the mean scores of the British, German, and Scandinavian Protestant groups. However, the deviation from the educational means of the Irish and "other" Protestants is eliminated in the former case and substantially reduced in the latter cases. The lower educational scores of these two groups in the first column, in other words, result from their rural and southern locations.

The low scores of the Italian, Polish, Slavic, French, and Spanish-speaking Catholics grow even lower when region and city size are held constant. If the southern and eastern European Catholics are compared with those who live in the places of the same size and the same region as they do, they are at even more of an educational disadvantage. The Poles, for example, have a minus deviation of 1.1 years of school—the same as the blacks.

The high scores of the Irish Catholics and the Jews are diminished somewhat by standardizing for region and size of place, but the educational success of these two groups cannot be explained merely by their non-South and metropolitan locations.

Surprisingly enough, the educational disadvantage of the eastern and southern European Catholics is not translated into income disadvantage (Table 2). While the Jews, the Irish Catholics, and the German Catholics have the highest gross incomes, the Italian, Polish, and French Catholics are all above the national average. The Irish Protestants are substantially ($566) beneath the national average, and the "other" Protestants are somewhat beneath the national average ($313). Indeed, Polish and Italian Catholics have a higher annual income than do any of the Protestant groups with the exception of the British Protestants. The incomes of the black and Spanish-speaking are deplorably beneath the national average.

In the second column of Table 2, education, region, and city size are all held constant. Irish, German, Italian, and Polish Catholics all have higher net incomes than do any of the Protestant groups under these circumstances.

The standardization in column 2 cuts income disadvantage in half for Spanish-speaking Catholics and reduces from $2163 to $1437 the income disadvantage of blacks. The data on the Irish Protestants continue to be surprising; they make on the average $500 less than the national average, and the standardization only slightly reduces that deficit. There is every reason to assume that the blacks and the Spanish-speaking have been the object of discrimination, but one wonders whether there is also discrimination against

Table 2. Deviation from Family Income Mean among American Religio-ethnic Groups for Head of Family (Mean = $7588)

Religio-ethnic Group	Gross Deviation (in dollars)	Net Deviation[a] (in dollars)
Protestants		
British	721	84
German	270	200
Scandinavian	281	305
Irish	−566	−491
Other	−313	−26
Catholics		
Irish	1637	809
German	1315	922
Italian	391	431
Polish	352	722
Slavic	165	166
French	110	245
Spanish-speaking	−1443	−724
Other	517	531
Jews	3324	1569
Blacks	−2163	−1437

[a] Standardized for region, size of place, and education.

Irish Protestants.[3] Equally surprising in Table 2 is the finding of the southern and eastern European Catholic groups, that both in the real world and the world created by standardization techniques they earn more money than the national average and in many cases more than their native American counterparts.

It becomes appropriate to wonder whether the surprising income levels of the Catholic ethnics may be the result of an "acculturation" process by which the children and grandchildren of immigrants have not only achieved some sort of rough parity in American society, but have actually managed to fight their way to the middle of the pack, if not to the top of the heap (as the Irish have nearly done). In the next four tables, we turn to a crude cross-sectional analysis that will attempt to throw some light on this question. Our technique will be to divide the population into age cohorts and then to compare each group with the mean score for its own age group. That the general educational level in the United States has gone up, and that younger people have far higher mean educations than older people are well known facts. Learning that younger Polish Americans have more education than older Polish Americans would therefore not prove "acculturation." However, if the relative position of Poles improved in the lower age group, that is, if the age group mean goes up while the Polish mean for the same group goes up even more, then we can point to relative Polish improvement and to an indication of Polish "acculturation"—at least in level of education—to American society.

In Table 3 we present the deviation from cohort mean for five age cohorts of each of the American religio-ethnic groups. Three ethnic groups are above the cohort mean at each level: Jews are two years higher than their respective cohort mean in all but one age level; the Irish Catholics are always at least a year above the group mean; and the British Protestants in three of five cases are more than a year above the mean, and in their thirties and twenties more than half a year above the mean. The Scandinavian Protestants are also about half a year above the group mean at each age level.

Four Catholic ethnic groups—German, Italian, Polish, and Slavic—begin beneath the group mean but cross it as age decreases. Thus, Germans in their forties are above the mean for that age group, and Italians, Poles, and Slavs have crossed the mean in their thirties. The comparison between the members of these three groups in their twenties and those in their sixties is striking and tells a fascinating story of adjustment to American society. Italians over age 60 are almost a full year beneath their cohort mean in education, Slavs are a year and a half beneath the mean, and Poles are more than two years beneath the mean. Italians and Slavs in their twenties, on the other hand, are both about one-tenth of a year above the mean, and Poles are a half-year above the mean.

Black and Spanish-speaking and French Catholic groups all remain beneath the group educational mean at the various age levels, but all three are moving up. Blacks have moved from almost two years beneath the mean for age 50 and over to less than a year beneath the mean for those in their twenties. The Spanish-speaking in their twenties are only about a third of a year beneath the mean, and the French Catholics are only about one-fifth of a year beneath the mean. All other Catholic groups in their twenties (excluding the residual "other" group) are above the group mean in educational achievement.

Finally, the Irish Protestants are not only beneath the group mean at all age levels but are receding from the mean. Irish Protestants under age 30 are even further from the group mean at that age level than are Spanish-speaking in the same group. Although this does not say that the absolute educational level of

Irish Protestants is going down, it does indicate that it is not going up at a time when the educational mean of the entire population is rising. Again, one is at a loss to explain this phenomenon.

Another interesting observation from Table 3 is that blacks under age 30 are closer to the group educational mean of their age group than are Poles or French Catholics in their forties and Italian, Polish, and Slavic Catholics in their fifties. Furthermore, blacks in their thirties are closer to their group mean than are Polish and Slavic Catholics in their sixties. No argument can be made about the comparability of experience of southern and eastern Europeans and that of blacks. Whatever prejudice and discrimination there may have been and may still be against Slavic and Latin Catholics (and we are persuaded that there still is such discrimination), it is surely relatively minor compared with what the blacks have had to and still do contend with. However, it is at least possible that older southern and eastern European Catholics may feel relatively educationally deprived compared to younger blacks.

Table 4 is addressed to the question of whether standardization for region and size of place affects the picture of educational change presented in Table 3. Jews, Irish Catholics,[4] and the British still continue to be above the group educational achievements. The score of Irish Protestants over age 30 is moving to or above the mean. One can thus say that the low scores of these Irish Protestants are a function of their living in rural and southern regions. However, Irish Protestants under age 30 are one-fifth of a year beneath the mean for that age group level, suggesting that even with region and city size held constant, there remains a problem of recession from the mean among that group.

The dramatic changes across age lines among southern and eastern European Catholic groups are as evident in Table 4 as they are in Table 3. Indeed, these groups may be said to have "started out" with even greater handicaps when they were compared with other Americans with the same regional and metropolitan distribution. The ethnics over age 60 are even lower than their group mean when region and metropolitanism are taken into account.

Similarly, standardization moves the achievement of educational parity down a decade in effect. Among the Catholic groups, the achievement of parity has been facilitated by the fact that the ethnics live in the big cities of the North where there are more educational opportunities. Nonetheless, the Italians and the Poles under age 40 and the French under 30 have achieved a rough parity with the rest of the population in education. The same cannot be said of the Spanish-speaking Catholics. In Table 3, their unstandardized de-

Table 3. Deviation from Educational Mean of Cohort by Age Group for American Religio-ethnic Groups (in Years)

Religio-ethnic Group	29 and Under	Thirties	Forties	Fifties	Sixty and Over
Protestants					
British	0.71 (195)	0.52 (251)	1.35 (248)	1.54 (233)	1.57 (374)
German	-0.01 (236)	0.34 (238)	0.09 (228)	0.07 (178)	0.26 (322)
Scandinavian	0.58 (85)	0.42 (66)	0.47 (57)	0.53 (56)	0.58 (94)
Irish	-0.42 (107)	-0.01 (83)	-0.06 (105)	-0.20 (107)	-0.16 (128)
Other	-0.34 (371)	-0.52 (386)	-0.29 (363)	-0.03 (266)	-0.34 (486)
Catholics					
Irish	1.07 (73)	1.18 (66)	1.55 (61)	1.65 (53)	1.33 (73)
German	0.54 (66)	0.56 (76)	0.40 (75)	-0.32 (55)	-0.01 (68)

Italian	0.10 (61)	0.37 (78)	−0.39 (79)	−0.82 (62)	−0.96 (64)
Polish	0.54 (19)	0.23 (28)	−0.89 (35)	−1.04 (28)	−2.30 (26)
Slavic	0.13 (42)	0.33 (45)	−0.58 (57)	−0.99 (49)	−1.53 (43)
French	−0.19 (37)	−0.85 (32)	−0.85 (27)	−0.05 (31)	−1.13 (29)
Spanish-speaking	−0.35 (45)	−2.13 (28)	−2.40 (26)	−3.06 (10)	−0.35 (13)
Other	−0.18 (169)	−0.27 (146)	−0.14 (127)	−0.30 (72)	−0.17 (92)
Jews	2.05 (42)	2.15 (48)	2.00 (55)	2.92 (46)	1.57 (45)
Blacks	−0.80 (309)	−1.14 (274)	−1.58 (273)	−1.92 (157)	−1.68 (267)
Cohort mean	12.2	11.9	11.3	10.5	10.0

Table 4.   Net Deviation*a* from Educational Mean of Cohort by Age for American Religio-ethnic Groups (in Years)

Religio-ethnic Group	29 and Under	Thirties	Forties	Fifties	Sixty and Over
Protestants					
British	0.81	0.64	1.47	1.46	2.05
German	0.02	0.38	0.38	−0.11	0.21
Scandinavian	0.50	0.34	0.33	0.33	0.30
Irish	−0.19	0.18	0.28	−0.03	0.20
Other	−0.10	−0.32	−0.04	−0.19	0.16
Catholics					
Irish	0.80	0.86	1.34	1.28	0.97
German	0.38	0.39	0.18	0.38	−0.24
Polish	−0.25	0.03	−0.87	−1.22	−1.82
Slavic	−0.09	−0.19	−0.80	−1.15	−1.80
French	0.16	−0.48	−0.89	−0.11	−1.96
Spanish-speaking	−2.61	−2.74	−2.72	−3.32	−0.96
Other	−0.39	−0.45	−0.43	−0.43	−0.28
Jews	1.74	1.79	2.14	2.14	1.02
Blacks	−0.70	1.07	−1.46	−2.00	−1.52

a Standardized by region and size of place.

viation from the mean for those under age 30 is .35; in Table 4 it is 2.61, perhaps due to the fact that almost half of our Spanish-speaking respondents apparently live in the Los Angeles metropolitan area.

To summarize briefly the evidence in Table 4, Irish Catholics, British Protestants, and Jews have made it in American society. They had met success in terms of their education before anyone in the present population was born. The southern and eastern European Catholic groups are in the process of making it. Those born since 1930 have achieved rough educational parity with the rest of the population, in part because they live in cities in the northern region of the country where there is more educational opportunity. But even taking this into account, the data in Tables 3 and 4 document a dramatic change in the educational achievement of Catholic ethnic groups and call into serious question much of the contemporary stereotyping of blue collar ethnics.

We should also note in passing the peculiar phenomenon of the Irish: The Irish Catholics are substantially higher in educational achievement than was expected; the Irish Protestants are somewhat lower than might have been expected. While their lower score results in part from their regional and rural distribution, there may also be other factors at work.

The dramatic change in the Catholic ethnics is further documented in Table 5, in which the annual family income for heads of family is presented with an age break at 40. (The dichotomy is necessary; since only heads of family are being considered, the number of cases is substantially diminished.) The most economically successful of those over age 40 are Jews and Irish Catholics, followed by German Catholics and British Protestants. All the other Catholic ethnic groups over age 40 earn less than the national average (with the exception of the residual "other" Catholic groups). If you are over 40, it "costs" $441 to be Polish, $566 to be Slavic, $260 to be French, and $10 to be Italian (and almost $300 to be an Irish Protestant). Among those under 40, there is a "payoff" over the cohort mean annual family income of $896 for Italians, $370 for Poles, and $1022 for Slavs. It "costs" $1786 to be black, $1334 to be Spanish-speaking, and $929 to be Irish Protestant. The fortunes of the southern and eastern European Catholics under age 40, in other words, have changed very notably when compared with those over 40. No comparable change has occurred for the blacks (with only $139 relative improvement), and only a moderate change has occurred for the Spanish-speaking Catholics ($504 improvement).

Standardizing for region, size of place, and education level in Table 6 indicates that at least as far as Italians and Poles go, those over age 40 earn more than the national average for their age and education, region, and size of place. The other eastern European Catholics, however, seem to pay a small penalty ($269), even when all the background factors are held constant. But they pay nothing like the penalty that blacks over and under age 40 pay;[5] nor, for that matter, do they pay anything like that of Irish Protestants under 40. With education, region, and city size held constant, it still costs more than $1000 a year to be an Irish Protestant, and $1468 to be a black.

Interestingly enough, when the background variables are held constant, the cost of being a Spanish-speaking Catholic is not high ($199). This finding—based, obviously, on a very small case of 28 respondents—suggests that once the Spanish-speaking are brought to educational levels comparable to the national average, they will experience only relatively minor income deprivation. On the basis of our data, such an assertion cannot be made about the blacks. Neither would it appear that it can be made about the Irish Protestants.

It is also worth noting that in the standardized world created for Table 6, all the Catholic ethnic groups (with the exception of the Spanish-speaking)

Table 5.　Deviation from Cohort Family Income Mean by Age for Head of Family (in Dollars)

Religio-ethnic Group	Under 40	40 and Over
Protestants		
British	139	774
	(205)	(429)
German	83	129
	(226)	(379)
Scandinavian	−517	430
	(75)	(112)
Irish	−929	299
	(83)	(159)
Other	156	217
	(289)	(494)
Catholics		
Irish	1682	1408
	(70)	(97)
German	1230	834
	(69)	(95)
Italian	896	−10
	(50)	(102)
Polish	370	−491
	(19)	(44)
Slavic	1022	−566
	(40)	(76)
French	91	−260
	(38)	(36)
Spanish-speaking	1334	−1838
	(28)	(37)
Other	874	83
	(124)	(137)
Jews	2575	3964
	(40)	(61)
Blacks	−1786	−1925
	(249)	(330)
Cohort mean	8231	7462

Table 6. Net Deviation[a] from Cohort Family Income Mean by Age for Head of Family (in Dollars)

Religio-ethnic Group	Under 40	40 and Over
Protestants		
British	91	114
German	306	137
Scandinavian	−521	819
Irish	−1051	128
Other	−10	−69
Catholics		
Irish	1165	654
German	1019	1058
Italian	786	165
Polish	836	659
Slavic	923	−269
French	457	174
Spanish-speaking	−199	−261
Other	1057	197
Jews	2756	2157
Blacks	−1468	−1508

[a] Standardized by region, size of place, and education.

under age 40 have higher annual family incomes than do any of the Protestant groups. Indeed, with the exception of the Germans, all Protestant groups under age 40 fall beneath the cohort income mean. It would appear, then, that with educational achievement held constant, Catholic ethnics, like Avis, try harder. Jews are Number One.

Finally, when we compare the proportion of male workers over age 40 who are white collar workers in the urban non-South with those under 40 (Table 7), the change in the southern and eastern European Catholics is striking. Both Poles and Italians over 40 are more than 10 percentage points below the national average (of northern urban males) in the proportion who have white collar jobs at that age level. In other words, the stereotype of the blue collar ethnic is accurate here. In the group under age 40, however, Poles and Italians are only 2 and 4 percentage points respectively below the national average; indeed, they are more likely to be white collar workers than British Protestants from similar cities outside the South. We note also that the Irish

Table 7. Deviation from Cohort Average Per Cent Male White Collar Workers in Urban non-South (Per Cent)

Religio-ethnic Group	Under 40	40 and Over
Protestants		
British	−6	11
	(84)	(179)
German	2	4
	(97)	(164)
Scandinavian	15	4
	(33)	(52)
Irish	−20	−6
	(27)	(39)
Other	−10	−1
	(98)	(176)
Catholics		
Irish	4	0
	(52)	(78)
German	3	−2
	(41)	(55)
Italian	−2	−11
	(50)	(88)
Polish	−4	−15
	(17)	(39)
Slavic	11	−15
	(29)	(52)
French	−10	−16
	(17)	(16)
Spanish-speaking	−18	−22
	(21)	(33)
Other	−3	−11
	(91)	(95)
Jews	28	34
	(30)	(63)
Blacks	−16	−18
	(102)	(121)
National average[a]	46	40
	(873)	(1360)

[a] For non-South urban males.

Protestants are 20 points below the national average in proportion of blue collar workers, even in cities outside the South. 'This score is lower than that of the blacks, who are 16 percentage points beneath the average.

The SRC election survey file that is available to us also contains data from the 1950 elections (1952, 1956, and 1958—the survey was not taken in 1954). Using this data, it is possible to measure change in income, occupation, and education among the various ethnic collectivities between the 1950s and the 1960s (Table 8). The per cent of managerial and professional workers increased nationally by 4 points between the two decades. The greatest changes were found in the German and Italian Catholics (both with 13 percentage points), and in the Irish Catholics (10 percentage points). The least change appears among the Irish Protestants and the Jews (2 percentage points) and the Poles (no change). It should be noted that the small change seen for the Jews probably reflects the fact that almost half of them were already in these occupational categories in the 1950s.

The Jews do however experience the greatest change in the per cent who attended college, rising from 26 per cent in the 1950s to 50 per cent in the 1960s. This finding suggests that Jews, already in the managerial class (small businessmen and shop keepers to a considerable extent, we presume) in the 1950s, were the most likely to take advantage of the increased educational advantages of the last two decades. Thus in terms of educational mobility the most striking advance has not been among the Catholic ethnics but among the Jews. Nonetheless, all the Catholic groups did increase their figures for the percentage attending college, with a greater than 5 per cent change between the two decades. Of the Protestant groups, only the Scandinavians improved their relative educational position during that time.

Finally, Jews, Italians, and Scandinavians are the most likely to have improved their financial positions during the two decades. We must note sadly that, whatever may have happened between the late 1960s and the present, gains for black Americans in income and level of occupation and education were less than those shown in national average between the two decades.

Since they include both the 1950s and the 1960s, the SRC data enable us to explore from a different perspective the question of the recent economic history of cohort religio-ethnic groups. We assume that those who were in their twenties during the 1950s are a representative sample of those born between 1931 and 1940, and that those who were in their thirties in the 1960s are a representative sample of that same group 10 years later. Thus by looking at those who were in their twenties in the 1950s and in their thirties in the 1960s, we are able to see how a specific segment of the population changed its income in the course of a decade. The technique of cohort analysis is elementary and frequent. But even though we are dealing with a sample of

Table 8. Occupation, Education, and Income of American Religio-ethnic Groups in the 1950s and the 1960s and the Change Between Decades from SRC Composite Sample

Religio-ethnic Group	Professional or Managerial (Per Cent)			College Attendance (Per Cent)			Mean Income (In Dollars)		
	1950s	1960s	Change	1950s	1960s	Change	1950s	1960s	Change
Protestants									
British	35	37	2	32	37	5	6246	8512	2266
Irish	19	25	6	25	24	−1	5110	7854	2434
German	24	31	7	19	27	8	5370	8146	2776
Scandinavian	23	33	10	19	33	14	5326	8963	3637
Catholics									
Irish	33	40	7	22	29	7	5882	8907	2025
German	17	30	13	11	25	14	5571	8615	2044
Italian	17	30	13	9	18	9	5263	8945	3622
Polish	20	20	0	29	18	9	5256	8317	2061
Jews	46	48	2	26	50	24	6960	10,940	3980
Spanish-speaking	7	15	8	7	18	11	3870	6360	2490
Blacks	7	9	2	10	11	1	2863	4860	1997
National average	24	28	4	19	24	5	5050	7812	2762

15,000 respondents, our analysis has a basic weakness. The cross-tabulation by age, decade, and ethnic group leaves us with rather small numbers of respondents for each ethnic cohort. Thus the most we can say is that we are dealing with very tentative and speculative data.

The figures in Table 10, sections A through K, represent deviations from a cohort mean, which is shown in Table 9. Thus to say that the English Protestants in Cohort I (between age 20 and 30 during the 1960s) have a score of −16 is to say that they earned $16 less than the mean for their cohort during that decade. The mean for Cohort I during the 1960s (Table 9) is $7723, which makes the mean for English Protestants $7707. If one reads down each column of Table 10, one can see the income differences among various age groups in the specific ethnic group during both of the decades. Thus during the 1950s, English Protestants in their twenties made $631 more than the average of all Americans at their age level. Those in their thirties made $1997 more than their age level average, those in their forties made $1781 more, and those in their fifties made $1060 more than their age level average. Similarly, reading down the second column, one can see that except for the English Protestants in their twenties, each age level among the English ethnic collectivity made more than the mean for the national cohort at that age level.

Table 9. Mean Income in Dollars for Age Cohorts in the 1950s and 1960s (SRC Composite Sample)

Cohort	1950s	1960s	Change
Cohort I Born 1941 to 1950. In its twenties during the 1960s.		7723	
Cohort II Born 1931 to 1940. In its twenties during the 1950s and its thirties during the 1960s.	4837	9345	4508
Cohort III Born 1921 to 1930. In its thirties during the 1950s and its forties during the 1960s.	5633	9459	3826
Cohort IV Born 1911 to 1920. In its forties during the 1950s and its fifties during the 1960s.	5888	8136	2248
Cohort V Born 1901 to 1910. In its fifties during the 1950s and its sixties during the 1960s.	5222	5478	256

Table 10. Income Deviation in Dollars of Ethnic Groups in the 1950s and the 1960s by Cohort (SRC Composite Sample)

A. English Protestants

	1950s	1960s	Net Change in Deviation from Cohort Mean
Cohort I Born 1941 to 1950. In its twenties during the 1960s.		−16 (193)	
Cohort II Born 1931 to 1940. In its twenties during the 1950s and its thirties during the 1960s.	+631 (51)	+1360 (168)	+729
Cohort III Born 1921 to 1930. In its thirties during the 1950s and its forties during the 1960s.	+1997 (106)	+748 (217)	−1252
Cohort IV Born 1911 to 1920. In its forties during the 1950s and its fifties during the 1960s.	+1781 (138)	+1443 (193)	−338
Cohort V Born 1901 to 1910. In its fifties during the 1950s and its sixties during the 1960s.	+1060 (139)	+1384 (155)	+324

B. Irish Protestants

	1950s	1960s	Net Change
Cohort I		+2260 (99)	
Cohort II	+1326 (39)	−243 (65)	−1569
Cohort III	+741 (51)	+127 (79)	−614
Cohort IV	−67 (39)	−957 (79)	−890

Table 10.   Continued

	1950s	1960s	Net Change in Deviation from Cohort Mean
Cohort V	+699 (32)	−101 (67)	−800

C. Scandinavian Protestants

	1950s	1960s	Net Change in Deviation from Cohort Mean
Cohort I		+663 (46)	
Cohort II	+548 (38)	+2160 (65)	+1612
Cohort III	+748 (34)	+670 (53)	−78
Cohort IV	+1054 (43)	+2859 (37)	+1779
Cohort V	+37 (49)	+329 (33)	+292

D. German Protestants

	1950s	1960s	Net Change in Deviation from Cohort Mean
Cohort I		+75 (200)	
Cohort II	+308 (93)	+977 (152)	+699
Cohort III	+530 (113)	+629 (156)	+99
Cohort IV	+449 (128)	+683 (143)	+234
Cohort V	+380 (85)	−144 (83)	−524

E. Other Protestants ("American")

	1950s	1960s	Net Change in Deviation from Cohort Mean
Cohort I		−134 (325)	
Cohort II	−155 (475)	−874 (287)	−719
Cohort III	−28 (606)	−1093 (305)	−1125
Cohort IV	−195 (457)	−1311 (263)	−1506

Table 10. Continued

	1950s	1960s	Net Change in Deviation from Cohort Mean
Cohort V	−456 (339)	−1111 (186)	−655

F. Irish Catholics

	1950s	1960s	
Cohort I		+1148 (50)	
Cohort II	+928 (24)	+1006 (44)	+78
Cohort III	+1821 (49)	+1046 (51)	−775
Cohort IV	+274 (40)	+680 (34)	+406
Cohort V	+288 (30)	+2349 (34)	+2061

G. German Catholics

	1950s	1960s	
Cohort I		+296 (52)	
Cohort II	+750 (27)	−172 (46)	−922
Cohort III	+640 (49)	+2145 (49)	+1501
Cohort IV	+122 (32)	+990 (30)	+968
Cohort V	+140 (20)	−139 (30)	−273

H. Polish Catholics

	1950s	1960s	
Cohort I		−345 (24)	
Cohort II	+706 (19)	+446 (15)	−260
Cohort III	−226 (28)	−245 (33)	+20
Cohort IV	−517 (35)	−429 (20)	+88
Cohort V	−1745 (13)	−342 (13)	+1403

Table 10. Continued

	1950s	1960s	Net Change in Deviation from Cohort Mean
I. Italian Catholics			
Cohort I		+1036	
		(46)	
Cohort II	−338	+426	+764
	(36)	(46)	
Cohort III	+102	+256	+154
	(61)	(48)	
Cohort IV	−152	+1073	+1225
	(50)	(37)	
Cohort V	+595	+2437	+1842
	(26)	(21)	
J. Jews			
Cohort I		+2804	
		(40)	
Cohort II	+2444	+2382	−72
	(24)	(41)	
Cohort III	+1681	+3769	+2088
	(42)	(37)	
Cohort IV	+2265	+2910	+645
	(51)	(26)	
Cohort V	+1522	+1358	−164
	(40)	(22)	
K. Blacks			
Cohort I		−2258	
		(148)	
Cohort II	−1495	−3613	−2118
	(192)	(148)	
Cohort III	−2556	−4198	−3826
	(148)	(121)	
Cohort IV	−2923	−5291	−2998
	(119)	(106)	
Cohort V	−2712	−2633	−79
	(77)	(69)	

Looking at the rows in Table 10, one can see how a specific age cohort improved its relative position in the 1950s and 1960s. Thus English Protestants born between 1931 and 1940 made $631 more than the national cohort mean in the 1950s, and $1360 more than the national cohort mean in the 1960s. They not only improved their absolute level of income, as did every ethnic group, they also improved their relative position. They were even further ahead of the mean for their age peers in the 1960s than they were in the 1950s.

The English Protestant Americans, then, are substantially ahead of the national average for their age group during the 1950s and remain ahead in the 1960s, except in Cohort I where they fall slightly beneath the national average for those who were in their twenties during the last decade. It may well be that the reason for the $16 deficit in Cohort I during the 1960s is that such a substantial segment of the English American population might still be in college or graduate school while in their twenties. However, it is also worth noting that in Cohorts III and IV, the relative advantage of English Protestant Americans over the national mean had diminished considerably.

A far different picture is presented by the Irish Protestants (Table 10, section B). While they are above their respective cohort averages in three of the four levels in the 1950s, they are below the national average in three of the five levels in the 1960s; and in all four cases they experience a negative change in deviation from the mean in the two decades. It is true that the Irish Protestants in their twenties during the 1960s are substantially above the national mean for that cohort. However, it should be noted that their predecessors who were in their twenties during the previous decade slipped badly ($1569) in the 1960s. This suggests that the income advantage of the Irish Protestants in their twenties in both decades may be the result of the fact that they begin their occupational lives early, thus earning more in their twenties than their age peers of other groups who may still be in college. However, by the time they get to their thirties, this initial advantage is canceled out by the college education of other groups. Thus while English Americans appear to maintain economic superiority, though perhaps with some erosion, SRC data, like the NORC data, indicate that the Irish Protestants— an ethnic group that seems to lack consciousness, organization, and visibility— are downwardly mobile.

The opposite can be seen in the case of the Scandinavian Protestants (Table 10, section C). In all cohorts in both decades the Scandinavians are higher than their cohort mean, and in three of the four cohorts they improved their relative position in the 1960s. Twenty years ago Scandinavians were already above the national income average, and in the course of the two decades they improved their position even more. The most notable improvements are among those who were in their twenties in the 1950s and those who were in their forties in the same decade. Cohort III of the Scandinavians did not improve greatly, possibly (and this is extremely speculative) because they were born or spent their childhood years during the worst years of the Great Depression.

Another group that has made the most of the last two decades is the German Protestant group, which is above the national average at all age cohorts in the 1950s and at four of the five age cohorts in the 1960s. Only in Cohort V during the 1960s does one German age group fall beneath the national mean. The $520 loss in relative position among German Protestants in their sixties during the 1960s may be due to the fact that this group is heavily composed of farmers. Farm income among people in their sixties may deteriorate more seriously than in other groups in the population. The relative improvement in the economic condition of German Protestants is not as strong as that of Scandinavian Protestants. Nonetheless, the former group continues to improve its relative position in the decade between 1960 and 1970 vis-à-vis the rest of American society.

But the "other Protestants" (for the most part, those who responded to the SRC ethnic question that they were "American") are the major losers among the white groups. All four age cohorts included in section E are beneath their respective means in the 1950s and even further beneath the mean in the 1960s. In two of the cohorts (III and IV) they suffer a loss in relative position of more than $1000. Granted that the "other Protestants" tend to be rural and farmers, Table 10 establishes that not only does a population segment concentrated in the rural areas earn less than more urban population segments, but also that its relative position is deteriorating. In each age cohort in the 1960s, income is even further away from the cohort mean than it was in the 1950s. Neither the Irish Protestants nor the "other Protestants" are an ethnic group in the sense that the Polish and the Italian Catholics are. Neither of the two Protestant groups has much in the way of self-conscious ethnic identity, nor are they so identified by the rest of American society. They include that element in the white American population which is not keeping pace with the general increase in income level, but precisely because they do not identify themselves as a group and are not so identified by others, their deteriorating position is not obvious to the rest of society. Perhaps it is not even obvious to many of them.

Irish Catholics are the most successful of the white immigrant groups. In all age cohorts in both decades the Irish are substantially ahead of the national average in their respective age cohorts. Indeed, in five cases they are more than $1000 ahead of it, and in one case more than $2000. Furthermore, the Irish who were under age 30 in the 1960s are $1000 ahead of the cohort mean for that group, indicating that the Irish movement upward continues unabated. In only one age cohort (III) was there a decline in relative advantage of the 1960s over the 1950s. Interestingly enough, it is this same Cohort III in which a $1252 decline in deviation from the mean was also recorded among the British Americans. We may specualte, just as we did in reporting on this phenomenon for the English Americans, that the Great Depression may have had some impact on this cohort's capacity to take advantage of the opportunities of the last 20 years. Let it be noted, however, that Cohort III is well above the national average for that cohort during the 1960s for both the English Protestant and Irish Catholic groups. It is not as far above as might be expected, given their performance in the 1950s.

Like German Protestants, German Catholics (Table 10, section G) suffer a decline beneath the cohort mean at the level of Cohort V (those who were in their fifties in the 1950s and in their sixties in the 1960s). In addition, however, German Catholics also suffer a decline in Cohort II (those who passed from their twenties to their thirties during the last two decades). NORC data for this age cohort does not indicate the same phenomenon. German Catholics improved their relative position in American society during the 1950s and 1960s, but not as much as the Irish Catholics did.

The Polish Catholic performance (section H) indicates a slow upward movement of the Polish population—though the number of respondents is sufficiently low to merit caution in appraising it. The three oldest age cohorts of Poles were beneath the national mean for their age cohorts in both the 1950s and the 1960s, though they improved their relative position somewhat during the two decades. Cohort II was the first Polish cohort to be above the national mean, though its relative advantage slipped somewhat from the 1950s to the 1960s. Polish Catholics, then, seem to be improving their relative position in American society, but far more slowly than the earlier Catholic immigrant groups.

However, the Italians (section I) are doing far better than the Poles. Indeed, they were substantially above the mean for their respective age levels, and all of them have improved their relative position notably since the 1950s. The Italians are in fact the only group to have improved their position in all four age cohorts between the two decades. Only the Jews have scored a greater increase in income between the 1950s and the 1960s. Thus, while the evidence about the upward mobility of American Poles is unclear, there is no doubt that the Italians are moving very rapidly into the upper middle class of American society.

The Jews (section J) are already solidly in the upper middle class. In all but the oldest age cohort, the relative Jewish advantage over the cohort income mean in both the 1950s and the 1960s exceeds $2000, and while Jews in Cohort II slipped a little ($72) in their relative advantage over the cohort mean between the 1950s and 1960s, they are still almost $2400 ahead of the average for their age level in the 1960s. Finally, Jews in their twenties in the 1960s have the greatest advantage over their age peers of any ethnic group ($2437). It is twice that of their nearest competitor, the Irish Catholics.

The last section (Table 10, K) is extremely depressing. Although better evidence can be made for the case with data more reliable than ours, and although in the late 1960s and early 1970s there has perhaps been some change, one is still forced to conclude from Table 10, K that in the two decades between 1950 and 1970, the upward mobility system, which worked extremely well for the Jews, the Irish, and the Italians, reasonably well for the Germans, and has at least begun to work for the Poles, has not yet worked at all for the blacks. Whether it may have begun working (at least for some) since 1965 is beyond the scope of this presentation.

While the findings reported here are as tentative as the rather shaky data base of the two composite samples, they nonetheless suggest that there is an important demographic story to be told about American religio-ethnic groups, a story with a past and a present and in all probability a future. To tell this story adequately, far better data will be required. In the continued absence of a religious question in the federal census, very large national samples will be necessary.

NOTES

1. The use of significance tests was considered and, on the advice of the NORC sampling experts, rejected. The differences among most groups in the first columns of Tables 1, 2, and 3 are based on large enough numbers of respondents as to be almost automatically significant, even if small. However, the complexities of standardization techniques when used with problematic composite samples are such that any attempt to use significance tests would give to the data an appearance of quality that they do not have. Our sampling advisers felt that the data should be presented as "suggestive" and for whatever use those concerned with the demography of religio-ethnicity might make of them, but with the caution that much better data is absolutely essential before one can generalize with any confidence—statistical or otherwise.

2. The formulas used for computing standardization were as follows:

Standardized Regression Scores

Independent Variables (Standardized)	Dependent Variables (Standardized)
	Income (standardized betas)
Education	.398
Size	−.088
Region	.104

Regression equation: $\bar{Y} = (\text{stdbeta}_1 \times X_1) + (\text{stdbeta}_2 \times X_2) + (\text{stdbeta}_3 \times X_3)$
where
$\qquad$ Y = Income
$\qquad$ X_1 = Education
$\qquad$ X_2 = Size
$\qquad$ X_3 = Region
$\qquad$ Stdbeta = standardized beta

Standardized Regression Scores

Independent Variables (Standardized)	Dependent Variables (Standardized)
	Education (standard beta)
Region	$-.102$
Size	$-.123$

Regression equation: $Y = (\text{beta-std}_1 \times X_1) + (\text{betastd}_2 \times X_2)$
Residual equation: $R = Y - ((\text{beta}_1 \times X_1) + (\text{beta}_2 \times X_2) + K)$
where
$\qquad$ Y = Education
$\qquad$ X_1 = Region
$\qquad$ X_2 = Size
$\qquad$ R = Residual
$\qquad$ Betastd = standardized beta
$\qquad$ Beta = beta for unstandardized variables
$\qquad$ K = constant

3. We are reminded of Arnold Toynbee's essay on the success of the Protestant ethic among the Scotch Presbyterians who migrated to Ulster and its failure among the Ulster Presbyterians who migrated to the United States.

4. It may be suggested that one of the reasons for the high educational achievement of Irish Catholics is that, as we pointed out in Table 5 of Chapter 2, they may be disproportionately male. Males, it could be argued, are more likely to go for further education, particularly among the Irish, and with a standardization for the Irish score formed for sex ratio, their score might be substantially diminished. However, an inspection of the deviation of Irish Catholic women from the group educational mean (the mean of men and women, not just women) indicates that if all Irish Catholic respondents merely had the educational achievement of Irish Catholic women, the picture described in the text would not be altered. Thus the deviation from educational cohort mean for Irish Catholic women would be as follows (in years):

Age	Mean
20	0.61
30	0.87
40	1.51
50	0.42
60 and over	0.82

5. Our composite sample is based on data collected through the 1960s. It may not measure notable changes in black educational and economic achievement that, according to some writers, occurred in the late 1960s. Better data on blacks are available in other data sets. Blacks are included here for rough comparative purposes. Still, information about blacks acquired by our composite sample is not inconsistent with the findings reported in other research on the "cost" of being black.

4.   DOES ETHNICITY MATTER?

W E PROPOSE IN THIS CHAPTER to ask one question and to provide a limited and imperfect answer that we hope will serve as one block for the construction of a grand theory of American ethnicity. Our question is, Do the cultural heritages of the Old World persist among the children and grandchildren of immigrants from the various European countries?

For our research we chose two ethnic groups—the Irish Catholics and the Italians—about whose countries of origin there exists something of an anthropological and sociological literature. From this literature we derived a number of hypotheses about their respective differences from the British American norm and from one another. To the extent that these hypotheses are sustained by the available evidence, we can assert that cultural differences persist within the United States that are predictable on the basis of the culture of the countries of origin.

We defined ethnic groups tentatively as "collectivities based on presumed common origin" (Chapter 1). Now we shall add that these groups act as bearers of cultural traits and, at least on occasion, contribute part of the self-definition of a person. We make no claim that our definition has any validity beyond the borders of the United States. American ethnic groups were created here and exist in a particular and peculiarly American context.

In our research we were not concerned with the explicit awareness of ethnic heritage, that is, that there might be differences between those Irish who are conscious of being Irish and those who are not, for example. Nor did we concentrate on the decline of ethnic attitudes and behaviors through the generations. When we asked a respondent what his nationality or background was, we assumed that his answer, "Irish" or "Italian," indicated the possible presence of a predisposition to attitudes, values, norms, and behavior that were part of the baggage the immigrant groups brought from their countries of origin and passed on to their children and grandchildren, largely through an implicit socialization process.

Not all differences among ethnic groups can be attributed exclusively to their Old World cultural heritages. The groups came to American society at different times in that nation's development, they settled in different regions of the country, and they have had different histories since their arrival. In this chapter, we limit ourselves to the differences that can be predicted from cultural patterns that existed in the country of origin, simply because in the absence of elaborate social histories for the immigrant groups these differences are far easier to sort out. The ethnic group as a self-conscious collectivity may

This chapter is adapted from a paper coauthored by Andrew M. Greeley and William C. McCready for presentation at the Seminar on Ethnicity at the Academy of Arts and Sciences, Boston, October 27, 1972.

be the result of the American experience, but Irish behavior with regard to drink and Italian behavior with regard to sex, for example, and the values of both groups about family life existed before immigration to the United States. Our hypotheses and the questions we asked reflected rather broad cultural traits that were clearly delineated in the anthropological and historical literature we used.

There were difficulties in pursuing these cultural traits and differences as they persist in Italian and Irish American ethnic groups.

1.   The anthropological literature was written after most of the immigrants left Italy and Ireland and came to the United States. There is a sufficient amount of historical information available, however, to persuade us that southern Italy and western Ireland remain similar to those regions as they were 50 to 100 years ago. But obviously some changes have taken place in Connaught and the Mezzogiorno between the time the immigrants left and the anthropologists arrived.

2.   There may well be deficiencies in the literature on Ireland and Italy of which we as Americans are unaware. The literature on Italy is more extensive and, as far as we know, has not been subject to much critical disagreement. The literature on Ireland is more limited and has been subject to considerable disagreement on the part of Irish scholars.

3.   Some of the hypotheses we derived from reading the literature on Italy and Ireland were of greater value than others, because they were based on observations that were at the core of all the descriptions of the two societies. Thus our hypothesis that Italian Americans would be more fatalistic than British was indeed substantiated. This validation was considerably more important than the nonvalidation of other hypotheses, because the theme of fatalism in the Mezzogiorno was of capital importance in all the writings on that area. Similarly, given both historical and anthropological evidence on drinking behavior in Ireland, the difference between the American Irish and the Italians and British in drinking behavior outweighed many nondifferences based on less important observations about Irish peasant culture.

4.   Finally, in our comparison of the Italians with the Irish we had to make certain decisions on the basis of descriptions that were scarcely written to facilitate such comparisons. For example, we predicted that the Irish would score higher on a measure of trust than the Italians because there seemed to be somewhat more emphasis in the Irish literature on the importance of religion as generating "Ultimate Trust." Similarly, we predicted that the Italians would score higher than the Irish on measures of fatalism, because the themes of fatalism seemed more obvious in the Italian literature. While these decisions were not completely arbitrary, they cannot be said to possess the precision that would be desirable in the best of all possible social science research.

Dominant Themes of the Literature. The literature on southern Italy[1] describes a society in which the *culture* postulates an extended family value system while the social *structure* is close to a state of collapse. The extreme poverty of daily life precludes the effective operation of the extended family and indeed dictates that individuals have as little to do with an extended family as possible, lest they be caught in the ancient web of obligation, which they cannot afford to honor.[2] This "amoral familism," to use Banfield's term, may have a value connotation that is unfortunate, but the reality to which he attaches that label is recorded by all other observers. Little trust persists beyond the nuclear family; it is difficult enough to honor the obligations to one's spouse and children.

The society is permeated by distrust and suspicion. Anxiety and fear are at a very high level. Men and women are caught in the grip of a fatalism that tells them that none of their efforts really matter very much. The principal proof of a man's quality as a father lies in his ability to protect the chastity of the female members of his family. An unfaithful wife or promiscuous daughter become an intolerable social disgrace. The Virgin, as the symbol of Italian Catholicism, is central to the southern Italian belief system because it emphasizes the importance of biological integrity and because it stresses the automatic and fatalistic elements of life. Relationships between man and woman tend to be formal and tense. The behavior of girls is rigidly controlled, although the behavior of boys is less closely supervised. Young men learn early the need to prove their maleness by being superior to women, which means protecting the chastity of one's own family and threatening the chastity of others—insofar as one can get away with it and not get caught.

The peasant society of Ireland[3] is not so grim and disorganized as that of Italy. Both societies have known poverty and oppression, but a comparison of the literature of the two countries shows that the social structure of western Ireland has been much less traumatized than that of the Mezzogiorno. In Ireland the demands and the support of the extended family are far more evident. The nuclear family displays a higher level of trust and indeed a capacity for political organization of a rather sophisticated variety, dating from Daniel Connell's Catholic Association of the early nineteenth century at least. In the west of Ireland there is a great concern about the transmission of family property, and, indeed, marriage contracts concerning the exchange of property in dowries are of the highest importance. The rearing of children and the planning of marriage, the assumption of the roles of wife and husband, and retirement from active direction of one's family are all decisively affected by the property at the time of marriage. Such concern would seem to indicate a more prosperous and better organized culture than that described in Sicily and in southern Italy.

On the other hand, there seems to be even more sexual repression in Ireland than in Italy, and hence a very high level of frustration. Repression and suppressed anger finds an outlet in prodigious feats of alcohol consumption. Precisely because the west of Ireland is apparently less disorganized than the south of Italy, there are external means of social control there that do not exist in Italy. For example, the highly skilled ridicule by the extended family and local community and the harsh, punitive, and omnipresent moralism of Irish Catholicism are very effective dampers on unconforming behavior.

While the Irish country family is almost as patriarchal as that of Italy, studies of country families migrating to Dublin indicate that matriarchy emerges rather quickly in the large cities—far more quickly than in southern Italian cities like Naples. Mothers "spoil" their sons by waiting on them and constraining their daughters to wait on them, yet the Irish male seems to have less freedom and independence than the Italian male, if only because the property settlements make it practically impossible for him to marry without parental approval. The Irish family structure seems somewhat less rigid than the Italian, but it is still rigid enough. While Connaught may not be as harsh and repressive a place as the Mezzogiorno, there is still substantial evidence in the available literature that the life of the peasants in the west of Ireland is filled with anxiety, insecurity, repression, and powerful conformity-oriented norms. Both Italy and Ireland, then, are presented in the literature as peasant societies with all the narrowness and conservatism characteristic of such societies, and with the special problems that come with poverty, oppression, and less than enlightened religious world views.

Hypotheses.   From the literature we derived a number of hypotheses about persisting cultural differences among the Irish and the Italians as compared with each other and as each compared with the British. These hypotheses were divided into four categories of variables: certain personality characteristics, political participation, attitudes and behavior about alcohol and sex, and respect for the democratic process. We have arranged six tables so that in each a comparison is made between Irish and British, Italian and British, and Irish and Italian. In the first column the measure is indicated, the second column is our hypothesis of which group will score higher, and the third and fourth columns provide the scores of the two groups. The next column indicates whether the hypothesis was sustained, and the last column (in the first four tables) shows the level of statistical significance.

Personality Variables.   In Table I we compare our three groups on seven personality variables derived from a survey of a national sample of American males.[4]

Table 1. Personality Variables

Variable	Hypothesis	Score		Con-firmed	Signif-icance
A. Irish and British		Irish	British		
Trust	Anglo	2.50	0.24	No	(.01)[a]
Fatalism	Irish	1.97	−1.34	Yes	.01
Authoritarianism	Irish	−1.24	−1.01	No	(.05)[a]
Anxiety	Irish	−2.10	−0.01	No	(.05)[a]
Conformity	Irish	1.00	0.01	No	
Moralistic	Irish	2.24	1.45	No	
Independence for children	Anglo	2.03	0.40	No	
B. Italian and British		Italian	British		
Trust	Anglo	0.50	0.24	No	
Fatalism	Italian	0.54	−1.34	Yes	.01
Authoritarianism	Italian	1.52	−0.01	No	
Anxiety	Italian	1.10	−0.01	No	
Conformity	Italian	−1.30	0.01	No	
Moralistic	Italian	1.40	1.45	No	
Independence for children	Anglo	−2.30	0.40	Yes	.01
C. Irish and Italian		Irish	Italian		
Trust	Irish	2.50	0.50	Yes	.05
Fatalism	Italian	1.97	0.54	No	
Authoritarianism	Italian	−1.24	1.52	Yes	.01
Anxiety	Italian	−2.10	1.10	Yes	.01
Conformity	Irish	1.00	−1.30	Yes	.01
Moralistic	Irish	2.24	1.40	Yes	.05
Independence for children	Irish	2.03	−2.30	Yes	.05

[a] Differences are significant in the opposite direction to the one hypothesized.

The hypotheses we generated on the basis of the literature were:

1. The rigid family structures, value systems and religious norms of Italy and Ireland should make both the Irish and the Italians less "trusting," more "fatalistic," more "authoritarian," more "anxious," more "conformist," more "moralistic," and less concerned about "independence for children" than British Americans, who represent the statistical "norm" of American society. However harsh and rigid American Protestantism may be in some of its manifestations, it certainly does not seem to compare with the situations described in southern Italy and the west of Ireland.

2. The Irish will be higher than the Italians on "trust," as well as "conformity" and "moralism." The Italians will score higher on "fatalism," "authoritarianism," and "anxiety." The Irish are probably somewhat more likely to stress "independence for children."

Our hypotheses had only a limited amount of success as far as the comparisons between the two Catholic immigrant groups and the British were concerned. Both the Irish and the Italians were significantly higher than the British in "fatalism," thus confirming in the United States one of the principal themes of the literature on the two countries, but significant differences between Italians and British exist only on one other scale. As predicted, the British are more likely than Italians to emphasize independence for children.

But only the fatalism hypothesis is validated for differences between the American Irish and their British fellow-citizens. Indeed, in four cases ("trust," "authoritarianism," "anxiety," and "independence for children") the differences between the Irish and the British are in the opposite of the hypothesized direction; and in three of these the differences are significant. The Irish are, despite our hypothesis, significantly less "anxious." Another difference, slightly less than significant, indicates the Irish are more likely than the British to value "independence for children."

On the other hand, on all but one of the scales the differences between the Irish and the Italians are significant in the direction hypothesized. The Italians are less fatalistic than the Irish, but in every other respect, the predicted differences do in fact exist. One way to summarize Table 1 would be to say that with the exception of fatalism, the Italians and the British are relatively similar to one another, while the Irish are significantly different from both, with the difference between the Irish and the Italians being in the direction predicted by our hypothesis, and the differences between the Irish and the British being in the *opposite* direction than those predicted by our hypothesis. Knowledge of the culture of the land of origin, then, is of some help in understanding the differences between the two ethnic groups but of rather little help in understanding their differences from the British—at least with regard to our personality scales.

Why are the Irish different in the opposite direction from what we predicted? Perhaps there are aspects of the Irish personality that are more complex than reported by the literature, or we misinterpreted the focus of the research. And why are the Irish—a group that came to the United States before the Italians—more likely to be significantly different from the British on personality measures than the Italians? Perhaps Irish Catholicism provided a far stronger structural and cultural force around which the Irish could rally and sustain their world view than that which was available to the Italians in their version of Catholicism.

Political Participation. We now turn to differences among the three groups on political participation measures.[5] Our hypotheses were that, given the high level of political activity and sophistication reported by historians and contemporary political scientists in Ireland,[6] one would predict that the Irish would be more likely to engage in voting and political campaigning than the British. They would however be less likely to engage in the organization joining "civic activity" type of political behavior, which Verba and Nie report to be a "Protestant mode" of participation. With a lack of viable political culture in southern Italy and Sicily, one would expect that both the Irish and the British would score higher on political participation than the Italians. This expectation was reinforced by the fact that the Irish learned their politics as part of a British system, and that after 1875 most of the Irish immigrants spoke English as their first language. (Before then western Ireland was primarily Irish-speaking.)

Table 2 indicates that in six of the nine cases our hypotheses were sustained at a significance level of .01. The Irish are indeed more likely to vote and to campaign than the British, but despite our prediction and despite the expectation based on the work of Verba and Nie, they are also more likely to engage in civic activities than the British. Similarly, both the Irish and the British are significantly more likely to campaign and engage in civic activity than are the Italians. Although the Irish are also more likely to vote than the Italians, the difference is not significant. The Italians are somewhat more likely to vote than the British, but once again the difference is not significant.

Our predictions, then, turn out to be considerably more successful when we are dealing with participation behavior than when we are dealing with personality variables, a finding that offered some consolation because political participation is, as social science measures go, something much "harder" than responses to sociopsychological personality scales.

Sex and Alcohol. Does knowledge of the culture of the country of origin enable us to predict attitudes toward sexuality and drinking behavior? For the groups we are studying it was hypothesized on the basis of the literature that

Table 2. Political Participation

Variable	Hypoth-esis	Score		Con-firmed	Signif-icance
A. Irish and British					
		Irish	British		
Voting	Irish	30.6	06.2	Yes	.01
Campaigning	Irish	42.4	06.8	Yes	.01
Civic activity	Anglo	22.3	13.7	No	
B. Italian and British					
		Italian	British		
Voting	Anglo	17.6	06.2	No	
Campaigning	Anglo	−15.4	06.8	Yes	.01
Civic activity	Anglo	−32.5	13.7	Yes	.01
C. Irish and Italian					
		Irish	Italian		
Voting	Irish	30.6	17.6	No	
Campaigning	Irish	42.4	−15.4	Yes	.01
Civic activity	Irish	22.3	−32.5	Yes	.01

the Irish would be more likely to drink alcohol than the British and would also be more likely to have serious drinking problems. It was also hypothesized that the Irish would be more restrictive than the British in their attitudes toward both male and female sexual permissiveness.

Little was said about drunkenness in southern Italy in the literature. One might conclude from that very fact that it did not plague that otherwise problem-burdened region. Hence, the Italians, we expected, would have lower scores on the alcohol scale than would the British. We would also expect that because of their sexual double standard the Italians would score lower on restrictiveness toward male sexual behavior but higher in restrictiveness toward female sexual behavior.

Finally, we hypothesized a greater alcohol problem for the Irish than for the

Italians, more sexual restrictiveness for the Italians with regard to female sexuality, and more restrictiveness for the Irish with regard to male sexuality.

Our hypotheses about the differences between the Irish and the British on alcohol and sexuality were not supported in anyway, but three of the four hypotheses about the differences between the Italians and the British were supported (Table 3). Our mistake was to assume that Italian sexual restrictiveness

Table 3. Alcohol and Sex

Variable	Hypothesis	Score		Con-firmed	Signif-icance
A. Irish and British					
		Irish	British		
Drink	Irish	1.63	1.64	No	
Drunk	Irish	4.17	4.05	No	
Male sex[a]	Anglo	3.53	3.71	No	
Female sex	Anglo	3.87	3.93	No	
B. Italian and British					
		Italian	British		
Drink	Anglo	0.43	1.64	Yes	.01
Drunk	Anglo	1.69	4.05	Yes	.01
Male sex	Anglo	4.06	3.71	No	(.01)[b]
Female sex	Italian	4.14	3.93	Yes	.01
C. Irish and Italian					
		Irish	Italian		
Drink	Irish	1.63	1.43	Yes	.01
Drunk	Irish	4.17	1.69	Yes	.01
Male sex	Irish	3.53	4.06	No	.01[b]
Female sex	Italian	3.87	4.14	No	

[a] The score measures restrictiveness in attitudes towards male sexual behavior.
[b] Differences are significant in the opposite direction to the one hypothesized.

would be limited to female sexual behavior. In fact, the Italians express a sexual restrictiveness for males and females. The Italians are also significantly less likely to have alcohol problems than the Irish, and they are more likely to be sexually restrictive than the Irish, but that was significantly so in only the case of male sexual behavior, and that was in opposite direction from our hypothesis.

Table 3, then, presents a picture that is exactly the opposite of Table 1. On the personality scales the Irish were significantly different from the Italians and the British, both of whom were quite similar to one another (save on "fatalism"). One might have concluded from Table 1 that the Italians had "assimilated" and that the Irish had not. However, in Table 3, the Irish and the British are similar while both differ from the Italians. It will be a truism, perhaps, to observe that the processes of differentiation and acculturation among the American ethnic groups are far more complicated than we expected.

Respect for the Democratic Process. A measurement of the respondents' respect for certain elements in the democratic process is the only scale presented in Table 4. Ireland became a political democracy long after most of the immigrants had left, and while the Irish were a politically involved people, their involvement was not such as to incline them to respect the niceties of the democratic process. (One need only look at the present situation in Ulster to see why.) Similarly, political democracy was never effectively established in Sicily or the Mezzogiorno. Furthermore, the low levels of trust and openness reported in the anthropological literature on both countries would indicate that there would be less concern for civil liberties among those affected by such cultures than there would be among native Americans. Finally, the allegedly authoritarian proclivities of Roman Catholicism might also ill equip Italians and Irish to respect the democratic processes. Hence one would predict that the British would be higher on the democratic process scale than either the Irish or the Italians, and that the Irish would probably be higher than the Italians.

Table 4 indicates that two of these expectations are supported. Both the Irish and the British have higher scores on the democratic process scale than do the Italians. However, the expectation of a higher score for the British over the Irish is dramatically disproven. The Irish are significantly, indeed overwhelmingly, higher on the democratic process scale. It may well be that a thousand years of revolutionary tradition does generate a respect for political democracy, a respect that survives even the passage of a society into a bourgeois mentality.

On the whole, our efforts to predict differences in attitudes and behaviors

Table 4. Respect for Democratic Processes

Hypothesis	Score		Con-firmed	Signif-icance
A. Irish and British				
	Irish	British		
British	.60	.05	No	(.01)[a]
B. Italian and British				
	Italian	British		
British	.05	−.16	Yes	.01
C. Irish and Italian				
	Irish	Italian		
Irish	.60	−.16	Yes	.01

[a] Differences are significant in the opposite direction to the one hypothesized.

among three American ethnic groups were moderately successful. Of 45 hypotheses, we were right at a statistically significant level—22 times. On the other hand, in six cases (mostly dealing with Irish personality) there were statistically significant differences in the *opposite* direction from what was predicted.

With the exception of "fatalism," the Italians were basically similar to the British in personality; but they were different in the predicted direction from the Irish. The Irish were different from the British in the opposite of the direction predicted. We were most successful in predicting political participation, with the Irish being the most and the Italians the least active politically. Both groups were significantly different from the British mean.

The Irish were rather like the British in their sexual attitudes and their drinking behavior. The Italians were both less likely to drink and more likely to be sexually restrictive than either of the other groups, as the literature on the country of origin had led us to believe. The Irish, unexpectedly, were more

likely to respect the democratic processes than the British, while the latter, ex-
pectedly, were more likely to respect such processes than the Italians.

What have we demonstrated with our exploratory research? It is apparent
that we can no longer believe that there are no important differences among
native Americans, Irish Americans, and Italian Americans. We are not all
alike. On the other hand, we cannot believe that ours is a mosaic society in
which differences among the three groups are to be expected on almost every
variable. The truth seems to lie somewhere in between. We are both similar
and different.

It is also clear that the differences that do in fact exist among the three
ethnic groups studied cannot be explained solely in terms of the cultural heritages they (or, more likely, their parents or grandparents) brought with them.
The majority of differences are of the sort that could be predicted by a study of
the literature of the two countries of origin, but a substantial minority of the
differences are exactly the opposite of the predictions the literature led us to
make. On the other hand, if one assumes (and many commentators in
American life seem to have made this assumption) that European heritages of
the American ethnic groups are irrelevant to an understanding of the present
attitudes and behaviors of such groups, one can find very little substantiation
in the research reported here. The European heritage may not be *all* important, but it is important, probably more so than many of us would have
thought.

We shall ask a final question. Are the differences among American ethnic
groups diminishing as social class differences diminish and as the number of
years the family has been in the United States increases? Tables 5 and 6
provide data with which to begin to fashion a response. Table 5 shows the
zero-order correlations between ethnicity and political participation for each of
the three comparisons, and then the standardized correlation with region and
educational level held constant. If an increase in education is leading to a decline in the differences in political behavior, the standardized coefficient should
be smaller than the zero-order coefficient. However, the data make it perfectly
clear that even taking into account the regional and educational differences
among the three ethnic groups, differences in political participation remained
unchanged.

Table 6 shows whether generation in the country has any effect on political
participation. Foreign born are the first generation; native born with foreign
parents, the second generation; and native born with native parents, the third.
The assimilationist theory would lead us to believe that the longer the immigrant family is in the country, the more likely it is to participate in political
activity. The high level of Irish political participation and the low level of
Italian political participation, then, would be seen as a function of the time the

Table 5. Zero-Order and Standardized Coefficients Between Ethnicity and Political Participation

Variable	Zero Order	Standardized for Region and Education
A. Irish and British		
Campaigning	.10[a]	.11
Civic participation	.03	.04
B. Italian and British		
Campaigning	− .07[b]	− .06
Civic participation	− .11	− .11
C. Irish and Italian		
Campaigning	.27[a]	.28
Civic participation	.28	.31

[a] Positive correlation with Irish.
[b] Positive correlation with British.

two immigrant groups were in the United States. However, as Table 6 makes clear, the small correlations between generation and political participation for the Italians and the Irish are small indeed. By contrast, the relationship between generation and active political participation for Jews indicates that the assimilationist model may be relevant for them, indicating that the complications do not cease when dealing with ethnicity.

Table 6. Correlations between Generation and Political Behavior

Variable	Irish	Italian	Jewish
Campaigning	.04	.04	.30
Civic participation	.04	.08	.34

Note: A positive correlation indicates that the longer a respondent's family has been in the United States, the more likely he is to participate.

We began with a very simple theoretical question, Does a knowledge of the cultural heritage of an immigrant group help us to understand its present behavior? On the basis of the evidence presented, we would answer yes. The heritage may not explain everything, but it appears to explain some things. The critical questions now become, how does the interaction between the Old World culture and the New World experience shape the phenomena of American ethnic group cultures? Why in the immigrant experience were some parts of the Old World culture ignored, others rejected, others vigorously reinforced and maintained with little conscious effort, and still others vigorously and tenaciously reinforced with full consciousness?

NOTES

1. See the pertinent section of the Bibliography, and especially Banfield and Banfield, Cronin, Ianni, and Parsons.

2. Cronin's study of Italian immigrants in Australia shows that when it becomes economically possible to sustain the values and norms of the extended family system, the extended family reemerges.

3. See the pertinent section of the Bibliography, and especially Arensberg, Humphrey, Kimball, Messenger, and Jackson.

4. The items in our scale are described in the appendix to this chapter.

5. These measures were devised by Sidney Verba and Norman Nie. See their *Participation in America: Political Democracy and Social Equality.* New York: Harper & Row, 1972.

6. See Bueil Chubb (Bibliography).

APPENDIX: SCALES USED IN THIS CHAPTER

I. Personality Scales

The seven personality measures used represented a number of the factors that emerged from a battery of 57 items. Here we list the items that had a factor loading of over .200 for each scale.

CONFORMING

According to your general impression, how often do your ideas and opinions about important matters differ from those of your relatives?

How often do your ideas and opinions differ from those of your friends?

How about from those of other people with your religious background?

How about from those of most people in the country?

How often do you feel that you can't tell what other people are likely to do, at times when it matters?

ANXIOUS

I feel useless at times.

At times I think I am no good at all.

On the whole I think I am quite a happy person.

How often do you feel that there isn't much purpose in being alive?

How often do you find that you can't get rid of some thought or idea that keeps running through your head?

How frequently do you find yourself anxious or worrying about something?

How often do you find yourself counting unimportant things, such as the number of cars passing by?

How often do you find that you are really enjoying yourself?

How often do you feel bored with everything?

How often do you feel powerless to get what you want out of life?

How often do you feel so restless that you cannot sit still?

How often do you feel that the world just isn't very understandable?

How often do you feel downcast and dejected?

How often do you feel that you are about to go to pieces?

How often do you feel guilty for having done something wrong?

How often do you feel uneasy about something without knowing why?

AUTHORITARIAN

Young people should not be allowed to read books that confuse them.

In this complicated world the only way to know what to do is to rely on leaders and experts.

People who question the old and accepted ways of doing things usually just end up causing trouble.

There are two kinds of people in the world, the weak and the strong.

Prison is too good for sex criminals; they should be publicly whipped or worse.

The most important thing to teach children is absolute obedience to their parents.

No decent man can respect a woman who has had sex relations before marriage.

MORALISM

When you get right down to it, no one cares much what happens to you.

If something works, it doesn't matter whether it's right or wrong.

It's all right to get around the law as long as you don't actually break it.

Once I've made up my mind I seldom change it.

You should obey your superiors whether or not you think they are right.

It's all right to do anything you want if you stay out of trouble.

It generally works out best to keep doing things the way they have been done before.

Do you believe that it's all right to do whatever the law allows, or are there some things that are wrong even if they are legal?

FATALISM

To what extent would you say you are to blame for the problems you have— mostly, partly, hardly at all?

Do you feel that most of the things that happen to you are the results of your own decisions or things over which you have no control?

When things go wrong for you, how often would you say it's your own fault?

How often do you feel that you are really enjoying yourself?

How often do you feel bored with everything?

How often do you feel guilty for having done something wrong?

TRUST

It's all right to get around the law so long as you don't actually break it.

Human nature is really cooperative.

You should be able to obey your superiors whether or not you think they are right.

If you don't watch out, people will take advantage of you.

Do you think most people can be trusted?

How often do you feel that you can't tell what other people are likely to do, at times when it matters?

INDEPENDENCE FOR CHILDREN

(Positive loadings)
Considerate of others
Interested in how and why things happen
Responsible
Self-control
Good sense and sound judgement

(Negative loadings)
Good manners
Neat and clean
Good student
Obey his parents

II. Political Participation Variables

The *Voting* variable was composed of four items: voting in last two presidential elections, last congressional election, frequency of voting in local elections.

The *Campaigning* scale was composed of four items: attending political meetings, contributing money to a campaign, working for a candidate, trying to persuade others to vote for a candidate.

The *Communal* (or *Civic*) scale was composed of items indicating membership in civic organizations and working for community improvement.

The *Particularized Contact* scale was composed of two items indicating direct approach to public officials either in person or through the mail.

III.   Moral Items

The items in the *Drink* scale were:

I neglect my regular meals when I am drinking.

Liquor has less effect on me than it used to.

I awaken next day not being able to remember some of the things I had done while I was drinking.

I don't nurse my drinks; I toss them down pretty fast.

I stay intoxicated for several days at a time.

Once I start drinking it is difficult for me to stop before I become completely intoxicated.

Without realizing what I am doing, I end up drinking more than I had planned to.

The items in the *Drunk* scale were:

Has an employer ever fired you or threatened to fire you if you did not cut down or quit drinking?

Has your spouse ever left you or threatened to leave you if you didn't do something about your drinking?

Has your spouse ever complained that you spend too much money on alcoholic beverages?

Have you ever been picked up or arrested by the police for intoxication or other charges involving alcoholic beverages?

Has your physician ever told you that drinking was injuring your health?

The *Permissiveness for Men* items were:

I believe that kissing is acceptable for the male before marriage when he is engaged to be married.

I believe that kissing is acceptable for the male before marriage when he is in love.

I believe that kissing is acceptable for the male before marriage when he feels strong affection for his partner.

I believe that kissing is acceptable for the male before marriage even if he does not feel particularly affectionate toward his partner.

I believe that petting is acceptable for the male before marriage when he is engaged to be married.

I believe that petting is acceptable for the male before marriage when he is in love.

I believe that petting is acceptable for the male partner before marriage when he feels strong affection for his partner.

I believe that petting is acceptable for the male before marriage even if he does not feel particularly affectionate toward his partner.

I believe that full sexual relations are acceptable for the male before marriage when he is engaged to be married.

I believe that full sexual relations are acceptable for the male before marriage when he is in love.

I believe that full sexual relations are acceptable for the male before marriage when he feels strong affection for his partner.

I believe that full sexual relations are acceptable for the male before marriage even if he does not feel particularly affectionate toward his partner.

The *Permissiveness for Women* items were the same as those for men, with "female" substituted for "male."

IV. Democratic Processes

The items in the *Democratic Process Scale* were:

If the government makes a decision that most people think is a good one, do you think other people should be allowed to criticize it—always, sometimes, or never?

Do you think people should be allowed to circulate petitions to ask the government to act on some issue—always, sometimes, or never?

Do you think people should be allowed to vote even if they are not well informed about the issues—always, sometimes, or never?

5.   ETHNICITY VERSUS RELIGION

WHEN A SOCIAL SCIENTIST ASSERTS that he has found differences in attitudes and behavior among American ethinc groups, there are normally two responses offered by the conventional wisdom.

The first is to suggest that the finding is not the result of ethnicity but of social class, and the second is to suggest that the finding is the result of religion and not ethnicity. Somehow diversity that is based on either social class or religion is more acceptable than diversity resulting from a "pure" ethnic factor. In a serious and thoughtful argument from the same perspective, Will Herberg, in his classic *Catholic-Protestant-Jew*, contended that a "triple melting pot" was developing in the United States, one for each of the major religious subdivisions.[1] Ethnic differences within the religious subdivisions were diminishing, but differences among the various subdivisions were not. In the Herbergian perspective, religion in American society had become *the* ethnic factor.

Both the social class and the religion explanations for ethnic diversity present complex methodological and theoretical problems for the researcher. As we shall see in a later chapter, a control for social class reduces Jewish political participation to the national average, for example. Does it therefore follow that their higher social status is the *cause* of Jewish propensity to higher levels of political participation, or is there some antecedent factor in the Jewish tradition that permits Jews to be both more politicized and more successful economically? Thus, even standardizing for social class does not solve the ethnicity versus social class argument—unless, of course, after standardization the differences persist.

In subsequent chapters we use a statistical technique called multiple classification analysis[2] to determine whether ethnicity makes a contribution to attitudes and behavior that is not the same as the contribution made by religion and social class. We inquire about the comparative power of ethnicity as a predictor of attitudes and behaviors in relation to the predictive power of religion and social class.

It should also be possible in theory to compare various ethnic groups within a given religious denomination, as well as the same ethnic groups with different religious denominations, in order to determine the relative importance of religion and ethnicity. Unfortunately, the history of American society and the history of Christianity make such comparisons extremely difficult. As noted in Chapter 2, almost half the Polish and Italian Catholics are of foreign stock, but only slightly more than one-tenth of the Irish are of foreign stock. Thus comparisons between the "older" and "newer" Catholic immigrant groups become very difficult, particularly when one is dealing with relatively small samples. There are not sufficient fourth generation Italians or first generation Irish to make comparisons in which generation (and social class) are controlled.

Furthermore, there are few Protestant Poles or Protestant Italians; and while there are many Protestant Irish (indeed, more than there are Catholic Irish), there is considerable reason to believe that most of them are descendants of the Ulster immigrants who came to the United States before 1800. They do not really belong to the same ethnic category as the Celtic Catholics from the south of Ireland.

We are therefore left with only one group, the Germans, in which there are enough Protestants and enough Catholics to enable us to ask directly whether ethnicity or religion is the more important determinant of attitudes and behavior. Are German Catholics more like their fellow Germans who are Protestant or their fellow Catholics who are not German? If the former is the case, then one can say that at least for the German Catholics ethnicity is a stronger predictor than religion. If the latter is the case, then one can say that at least for German Catholics, religion is a stronger predictor than ethnicity.

The Germans are an invisible ethnic group. They are not quite as invisible, perhaps, as the Irish Protestants, who scarcely appear to be an ethnic group at all in any organized sense. Throughout this book there is little comment about Germans. The Irish Protestants are mentioned more often, if only because their existence and their scores on our measures come as a surprise. Because the Germans are sufficiently different from the national average in most of our tables, differences will be noted in passing, but they are not of a magnitude to occasion much comment. They are not quite as economically successful as the Irish, though far more successful than the Poles. They are not moving upward at the same rate as the Italians nor as slowly as the Poles. We notice the Irish because of their unexpected economic success and, as we shall see in subsequent chapters, their equally unexpected political liberalism. We notice the Poles and the Italians because they are the white ethnics par excellence with which American society has become concerned in recent years. We notice the Jews because they are America's most impressive success story, and we notice the blacks because they are the omnipresent failure of American society. The Germans we hardly notice. If ever an American ethnic group vanished, it is the Germans.

And yet, one-fifth of the respondents in the NORC composite sample gave their first ethnic identification as German. Even in the SRC and CPS samples, there were about as many Americans who described themselves as German as there were blacks. Germans are the largest non-British ethnic group in American society. Their migration began as far back as the seventeenth century, and there was a substantial German population at the time of the revolutionary war. The migration continued through the nineteenth and even the twentieth centuries, and there are German immigrants in the United States even today. With the possible exception of the British, no ethnic group has had such a sustained movement to the United States. Furthermore, with a few exceptions, the Germans did not come as poor, hungry, oppressed peasants like the Famine Irish, or, later, the Italians and the Poles. Although there was great diversity in German immigration, including socialist refugees in 1848 and Catholic refugees from Bismarck's *Kulturkampf* in the 1870s, most German immigrants were neither uneducated nor unskilled. They ranged from farmer to professional person. Because of their superior education and occupational skills, the German immigrants came equipped with resources for sustaining a separate German ethnic identity in America. Many German organizations in the old country were prepared to provide financial and cultural support for the German immigrants. It would not be an exaggeration to say that immigration was easier for them than for most other groups.

The nineteenth-century German immigrants took America at its word that one did not have to give up one's religion or culture or language to be an American. Although not all Germans endorsed the idea of "Germania," that is, separate geographic and cultural enclaves that were simultaneously German and American, the Germania movement was powerful and important before World War I.[3]

Among German American Catholics the demand for cultural separatism was so powerful that in the famous Cahensley memo it was recommended that Rome establish what was for all practical purposes a separate German American Church. The Irish American hierarchy, led by Cardinal Gibbons, responded vigorously to the interference in Church matters by Peter Paul Cahensley, who was not even an American citizen but the head of a German association concerned with the religious welfare of immigrants. While Cahensley and the German American bishops lost the battle, they may have won the war—German national parishes and German-language parochial schools flourished during the early part of the present century, and certain dioceses were normally assigned to German bishops by informal arrangement.[4]

There is every reason to suppose that German American separatism could have been maintained had it not been for World War I. Germans had the financial, intellectual, and cultural resources, along with the administrative and technical skills to make separatism a reality. If such separate Germanic enclaves had persisted, it is altogether possible that they would have provided models for later groups, especially the Italians and the Poles.[5] But Germania came to an end with World War I for most parts of American society and in most aspects of American life. And American cultural pluralism developed in a very different direction.

The First World War was a disaster for German Americans. While many German organizations, newspapers, and individuals sided with the Central Powers against the Allies before the United States entered the war, the overwhelming majority of German Americans were patriotic Americans first and Germans second. When push came to shove, there was little doubt as to which side they would be on—at least in *their* minds. However, the xenophobia of the era required that German Americans be punished not merely as foreigners but also as enemies. German music could not be played in some cities, and hamburgers became salisbury steaks. German culture went underground.[6]

Individual German citizens as well as the leaders of German organizations soon understood that the best thing for a German ethnic group to do in the 1920s was to become invisible. Their strategy worked. Beethoven can now be played, and only in fancy restaurants is hamburger called salisbury steak. In the process, however, an immense amount of cultural richness was lost to American society.

By 1939, most Americans were willing to believe that Fritz Kuhn and the German American Bund represented only a tiny fraction of the German American population. There was little doubt in the national mind that citizens of German nationality would be loyal allies in the war against Hitler. It was now the Japanese Americans' turn to be the national scapegoat.

If most German Americans are not highly conscious about their Germanness and if, by and large, German ethnic organizations maintain low profiles out of force of habit if nothing else, the German American ethnic group has nevertheless not completely vanished from the society. There are German newspapers, German radio programs, German cultural and fraternal organizations.[7] Certain towns in Ohio, Iowa, Wisconsin, and Minnesota are overwhelmingly German in both national origin of their citizens and in cultural style. Some such towns are still bilingual; in places like Stearns County, Minnesota, for example, the profile of the German ethnics is hardly low. These rural German enclaves lead one to suspect that had it not been for World War I Germania might have had an extraordinarily powerful influence on American life.

It is worth noting, incidentally, that of all the non-British American ethnic groups, the Germans are the most likely to be Republicans and politically conservative on a wide range of issues. Their political position does not seem to result only from the fact that they are more frequently rural than are other ethnic groups. The German collectivity may well retain some kind of unconscious collective memory that it was the Democratic party that twice presided over United States involvements with Germany in war. The German Americans may dimly remember that the liberal Democrats were their enemies.

But our concern in this chapter is whether German Catholics are more like German Protestants than they are like other Catholics. Catholic immigrants came at different times (more in the second half of the nineteenth century than at other periods) and from different regions in Germany (mostly the south) than did German Protestants. Thus the differences between the two groups are not merely religious but regional and generational. A careful inspection of the tables in Chapter 3 indicates however that the social and economic differences between German Catholics and German Protestants are minor.

For the purposes of this chapter, an appropriate comparison group was needed. Because they are relatively similar in econmic status to German Catholics and because they arrived in the United States as part of the "old" immigration, the Irish Catholics were chosen. The problem with this comparison is of course that Irish Catholics are somewhat more likely to be urban than are German Catholics; but as no other Catholic group is so nonurban as the Germans, we had no choice but to make the comparison. The data presented in this chapter are adequate for answering only one question: Do German Catholics more closely resemble German Protestants or Irish Catholics? If they are closer to German Protestants, the contention that ethnic differences are melting into religious differences must be called into serious question, at least as far as the Germans are concerned. And if ethnicity is a more important predictor of behavior than religion for German Catholics, who have been in the United States for a substantial period of time and for whom a low ethnic profile has been characteristic for more than half a century, then the burden of proof must surely shift back to those who see religion replacing nationality as the principal focus for ethnic diversity in American society.

The data presented in Table 1 indicate differences in Z scores in the variables listed. The first column in each section represents the mean difference between German Protestants and German Catholics, and the second column represents the difference in mean between German Catholics and Irish Catholics. If the figure in the first column is larger than the figure in the second column, religion is a stronger predictor than ethnicity, because in such a case German Catholics will be more like Irish Catholics than they are like German Protestants. If the figure in the second column is larger than that in the first column, it follows that ethnicity is the stronger predictor, because German Catholics are more like German Protestants than they are like their Irish co-religionists.

Section A of Table 1 is concerned with personality characteristics, as measured by the sociopsychological scales devised by Melvin Kohn. On "authoritarianism," "fatalism," "trust," "independence for children," "anxiety," and "conformity," the German Catholics are far more like German Protestants than they are like Irish Catholics. Only on the "moralism" scale does religion have a greater impact than ethnicity, perhaps because of the heavy emphasis on moralism in American Catholicism—at least that of the pre-Vatican Council variety.

In section B we observe that religion is the stronger predictor on only one of the four political participation measures. German Catholics are more like Irish Catholics than they are like German Protestants when it comes to voting. But in "campaigning," "civic activity," and "particularized contact,"[8] German

Table 1. Ethnicity and Religion: A Comparison Between German Americans, Protestant and Catholic, and Irish American Catholics (Mean Differences in z Scores)

A. Personality Characteristics

	Differences Between German Protestants and German Catholics	Differences Between German Catholics and Irish Catholics
Authoritarianism	1.5	17.0
Fatalism	2.0	11.0
Trust	0.1	17.9
Independence for children	7.6	25.8
Anxiety	4.5	11.3
Conformity	2.0	5.4
Moralism	12.4	5.8

B. Political Participation

Voting	20.6	1.4
Campaigning	2.8	35.4
Civic activity	9.8	21.6
Particularized contact with political leadership	9.5	8.0

C. Civil Liberties and Civil Rights

Support for democratic principles[a]	8.0	45.0
Sympathy for inter-racial contact[b]	0.0	12.0
Would vote for black mayor[b]	0.0	22.0
Perception of discrimination against blacks[b]	13.0	28.0
Support for civil rights legislation[b]	10.0	20.0

Table 1. Continued

D. Family Structure (College alumnae)

	Differences Between German Protestants and German Catholics	Differences Between German Catholics and Irish Catholics
Traditional role of women	0.0	43.0
Importance of maintaining family contact	1.0	16.0
More interaction with mother than with father	6.6	5.0
More affection from mother than from father	16.0	11.0
More achievement emphasis from someone other than father	1.0	3.0
More support from someone other than father	10.0	15.0
Marital happiness	23.0	20.0
Sexual adjustment	16.0	3.0

[a] Variable explained in Chapter 3.
[b] Variable explained in Chapter 9.

Catholics are far more like German Protestants than they are like their Irish coreligionists.

On matters of civil liberties and civil rights (section C), German Protestants and German Catholics are fairly similar. Both are very different from the far more liberal Irish Catholics. Indeed, on the subjects of voting for a black mayor and the repression of urban unrest there are no differences between German Catholics and German Protestants. Perhaps the Irish are more politically and racially liberal than the Germans because the Irish never underwent the experience of being identified despite themselves with an enemy nation.

Young college graduates who are German Catholic are more like German

Protestants than they are like Irish Catholics in their conception of the role of women. The Irish are extremely traditional in this area. Section D of Table 1 shows that the Irish place importance on maintaining family contact and recollect experiencing more encouragement for achievement and receiving more social support from their mothers than from their fathers.[9] But on half the items in this section (marital happiness, sexual adjustment in marriage, dominance of mother in family interaction, and in the exchange in affection), it is surprising that ethnicity is more important than religion in determining a young woman's view of the role of women. Religion is more important in predicting marital happiness and slightly more important in predicting sexual adjustment. The differences on these four factors for young women are so similar in the two comparisons that one could say that religion and ethnicity are virtually equal in their predictive power on the subject of family structure. German Catholics are about as different from German Protestants as they are from Irish Catholics.

Twenty-four sets of comparisons have been made in this brief chapter. In two-thirds of the instances, the differences between German Catholics and Irish Catholics were greater than those between German Protestants and German Catholics, and in most of those cases the differences were considerable. Religion is a more important predictor than ethnicity only in scores on the moralistic personality scale, voting behavior, and certain kinds of family relationships, particularly those dealing with sexual adjustment and marital happiness. In short, ethnicity is generally but not always more important than religion in predicting behavior of German Catholics. Catholic Germans and Catholic Irish are similar to one another in that they are more moralistic and more likely to report happiness in marriage. Morality and marriage are both issues about which Catholicism has been profoundly concerned. Under circumstances where religious doctrine is highly salient, one can apparently expect religion to be more powerful an influence than ethnicity. Interestingly enough, on the subject of the traditional role of women—which the Roman church, at least at one time, strongly espoused—there is no difference between German Protestants and German Catholics, and both are strikingly different from the very traditional Irish Catholic.

It is worth noting that for Germans religion is a much stronger predictor than ethnicity as far as voting is concerned. Table 2 is based on data from a longitudinal research project currently under way at NORC to reanalyze election data from the University of Michigan Survey Research Center. While German Catholics were substantially more likely to vote for Republicans than were Irish Catholics in both presidential and congressional elections, they were still solidly on the Democratic side with a 55 per cent Democratic presidential vote in the years between 1952 and 1968 and a 57 per cent congressional vote in the years between 1952 and 1970. But the German Protestants were well below the national average in Democratic voting (28 per cent in the presidential elections, 39 per cent in the congressional elections). Both German groups are the least Democratic ethnic group of their respective denominations, but Catholic Germans are far more likely to be Democrats than their Protestant counterparts.

In the previous chapter we focused on two Catholic groups to see if a knowledge of their cultural heritages would enable us to predict certain things about their attitudes and behavior. Continuing our "building block" approach in this chapter, we focused on two German groups to see whether a knowledge of their religion is of any assistance in predicting certain things about their attitudes and behavior. We concluded in Chapter 4 that under certain circumstances the cultural heritage of the land of origin seems to continue to exercise influence in the United States, even after a group has been here for several generations. In this chapter we conclude that under some circumstances cultural heritage is a more important predictor of attitudes and behavior than religion is.

In the next two chapters the strategy shifts. Instead of focusing on comparisons between two groups, we study all the major American ethnic groups to determine whether there are substantial differences among them in political participation and family structure and how ethnicity compares with social class as a predictor of family structure and political participation. This approach may seem tedious and perhaps even simpleminded. Yet by definition this book is a preliminary reconnaissance, and in a reconnaissance mission the ground traveled must be mapped with great care—particularly when a considerable number of people seem reluctant to acknowledge that the land exists.

Table 2. Voting of Americans of German Descent (Per Cent Democratic)

	German Protestants	German Catholics	Irish Catholics	All United States
Average in presidential elections, 1952–1968	28	55	65	55
Average in congressional elections, 1952–1970	39	57	70	48
Presidential, 1968	22	55	65	44

Source: Composite sample of University of Michigan Survey Research Center biennial election surveys, 1952–1970.

NOTES

1. Herberg, *Catholic-Protestant-Jew*. New York: Doubleday, 1955. See also Ruby Jo, Reeves Kennedy, "Single or Triple Melting Pot? Intermarriage Trends in New Haven." *American Journal of Sociology*. (January 1944).

2. Frank Andrews, James Morgan, John Sonquist. *Multiple Classification Analysis: A Report on a Computer Program for Multiple Regression Using Categorical Predictors*. Survey Research Center, Institute for Social Research, The University of Michigan, Ann Arbor, Michigan, May 1967.

3. See John A. Hawgood, *The Tragedy of German-America: The Germans in the United States of America During the Nineteenth Century and After*. New York: Arno Press, 1970.

4. Chicago was one such diocese. The thoroughly Americanized bishop from Brooklyn, George William Mundelein, was sent to Chicago in 1916 to mediate the conflict between the Germans and the Irish. Because of his German name, Mundelein was able to side with the Irish, leaving the German clergy of the diocese fuming in impotent anger. After Mundelein's death, Rome assigned the Archbishop of Milwaukee, Samuel Alphonsus Stritch, to Chicago, confident that Stritch was German. Someone in the Curia slipped up, however (a not infrequent occurrence with that illustrious body). Stritch was vigorously and enthusiastically Irish. His successor, Albert Meyer, was one of the greatest Catholic churchmen in the history of the United States and a German from Milwaukee. For a discussion of the Cahensley conflict that is sympathetic to the German viewpoint, see Coleman Barry, *The Catholic Church and the German Americans*. Milwaukee: Bruce Books, 1953. And for a study of a curious but very influential German Catholic social movement, see Philip Gleason, *The Conservative Reformers: German-American Catholics in the Social Order*. Notre Dame, Ind.: University of Notre Dame Press, 1968.

5. Actually, the German national parish did become a model for later Catholic immigrant groups, so that by 1940 the American Catholic Church had become in effect a loose confederation of relatively independent national churches usually presided over by an Irish bishop within the diocese and an Irish-dominated national hierarchy. In the Archdiocese of Chicago, for example, the chancery office did its best to be as little involved as possible in the affairs of the Polish, Lithuanian, Italian, and, for a while, German churches in the diocese. National parishes, separate cemeterys, and separate orphanages and fraternal organizations as well as separate lay and clerical ruling elites formed a remarkable model of cultural pluralism.

6. In describing his fieldwork in German towns in Ohio during the late 1950s, Peter Rossi observes that although the cooking of many of the restaurants was German, all the offerings on the menus were given in English.

7. For example, on Sunday evenings, FM station 100 in Benton Harbor, Michigan, broadcasts three hours of delightful German schmaltz, partly sponsored by the Benton Harbor German rugby team.

8. "Campaigning," "civic activity," and "particularized contact" are modes of political participation devised and computed by Sidney Verba and Norman H. Nie. For full details see their book *Participation in America: Political Democracy and Social Equality*. New York: Harper & Row, 1972. "Campaigning" is based on measures of campaign and election activity (including financial, excluding voting); "civic" or "communal" (Verba-Nie's term) is based on measures of membership in groups and organizations actively engaged in attempting to solve community problems; "particularized contact" is based on measures of individual effort to contact individuals of influence or representatives of the community or government.

9. The scales used in Table 1D are explained in Chapter 7.

6. POLITICAL PARTICIPATION AMONG ETHNIC GROUPS IN THE UNITED STATES

C ONSIDERABLE WORK, most of it cross-national, has been done recently on the subject of political participation, or political "mobilization" as it is sometimes called. Nie, Powell, and Prewitt[1] spelled out the relationship between economic growth, attitudinal change, and political participation in six nations, for the most part using data from the civic culture study.[2] Verba, Nie, and Kim[3] developed causal models to explain political participation in five countries (using data from the political participation study).[4] These models were generally satisfactory in explaining four different kinds of political participation in the five countries. Verba, Ahmed, and Bhatt[5] have traced the similarities and differences in political participation models to be observed among blacks in the United States and Harijans in India.

All three studies are based on an explanatory model that is described in its simple form by Verba, Nie, and Kim:

> According to this model, rising levels of socioeconomic status—in particular increased education, but also higher income and higher-status occupations—are accompanied by increased civic orientations such as interest and involvement in politics, sense of efficacy, and norms that one ought to participate. This leads to participation. The model looks something like the following:
>
> socioeconomic status $\longrightarrow$ civic attitudes $\longrightarrow$ participation[6]

The Modes of Democratic Participation addresses itself not only to between-system variation but also to within-system variation. It discusses not only the similarities and differences in political participation in the United States and India but also compares white and black political participation in the United States and the participation of the Harijans and caste Hindus in India. In large societies like the United States the division of the society into "nonoppressed" and "oppressed" groups, however useful it may be for asking certain questions, does not exhaust the possibilities for exploring within-system variations.

In this chapter we explore within-system variation in political participation among the white[7] religio-ethnic groups in American society,[8] and address the following six questions:

1. Are there differences in levels of political participation among the major religio-ethnic groups in American society?
2. Do these differences persist when controls for social class, region, age, and sex are applied?
3. How important as a predictor of political participation behavior is ethnicity?

4. Are there differences in political participation "style" as well as in levels of participation among American religio-ethnic groups?

5. Are there different causal models to explain political "mobilization" in the various American religio-ethnic collectivities?

6. Is there a relationship between ethnic identification and political participation or nonparticipation?

The analysis labors under two major weaknesses:

1. It will be for the most part a descriptive chapter. The normal method of social research is to use data to test hypotheses that have been derived either from general theory or from previous research. However, there is presently no theory of ethnic diversity in the United States, and practically no empirical research has been done on many of the major religio-ethnic collectivities. (For example, the only major work done on the Poles, a group that is extremely interesting in its modes of political participation, is *The Polish Peasant in Europe and America,* Thomas and Znaniecki, published more than half a century ago.)

2. Even though the national sample used in the political participation study (which is being reanalyzed in this chapter) had a weighted size in excess of 3,000 respondents, many of the more interesting American ethnic groups have a relatively small number of respondents, as Table 1 makes clear. Hence material presented here must be considered not as a definitive study of the Irish, the Italians, the Poles, or the French but as a tentative initial investigation.

Table 1 includes three principal residual groups: "Other" Protestant, "Other" Catholic, and "Other." Those assigned to these three groups either were unable to describe their ethnic backgrounds (which was the case in most of the "other" Protestants, who described themselves as "American") or were from ethnic groups too small to include in our analysis (Greeks, Lebanese, Armenians, etc.) or had such a complicated ethnic background that they were unable to specify an identification. Finally, the "Slavic" group is a combination of all the non-Polish eastern European Catholics. Clearly the three "other" groups pose complicated theoretical and methodological problems. They are excluded from the present analysis because we wish to simplify what should be considered only a first step in research on ethnic political behavior and because the sample is not large enough to cope with the many possible combinations of ethnic background found in American society. This chapter, then, is concerned only with the major ethnic groups and only with those people who have little trouble placing themselves within one such group. However, such a concern enables us to deal with approximately three-quarters of the American population.

Table 1. Distribution of Major Religio-ethnic
Groups in Political Participation Sample

Religio-ethnic Group	Number
Protestants	
Anglo-Saxon	591
Scandinavian	110
German	333
Irish	188
Other	447
Catholics	
Irish	95
German	97
Italian	109
French	40
Polish	56
Slavic (Other Eastern European)	41
Spanish-speaking	89
Other	182
Jews	72
Blacks	406
Other	230
Total	3095

The descriptions presented in this chapter have two principal goals.

First, we wish to assert that ethnicity is an important predictor of political behavior in American society and ought not to be excluded from any serious analysis of such behavior. Second, we argue that in the United States cross-cultural research can deal with within-system variation as well as with cross-system variation.

Given the paucity of research done on American ethnic groups, it is impossible to generate any hypotheses about their political participation. We may, however, list certain "expectations" based on folklore, impression, journalistic commentary, and the occasional research document available.

1. *Anglo-Saxon Protestants.* Because they are the largest group in the country, their political behavior will constitute the statistical norm. It also seems not unreasonable to assume that as first arrivals and as those who

created the American republic their behavior will also constitute the cultural norm.[9]

2. *Germans*. There are two reasons for assuming that German political participation will be rather like that of the Anglo-Saxons. Their immigration to the United States has been spread over the longest time, and they are part of the northern European cultural heritage. It may well be however that the traumatic experience of two world wars will lead to slightly lower political participation among them.

3. *Scandinavians*. One would expect the Scandinavians to show high levels of political participation because of the long tradition of political democracy in the Scandinavian countries and because of the general reputation of civic-mindedness attributed to members of the Scandinavian-American community.

4. *Protestant Irish*. The Protestant Irish—perhaps for the most part the so-called Scotch-Irish—can be expected to be rather like the Anglo-Saxons because of their early arrival in the United States and because they have been the main partners of the Anglo-Saxons in the American enterprise for so long that they have become almost indistinguishable from them.

5. *Irish Catholics*. It seems safe to assume that the Irish, by reputation a highly political people, will be more involved in political behavior than any of the other Catholic groups (with the possible exception of the Germans) if only because they came first, understood the language, and developed in the penal time of Ireland a high level of political sophistication and skill. The Irish, like all the Catholic groups, may very well end up low on the communal activity variable because the civic-minded traditions, which were so much a part of the Anglo-Saxon culture, may not yet have had time to develop among the Catholic groups.

6. *French*. About the French-American community very little is known.

7. *Italians*. Given the findings of a number of authors indicating that the Italians are low on social trust and proclivity for cooperation, it might be expected that they will score low on most political participation measures, though perhaps high on the particularized contact scale.[10]

8. *Slavs and Poles*. Very little is known about the Polish and other eastern European Catholic groups. However, given their more recent arrival, their lack of English language skills when they came, and also the absence of a tradition of political democracy in eastern Europe, it may well follow that eastern European Catholic groups will also be low in political participation, save on the particularized contact scale.

9. *Jews*. The Jews could easily be the most active political participants in America since American Jews generally appear to be politically and socially active. But it may well be that just as the Catholic groups are high on particularized contact, so the Jews will be low on this type of political behavior.

I. Differences in Political Behavior

Political Participation Scale.[11]   Figure 1 shows that there are considerable differences in the general participation scores of American ethnic collectivities. The Irish Protestants, the Italian Catholics, and blacks have scores substantially below the mean, with blacks having a slightly larger negative score than the Irish Protestants. ("Substantial" will be used in this discussion to indicate a difference from the mean in excess of 10 standardized units.) The highest scores in political participation are registered by the Irish Catholics (41 standardized units), the Scandinavian Protestants (32 units), and the Jews (19 units). Polish Catholics, German Catholics, and Anglo-Saxon Protestants are all slightly above the score of 10 units.

Several observations are pertinent with regard to Figure 1. First, there are major differences within religious groups. The highest scores are registered by a Catholic group, the Irish, and by a Protestant group, the Scandinavians. The two lowest scores for white groups are also registered by a Catholic group, the Italians, and by a Protestant group, the Irish. Second, there is almost no difference between the scores of German Catholics and German Protestants, but there are substantial differences between the scores of Irish Catholics and Irish Protestants. Finally, the expectation that Italian Catholics and French Catholics

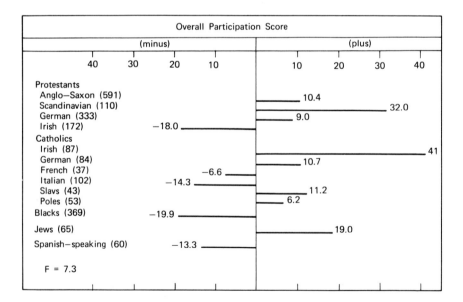

Figure 1. Political participation for American ethnic groups (deviations from the mean).

might score low on political participation is upheld. On the other hand, both the eastern European and Polish Catholics have positive scores.

Voting Scale.[12] Figure 2 shows that the two eastern European Catholic groups, Slavs (non-Polish eastern Europeans) and Poles, are the most likely to score high on the voting scale. The Irish Catholic and Scandinavian Protestants are slightly behind them, with scores still in excess of 30 units. The only negative scores on the voting scale are registered by Irish Protestants and by the blacks. The −24.9 score of the blacks occupies the lowest range.

The following observations are pertinent. First, all the Catholic groups score higher on the voting scale than do the non-Scandinavian Protestants. Thus it seems safe to conclude that a high voting score tends to be a Catholic phenomenon even though Scandinavians also rank high on this scale. Second, among the Catholic groups, the French and the Italians have the lowest scores, suggesting that even in this "Catholic" modality of participation they do less well than the other groups. Finally, the differences between the Irish Catholics and the Irish Protestants are substantial, but there is also a difference of 19 units between the German Protestants and the German Catholics, indicating perhaps that as far as voting is concerned, Catholicism is more important than "Germanness."

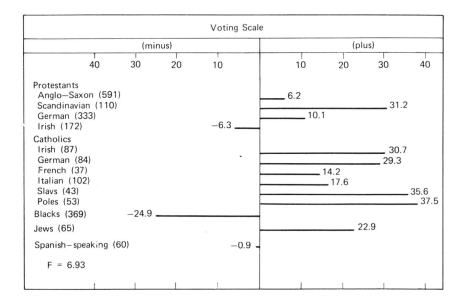

Figure 2. Political participation for American ethnic groups (deviations from the mean).

Campaigning Scale.[13] As is perhaps appropriate for a group that is reputed to have mastered the art of being precinct captains, the American Irish have the overwhelming lead on the political campaigning scale of Figure 3. Indeed, their score is more than twice that of the nearest group, the Scandinavian Protestants. The French and Italian Catholics and the Irish Protestants have substantial negative scores, while the Jews have a substantial positive score (as they also do on the voting scale). There is considerable difference between Irish Catholics and Irish Protestants and relatively little difference between German Catholics and German Protestants.

Communal Participation Scale.[14] Verba and Nie observe in their book that communal participation is a specifically Protestant form of political participation. There is some clarification of this observation (made from the same data, of course) in Figure 4. Three of the four Protestant groups have positive scores on the scale and four Catholic groups have negative scores (the Italians score −32.5). The Scandinavians have the highest positive score (23.3), followed by the Anglo-Saxons (13.6), the Jews (12.0), and the German Protestants (11.5).

We observe therefore that Irish Catholics and Irish Protestants continue to differ. German Protestants score somewhat higher on the communal partici-

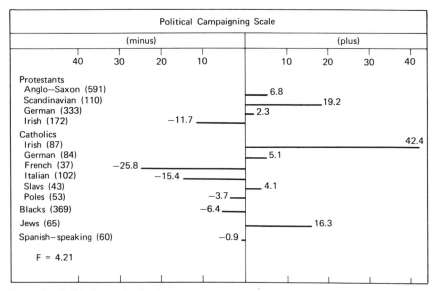

Figure 3. Political participation for American ethnic groups (deviations from the mean).

pation scale than do German Catholics, a reversal of the finding on the voting scale. Voting is an especially Catholic mode of political participation, in which German Catholics lead German Protestants. But communal participation is an especially Protestant form of political participation, in which German Protestants lead German Catholics. The black score continues to be negative, as it has been in all previous figures. The Jewish score continues to be positive.

Particularized Contact Scale.[15]   The French, who were low on both communal participation and campaigning, score very high on this measure (33.4). The non-Polish eastern Europeans, the Irish Catholics, and the Italians also have scores above 10. The second highest score (19.1) on the particularized contact indicator is registered by the Scandinavian Protestants.

The following comments are appropriate to Figure 5. First, as on all previous scales, the scores of the Irish Protestants and the blacks are negative. Second, as on all previous scales, the score of the Jews is positive, but only very slightly so. Finally, Irish Protestants and Irish Catholics continue to be quite different; German Catholics and German Protestants, relatively similar.

The picture that emerges from these five figures seems to indicate that on the general participation scale as well as on all of the specific scales the most

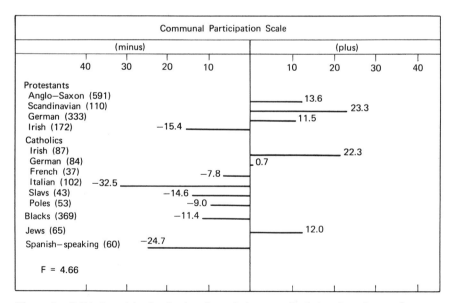

Figure 4.   Political participation for American ethnic groups (deviations from the mean).

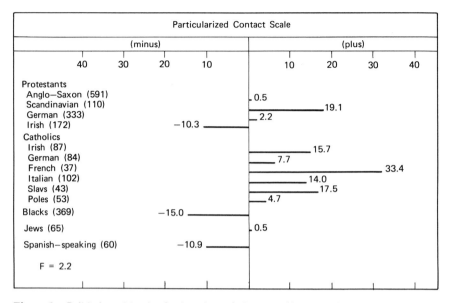

Figure 5. Political participation for American ethnic groups (deviations from the mean).

active politically are the Irish and the Scandinavians. The Irish Protestants and the blacks tend to be low, and in most instances the Jews are in third position behind the Irish Catholics and the Scandinavians. French, Italian, Slavic, and Polish Catholics are positive on voting and particularized contact and negative on political campaigning and communal participation. Italians and the French are lowest on campaigning and participation. The Poles and other eastern Europeans are highest on voting and the French are highest on particularized contact. The Spanish-speaking are on the mean on both voting and political campaigning, though substantially below the mean in communal participation and somewhat below it on particularized contact.

II. Differences with Social Class and Region Controlled. In Figures 6 to 10 we leave behind the real world of actual collectivities and ask what the scores of various groups would be like if their social class and region were the same. It is worth noting that this analysis does not assume that the cause of ethnic differences is social class. A persuasive case might be made that on the contrary the differences in behavior recorded in the previous five figures may represent dimensions of cultural heritage that are the cause rather than the effect—or at least a partial cause as well as a partial effect—of social class differences.

By comparing Figure 6 with Figure 1 we see that the Irish and the Scandinavians continue to be the most active participators. The scores for the eastern Europeans go up. The negative scores of the blacks and the Irish Protestants become slightly positive. Perhaps the most interesting comparison between Figures 6 and 1 is that the relatively high Jewish score on Figure 1 becomes negative on Figure 6. In other words, in the abstract model created by holding region and social class constant, the Irish Catholics, the eastern European Catholics, and the Scandinavian Protestants emerge as exceptionally active political participators while the Jews emerge as the least active of all the groups. One might then conclude that at least as far as the Jews are concerned, the reason for their high level of general political participation is their social class.

When social class and region are held constant the differences in voting behavior also decline somewhat (Figure 7). Although the non-Irish Catholic groups continue to have the highest scores and the Irish Catholic and Scandinavian Protestants continue to score higher than the rest of the Protestant population, the Protestant Irish negative score becomes slightly positive, the black negative score is reduced almost to the mean, and the positive Jewish score becomes negative.

Control for social class and region does little to deprive the Irish Catholic of his rating as a confirmed campaigner (comparison of Figure 8 with Figure 3). The score of 42.4 in Figure 3 declines to 37.0 in Figure 8, a much smaller pro-

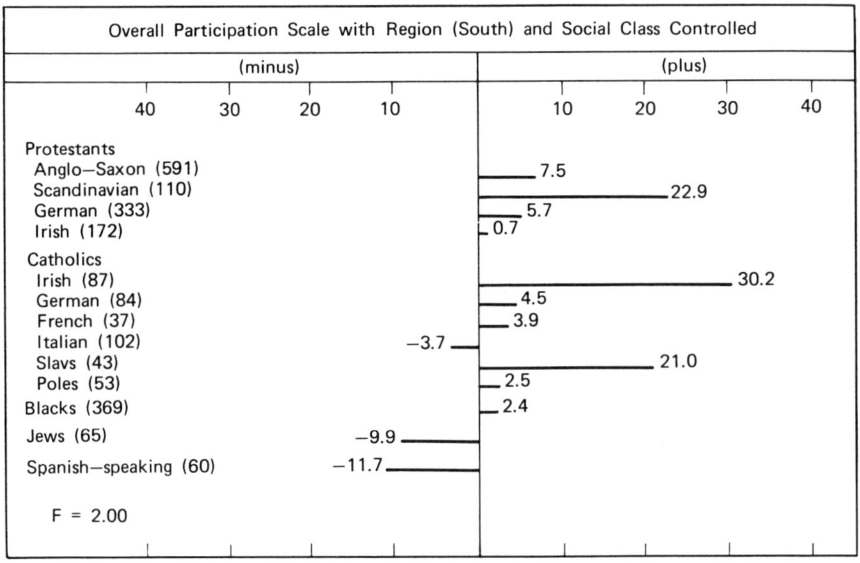

Overall Participation Scale with Region (South) and Social Class Controlled		
(minus)	(plus)	
40 30 20 10	10 20 30 40	

```
Protestants
  Anglo–Saxon (591)                        ___ 7.5
  Scandinavian (110)                              _____ 22.9
  German (333)                              __ 5.7
  Irish (172)                              _ 0.7

Catholics
  Irish (87)                                      _____ 30.2
  German (84)                               __ 4.5
  French (37)                               __ 3.9
  Italian (102)                 -3.7 __
  Slavs (43)                                      ____ 21.0
  Poles (53)                               _ 2.5
Blacks (369)                               _ 2.4

Jews (65)                      -9.9 ___

Spanish–speaking (60)       -11.7 ___

  F = 2.00
```

Figure 6.   Political participation for American ethnic groups (deviations from the mean).

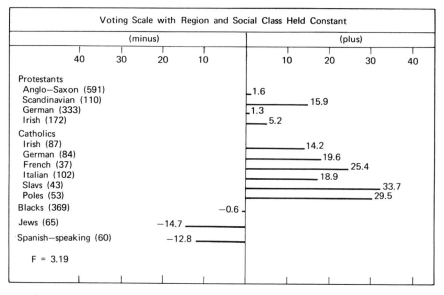

Figure 7. Political participation for American ethnic groups (deviations from the mean).

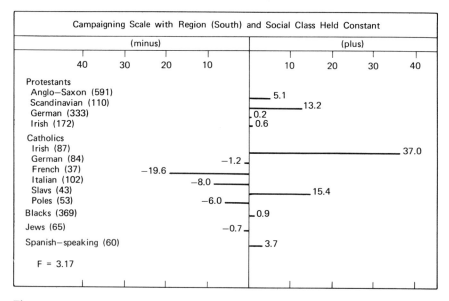

Figure 8. Political participation for American ethnic groups (deviations from the mean).

portional loss than that of the Scandinavians, whose score declines from 19.2 to 13.2. The social class and regional controls improve the scores of Slavs, who in the world created by the controls forge ahead of the Scandinavians. All the negative scores in Figure 3 are reduced somewhat, though the French (−19.6) still have the largest negative score. Once again, the fairly substantial positive Jewish score become negative.

Control for region and social class has practically no impact on the pattern of communal activity that was reported in Figure 4. As we note in Figure 9, negative scores of the Italians and the Spanish-speaking diminish somewhat. The negative scores of the French increase, but there is virtually no change among the groups on the positive side of the scale (Figure 9).

Holding social class and region constant creates a situation in which the French score goes up (comparing Figures 5 and 10). The French score on particularized contact (42.0) is more than twice as large as that of the Scandinavians. Furthermore, the Italians' score is cut almost in half, suggesting that if there is an Italian tendency to appeal to the "padrone" or "godfather," it is substantially reduced when social class is taken into account. The large negative score for blacks is reduced in Figure 10 to practically the mean, and the slight positive Jewish score becomes negative. The Irish Protestant's negative score declines somewhat. Thus in four of the five figures generated to describe a world where the effect of region and social class is removed, the Jewish score moves from positive to negative.

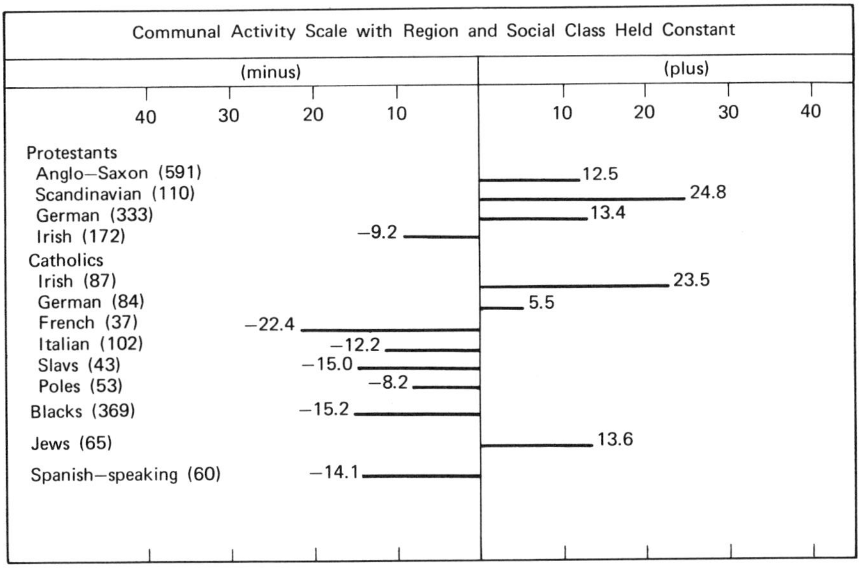

Communal Activity Scale with Region and Social Class Held Constant								
(minus)				(plus)				
40	30	20	10	10	20	30	40

Protestants
  Anglo–Saxon (591)   12.5
  Scandinavian (110)   24.8
  German (333)   13.4
  Irish (172)   −9.2
Catholics
  Irish (87)   23.5
  German (84)   5.5
  French (37)   −22.4
  Italian (102)   −12.2
  Slavs (43)   −15.0
  Poles (53)   −8.2
Blacks (369)   −15.2

Jews (65)   13.6

Spanish–speaking (60)   −14.1

Figure 9.   Political participation for American ethnic groups (deviations from the mean).

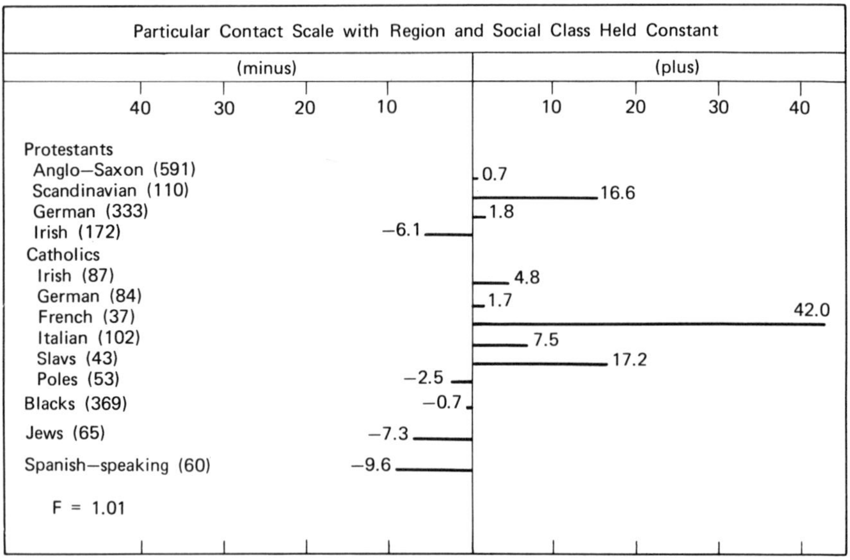

Particular Contact Scale with Region and Social Class Held Constant								
(minus)					(plus)			
40	30	20	10		10	20	30	40

```
Protestants
  Anglo–Saxon (591)                              0.7
  Scandinavian (110)                                   16.6
  German (333)                                   1.8
  Irish (172)                     –6.1

Catholics
  Irish (87)                                      4.8
  German (84)                                    1.7
  French (37)                                                          42.0
  Italian (102)                                    7.5
  Slavs (43)                                         17.2
  Poles (53)                    –2.5
Blacks (369)                    –0.7

Jews (65)                 –7.3

Spanish–speaking (60)   –9.6

  F = 1.01
```

Figure 10. Political participation for American ethnic groups (deviations from the mean).

We may summarize the results of holding social class and region constant as follows:

1. Even under such controls the Irish Catholics remain the most active political participants in American society. Not only are they high on voting and campaigning, as might be expected, they are also moderately high on communal participation and relatively low only on particular contact, which is the "Catholic" modality of political behavior in the sense that other Catholic groups tend to score high on it.

2. Scandinavian Protestants are the second most active political group in America, even in a world where differences of social class and region are eliminated.

3. The non-Irish Catholic groups continue to have higher scores than do the Protestant groups (except the Scandinavians) on voting. The French, Italians, and other eastern Europeans are also higher on particularized contact.

4. The negative scores of the Irish Protestants and the blacks are substantially reduced if not eliminated when region and social class are held constant.

5. The positive scores of Jews become negative when social class is held constant.

In summary then, the Irish and the Scandinavians are not only the most politically active, they are also the ones who deviate the most from the behavior characteristics of their coreligionists. Blacks and Irish Protestants would not be much different in their political participation from the American mean if differences of region and social class were eliminated. Finally, the high level of Jewish political participation seems to be almost entirely a social class phenomenon. (Which is not to say that it is "caused" by social class.)

III. Political Styles. The next step in our strategy was to attempt to determine whether there were "styles" of political participation that were unique to the various ethnic collectivities. To do this, a higher order factor analysis was prepared for each of the American ethnic groups. A differential distribution of factor loadings would suggest differential political styles.[16]

In Table 2 we present the results of the higher order factor analysis.[17] In discussing it we assume that the loadings on the Anglo-Saxon factor are the basis for comparison. The following comments may be made on Table 2.

Table 2. Political "Styles" of American Ethnic Groups (Higher Order Factor Analyses)

	Voting	Campaigning	Communal Activity	Particularized Contact
Protestants				
Anglo-Saxon	.65	.82	.80	.17
Scandinavian	.46	.89	.85	.29
German	.60	.80	.69	.41
Irish	.64	.80	.80	.05
Catholics				
Irish	.67	.88	.80	.07
German	.71	.79	.73	.55
French	.29	.90	.83	.42
Italian	.56	.87	.87	.01
Slavic	.37	.90	.89	.03
Polish	.39	.87	.81	.32
Blacks	.72	.74	.67	.31
Jews	.65	.85	.79	.15

1. There are relatively few differences among the various groups in loading on either campaigning or communal activity. The highest loading on campaigning is .9 for the French Catholics, and the lowest (among whites) is .79 for German Catholics. (The black loading is .74.) Similarly, eight of the collectivities have loadings in the .80s on communal activity. Somewhat lower scores are observed for the German Protestants (.69), German Catholics (.73), and blacks (.67).

2. But while there is relatively little variation in the loadings on these two items, there are considerable variations in loadings on voting and particularized contact. German Protestants, Irish Protestants, Irish Catholics, German Catholics, Italian Catholics, blacks, and Jews have relatively high loadings, while Scandinavian Protestants and Polish and Slavic Catholics have relatively low loadings. French Catholics have a very low loading (.29).

3. If the Anglo-Saxon loading of .17 is considered "typical" for particularized contacts, then the Scandinavians, German Protestants, German Catholics, French Catholics, Poles, and blacks have high loadings, while Irish Catholics, Irish Protestants, Italians, and Slavs have very low loadings.

4. Another way of looking at the data in Table 2 is to observe that the three British groups and the Jews have very similar political "styles," with the principal difference being that the two Irish groups score relatively lower on the particularized contact item and the Jewish and Anglo-Saxon groups score relatively higher.

5. Similarly, the German Catholics and German Protestants have relatively similar "styles." Both are substantially higher than most other groups on particularized contact. They are similar to the Jews, the Irish, and the Anglo-Saxons on the other three items.

6. One of the more deviant groups in their political "styles" are the French Catholics, who have a lower loading on voting than they do on particularized contact. The Poles, whose loading on voting is only slightly higher than their loading on particular contacts, are also noteworthy. The Scandinavians are lower than most in their loading on voting and relatively high on their loading on particularized contact. The blacks, finally, tend to be lower than other groups on the first three items and higher than some other groups on their loading on particular contacts.

In summary then, insofar as political "styles" are accurately described in Table 2, the Jews are the most like the Anglo-Saxons and the Germans (Catholic and Protestant), and the Irish (Catholic and Protestant) are relatively similar to the Anglo-Saxons and the Jews. The Germans are slightly higher than the Anglo-Saxon-Jewish "norm" on particularized contact, and the Irish Catholics and the Irish Protestants are lower than the "normal" loading on this variable.

The fact that the Irish Catholics, who are the most active political participants, and the Irish Protestants, who are the least active, are relatively similar to each other (as well as to the Anglo-Saxon and Jewish norm) in their political styles would seem to indicate that there may be substantially different levels of participation among these three groups. The components of their participation are relatively similar. While the Irish Catholics may be far more active politically than the Anglo-Saxons and the Irish Protestants far less active politically, the "mix" of their political behaviors tends to be similar. The Irish Catholics "do" more than Anglo-Saxons and much more than Irish Protestants, but the "blend" of what they do is almost identical.

It is possible to speculate about the Irish Catholics and the Irish Protestants. Both groups had experience with the Anglo-Saxon political system in Ireland, learning both to live with it and to exploit it. (It should not be forgotten that the Ulster Irish were dissidents against the established Church of Ireland as much as were the Celtic Catholics.) The "rotten borough" politics of the British parliament of that time gave Irish Catholic immigrants excellent preparation for the politics of the large cities in the northeastern and north central part of the United States, providing them with certain appropriate political skills for the American environment. Thus the Irish Catholics discovered that politics in the United States was a way to respectability, power, and affluence. They became involved in party politics and in political or politically related jobs, such as those in the fire department, the police force, and public transportation. Their children and grandchildren continued the political interest as they chose careers in law and government service. Irish Protestants, on the other hand, settled for the most part in the Piedmont area of the southeast and moved into an environment where there was less political activity and where politics was not a way to affluence and respectability. The two groups, coming from an Anglo-Saxon political system, became either hyperpolitical or hypopolitical as the result of the environment into which they moved at immigration and their subsequent developmental history.

Considerably more research must be done on the social history of the American religio-ethnic groups before even tentative explanations such as the foregoing can be possible for the different political "styles" of the various ethnic subcomponents within American society.

IV. Ethnicity and Social Class. We have thus far established that there is a relationship between ethnicity and political participation and that this relationship is not just a function of social class. But how "important" is ethnicity as a predictor variable? Even if it is distinct from social class, how much explanatory power does it have? What is the impact of ethnicity net of social class, compared to the impact of social class net of ethnicity?

When dealing with ordered variables in social research, the obvious technique to use for such questions is multiple regression analysis. The simple correlation coefficient (r) indicates the relationship between a predictor variable and a dependent variable, and the standardized coefficient (beta) indicates the relationship between the two net of all other predictor variables put into the equation.

Unfortunately for our purposes neither ethnicity nor religion is an ordered variable. However, an analytic technique called "multiple classification analysis" (MCA) has been developed at the University of Michigan Survey Research Center.[18] This technique enables us to analyze variables that are not ordered. The program produces "eta" and "beta" that are standardized measures for nonordered variables equivalent to r and beta in multiple regression analysis. The MCA eta is a zero-order correlation; the MCA beta, a partial-order correlation.

With the assistance of John Petrocik of the NORC staff, a set of MCA equations were prepared for the political participation variable and six predictor variables—income, education, occupation, region, religion, and religio-ethnicity. The betas that emerged from this analysis enabled us to compare the *relative* impact of ethnicity on political behavior, compared to those social class and religion variables that Verba and Nie found important in their analysis.

An inspection of Table 3 reveals that ethnicity is a relatively important predictor of political behavior. It is stronger than religion, region, and occupation for all four of the variables, equal to or stronger than income on two variables (voting and contact), and stronger than education on two variables (voting and contact). It is the strongest predictor of both voting (though tied with income) and particularized contact, and in third place on both campaigning and civic activity. The differences among the various predictor variables are relatively small and not much should be made of one predictor being more powerful than another. However, it does seem safe to say that at least as far as political participation is concerned, ethnicity is a not unimportant variable compared to other predictors. One could as well leave occupation off a questionnaire as ethnicity.

Ethnic diversity in the United States is greatest in the northeast (New England and Middle Atlantic states) and north central (the Midwest and plains states) regions because the largest number of immigrants settled there. Hence, it is fair to ask whether the predictive power of ethnicity increases when only respondents from those regions are the subject of multiple classification analysis.

Table 3. Coefficients of Multiple Classification Analysis for Political
Participation Variables (Betas)

Predictor Variables	Voting	Cam-paigning	Civic Activity	Particu-larized Contact
A. United States				
Religion	.13	.09	.10	.04
Income	.17	.15	.16	.09
Education	.14	.20	.23	.06
Ethnicity	.17	.13	.14	.10
Region	.06	.09	.10	.06
Occupation	.11	.08	.13	.07
B. Northeast and North Central only				
Religion	.16	.12	.17	.08
Income	.17	.19	.15	.11
Education	.13	.21	.28	.09
Ethnicity	.20	.16	.16	.16
Occupation	.14	.06	.15	.06

We note in Section B of Table 3 that there is indeed a moderate increase in
the predictive power of ethnicity when the analysis is limited to those regions.
The differences are not however of such a magnitude as to appreciably change
the picture presented in section A. Perhaps the most interesting question that
might be asked cannot be answered with our data. In the big heavily ethnic
cities of the "quaradcali" (to use Scammon and Wattenberg's word), does
ethnic diversity become the most important predictor of political participation?
Furthermore, one might also wonder if the various urban ethnic groups have
different styles of political participation in different cities. Are the New York
Irish, for example, as active as the Chicago Irish? Do the Detroit Poles vote as
much as the Milwaukee Poles? The answer to such questions must await an
extensive and systematic series of research projects on the relationship between
ethnicity and politics in American life. The data presented in Table 3,
however tentative and limited they may be, suggest that such systematic research would be no more out of place than systematic research on the relationship between social class and political participation in the United States.

V. Causal Models of Political Mobilization. Nie, Powell, and Prewitt; Verba, Nie, and Kim; and Verba, Ahmed, and Bhatt all insist on the importance of social class (as usually measured by educational level) as a cause of higher levels of political participation. Verba, Nie, and Kim, for example, present models[19] showing that campaign activity, voting, and communal activity are strongly related to education in the United States. It is therefore legitimate to ask whether this general correlation persists among the various religio-ethnic groups within the American social and political system. The data presented in Table 4 seem to indicate that although the picture is complicated, educational level does not affect all the ethnic groups' political behavior in the same way. There are virtually no differences in the correlations between voting and educational level for the first five groups. However, among the German Catholics, the French, the Italians, the Poles, the Spanish-speaking, and the Jews, the relationship between voting and education is far lower than it is among other groups. This cannot be described as a Catholic-Jewish phenomenon because the correlation between education and voting for the Irish and Slavic Catholics is virtually the same as that for the Anglo-Saxon Protestants.

Table 4. Correlations Between Political Participation and Educational Level for Major American Religio-ethnic Groups

Religio-ethnic Group	Voting	Cam-paigning	Communal Activity	Particu-larized Contact
Protestants				
Anglo-Saxon	.22	.29	.32	.06
Scandinavian	.20	.28	.23	.06
German	.19	.29	.33	.03
Irish	.29	.24	.27	.04
Catholics				
Irish	.23	.25	.30	.06
German	.06	.27	.02	.02
French	.00	.33	.33	.09
Italian	.13	.13	.23	.16
Slavic	.20	.33	.53	.06
Polish	.03	.02	.07	.23
Spanish-speaking	.00	.21	.35	.24
Blacks	.21	.14	.22	.00
Jews	.07	.50	.44	.00

Similarly, while there is a strong correlation (in the neighborhood of .3) between education and political campaigning for most American religio-ethnic groups, this correlation does not exist at all for the Poles and is substantially below .3 for the Italians and the blacks. On the other hand, the relationship between education and political campaigning for Jews is .5.

For two groups there are very low correlations between education and communal activity. For German Catholics the relation is .02, for the Polish Catholics, .07. For Jews (.44) and for Slavic Catholics (.53), the correlation is far higher than that of the Anglo-Saxons (.32). Finally, while education in the United States correlates in general at a very low level with particularized contact, it is substantially higher both for the Poles and the Spanish-speaking (.23 and .24 respectively) and somewhat higher than the average for the Italians (.16).

To summarize the data in Table 4, the blacks and the French depart once from the ordinary pattern of relationship between education and political participation. German Catholics and the Spanish-speaking depart from the pattern twice. The Jews and the Italians depart from the pattern three times, and the Poles four times, displaying practically no correlation between education and political behavior for voting, campaigning, and communal activity, and a relatively high correlation between education and particularized contact. Education does correlate with political participation in American society, but not for all ethnic groups. One ethnic group in particular, the Poles, seem to represent a phenomenon completely at variance with that described by Nie, Powell, and Prewitt in their study of six nations.

Given the fact that there is some relationship between education and political participation for American ethnic groups, we can now turn to the replication of the causal models developed by Verba, Nie, and Kim and Verba, Ahmed, and Bhatt to explain political mobilization. According to these models, a rise in educational levels leads to an increase in psychological involvement in politics, partisan affiliation, and a sense of responsibility to contribute to the community.[20] The various possible causal models presented in the two publications differ somewhat. However, they may be rearranged for our purposes according to the following six types (see Figure 11):[21]

1. The *"normal" socioeconomic status model* of mobilization. In this model an increase in education leads to an increase in psychological concern with politics and hence to an increased level of participation.

2. The *civic responsibility model.* Although this model is not explicitly stated by Verba and his colleagues, it is at least a logical possibility. An increase in education leads to an increase in a sense of responsibility to contribute to the welfare of the community. Education, in other words, produces altruism, which in turn produces political participation.

3. The *partisan mobilization model.* In this model an increase in

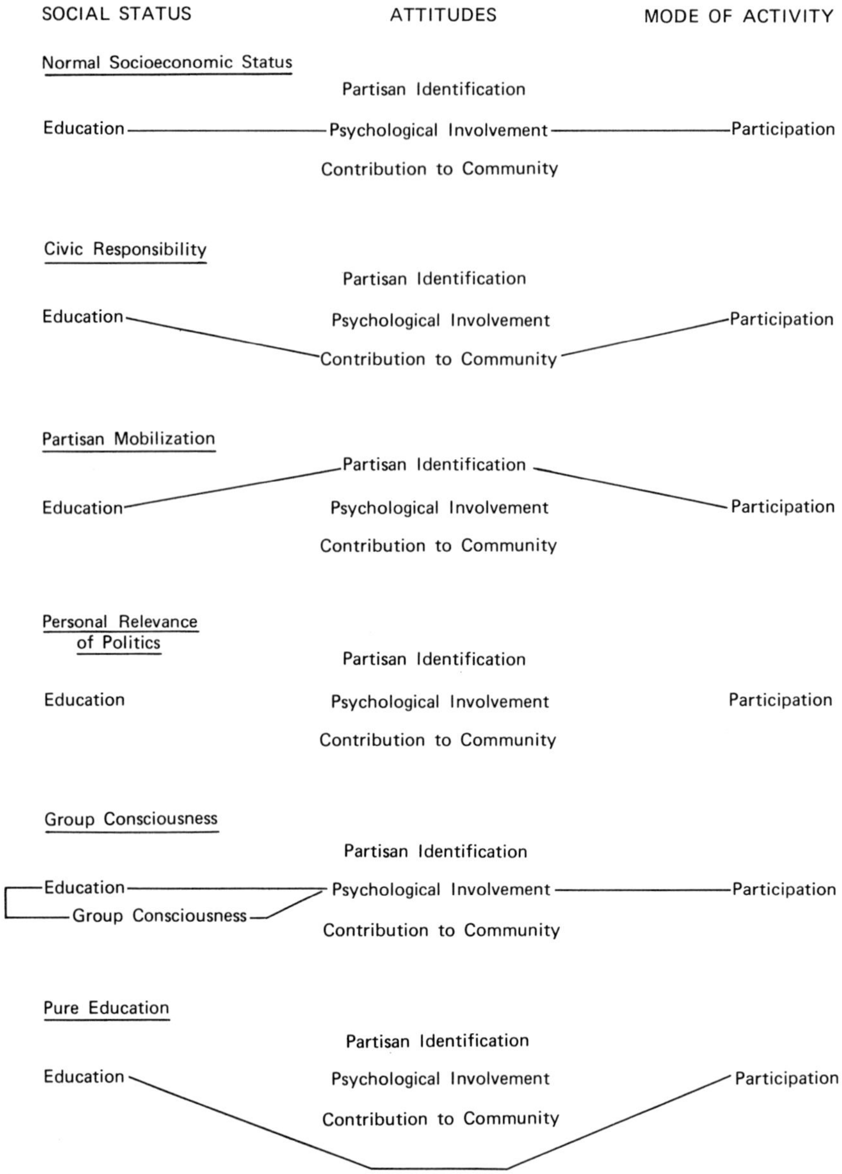

SOCIAL STATUS	ATTITUDES	MODE OF ACTIVITY

Normal Socioeconomic Status

Partisan Identification

Education ——————————— Psychological Involvement ——————————— Participation

Contribution to Community

Civic Responsibility

Partisan Identification

Education

Psychological Involvement

Participation

Contribution to Community

Partisan Mobilization

Partisan Identification

Education

Psychological Involvement

Participation

Contribution to Community

Personal Relevance
of Politics

Partisan Identification

Education

Psychological Involvement

Participation

Contribution to Community

Group Consciousness

Partisan Identification

Education ——————————— Psychological Involvement ——————————— Participation

Group Consciousness

Contribution to Community

Pure Education

Partisan Identification

Education

Psychological Involvement

Participation

Contribution to Community

Figure 11. Theoretical models of political mobilization.

142

education leads, perhaps through an increase in awareness of one's class identification in politics, to a higher level of identification with a political party, which in turn makes for higher levels of political participation.

4. The *personal relevance of politics model*. In this model political participation is unaffected by education, party identification, psychological involvement, and a sense of community contribution. Those who participate politically do so for reasons of their own that are not related to any of these variables.

5. The *group consciousness model*. This model adds group consciousness as an antecedent independent variable at the same level in the model with education. Verba, Ahmed, and Bhatt investigate the workings of this model both for the blacks in the United States and the Harijans in India. In the present analysis it is not possible to investigate this model directly since we do not have items that would tap group consciousness as a political variable among white ethnic groups in the United States. However, as we shall see in the next section, it is possible to ask whether "ethnic" behavior does have some political effect even among white groups in the United States.

6. The *pure education model*. This model is also not discussed explicitly by Verba and his colleagues but is a logical possibility. It is conceivable that education would influence political participation directly, or at least if not directly then as mediated by variables other than party identification, psychological involvement, and a sense of contribution to the community.

Figure 12 enables us to ascertain which of the various models are most pertinent to explain voting behavior among the various American religio-ethnic groups. We will discuss first the relationship between education and the three intervening variables.[22] Education does not lead to a heightened sense of partisan political identification for any of the four Protestant groups, nor is there an important relationship between education and identification for German Catholics, French Catholics, Slavic Catholics, or Poles, Jews, or blacks. However, there is a positive relationship between education and party identification for the Irish, Italians, and Spanish-speaking; and in the case of the Irish and Italians the correlation is moderately high (.24 and .29 respectively).

There is an important correlation, on the other hand, between education and psychological involvement in politics for all the ethnic groups under consideration. This segment, then, of the "normal" socioeconomic status model is verified for all American ethnic groups.

Finally, only among the Irish Catholics, the Slavic Catholics, and the Jews is there an important correlation between education and a sense of contribution to the community. The correlation is .23 for the Irish, .17 for the Slavs, and .35 for the Jews.

Having investigated the first segments of the causal models in Figure 12, we are now in a position to evaluate the entire model. It is first clear that the

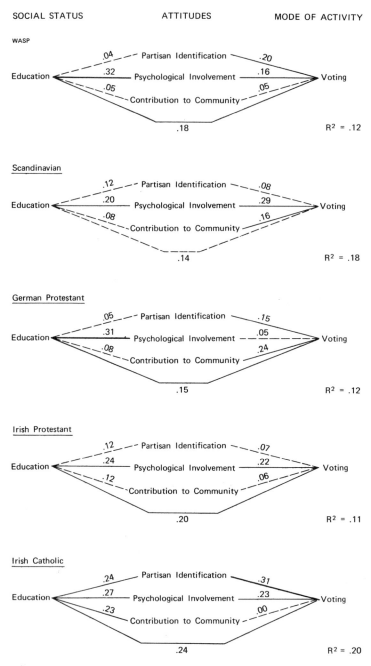

Figure 12. Paths to voting participation: American ethnic groups.

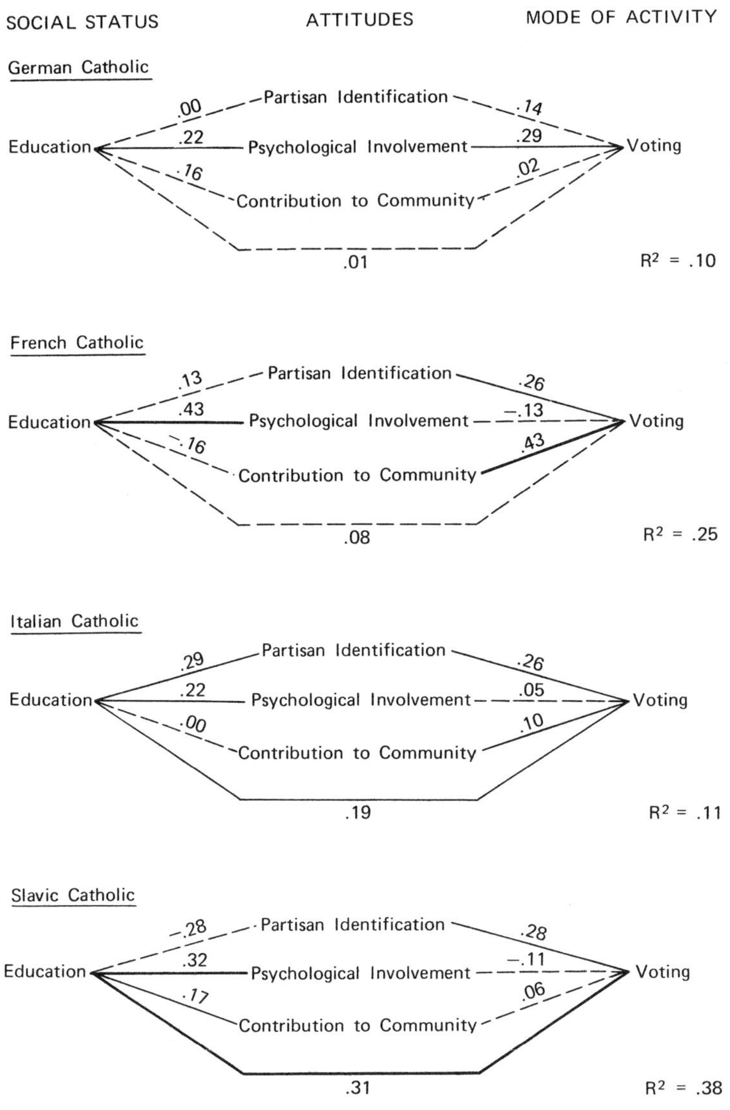

SOCIAL STATUS   ATTITUDES   MODE OF ACTIVITY

German Catholic

French Catholic

Italian Catholic

Slavic Catholic

Figure 12. (Continued)

145

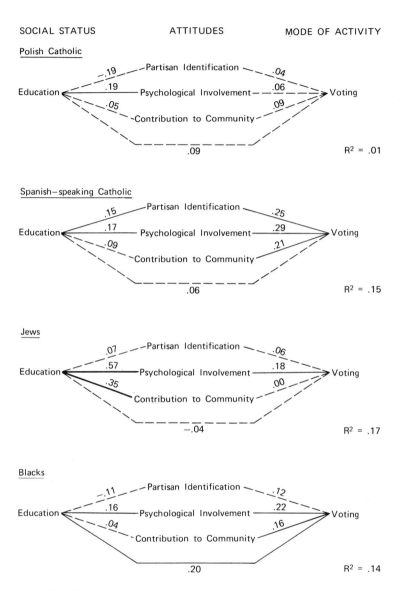

Figure 12. (*Continued*)

"normal" social class model applies to many of the groups—the WASPS, the Scandinavians, the Irish Protestants, the Irish Catholics, the German Catholics, the Spanish-speaking, the Jews, and the blacks. However, this model does not apply to German Protestants, French Catholics, Italian Catholics, Slavic Catholics, or Poles. German Protestant voting behavior, insofar as it can be explained, relates directly to education, party identification, and to a sense of community responsibility, but the latter two variables are not influenced by education. Thus, insofar as education influences voting among German Protestants, it does so through a form of the "pure" education model.

The Irish Catholic model looks like a combination in approximately equal parts of the "normal" socioeconomic status model and the partisan political model, perhaps a function of the strong Irish identification with the Democratic party and the considerable control over it that the Irish have exercised in the major cities of the United States.

French political mobilization does not fit any of the general models. It is strongly influenced by party identification and a sense of community responsibility, but not at all by education. Essentially then, French political behavior cannot be subsumed under the general explanatory model developed by Verba and his colleagues.

Italian voting behavior seems to fit the partisan model rather well, although there is also a strong direct relationship between education and voting for Italians. There is also a strong relationship between education and voting for Slavic Catholics (.31). In other respects the Slavic model does not fit too well into the general model provided by Verba and his colleagues. In addition to education, only party identification correlates strongly with voting, yet party identification is not influenced by education. The Slavs, then, may be considered like the Italians and the Irish to be mobilized by party identification and, as in the case of the French, education has no influence on the strength of this identification.

Polish Catholics represent the most fascinating model in the figure because no variable in the model explains their voting behavior. It must also be remembered that the Poles are the American ethnic group that is most likely to vote. Is it that, coming recently from a country where they did not possess the vote, American Poles have defined voting as such an important symbol of their Americanism that they cast the vote enthusiastically and quite independently of education or social psychological attitudes?

Figure 13 enables us to determine whether the normal social class model of political behavior explains mobilization for campaign activity among American ethnic groups. A brief inspection of the figure reveals that the normal social class model is verified in each of the groups. However, the mobilization styles of the groups are still substantially different, as one can see by considering the striking differences in the power of the models to explain variance for the dif-

SOCIAL STATUS   ATTITUDES   MODES OF ACTIVITY

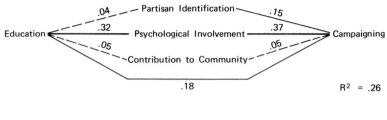

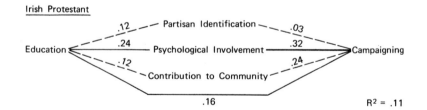

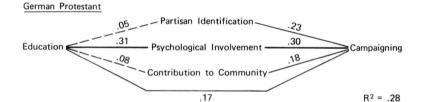

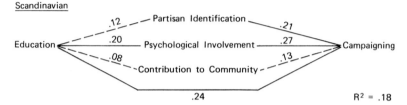

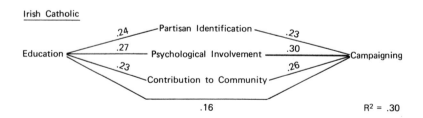

Figure 13. Paths to campaigning participation: American ethnic groups.

German Catholic

French Catholic

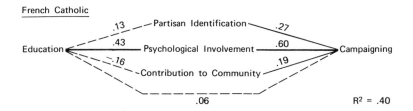

Italian Catholic

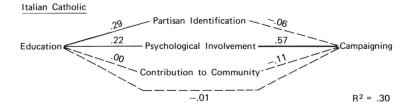

Slavic Catholic

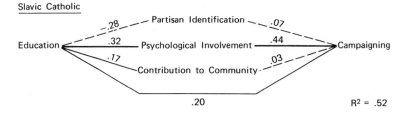

Figure 13. (*Continued*)

SOCIAL STATUS   ATTITUDES   MODES OF ACTIVITY

Polish Catholic

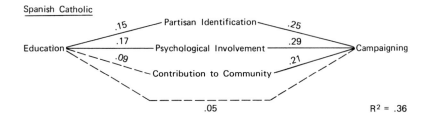

Education ← Partisan Identification — Campaigning
-.19 / .19 / .05
Partisan Identification — .07
Psychological Involvement — .24
Contribution to Community — .14
−.06 $R^2 = .09$

Spanish Catholic

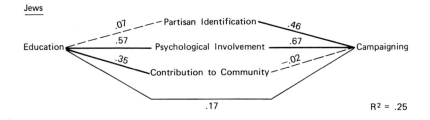

Education ← Campaigning
.15 / .17 / .09
Partisan Identification — .25
Psychological Involvement — .29
Contribution to Community — .21
.05 $R^2 = .36$

Jews

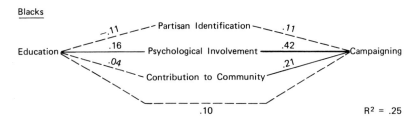

Education ← Campaigning
.07 / .57 / .35
Partisan Identification — .46
Psychological Involvement — .67
Contribution to Community — −.02
.17 $R^2 = .25$

Blacks

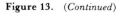

Education ← Campaigning
-.11 / .16 / .04
Partisan Identification — .11
Psychological Involvement — .42
Contribution to Community — .21
.10 $R^2 = .25$

Figure 13. *(Continued)*

150

ferent groups. The R^2 ranges from a low of .09 for Polish Catholics to a high of .68 for the Jews. The normal social class model, then, does indeed explain campaign behavior among American ethnic groups, but explains it in very different ways.

In the Irish Catholic graph, for example, there are solid lines between all possible relationships, suggesting that this most politically mobilized of American ethnic groups is mobilized by a combination of four models: the normal social class, the partisanship, the civic responsibility, and the pure education. For American Jews the strongest predictors of campaigning are psychological involvement and party identification and education through psychological involvement.

Party identification predicts campaigning for all the groups except Irish Protestants, blacks, and Italian, Slavic, and Polish Catholics. Community responsibility on the other hand relates to campaigning only for German Protestants, Irish Catholics, Spanish-speaking, and blacks. There is, finally, a direct relationship, independent of three intervening variables, between education and campaigning for all the groups except the French, Italian, Polish, and Spanish-speaking Catholics, and the blacks.

We can summarize the findings presented in Figures 12 and 13 by saying that they suggest a wider variety of diverse paths to political mobilization among American ethnic groups than previous researchers have been able to find among the various nations that have been studied in cross-national research projects. One need only consider, for example, the Irish and the Polish Catholics. The former are the most likely to campaign, and they are mobilized for their campaign behavior by a combination of four of the six possible models, whereas the Polish Catholics are the most likely to vote. The only model that fits their voting behavior is the individual relevance of politics model, which is in effect a denial of the relevance of social class and the intervening social psychological variables in explaining this particular voting behavior. We may speculate that the Irish are mobilized to campaign by all the variables in the model as a result of their discovery of big city politics as a means of upward mobility. The Poles are mobilized to vote by the vote symbolism as "American behavior" quite independently of education or psychological attitudes.

Further research would be required to test such speculations and to make similar speculations possible for the other American ethnic groups represented in Figures 12 and 13. Those interested in cross-cultural comparative political studies, then, should surely continue to explore the paths dictated by the multinational approach. But they would be wrong to think that there are no mysteries to be explained by comparative research within the boundaries of the United States.

VI. Ethnic Consciousness and Political Participation. While it is impossible to test with these data the group consciousness model of political participation that Verba, Ahmed, and Bhatt used in their research, we may still ask whether ethnic identification does influence those particular kinds of political behavior that seem to be especially characteristic of certain groups.[23] For example, if ethnic identification does reinforce a particular kind of political behavior to which an ethnic group is predisposed, we could predict a positive correlation between ethnic identification and voting for the Poles and the Slavs; a positive correlation between ethnic identification and campaigning for the Scandinavians, Jews, and Irish; and a negative correlation between political participation and ethnic identification for Italians. In Table 5 we see that there is modest support for five or these six expectations. Ethnic identification does indeed lead to higher levels of voting for Poles and Slavs and to higher levels of campaigning for the Jews and the Irish (though not for the Scandinavians). Finally, among the Italians, whose political participation level is low, identification as Italian leads to an even lower level of political participation.

One could speculate that since for the Irish political campaigning was a way to upward mobility, it is not unreasonable that those who are still conscious of their Irishness would be even more interested in the power and affluence that comes to members of this group from upward mobility. It is even more interesting to speculate that if the vote is a symbol of Americanism for the Poles, then it is precisely those Poles who are most conscious of being Polish who find the greatest need to manifest this American symbolism.

Conclusions. The descriptions presented in this chapter seem to support a plausible case for the two basic arguments being made: Ethnicity still is an important variable in American society, and cross-cultural research can be done not only among nations but among diverse groups within large nations. Un-

Table 5. Correlation Between Ethnic Identification and Certain Forms of Political Participation

Polish voting	.19
Slavic voting	.16
Scandinavian campaigning	− .03
Jewish campaigning	.13
Irish campaigning	.14
Italian political participation	− .11

fortunately we need to know far more than we presently do about American religio-ethnic groups to be able to fully exploit the possibilities of such research. If the findings reported in this chapter can be substantiated in research with a much larger sample (and clearly such research is of the first order of importance), we will have conclusively established that the levels, the "styles," and the causes of political participation among the major ethnic groups in American society are different. Being able to define these differences is of course an important accomplishment, but serious scholarly research cannot be content with differences that are unexplained.

NOTES

1. Norman H. Nie, G. Bingham Powell, and Kenneth Prewitt. "Social Structure and Political Participation Developmental Relations, Part I and Part II." *American Political Science Review,* **63** (June 1969), pp. 361–378; and (September 1969), pp. 808–832.

2. Gabriel Almond and Sidney Verba. *The Civic Culture.* Boston: Little, Brown and Company, 1965.

3. Sidney Verba, Norman H. Nie, and Jae-on Kim. *The Modes of Democratic Participation: A Cross-National Comparison,* Comparative Politics Series. Beverly Hills, Calif.: Sage Publications, 1971.

4. Sidney Verba and Norman H. Nie. *Participation in America: Political Democracy and Social Equality.* New York: Harper & Row, 1972.

5. Sidney Verba, Bashirubdin Ahmed, and Anil Bhatt. *Caste, Race, and Politics: Comparative Study, India and the United States,* Comparative Politics Series. Beverly Hills, Calif.: Sage Publications, 1971.

6. Verba, Nie, and Kim, *op. cit.,* p. 55.

7. Data on blacks are included for comparative purposes.

8. Respondents answered these questions:
   In what country were you born?
       A.   In what country was your mother born?
       B.   In what country was your father born?
       C.   If both parents born in U.S.:
           What is the nationality of most of your ancestors?

   What is your religion?
   Protestant
   Catholic
   Jewish
   Other (specify)
   None

9. In the figures and tables for this chapter, the Anglo-Saxon scores will tend to be somewhat higher than the mean and more groups will have positive scores than negative ones. The reason is that the "Other" Protestants (a substantial proportion of whom are from the South) tend to have negative scores.

10. The particularized contact scale measures whether the respondent attempts to contact either personally or in writing a government representative outside the local community.

11. The generalized participation score is a combination of the four particular participation scores to be discussed subsequently.

12. Voting score represents the respondents' participation in the 1960 and 1964 presidential elections and the 1966 congressional election.

13. The campaigning scale is composed of four items: whether the respondent had worked for a party or a candidate in an election, whether he had attended political meetings, whether he had contributed money to a political party or candidate, whether he had ever tried to persuade others to vote for a candidate or a party.

14. The communal participation scale measures membership in a "civic" organization, working with others to solve community problems, forming a community organization, or trying to influence somebody in the community on a matter of community concern.

15. See note 10 for a definition of the particularized contact scale.

16. The given factor loading tells the relationship between, let us say, voting for a given group and an underlying dimension of political behavior for the group in question. A high loading means that the scale in question relates at a high level with the dimension that is characteristic of the particular group.

17. The logic of higher order factor analysis is explained in detail in Verba, Nie, and Kim. Briefly, the technique involves doing a factor analysis over the four factors for each of the population groups under consideration. What emerges is a factor representing the pattern of relationships among the four lower order factors for each of the ethnic groups. Thus, for example, on the Irish Catholic political factor (we might call it "Irishness"), voting loads .67, campaigning .88, communal activity .80, and particularized contact .07. One might say in shorthand fashion that the pattern of interrelationship among the four lower order factors represents the "political style" of a given ethnic group, at least the style as far as the mix of these four factors is concerned.

18. Frank M. Andrews, James N. Morgan, and John A. Sonquist. *Multiple Classification Analysis: A Report on a Computer Program for Multiple Regression Using Categorial Predictors.* Survey Research Center, Institute for Social Research. Ann Arbor: University of Michigan, May 1967.

19. Verba, Nie, and Kim, *op. cit.*, p. 59.

20. Verba, Nie, and Kim, *op. cit.*, pp. 55–61.

21. Verba, Nie, and Kim (*op. cit.*, pp. 44–45) describe the three scales of psychological involvement, partisan identification, and contribution to the community that we use:

"*General psychological involvement* refers to the degree to which citizens are interested in and attentive to politics and public affairs. At one extreme, there are individuals who are totally preoccupied with their work, their families, and other aspects of their private lives and who have little or no interest in or commitment to public life. At the other end of the spectrum are those who are highly interested in social and political isssues and the collective life of the community. We place citizens on this continuum of psychological involvement according to the frequency with which they engage in discussions of politics and public affairs with others, and by their expressed interest in such matters.

"*Strength of partisan identification* refers to the presence and intensity of the citizen's psychological attachment to a political party. We are not concerned with the direction of affiliation, but only with whether such an identification is present, and, if present, whether it is weak or strong. Strength of partisan identity was measured by what has become an almost standard procedure, whereby citizens are classified into four categories, from those who have no partisan attachment whatsoever to those who strongly identify with one or another political party.

"*Sense of contribution to the community welfare.* The third and final political orientation we will examine pertains to the citizens' belief about his contribution to the general welfare of the community in which he lives. Based on a self-anchoring ladder, the respondent was asked to place himself on the rung that best reflected his civic contribution relative to others in the community—i.e., compared to those he thought contributed most and those who contributed least."

22. In Figures 12 and 13 we follow the convention of Verba, Nie, and Kim of using thick lines for relationships over .3, thin lines for relationships between .15 and .29, and broken lines for relationships under .15. In addition we follow their convention of eliminating the inter-correlations among the three intervening variables.

23. Ethnic identification items:

1. What proportion of your friends are of your own nationality?

All. . . . .

Most. . . . .

About half. . . . .

Less than half. . . . .

None. . . . .

2. Do you or your family observe any customs connected with the country from which your family originally came such as cooking special food or observing particular holidays or anything like that? Do you observe a lot of such customs?

Some. . . . .

Only a few. . . . .

No such customs at all. . . . .

3. Could you tell me if you belong to any nationality groups? (In the context of the questionnaire "nationality groups" means nationality based membership organizations.)

7. THE PERSISTENCE OF ETHNIC VARIATION IN AMERICAN FAMILIES

WILLIAM C. McCREADY

I N THIS CHAPTER we consider whether ethnic heritage continues to have an influence on the relationships within the contemporary American family despite the process of assimilation and homogenization that was the American context of the immigrant family. The essential technique is to compare the family as described in ethnographic and literary sources of the country of origin with the family as described by data from contemporary American survey research. To the extent that the data confirm hypotheses formulated from the literature, we will have demonstrated the persistence of ethnic variation in current family structures.

The family is particularly important in studying the persistence of ethnicity because of its dual function as the repository of the cultural legacy and as the situs of the process by which that legacy is transmitted from one generation to the next. The center of social interaction for most of the immigrants in their countries of origin was the family. It played an essential organizing role in the life of the villages they left behind. Families were where the young were trained by the old, a process that insured generational continuity.

Migration to a new land changed the context for the family. The city replaced the village. The cultural values transmitted within the family no longer reflected the outside society and were not necessarily operative within it. The family was no longer insured of its traditional preeminent position in the lives of its members. Children now had to move away from their parents in order to survive and prosper. The new land encouraged independence and "striking out on one's own." Oscar Handlin describes the dilemma of the immigrant parents most poignantly:

> Perhaps they never took the time to make a balance sheet of their lives, those two old ones left alone, never stopped to reckon up how much they had gained and how much lost by coming. But certainly they must occasionally have faced the wry irony of their relationships with their offspring. What hope the early seasons of their years had held was hope of efforts for their children's sake. What dreams they had had were dreams of the family transplanted, that generation after generation would bear witness to the achievement of migration. In the end, all was tinged with vanity, with success as cruel as failure. Whatever lot their sons had drawn in this new contentious world, the family's oneness would not survive it. It was a sad satisfaction to watch the young advance, knowing that every step forward was a step away from home.[1]

A "step forward" was indeed a step away from home in many ways, but the immigrant could never really leave that home behind. Roots planted there would remain to influence the future growth of his children as they made their own ways.

157

Migration was only the beginning point of the life of an ethnic group. Such a group had no function in the country of origin; it was a product of the migration experience. An ethnic group begins with a cultural legacy from the native land that helps the individual interpret and understand the world around him. This legacy is most useful to the first generation; it provides instructions about how to carry life forward in the new surroundings. As time and generations go by, mutations in the instructions occur. We can see the results of these mutations in successive generations. It is important to note that we are not observing a phenomenon that is disappearing at a linear rate; rather we are seeing one that is changing from point to point and adapting to various contexts. Ethnicity appears in different forms from one generation to the next. Its influence on family relationships is of particular interest to us in this chapter.

The immigrants brought many pieces of cultural baggage with them when they came to the New World. Art, political styles, religious perspective are but a few such pieces. But none was as important as the "how" of being a family. It provided a stable continuous pattern of development in the new surroundings. The groups represented in this study all have different traditions and expectations about the meaning and definition of "family."

Family styles differ from one culture to another. The appropriate behavior toward one's most intimate relations is specified and encoded in the cultural definition of family. Basic identity and basic values are formed in the family at an early age. The struggle for independence and intimacy is enjoined in the family of origin and continues on in the family of choice. For all of these reasons the family provides an excellent location from which to view the mutations of an ethnic heritage.

The five groups examined in this chapter (Italians, Irish, Jews, Poles, and blacks) came to this country at least two generations ago. Therefore it is impossible to obtain precise data about the nature of family structure in the countries of origin. However, there are some ethnographic and literary descriptions of family life, and these will supply the data for comparisons. Rita Stein has used this method to good effect in her work *Disturbed Youth and Ethnic Family Patterns,*[2] in which she demonstrates the association between the culture of origin and the kinds of emotional disturbance of Irish and Italian adolescent males.

Here, as in Chapter 3, the essential theoretical question is, Does knowledge about the cultural heritage of an immigrant group provide an increased understanding of the present behavior or attitudes of the members of that group? Hypothetical expectations about the nature of familial relationships are adduced from the ethnoliterary sources for each of the five groups studied. These expectations are then compared with survey data about contemporary family structure. If the hypotheses are confirmed, the case for the persistence of ethnic variation will be demonstrated. Before proceeding with these comparisons, however, we briefly describe the sample and define the variables to be used.

Definition and Description. The data about contemporary family relationships were generated from the NORC 1961 College Alumni Study. Findings from this study have been reported in James A. Davis' *Great Aspirations*.[3] That volume also contains a detailed account of the two-stage sampling frame used in the project. The essential factor for our present purpose is that all the respondents were college graduates. The questions that form our variables were included in a follow-up to the 1961 study that was completed in 1964.

The fact that all the respondents were graduated from college in 1961 effectively controls for both educational level and generation in the United States. (This is true only for the data presented in this chapter.) These respondents are well removed from the experience of migration. If the assimilationist theory is correct, they should be immune from the influence of their heritage. If, however, there has been a persistence of some cultural instructions, as we predict, traces of it should be perceivable in the family structure and role definitions revealed by the data.

In the study, ethnicity was determined by the respondent's answer to the question, "What is your father's main national background?" The dependent variables used in this analysis are described below. All seven were administered to female respondents; only the first four to male respondents.

1. "Mother salience" represents the relative important to the respondent of mother over father. A plus score indicates that the mother was mentioned more often as important to the respondent; a minus score indicates that the father was mentioned more often.

2. "Mother salience: warmth" indicates the relative importance of the mother for giving affection to the respondent.

3. "Mother salience: achievement" indicates the relative importance of the mother in giving the respondent support for achieving educational goals.

4. "Traditional role" measures the extent to which the respondent thinks the most desirable pattern of life for a woman centers on the home and family rather than on a career or fulfillment of personal goals.

5. "Domestic skills" measures the respondent's self-description of competence at cooking, home management, and so forth.

6. "Attractiveness" measures the respondent's satisfaction with her own physical appearance.

7. "Sex appeal" measures the respondent's satisfaction with her ability to attract the opposite sex.

Items 5, 6, and 7 were measured by asking the female respondents to rate themselves on a scale of 1 (very low satisfaction) to 5 (very high satisfaction).

Many observers have assumed that family patterns of the various immigrant groups have blended into one more or less uniform American pattern. The common school, mass media, loss of native language, and the common experience of American culture were all supposed to produce homogenization. If differences persist, even among college-educated people, in their memories of family experiences and in their own values and attitudes about family, it follows that ethnic heritage is an important factor in family structure, and that it persists through the "assimilation" experience.

The Italians. In the period of their mass migration, most Italian immigrants came from southern Italy and Sicily. Schermerhorn indicates that by the Depression years the majority of Italian Americans had lived in the United States for an average of 17 years (as compared to an average of 40 or 50 years for Irish Americans and English Americans).[4]

The literature about the Italian family and the impact of family structure on the behavior of its members is diverse. One of the best and most recent of these analyses is Lydio Tomasi's *Italian American Family*.[5] One thing that most of the divergent views of Italian family structure agree upon is that only one institution of importance exists in the Italian social structure—the family. The concept of "family" actually subsumes two institutions. The larger of the two refers to the family as a social group—*la famiglia*—and includes blood relatives and relatives by marriage up to the fourth degree. The smaller, but more important of the two institutions—the nuclear family—has reference to the family of procreation and one's godparents. This unit is headed by the oldest male, usually the father. In discussing the wife, Chapman gives us a glimpse of the familial doctrine commonly found among southern Italians:

> Like a good weapon, she should be cared for properly; like a hat she should be kept straight; like a mule, should be given plenty of work and occasional beatings. Above all, she should be kept in her place as a subordinate, for there is no peace in the house where a woman leads her husband.[6]

The mother functions as an interpreter of her husband's wishes, the selector of wives for her sons, and the family treasurer.

The Italian family consists of the "only people in the world you can really trust," that is, those with immediate blood ties to each other. The southern Italian shows an intense distrust of any outsider: "You can trust members of your own family first, relatives second, Sicilians third, Italians fourth and forget about the rest of them."[7] The Italian peasantry never formed deep and lasting attachments to the land, since land could be taken from them at any moment by the noblemen, clergy, and other powerful people. For many peasant cultures family security was rooted in the land, but for Italians intimate relationships among members of the family provided the roots of security. The widespread poverty and social disorganization in southern Italy placed the burden for sustaining the individual directly onto the family. It was the only social unit capable of defending its members from enemies and of protecting land and properties from rapacious authorities. This cohesive nuclear group was brought to America intact and replanted in a new context.

Campesi[8] reports that the family structure was strongly patriarchal, and that the father's domination was based largely on fear. The closest ties outside the family were the godparents. All of these familial relations were closely bounded by duties and obligations, and provided not only the security against the outside world but also a very definite and specific set of instructions as to how life ought to be lived. It would seem logical that such a tight, inward-looking family structure would not disappear immediately upon migration to a new country but would retain to some degree the influence that it had over its members.

Banfield and Ware[9] also recognize the father's dominance in the Italian family and add that his control stops at the kitchen door. The mother is a strong figure within her own world, the household. This strict division of labor and roles is an important characteristic of the Italian family. The mother supplies affection to the children; discipline is provided by the father.

Boys and girls are raised according to different sets of rules. Sons are regarded as more important assets in the social system—they are potential patriarchs. Girls are regarded as debts bound to come due because of the dowry system. Boys are encouraged to become aggressive and spontaneous, while girls are encouraged to be shy and reserved. Tomasi describes the experience of the onset of puberty for girls as follows:

> The appearance of heterosexual interest in males is frankly recognized. [As a contrast] premarital lives of girls are marked by careful surveillance and always under their mother's watchful eye, otherwise both would be criticized and lose status.[10]

This description leads us to expect that Italian girls would tend to focus on their mothers as objects of attention, while Italian boys would tend to focus on their fathers. Girls would tend to be secure in their roles as women. (Cottle[11] relates the story of interviewing a young Italian college girl who was so upset after having a conversation with a friend's mother about the mother's enrollment in college courses that the girl immediately telephoned her own mother. She wanted reassurance that her mother was performing her proper duties, such as keeping house and taking care of her husband and children.) We would hypothesize that the Italian women in our sample would be quite close to their mothers, that they would score high on the "mother salience" variables. They should also be rather high on estimation of self-worth, and agree with the traditional definition of the woman's role. The Italian men in our sample should be close to their fathers. They too should tend to agree with the traditional definition of the woman's role.

An inspection of Table 1 indicates that generally the hypotheses are confirmed. The mother is indeed more salient for the Italian females than for the Italian males in every instance. The only hypotheses not confirmed are the two concerning the traditional role and domestic skills for women. These scores are rather low. The males' acceptance of the traditional role of women is particularly high. It is interesting to note that there is a difference for women respondents between the internal perceptual items, attractiveness and sex appeal, and the external behavior items, traditional role and domestic skills. It may be that the Italian girls, armed with high self-esteem and their college educations, are willing to experiment more with changing the traditional roles.

The Irish. Most of the Irish immigrants to America came during the Great Famine period in Ireland (1850–1870). Irish did come to this country prior to 1850, but most of them were artisans and well-to-do farmers from the Protestant north. During the 1850s, immigration increased sevenfold. The starving Irish peasantry of the Catholic south, attempting to escape the potato

Table 1. Male and Female Italians' Scores on Mother Salience, and Female Scores on Three Measures of Self-Esteem (z Scores)

Mother Salience and Self-Esteem Variables	Female	Male
Mother salience	.25	− .07
Mother salience: warmth	.35	− .02
Mother salience: achievement	.06	− .18
Espouse traditional role for women	.02	.35
Domestic skills	.05	
Attractiveness	.23	
Sex appeal	.23	
N =	(48)	(114)

Note: Z scores have a mean of 0 and a standard deviation of 1.

famine and the oppressive rule of Great Britain, poured into this country. The relevant descriptions of Irish family life are those of the south of Ireland.

A dominant feature of Irish family structure was the "stem" family system, in which only one child in each generation was allowed to marry, bear children, and hold the family land. (This is in contrast to the "joint" family system in which the land is held by all the members of the family.) The demographic consequences of this practice were that some siblings never married, although they frequently remained at home living under the rule of the son who had inherited the family farm. One of the common by-products of the "stem" family system is that family relationships can become second to economic considerations. This meant that there was a certain quality of pragmatism that crept into the Irish family structure, which was at the same time a weakness and a strength. It was a weakness because it promoted factionalism and disputes among the members of a family; it was a strength because it enabled the family to survive as a unit during exceedingly difficult and trying times.

Arensberg and Kimball[12] describe the southern-county Irish family of the mid-nineteenth century as nuclear, consisting of parents and children in a rural farm economy. The family is typically described as mother-dominated, with the mother remaining somewhat distant from the family emotionally. The wife and mother pervaded all areas of family life, doing household chores and also participating in farm work. Within the family the husband had nominal authority, but he was always subject to the expectations of his wife.

In the New World in an urban setting, the responsibility of economic support remained with the father. The mother, who had never been economically crucial in Ireland, was in no danger of losing status, but the father who could not now fulfill the role of provider became even more dependent; he increasingly took on the character of someone who needed caring for. The mother, often bitter and resentful, became the strong bond that held the family together.

The traditional way of raising children in Ireland was for the mother to keep them as her constant companions until about the age of 7. Children learned speech and behavior patterns from her in a flood of endearments, admonitions, and encouragements. The stereotype of the Irish male as a man who drinks great quantities of alcohol and who occupies a passive-dependent role within the family is not always accurate, but it is an indication of a chronic problem in Irish family life.

Handlin[13] observed that there was a deep pessimism bred from poor economic conditions in Ireland. He concluded that this pessimism was not relieved when the Irish encountered job discrimination in the New World. This pessimism pervaded religion, which was perceived in Ireland as a consolation for the suffering in this world and a promise of grace in the next.

According to prevalent religious doctrine, man was supposed to receive his true reward in an eternal scheme, not in the painful and frustrating temporal world. The feminine religious symbol of the Virgin had a peculiarly Irish tone quite unlike that of mediating protector of young girls in Italy. In Ireland she was a spiritual figure with divine power in her own right. In effect, the Virgin was a maternal deity to whom one could appeal directly for solace, protection, and security in times of trouble.

Given the cultural situation just described, we would expect that the reaction of Irish children toward their mothers would be ambivalent. The mother in the Irish family emerges from the literature as a dominating and not very attractive person. As a result we would expect her children to be distant from her. We would also expect the Irish women to be ambivalent about their own self-conception. With a role model whose major characteristic is domination of her husband, we would expect Irish women to be in some doubt and confusion about what constitutes an attractive self-image.

The data in Table 2 show that indeed both males and females report low mother salience scores. At the same time, the females indicate that they do espouse the traditional role for women, and they do so to a greater degree than the males. Also, the self-esteem of the females, as indicated by domestic skills, attractiveness, and sex appeal, is relatively low.

The females espouse the traditional role rather strongly, yet they describe themselves as rather ill-equipped to fulfill it. Why? We note that the Irish mother in the family simultaneously presents an attractive and repellent role model to her daughter. A mother competent in her tasks about the home (perhaps more so than a daughter could ever hope to be), who at the same

Table 2. Male and Female Irish Scores on Mother Salience, and Female Scores on Three Measures of Self-Esteem (z Scores)

Mother Salience and Self-Esteem Variables	Female	Male
Mother salience	−.01	−.04
Mother salience: warmth	−.02	.02
Mother salience: achievement	.02	−.10
Espouse traditional role for women	.43	.23
Domestic skills	−.19	
Attractiveness	−.01	
Sex appeal	−.05	
N =	(72)	(174)

Note: Z scores have a mean of 0 and a standard deviation of 1.

time dominates and humiliates her husband in a way that may well repel her daughter, may partly explain why the young Irish women in the sample agree with the traditional role definition for women and at the same time feel as though they do not fit the description.

The Jews. Landes and Zborowski[14] describe the Jewish family as a highly structured social unit. Behavior is standardized and codified. The bulk of the Jewish migration to this country came from eastern Europe. The dynamic of intimate relationships within the peasant family was well structured by three major bonds—between man and wife, mother and son, father and daughter.

A man and woman married primarily to have offspring, and their duties and roles were carefully delineated by tradition. The formal structuring of the husband's role placed upon him the responsibility for propagating the family that carried his name, but failure to propagate was blamed on the wife. It was common practice that after 10 years of a barren marriage, a man was enjoined by law to request a divorce and to remarry fruitfully. The Jewish father was more closely connected to his family than the Irish father. He was an authoritarian figure for the children throughout their lives.

The wife's role in a legalistic sense was regarded as being complementary to the husband, and she was subordinate to and dependent upon him. The Jewish mother fulfilled the role of one who prodded her children under the authoritative eye of the father. Wolfenstein[15] comments that the Jewish mother was both righteous and long-suffering. Since she had no productive work function in the peasant family, she lost no status during migration. As a result, her position vis-à-vis the father was strengthened in the new land. Both parents, according to Wolfenstein, tended to be ambitious for the success of their children. Landes and Zborowski[16] hypothesize that children internalized parental standards successfully, and that much of their behavior could be understood as being modeled after the parent of the same sex.

The Jewish home was defined primarily as a place for rearing children. "She kills herself," people said of a good Jewish mother, "in order to bring up her children." The father in the Jewish family had a tendency to be childlike in the home. It was only outside the home that he seemed to exercise a fully adult role. Mothers were described as "despotic," "nagging," "last court of appeal," and "smotheringly affectionate."[17]

The relationship between mother and son was affectionate and, according to most of the literature, more affectionate than that between husband and wife.[18] Mother-daughter relationships contained some rivalry and even hostility, due to competition centered on the father. Father-daughter relationships, too, tended to be very affectionate. The mother-daughter relationship existed in the home and centered on the mother teaching the daughter various domestic skills in a "master-apprentice" pattern, in which the daughter progressed from the role of unskilled assistant to journeyman housewife.[19]

From this literature we would hypothesize that Jewish mothers are more salient to their sons than to their daughters. We would also hypothesize that the daughters would have a rather high self-esteem, and that they would appreciate the traditional role of women.

The data in Table 3 support some of these hypotheses and fail to support others. Indeed the female Jewish college graduate is more likely to say that her mother was not very important to her. The male, however, is not much more likely than the female to say that his mother was important to him. In fact, the only positive response to "mother salience" is the one that taps warmth. Both males and females in the sample tend to reject the traditional role for women, and the young Jewish women do tend to have a rather high opinion of their domestic skills and attractiveness. The Jewish mother seems to be more successful than the Irish mother in encouraging a sense of competence and self-esteem in her daughter.

The negative opinion of the males and females about the traditional role of women may attest to the influence of higher education or to the supremacy of parental encouragement over traditional restraints. That is, parents encourage their children to choose occupations and careers of high status. In the present society a housewife does not have very high status. Therefore, Jewish college graduates may be reacting more to parental encouragement than to traditional conceptions of the female role.

Table 3. Male and Female Jewish Scores on Mother Salience, and Female Scores on Three Measures of Self-Esteem (z Scores)

Mother Salience and Self-Esteem Variables	Female	Male
Mother salience	−.09	−.05
Mother salience: warmth	−.13	.10
Mother salience: achievement	−.03	−.05
Espouse traditional role for women	−.20	−.16
Domestic skills	.26	
Attractiveness	.31	
Sex appeal	.10	
N =	(147)	(296)

Note: Z scores have a mean of 0 and a standard deviation of 1.

The Poles. The literature about the Poles is sparse and not very detailed. The Polish family was an extended one that underwent a severe crisis at migration. Thomas and Znaniecki[20] relate some of the differences between the Polish family in Poland and the Polish family in the United States. The family in the United States is marked by social disorganization. Warner[21] mentions the phenomenon of "Polish murder," an act of violence between two family members. He concludes that it results from a breakdown of the social order with the family unit.

The father's power in the traditional Polish family rested upon his ability to support and provide the economic base for the family. He was a patriarchal ruler of the household and a rather distant disciplinarian. Zand[22] relates that parental authority and discipline were strict in the traditional Polish home. The mother usually meted out the punishment to the smaller children and punished older children for minor infractions. More serious offenses of older children were left for the father to deal with, and the threat to "tell father" was used efficaciously by most mothers. This did not indicate real power on the father's part; it was, rather, a vestigial power that resulted from the traditions of the peasant society. Radzialowski[23] comments that the mother did not exert a strong influence in the raising of her children because of the dependence on the extended family in the peasant society. The utilization of significant ancestors played an important part in the family's emotional life. Grandparents were appealed to often by parents for help in raising children.

Neither parent was very ambitious for their children, and the traditional view of child rearing was that too much education would lead the child away from the family and therefore away from his cultural roots. Thomas and Znaniecki comment that the parent who aspired to a better life for the children was marked as a "strange" person in the traditional Polish community.[24]

All the members of the postmigration Polish family exhibited a concern for the well-being of the father, who seemed to have suffered most in the move from village to city. The literature on the Polish family in America describes two types of Polish father. One was the man who had been a strong patriarchal figure in Poland, was unable to maintain that role in the new country, and became a dependent person. Warner reviewed literature that indicated that this type of Polish father eventually became a child to his own children. The children were his disciplinarians and protectors. The second type was the man who had been a strong patriarchal figure in Poland and was able to maintain that role in this country. A common technique for retaining this position in the family was to ignore his own employment opportunities and retain control over the economic resources of the family by confiscating the paychecks of his employed children. Warner describes the potential source of conflict between fathers and children represented by this practice.[25]

This concern of Polish children for their father would lead us to hypothesize that both males and females would find the mother less salient in their lives than the father. This is likely to be more true for women than for men, because the traditional role for women dictated that she was the one to take care of a disabled or aging father.

We would also hypothesize that young Polish women would be attracted to and confident in the traditional feminine role, since there is nothing in their mothers' behavior to produce strain in the family. This lack of strain should insure that both males and females would think highly of the traditional feminine role description.

The data in Table 4 reveal that, as predicted, the mother is less salient for Poles than for the other groups we have seen. The high negative scores for the females would indicate that the father is a focus of their attention. The Polish males report that their mother is a bit more salient than their father in the first two categories of Table 4. Only in the achievement category is the father more salient than the mother. It would appear that the Polish father has been able to maintain the image of patriarch even during times of great stress and social mobility. Just as the Polish father who was unemployed was able to hang onto his children's fealty by collecting their paychecks and maintaining economic control of the family, so the Polish father who appeared to be incompetent and inadequate in the New World was able to hang onto his children's loyalty and attention by needing their care and trading approval for it.

The young Polish women rate themselves high on domestic skills, attractiveness, and sex appeal, indicating that they do espouse the traditional values for women in the society. Their low saliency scores for mother indicate that they have received these values from their fathers rather than emulating their

Table 4. Male and Female Polish Scores on Mother Salience, and Female Scores on Three Measures of Self-Esteem (z Scores)

Mother Salience and Self-Esteem Variables	Female	Male
Mother salience	− .49	.07
Mother salience: warmth	− .45	.13
Mother salience: achievement	− .28	− .21
Espouse traditional role for women	.25	.52
Domestic skills	.29	
Attractiveness	.21	
Sex appeal	.28	
N =	(28)	(71)

Note: Z scores have a mean of 0 and a standard deviation of 1.

mothers as role models. In other words, they think of themselves as attractive, competent women because their fathers told them they were.

The Blacks. Research on the dynamic and history of the black family is fraught with controversy. Frazer[26] outlines the broad effects of slavery on the black family and the conditions that led to what he calls an "amorphous" family style. This was reminiscent of an extended family of a somewhat looser structure than is usually found in that situation. The amorphous black family is closer to the definition of a pure primary group than other families we have studied here. It is likely that the term "relatives" applied in the black family includes not only persons related by blood (illegitimate as well as legitimate children), but also adopted children, in-laws, and semipermanent visitors. In many ways, anyone who was living in the household and who was being cared for by the family unit was considered a member of the family.[27] Frazer also observes the problem of the male-absent and mother-dominant family, which seems to occur so frequently in the descriptive literature of the black family in the United States.

The work of the historian Herbert Gutman has shed much light on the nature of the relationship between black male and female in the Civil War period.[28] By examining army records of marriage registration, he found that many of the unions registered after the war were those that had lasted from 10 to 20 years. They were, in effect, what a sociologist would call "stable pair-bond relationships" rather than casual associations of convenience or necessity. It was when the black family moved into the cities, according to Gutman, that disorganization became a mark of the style of the black family.[29] The males suffered more from the discrimination in housing and employment in the North, and were unable to get the kinds of jobs that could offer them a stable base on which to build a family. As a result, much of the authority in the family and much of the responsibility for its survival was borne by the women.

Blood and Wolfe[30] note in a study of Detroit families that "Negro husbands have unusually low power," and while this is characteristic of all low income families, the pattern pervades the black social structure.[31] Discrimination in jobs and the poor schooling of blacks are generally considered responsible—for many years black females were better educated than the males, and, while this is currently changing, it still remains true for the black population as a whole.[32] Robin Williams[33] reports that only 57 per cent of Negro adults reported their "married spouse present" as compared to 78 per cent of native white American Gentiles, 91 per cent of Italian Americans, and 96 per cent of Jewish respondents. Many black children grow up with no knowledge of their fathers, and the father who is present in the family frequently has little influence on the pattern of child rearing. The black family has been described as a matriarchy, with the mother providing all the discipline and affection for the children. She is usually better educated than her husband, and in general has more of an impact on the lives of the children.

We would hypothesize that both the men and women in our sample focus more upon their mothers than on their fathers and find their mothers more salient in every category. Since the mothers are frequently in the "male" role of head of the family, we would also expect that the respondents would reject the traditional, submissive role of women as being normative. We also hypothesize that black women find themselves competent, attractive, and have high self-esteem.

The data support the mother salient hypothesis very well. We see in Table 5 that the mother is more salient than the father in every category for both young black males and females. We are tentative in our interpretations of this table because the case base is so small. However, the direction of the differences indicates that these responses are quite in agreement with what the literature would lead us to expect. We can speculate that the higher salience of the mother for the black males as opposed to the black females in the sample is indicative of their greater psychological and emotional reliance on the mother. It is the young black males who are in the position of having to "make it" in a world that is hostile and alien to them, one that actively discriminates against them. They need all the supports they can find, and it may be that they report a higher importance for mother simply because they need her support more.

As we predicted, black men and women reject the traditional role for women, indeed more strongly than any of the other groups in this study. This indicates that the traditional division of labor, that is, the man working outside

Table 5. Male and Female Black Scores on Mother Salience, and Female Scores on Three Measures of Self-Esteem (z Scores)

Mother Salience and Self-Esteem Variables	Female	Male
Mother salience	.45	.92
Mother salience: warmth	.45	.76
Mother salience: achievement	.35	.73
Espouse traditional role for women	− .42	− .83
Domestic skills	− .07	
Attractiveness	.14	
Sex appeal	.42	
N =	(20)	(12)

Note: Z scores have a mean of 0 and a standard deviation of 1.

the home while the woman does the work inside the home, is not an acceptable practice for these young black people. (Could it be that educated black families will become the leading edge of a "family liberation" movement?)

The black female respondents rate themselves low on domestic skills, moderately high on attractiveness, and very high on sex appeal. This reflects an interesting self-conception. While they do not think themselves to be quite as attractive as the Italian and Polish girls do, they obviously consider themselves to be more attractive to men than any of the other groups did. It is almost as though they are saying, "I think I am very attractive to men, but I don't want to be caught like my mother where everything depends on me." In general, the hypotheses about black family structure are well supported.

Conclusion

Knowing about the cultures of origin of the groups studied allows us to give more meaning, richness, and depth to these family data. Table 6 presents a summary of the previous tables. The general relationship between the data and the hypotheses can be readily examined.

The agreement between data and hypotheses does not mean that all of the personality theories have been proved; it does mean, however, that the ethnic factor has persisted to a greater extent than two or three generations of "assimilation" might lead us to believe.

A final piece of evidence is presented in Table 7. The numbers in this table are coefficients produced by multiple classification analysis (see Chapter 4). Eta represents the interaction between the two variables much as a zero-order correlation represents association. Beta represents the interaction between the variables controlling for all of the other variables in the analysis, and is similar to a partial correlation. In other words, one should examine the coefficients to see if the size of the eta is decreased when controls are inserted into the equation. This can be done by comparing eta to beta. If the beta is smaller, the controls have accounted for much of the interaction; if it is larger, the interaction between the two variables is even stronger when controls are introduced.

The independent variables in Table 7 are the ethnic identities of the respondent's mother and father. The dependent variables are the respondent's perception of sex roles and the "mother salience" items that have been used previously. There is clearly not very much difference between eta and beta in most instances. When the other variables in the analysis, that is, religion, parental educational level, and region are controlled, the impact of ethnicity increases in all but one instance. This table does not claim that ethnicity is more important than other social factors, but that it is clearly as important as religion, education, and region. We are severely limited in this endeavor be-

Table 6. Summary Table of Male and Female Ethnic Scores on Mother Salience, and Female Scores on Three Measures of Self-Esteem (z Scores)

Mother Salience and Self-Esteem Variables	Italian		Irish		Jewish		Polish		Black	
	Female	Male	Female	Male	Female	Male	Female	Male	Female	Male
Mother salience	.25	−.07	−.01	−.04	−.09	−.05	−.49	.07	.45	.92
Mother salience: warmth	.35	−.02	−.02	.02	−.13	.10	−.45	.13	.45	.76
Mother salience: achievement	.06	−.18	.02	−.10	−.03	−.05	−.28	−.21	.35	.73
Espousal of traditional role for women	.02	.35	.43	.23	−.20	−.16	.25	.52	−.42	−.83
Domestic skills	.05	n.a.[a]	−.19	n.a.	.26	n.a.	.29	n.a.	−.07	n.a.
Attractiveness	.23	n.a.	−.01	n.a.	.31	n.a.	.21	n.a.	.14	n.a.
Sex appeal	.23	n.a.	−.05	n.a.	.10	n.a.	.28	n.a.	.42	n.a.
Sample size	(48)	(114)	(72)	(174)	(147)	(296)	(28)	(71)	(20)	(12)

Note: Z scores have a mean of 0 and a standard deviation of 1.
[a] No data available because these items were not asked of the males in the sample.

Table 7. Multiple Classification Coefficients Between Parental Ethnicity and Female Scores and Mother Salience

Parental Ethnicity	Respondent's Behavior is Traditional for Woman		Respondent Espouses the Traditional Female Role		Mother Salience		Mother Salience for Affection		Mother Salience for Achievement		Mother Salience for Support	
	eta	beta	eta	beta	eta	beta	eta	beta	eta	beta	eta	beta
Father	.14	.17	.16	.19	.12	.18	.13	.21	.08	.14	.08	.11
Mother	.13	.12	.15	.17	.09	.13	.09	.14	.09	.13	.07	.11

cause of the quality of the data. Better data would yield more information and clearer insights.

Man's most primal needs and emotions declare themselves first within the family. Man learns his greatest fears, loves, hatreds, and hopes within this social unit. Peter Berger has described socialization as possibly the greatest confidence trick that society plays on the individual. It makes what is in fact a bundle of contingencies appear as a necessity, and thus makes meaningful the accident of birth.[34] If we ever hope to find out how people go about building their subjective worlds, we need to know a great deal more about what happens in this very elemental and primary kind of triadic relationship, the family.

We know very little about the role the family plays in socialization, though we know it is extremely important. We know little about what forces influence it and how and to what degree. The family is the greatest consumer of our social services, and we don't know very much about what it needs. We spend great sums of money trying to care for families, and we seem to be improving their situations very little. The mysterious processes by which families socialize their young must be understood if we are to create meaningful and accurate models about the family and incorporate these models into our designs for social policies.

Most social services, social work, therapeutic activity, and even most education still takes place within the family unit. Increasingly, we hear from directors of social institutions that they cannot undo what the family has done, nor can they do what the family has left undone. Much criticism from the people responsible for these massive institutions goes directly back to the family and asks why something wasn't done there.

The congruences between the hypotheses and the data reported in this chapter give me a somewhat uncomfortable feeling. Usually hypotheses collapse; rarely do they fit "reality," as represented by data, so closely. Despite this neatness of fit, I am not prepared to contend that I have "proven" the persistence of diversity in family structure among American ethnic groups. What can be said is that hypotheses derived from an assumption of the persistence of diversity are supported with remarkable regularity. It would seem that given the great need to understand family processes and to understand the place of the family in society, these data suggest that social policy that involves the family must either take ethnic diversity into account or run the risk of grossly oversimplifying the complexity of the object of concern.

NOTES

1. Oscar Handlin. *The Uprooted.* New York: Little, Brown and Company, 1951, p. 258.
2. Rita Stein, *Disturbed Youth and Ethnic Family Patterns.* Albany: State University of New York, 1972.

3. James A. Davis. *Great Aspirations*. Chicago: Aldine Publishing Company, 1964, Appendix 5, pp. 278–294.

4. Richard A. Schermerhorn. *These Our People*. Boston: D. A. Heath and Co., 1949.

5. Tomasi, Lydio F. *The Italian American Family*. New York: Center for Migration Studies, 1972.

6. Chapman, C. G. *Milocca: A Sicilian Village*. Cambridge: Schenkman Publishing Co., 1971.

7. Ferretti, F. "A Crime Family's Journey into Legitimacy." *New York Times*, May 29, 1971.

8. Paul J. Campesi. "Ethnic Family Patterns: The Italian Family in the United States." *American Journal of Sociology*, 00 (May 1948), pp. 443–449.

9. Carolyn F. Ware. *Greenwich Village, 1920–1930*. New York: Houghton Mifflin Company, 1935, p. 156.

10. Tomasi, *op. cit.*

11. Thomas J. Cottle. *Time's Children*. Boston: Little, Brown and Company, 1967.

12. C. Arensberg and S. T. Kimball. *Family and Community in Ireland*. Cambridge: Harvard University Press, 1948.

13. Handlin, *op. cit.*

14. Ruth Landes and Mark Zborowski. "Hypotheses Concerning the Eastern European Jewish Family," in *Social Perspectives on Behavior*, edited by Stein and Cloward. Glenview, Ill.: The Free Press, 1958.

15. Martha Wolfenstein, "Two Types of Jewish Mothers," in *Childhood in Contemporary Cultures*, Margaret Mean and Martha Wolfenstein, eds. Chicago: University of Chicago Press, 1955.

16. Landes and Zborowski, *op. cit.*

17. Wolfenstein, *op. cit.*

18. *Ibid.*

19. *Ibid.*

20. William I. Thomas and Florjan Znaniecki. *The Polish Peasant in Europe and America*. Chicago: University of Chicago Press, 1918.

21. L. W. Warner. *Yankee City Series Vol. III*. New Haven: Yale University Press, 1945, p. 132.

22. H. S. Zand. "Polish-American Childways." *Polish American Studies*, 00 (July–December 1959), pp. 78–79.

23. Thaddeus Radzialowski, "The View from the Polish Ghetto: Some Observations on the First Hundred Years in Detroit." *Ethnicity*, **1**,1 (April 1974).

24. Thomas and Znaniecki, *op. cit.*

25. Warner, *op. cit.*, p. 128.

26. E. Franklin Frazer. "The Negro Family in the United States." *American Journal of Sociology*, (May 1948), pp. 435–438.

27. *Ibid.*

28. Herbert Gutman. "Family Structure in American Ethnic Groups." Paper presented at a seminar at the Center for the Study of American Pluralism, NORC. Chicago, May 10, 1971.

29. *Ibid.*

30. R. O. Blood and D. M. Wolfe. *Husbands and Wives: The Dynamics of Married Living*. Glenview, Ill.: The Free Press, 1960, p. 34.

31. *Ibid.*, p. 35.

32. *Ibid.*, p. 35.

33. Robin M. Williams. *Strangers Next Door.* Englewood Cliffs, N.J.: Prentice-Hall, Inc., 1964, p. 240.

34. Peter Berger and Thomas Luckmann. *The Social Construction of Reality.* Garden City, N.Y.: Doubleday, 1967, p. 135.

8. THE ETHNIC AND RELIGIOUS ORIGINS OF YOUNG AMERICAN SCIENTISTS AND ENGINEERS

D ESPITE THE RECENT INTEREST in American ethnic groups, there is little evidence available on the relationship between religio-ethnicity and occupational career choice. It has generally been assumed that Jews are more likely to choose scientific careers than Gentiles, and that Protestants are more likely to choose such careers than Catholics.[1] But practically nothing is known of differential behavior among various Protestant and Catholic ethnic groups. If one accepts the evidence of widely different political and social attitudes and personality constellations among these ethnic groups, one has reason to expect that the climate and perhaps the direction of the scientific professions may be altered by changing the balance of components in the religio-ethnic mix of the scientific professions.

Although there are virtually no data available from the past, information from NORC's ongoing study of June, 1961 college graduates[2] enables us to make some observations about the religio-ethnic composition of the American scientific and engineering professions at the present time.

It must be noted first of all that there are strong correlations between ethnic background and occupational choice of those who were graduated in 1961 and interviewed in 1968. Irish Catholics are three times more likely than the national average to choose the legal profession. Jews are more than three times as likely as the national average to choose medicine. The Jews also overchoose social science—they are 25 per cent more likely to enter these fields than the national average—and to underchoose the humanities—they are only 86 per cent as likely as the national average to select careers in the humanities.

When one turns to the physical sciences,[3] biological sciences, and engineering, one may be surprised to discover that the three Catholic ethnic groups (Polish, German, and Irish) are overrepresented in the physical sciences while Jews are somewhat underrepresented in these disciplines. Irish Catholics[4] are overrepresented in the biological sciences, as are Jews. Germans, whether Protestant or Catholic, are overrepresented in engineering, as are Polish Catholics. Both the Jews and the Irish are drastically underrepresented in engineering.

Although the Italian Catholics are underrepresented in all three of these broad areas of scientific enterprise, the data in Table 1 suggest that, among younger scientists, Catholics are more numerous than past impressions would have led us to expect and Jews are perhaps less numerous.

The data in Table 2 are even more surprising. Even though none of them had attended high quality graduate schools, the Irish are the most likely of those in the scientific disciplines to have Ph.D.'s, and they are also the most likely to be working in an academic or research setting. In both instances, the "lead" of the Irish over the Jews is substantial: 16 percentage points in possession of Ph.D's and 28 percentage points in academic employment. Both

178

Table 1. Rank Order of American Ethnic Groups in Scientific Career Choices (Ratio of Actual to Expected Career Choice)

Physical Sciences (n = 231)		Biological Sciences (n = 74)		Engineering (n = 423)	
Polish Catholic (219)	3.28	Irish Catholic	1.25	German Protestant	1.41
German Catholic (326)	1.54	Jewish	1.08	Polish Catholic	1.40
Irish Catholic (355)	1.02	Anglo-Saxon Protestant	1.02	German Catholic	1.24
Anglo-Saxon Protestant (1599)	1.00	Italian Catholic	.87	Scandinavian Protestant	1.00
Jewish (360)	.90	German Catholic	.77	Italian Catholic	.96
Italian Catholic (219)	.82	Scandinavian Protestant	.75	Anglo-Saxon Protestant	.95
German Protestant (1025)	.77	German Protestant	.68	Jewish	.75
Scandinavian Protestant (275)	.50	Polish Catholic	.56	Irish Catholic	.46

Source: A national sample of American college graduates of June, 1961, interviewed in 1968.

Table 2.   Career Behavior of American Ethnic Scientists and Engineers (Per Cent)

Religio-ethnic Group	High Quality Undergradu- ate College	Ph.D	Employer (University, College, or Research)	Presently Earn More Than $15,000	Expect More than $20,000 in 6 Years
Protestants					
Anglo-Saxon (295)	31	19	24	28	39
German (181)	14	15	21	34	40
Scandinavian (27)	14	22	29	15	35
Catholics					
Irish (40)	0	43	58	33	56
German (66)	38	29	12	28	42
Italian (31)	20	10	6	50	68
Polish (34)	6	23	37	28	34
Jews (27)	33	27	30	44	59

groups are ahead of Anglo-Saxon Protestants, and in most cases Jews are ahead of the other Catholic ethnics. Polish Catholics compare favorably with Anglo-Saxon Protestants in both Ph.D.'s and academic employment, while German Catholics lead Anglo-Saxon Protestants in the former and trail them in the latter. Jews and Italian Catholics seem to be enjoying the most economic prosperity, although there is little difference between Jews and the Irish in their expectations of income six years after the time of the interview.

The Irish (Table 3) are also the most likely of all the religio-ethnic groups to say that they expect their major satisfactions to come from their scientific careers and to report that challenge is important in their work. The Jews also consider challenge important and put stronger emphasis than any other group both on controlling their own work and on controlling the work of others. The Italians and the Irish are the most likely to emphasize variety and responsibility. If career commitment and the search for challenge, variety, and responsibility in one's work are important qualities in an academic professional, the data in Table 3 would suggest that the Catholic ethnic groups, and the Irish in particular, compare favorably with American Jews in these qualities.

Furthermore, if there are political and cultural attitudes that have traditionally been linked with the scientific enterprise, the young Irish scientists

Table 3. Job Expectations for American Scientists and Engineers According to Their Religio-ethnic Background (Per Cent)

Religio-ethnic Group	Responsibility "Very Important"	Variety "Very Important"	Control over Own Work "Very Important"	Control over Other's Work "Very Important"	Challenge "Very Important"	Expect Major Satisfaction from Career
Protestants						
Anglo-Saxon	57	63	48	14	81	28
German	58	60	53	11	71	31
Scandinavian	57	70	33	11	67	28
Catholics						
Irish	65	80	55	10	90	51
German	36	62	52	13	55	40
Italian	74	81	37	10	77	15
Polish	29	51	37	9	54	6
Jews	62	72	70	26	88	25

seem to possess these characteristics (Table 4). Along with Polish Catholics, they are second only to Jews in their support for student and black militancy. They are the least likely of all the ethnic groups in the sample to score high on an index designed to measure suspicion of expertise. They are the most likely to score high on an index indicating frequency of serious reading. They are second only to the Jews on an index measuring a wide variety of artistic interests. Finally, they are in third place behind the Jews and the Poles in describing themselves as "liberal Democrats."

Both of the other Catholic ethnic groups are more likely than Protestants to be pro-militant and liberal Democrats, but they are also more likely than Protestants (though in the case of German Catholics, only slightly) to be high on the anti-expert index, and they lag behind Anglo-Saxon Protestants in both their reading and artistic activities.

Finally, Irish Catholics in the scientific and engineering fields (Table 5) are the most likely to have an "intellectual orientation" and the least likely to have a "security orientation."[5] The other Catholic ethnics, however, are more likely than Protestants to be concerned with security, although German Catholics are more likely to have an "intellectual orientation" than are any of the Protestant groups. The vigorous orientation toward intellectual and scholarly careers that seems to characterize the Irish Catholic scientists in our sample has apparently not interfered with their relationship to the Catholic Church. Nine-tenths of

Table 4. Political and Cultural Attitudes and Behavior of American Scientists and Engineers According to Their Religio-ethnic Backgrounds

Religio-ethnic Group	Per Cent High on Pro-militancy Index	Per Cent High on Anti-expert Index	Per Cent High on Reading Index	Per Cent High on Arts Index	Liberal Democrats
Protestants					
Anglo-Saxon	20	15	15	17	8
German	14	19	10	12	5
Scandinavian	8	8	10	15	4
Catholics					
Irish	32	3	32	25	21
German	23	18	12	8	14
Italian	20	41	4	11	16
Polish	32	23	2	6	26
Jews	51	16	25	35	35

Table 5. Personality Values and Religious Affiliation and Behavior for American Scientists by Religio-ethnic Background (Per Cent)

Religio-ethnic Group	"Intellectual Orientation"	"People Orientation"	"Security Orientation"	Same Religion as Raised in	Weekly Church	Church Never
Protestants						
Anglo-Saxon	47	14	14	70	28	17
German	48	21	15	70	33	15
Scandinavian	52	26	11	89	44	3
Catholics						
Irish	75	23	5	90	73	5
German	65	12	26	85	58	13
Italian	33	13	23	87	51	3
Polish	44	27	18	100	91	0
Jews	64	20	12	98	10	10

them still describe themselves as Catholics; about three-quarters attend church weekly.

Even though our data are based on a very large national sample, the number in that sample who chose scientific careers is necessarily limited. In addition, the data are based on only one college graduating class in a sample that was interviewed in 1968. Finally, there is nothing in our data that would enable us to evaluate the quality of the scientific work of the young scientists in the study.

As far as quantity goes, however, our data would indicate that the Catholic ethnics are not underrepresented in the scientific disciplines and that the Irish in particular display a pattern of attitudes and behavior that seems consistent with productive scientific careers. It may be that the Irish, who came as the first Catholic immigrant group and who already spoke the language of the land, have acculturated to American life more quickly than the other groups. They have now reached a sufficient level of social and economic security to be able to vigorously pursue scientific careers in about the same proportion as American Jews—most of whom, of course, came later than the Irish and did not speak English as a native tongue.

Whether this apparent influx of Catholics into the scientific enterprise has changed the nature of these professions remains to be seen. Relatively little is known about the differential impact of personality styles on professional behavior. However, there is now persuasive evidence that there are different personality profiles among the American religio-ethnic groups. Jews, for example, are consistently and strongly "liberal" on a number of scales, being low on "moralism," high on "self-confidence," and low on "self-depreciation." They are high on stressing "initiative" for children and low on stressing "obedience." Protestant and Catholic Germans and Anglo-Saxon Protestants steer a moderate but consistent middle course, being neither very high nor very low on available personality scales. Irish Catholics display a remarkably inconsistent personality profile, being high on "moralism" but low on "authoritarianism"; high on "fatalism" and also high on "trust"; low on both "self-confidence" and "self-depreciation" and high on both "inner direction" and "other direction."

Whether a substantial infusion of professionals with different interests and different personality profiles into scientific disciplines may change the climate of American science is at present an unanswerable question, but the apparent increase in the number of young scientists from "ethnic" families and the apparent diversity of personality constellations among ethnic groups makes this question one that should be carefully considered by scientists in years to come.[6]

NOTES

1. Among the works to be found on the relationship between religious background and science are Charles Y. Glock and Rodney Stark, "On the Incompatibility of Religion and Science," in *Religion and Society in Tension,* Chicago: Rand McNally, 1965; John Tracy Ellis, "American Catholics and the Intellectual Life," *Thought,* 00 (Fall 1955) pp. 000–000; Thomas F. O'Dea, *American Catholic Dilemma: An Inquiry into the Intellectual Life,* New York: Sheed & Ward, 1958; G. H. Knapp and H. B. Goodrich, *Origins of American Scientists,* Chicago: University of Chicago Press, 1952; R. H. Knapp and J. J. Greenbaum, *The Younger American Scholar,* Chicago: University of Chicago Press, 1953; and Gerhard Lenski, *The Religious Factor,* New York: Doubleday, 1961.

2. The study is based on a sample of 40,000 graduates of 135 accredited large colleges and universities. Data were collected in 1961, 1962, 1963, 1964, and 1968. The 1968 wave, commissioned by the Carnegie Commission on Higher Education, was based on a subsample of 30 per cent of the respondents who had returned all four previous questionnaires. Of the 6005 persons drawn, 4868 returned completed questionnaires—a response rate of 81 per cent. The original sample was a multistage national probability sample of 1961 June graduates of all American four-year colleges and universities. Details of the sample design can be found in James A. Davis, *Great Aspirations,* Chicago: Aldine Publishing Company, 1964. The report of the 1968 wave is contained in Joe L. Spaeth and Andrew M. Greeley, *Recent Alumni and Higher Education, A Survey of College Graduates,* New York: McGraw-Hill, 1970.

3. Physical science in this case includes chemistry and mathematics.

4. The Irish Catholics are almost twice as likely to be college graduates than the general American population. The other Catholic groups are in the college graduate population in about the same proportion as they are in the total population. Jewish Americans are a little more than twice as likely to be college graduates than is the general population.

5. These scales are based on the values a respondent considers important in his job. The scale is a modification of the Rosenberg Occupational Value Scale. See Davis, *op. cit.*

6. Lipset and Ladd analyzed the "religious factor" and its influence on the attitudes, beliefs, and behavior of college faculty. They drew their data from the extensive Carnegie Commission study of American university faculty members. With the permission of Lipset and the Carnegie Commission, I reanalyzed the data to investigate whether Catholicism interfered with an academic career. (See Seymour Martin Lipset and Everett C. Ladd, "Jewish Academics in the United States: Their Achievements, Culture, and Politics," in Michail Wallace, *Jewish Year Book,* Hartford, Conn.: Prayer Book, 1971; and Andrew M. Greeley, "The 'Religious Factor' and Academic Careers: Another Communication," *American Journal of Sociology,* **78,** 5 (March 1973) pp. 1247–1255. The Carnegie Commission data seem to confirm the findings of this chapter, reporting a notable move toward scholarly professions on the part of the Catholic ethnics. Unfortunately the Carnegie questionnaire did not ask an ethnic question. Therefore one cannot say conclusively that this Catholic invasion of the upper levels of the academy is primarily an Irish Catholic invasion. Nonetheless, given the fact established in Chapter 2 that the Irish have the highest educational level of the American Catholic population, it does seem probable that they are disproportionately represented among the Carnegie-Lipset elite university professors under age 35, just as they are so disproportionately represented among the young scientists and engineers of this chapter.

9. POLITICAL ATTITUDES AMONG AMERICAN ETHNICS

A STUDY OF PERCEPTUAL DISTORTION

NORMAN H. NIE, BARBARA CURRIE, AND
ANDREW M. GREELEY

THE MASSIVE EUROPEAN IMMIGRATION to the United States at the end of the last century and the beginning of this one has had a substantial impact on American social and political patterns. The immigrants and their children are credited with a decisive role in the major political realignment of the Roosevelt era. As the backbone of Democratic party support in the 1930s, the immigrants remained the core of the New Deal liberal economic coalition through the 1950s. But times have changed for the white ethnics, the heirs of the great European immigration. No longer victims of severe discrimination, the immigrants and their children have "made it" in American society today. Economically and socially many have moved into the middle class or higher. Politically they have attained national acceptance to the extent that one of their Irish Catholic number was elected president.

Does ethnicity persist as a distinctive factor in American political life? Forecasts of a major political realignment in the 1970s that suggest the emergence of the social issues—race, crime, and the quality of patriotism—as the central political concerns of the American electorate frequently focus on the white ethnic.[1] As immigrant economic views proved decisive in the 1930s, so ethnic social views are given an important part to play in the 1970s. But do the children of the massive European immigration continue to play a distinctive role in American political life? The white ethnics are far removed in time and, for many, in generation from the European and American experiences of that immigration. Ethnicity often seems to serve as surrogate for social class, for while the ethnics have moved beyond poverty, most of them have not moved beyond the lower middle class, and the terms "white ethnic" and "hard hat" are often used interchangeably.

Yet many social scientists describe the continued existence of a distinctive ethnic political ethos.[2] Banfield and Wilson, for example, argue that in the ethnic vision, politics is limited to the service of individual and group self-interest.[3] This perspective might suggest that the ethnics have never espoused the liberalism associated with them on the basis of their New Deal economic preferences. Indeed those self-serving preferences might require a new translation in the current context of ethnic economic security and relative affluence. On the social issues that are especially relevant to the current forecasts of political change the ethnic position has historically been understood as conservative.[4] White ethnics have long been thought particularly hostile toward blacks.[5] Certainly, conflict between blacks and ethnics over jobs, schools, and housing is highly visible in American society today. Indeed, confrontations

We thank Sidney Verba and the other members of the cross-national research program in political and social change for allowing us to use their data for this study. We owe similar thanks to Paul Sheatsley and his collaborators on the Integrated Neighborhood Study for permitting us access to their data.

187

between black and white outside the South seem to be confrontations between black and ethnic.

Is there a distinctive ethnic political conservatism? America seems to think so. Television and the press focus on ethnic conflicts with blacks, student activists, and hippies; political pundits write of the increasingly conservative ethnics; social scientists evolve theories to explain differences between ethnics and other Americans. But how reliable are the images created by these normal reportorial processes? Do they accurately reflect social reality or do they distort it? The question is critical, for social images tend to be self-fulfilling prophecies. Political and social leaders act on the basis of apparent social reality; and groups form images of themselves based upon that apparent reality. Even if the images that emerge from these monitors of the social process are not current reality, they may well become it.

This chapter is an attempt to use systematic survey data to describe the attitudes of white ethnic Americans on some of the major social and political issues of the day and to compare these attitudes with accepted images. The political attitudes of the large American ethnic groups are crucial for an understanding of American society as it is now and as it may become. The study of how social images are formed is one of the most critical issues in the social sciences.

Ethnicity is conceptually and empirically complex. As a concept it may be used to classify individuals into groups on the basis of shared, observable traits. These traits may be various indeed: shared physical characteristics, shared historical experiences, and shared religious identities are particularly relevant. At the same time, ethnicity is a concept that characterizes the bonds generated by shared traits. Thus Edward Shils speaks of "primordial ties" that have an "ineffable significance."[6] Clifford Geertz calls these primoridal attachments the "givens" of social science. They involve "immediate continuity in kin connection mainly, but beyond them, the givenness that stems from being born into a particular religious community, speaking a particular language or even a dialect of language, and following particular social patterns."[7] The bonds established by such ties are "of some unaccountable absolute import," and they are distinguishable from other ties such as class, party, or profession.

"White ethnic" in mid-twentieth century parlance frequently refers to the non-English, non-Protestant heirs of the great waves of European immigration (see Table 1). The classification would seem to be based upon the common experience of past nationhood, shared religious identity, and coincident arrival on American shores. Perhaps a more important basis for the classification arises from these characteristics not as they are shared but as they suggest differences from what is understood as the dominant American experience—differences of nationality, religious affiliation, and time of immi-

Table 1. Ethnic Proportions in the Survey Population

	Per Cent of Total Sample	Per Cent of Classifiable Sample
Nonethnics		
Sans Hyphens	10 (322)	14
Hybrids	4 (121)	5
Western European Protestants	40 (1220)	54
Ethnics		
Western European Catholics	10 (311)	14
Southern Europeans	4 (118)	5
Eastern Europeans	4 (112)	5
Jews	2 (67)	3
		——
		100
Extras		
Blacks	13 (406)	
Other Nonwhites[a]	4 (119)	
Nonclassifiable[b]	10 (299)	
Total	100 (3095)	

Note: Numbers in parentheses indicate the number of individuals in each group. Total weighted sample is 3095 cases. The actual number of interviews is 2549.

[a] Includes American Indians, Latin Americans, and Orientals.

[b] Nonclassifiable are those who failed to answer questions about nationality and/or religion, those with mixed ancestry, and those with no religious affiliation.

gration. The white ethnic may be Italian, Polish, or Irish Catholic; but what he is *not* is more certain and more critical. He is not a white Anglo-Saxon Protestant.

To define the heirs of one immigrant group as relevantly different from the heirs of another immigrant group, however, presents some conceptual problems in this nation of immigrants. On an empirical level the task of identifying individuals on the basis of ethnic differences is even more complex. While various groups may be theoretically distinct and identifiable at the point of their immigration, differences in the precise timing of that immigration, differences in the passage of generational time, complicated patterns of internal migration, and increasing intermarriage make an operational definition of ethnicity extremely difficult over a large survey population. Our ethnic classification can only attempt to capture the essence of the current usage and through it the historical, social, and psychological aspects of the particular immigrant experience.[8]

The typology is based on data from a national survey study conducted in the spring of 1967.[9] We have chosen this particular survey because it combines an unusually large number of interviews with questions on both ethnic background and current political issues.[10] The survey, however, also has shortcomings. It reports nationality only in broad geographic groupings—western Europe, for example, rather than France and Germany. Another is that while we can identify first and second generation Americans, we cannot determine the time of immigration beyond two generations. Third, even with the enlarged sample and the crude classification of national backgrounds, the number of cases in many of our ethnic categories remains smaller than is desirable for detailed analysis. Despite its flaws, however, our typology does enable us to classify large numbers of people according to relatively distinct ethnic backgrounds. We also report data from several smaller surveys in an attempt to validate and elaborate the findings in the central survey.

The ethnic typology of the white American population is comprised of the following groups:

Western European Protestants, whose forefathers are primarily from the United Kingdom, Germany, and Scandinavia. Canadians are included as well. Almost all members of this group come from families that have been in America more than two generations.

Sans Hyphens are self-described unhyphenated Americans. When asked from what country most of their ancestors came, these individuals answered "just America." They are all Protestant and their families have been in America for a very long time.

Hybrids have mixed western, eastern, and southern European heritages. All are Protestant and all come from families that have been in America at least two generations. When asked about their national origins these individuals often replied with a series of complex fractions (half English, one-fourth Dutch, one-eighth German, and one-eighth French, for example), which is perhaps an indication of both the complexity and the saliency of ethnicity in America.

Western European Catholics come from the same countries as the western European Protestants, though their Catholicism suggests that this group is preponderantly Irish and German. Most of them have been here more than a generation or two, and their forefathers formed part of the late nineteenth-century wave of American immigration.

Southern Europeans are primarily first and second generation Americans. Most are from Italy. Nearly all are Roman Catholic.

Eastern Europeans are primarily from Poland, Czechoslovakia, and Russia. Like the southern Europeans they are almost all first and second generation Americans, but religiously they are more split, as three-quarters are Catholic and the remaining quarter Protestant.

Jews are grouped together here regardless of nationality. The unique historical and spiritual experience of the Jews suggests their inclusion as a separate group rather than as participants in a distinctly Western or Eastern culture. Although for the most part Jews are thought to have assimilated to the dominant Protestant political ethic,[11] we include them in our ethnic typology, since substantial Jewish immigration occurred during the period of massive European immigration to the United States and since the early economical and social experiences of the Jewish immigrants closely parallel the experiences of other late immigrant groups. Somewhat more than half the Jews in our sample are first or second generation Americans, most of them from eastern Europe.

Ethnic Political Attitudes on Race, Welfare, and Vietnam.   Are there distinct ethnic political attitudes? Are ethnics more or less conservative than nonethnics? We examine attitudes about three major issues in the politics of the late 1960s and early 1970s, attitudes that are often linked to the emergence of the social issues of race, social welfare, and the war in Vietnam.

Race.   Table 2 suggests that the ethnic stand on race is exactly contrary to the prevailing image. Differences between ethnic and nonethnic groups are not overwhelming in most cases, but the ethnic groups are minimally 15 percentage points more pro-black on race scale responses than sans hyphens and hybrids. They are at least 7 percentage points more pro-black than western European Protestants. The race scale is comprised of responses to three questions about blacks: Is the improvement in the position of blacks in American society happening too quickly? Should the government see to it that black and white children go to the same schools? Should the government see to it that blacks can buy homes without discrimination? On the composite scale, ethnics are more pro-black than nonethnics. More detailed analysis indicates that the relative positions of the groups are maintained on each question that makes up the scale.

Welfare.   Two distinct measures are used to define welfare attitudes. The first is based on five questions that ask whether the government or individuals and private groups should have major responsibility for meeting the needs of the people in the areas of housing, medical care, schooling, employment, and

Table 2. Political Attitude of Ethnic and Nonethnic Americans

	Attitudes on Race	Attitudes on Welfare		Attitudes on Vietnam
	Race Scale: Per Cent Pro-black	Service: Favor Government (Per Cent)	Help for Poor: Government Responsibility (Per Cent)	Hawk-Dove Scale Per Cent Doves
Nonethnics				
Sans Hyphens (322)[a]	50	57	58	43 (104)[b]
Hybrids (121)	52	66	57	31 (55)
Western European Protestants (1220)	58	60	57	43 (499)
Ethnics				
Western European Catholics (311)	65	65	58	54 (149)
Southern Europeans (118)	67	78	70	60 (69)
Eastern Europeans (112)	66	75	69	38 (42)
Jews	68	75	63	71 (44)

Note: Exact questions and scale construction techniques appear in Appendix A.

[a] Numbers of cases on which the percentages are based vary slightly from item to item depending upon missing data.

[b] The Vietnam questions were asked of approximately 1500 of the 2500 respondents. The number of cases is therefore accordingly smaller.

care of the aged. The second measure is based on a single question that asks whether government should have major responsibility for helping the poor. While the first measure may tap the attitudes of traditional economic liberalism and includes the possibility that individual response is predicated on expected benefits from government social welfarism, the second measure offers an opportunity to test more directly an individual's preference about the government's role in helping others. Table 2 makes clear that on both indices of social welfare, ethnics are considerably more liberal than nonethnics.

Vietnam. Attitudes toward foreign policy have not traditionally served to distinguish liberals from conservatives. However, in recent years it has been suggested that the "hawkish" predispositions of ethnic groups prevented the Democratic party from coalescing around an antiwar position. That predisposition, particularly prevalent in the ethnic-dominated union leadership, has explained for some the lack of an antiwar stance among Democrats even after the withdrawal of Lyndon Johnson from the presidential competition in 1968. Table 2 presents "dovish" attitudes about Vietnam among ethnic groups. The Vietnam index is composed of a series of questions about preferences for withdrawal rather than continued fighting, preferences about sending additional American troops to Vietnam, and preferences about halting or continuing bombing operations. Once again the ethnics would seem innocent of the charges brought against them. Their responses on the Vietnam scale are not those of a new American superpatriot group. With the exception of the eastern Europeans, each of the ethnic groups is more dovish than the nonethnics.

In every instance, then, far from being more conservative on race, social welfare, and the war in Vietnam, ethnic groups are more liberal than nonethnic Americans. Because our findings are so diametrically opposed to prevailing beliefs about ethnics we shall attempt to validate them by presenting data from several other surveys—surveys that ask different questions, were taken at later points in time, and that enable us to use slightly different types of ethnic classification.

Data from the Integrated Neighborhood Study conducted by NORC in 1968 permit us to delve more deeply into the racial attitudes of ethnic and nonethnic white Americans.[12] This survey contains a rich battery of precise countries of national origin. Though the number of cases within each ethnic category is small, the patterns are quite clear and confirm those reported in Table 2.

In terms of the individual questions on integration of schools (having blacks in one's home and neighborhood, permitting racial intermarriage, etc.) the five ethnic groups consistently respond with more favorable and tolerant views toward blacks. In many areas, all five ethnic groups are 15 to 20 percentage points more liberal than the western European Protestants. In only two instances in Table 3 is any ethnic group less favorable toward blacks than the western European Protestants; and in both of these instances only two percentage points separate the two groups. On several other questions there is little or no difference in attitude between ethnics and nonethnics. The overall pattern is reflected in the summary scale, where each of the five ethnic groups is at least 10 and more often 15 percentage points more pro-black than the native Protestant segment of the population.

A study conducted by the Louis Harris organization in 1970 also finds evidence of more tolerant attitudes toward blacks among ethnics than among nonethnics.[13]

Table 3. Racial Attitudes among Ethnic Groups from the NORC Integrated Neighborhood Study (Per Cent)

Religio-ethnic Group	Favor School Integration	Would Bring Black to Dinner	Oppose Keeping Blacks out of Neighborhood	Oppose Laws Against Racial Intermarriage	Disagree that Blacks Should Not Push	Summary Scale[a]
West European Protestants (783)[b]	70	59	45	42	13	25
Irish Catholics (56)	82	79	68	61	20	43
German Catholics (47)	79	68	60	57	17	40
Southern European Catholics (39)	80	69	54	56	13	39
East European Catholics (54)	78	57	43	59	13	35
Jews (24)	100	92	79	75	33	67

Note: Exact questions and scale construction techniques appear in Appendix A.

[a] Per cent giving four or five pro-black answers.

[b] Numbers of cases on which the percentages are based vary slightly from item to item depending upon missing data.

Table 4 reports findings from several Gallup polls.[14] Lacking nationality identification, the surveys distinguish Protestant and Catholic blue collar workers living outside the South. In current usage, the Catholic blue collar worker is virtually synonomous with white ethnic. While differences between the two groups are not great on Vietnam and on willingness to vote for a black President, Catholic blue collar workers outside the South are considerably more likely than their Protestant counterparts to favor a guaranteed annual wage. They are considerably less likely to say that racial integration is moving too fast.

Thus the data from four separate studies over the past six years indicate that ethnics are more liberal than nonethnics on the issues of race and welfare. On the issue of Vietnam the ethnics appear at least as liberal as the nonethnics. The question now becomes whether it is the ethnicity of these groups that explains their more liberal political attitudes or whether other more significant differences are caught in our ethnic typology.

Ethnics differ from nonethnics in a number of important ways that are not directly related to their ethnicity. First, few ethnics live in the South. Given the particular political and historical traditions of the South, especially as they relate to the racial issue, we might wonder whether the apparent differences between ethnics and nonethnics might simply reflect the very different proportions of ethnic and western European groups living there. Second, the ethnic

Table 4. Political Attitudes of White Blue Collar Workers Outside the South

Attitudes	Blue Collar Workers	
	Protestants	Catholics
Per cent favoring guaranteed annual wage	29 (228)	47 (134)
Per cent who would vote for a black president	72 (193)	78 (142)
Per cent saying school integration is moving too fast	57 (280)	42 (127)
Per cent favoring withdrawal from Vietnam immediately or within 18 months	50 (195)	47 (114)

Note: Exact questions appear in Appendix A.

groups differ from the native Protestant population in their levels of wealth and status.[15] Because members of each of the ethnic groups are particularly likely to share similar income levels and because they differ from each other and from the nonethnic portions of the population in this respect, it may be that the differences in attitudes are primarily a reflection of differences in status and wealth rather than ethnicity itself. To determine whether it is ethnicity per se or these other related factors that are responsible for the observed attitude patterns, we must attempt to control for their potentially confounding effects.

Ethnic Attitudes with a Control for Region and Income. Table 5 presents a comparison of the political attitudes of ethnics and nonethnics when we control for differences among the groups in regional location and annual income. The table displays the proportions of each religio-ethnic group taking liberal positions on our measures of race, welfare, and Vietnam among those living outside the South[16] and within three categories of family income.[17] For simplicity of presentation and to insure a sufficient number of cases in each category, we have combined the southern and eastern Europeans into a single category of late-arrival immigrants. Western European Protestants, hybrids, and sans hyphens have been grouped together as "native Protestants." We thus have one group of nonethnics and three groups of ethnics: the western European Catholics, a combined group of eastern and southern Europeans, and the Jews.

Race. Region appears to account for much of the difference in the racial attitudes between ethnics and nonethnics. The total proportions of each of the religio-ethnic groups giving responses favorable to blacks become nearly identical when the South is excluded from the scale. A comparison of the final column of percentages in the race breakdown portion of Table 5 with the similar breakdown in Table 2 (which includes the South) tells us quite clearly why this is the case. The proportion of each of the ethnic groups favorable to blacks changes little, primarily because such a small fraction of each of these groups lives in the South. However, there is a significant shift upward in the proportion of the native Protestants who report favorable attitudes toward blacks when the southern component of this group is excluded.

The data in Table 5 suggest that when it comes to racial attitudes, ethnic background appears to matter very little for those who live outside the South and earn more than $5000 a year. Among those who earn less than $5000 a year the situation changes. Low income ethnic groups are considerably more pro-black on our measure than are either their native Protestant counterparts

Table 5. Political Attitudes of Ethnics and Nonethnics by Family Income Outside the South

Religio-ethnic Group	Less than $5000		$5000– 9000		$9000 +		Total Non-South
Race scale (per cent pro-black)							
Native Protestants	66	(250)	66	(325)	63	(325)	65
Western European							
Catholics	76	(49)	68	(85)	66	(110)	69
Southern/Eastern							
Europeans	83	(56)	60	(70)	60	(65)	67
Jews	—	(6)[a]	57	(14)	64	(30)	62
Service scale (per cent favoring government help)							
Native Protestants	76		57		50		60
Western European							
Catholics	75		71		57		65
Southern/Eastern							
Europeans	82		80		72		78
Jews	—		86		71		76
Help poor (per cent favoring government help)							
Native Protestants	68		53		49		56
Western European							
Catholics	67		66		51		59
Southern/Eastern							
Europeans	74		69		62		68
Jews	—		57		64		64
Hawk-dove scale (per cent dove)							
Native Protestants	49	(99)[b]	38	(151)	40	(176)	41
Western European							
Catholics	23	(21)	50	(47)	59	(68)	50
Southern/Eastern							
Europeans	46	(22)	39	(38)	66	(32)	50
Jews	—	(2)	—	(7)	94	(18)	—

[a] Too few cases for percentaging.
[b] Vietnam questions asked of only half the total sample.

or their wealthier ethnic cousins. Contrary to popular image, the poor northern ethnics appear to be the most liberal segment of the population in their willingness to satisfy black aspirations.

Welfare. The pattern of differences among ethnic group attitudes toward an active government policy for solving social and economic problems and government responsibility for the poor is not much affected by region or level of income. Although increases in income are accompanied by decreases in pro-welfare responses among all groups on both measures, western European Catholics, southern and eastern Europeans, and Jews are always more pro-welfare than the native Protestants. Ethnics and nonethnics are most like each other in the proportions favoring government responsibility for solving social problems and helping the poor. All groups in the lowest income category are heavily pro-welfare. As their family incomes increase, the ethnics tend to continue to support government responsibility for social problems and, perhaps more significantly, government responsibility for the poor more strongly than does the native Protestant group. In these data, more affluent ethnics show a stronger commitment to government social and welfare policies than do the more affluent native Protestants.

Vietnam. Controlling for income and region does not clarify differences between ethnics and nonethnics in their attitudes toward the war in Vietnam. All the high income ethnic groups were the most dovish portions of the population in 1967. Among those with low incomes the western European Catholics were the most hawkish. Perhaps the most interesting pattern in Table 5 is that an increase in income among native Protestants appears to be associated with an increase in support for the war. Exactly the opposite holds true for the ethnics. The meaning of that pattern, however, is not clear to us.[18]

The data presented thus far suggest that, in general, ethnics appear more liberal than the native Protestants in the United States. When we control for the effects of region and income, most of the differences in racial attitudes disappear for those who earned $5000 or more in 1967. Low income ethnics, however, appear to be the most favorably disposed segment of the population to support rapid government-fostered social equality for blacks. In the area of government responsibility for solving social and economic problems, ethnics are consistently more liberal than the native Protestant stock, regardless of level of income. On the question of government responsibility for aiding the poor, higher income ethnics are more likely to support a strong government role than are higher income native Protestants. On attitudes toward the war in Vietnam, differences between groups are less clear-cut, except for the somewhat more dovish position of the higher income ethnics, a position that becomes overwhelmingly dovish in the case of the Jews. Although the Jewish ethos is thought to be very like that of well-to-do native Protestants on political issues, in our data Jewish response in general resembles most closely the response of other late-arrival immigrant groups.

How can one reconcile these findings with the prevailing image of the increasingly conservative ethnic? Why do these survey data, across several independent studies, stand at such complete odds to those impressions that come from our society's more informal reportorial channels?

Ethnicity and Proximity: An Explanation? The reason ethnics have come to be seen as an increasingly conservative force in American society can perhaps be understood by examining the factors that have led them to be viewed as anti-black, an image that may itself help to account for the expectation of a general ethnic conservatism. Racial tensions in ethnic neighborhoods have undeniably increased. Clashes of interest between blacks and urban ethnics are highly visible and not infrequently violent. Increasingly, ethnic neighborhoods have organized and found leadership around those taking hard positions on black encroachment. But does this mean that ethnics are more hostile to blacks than other segments of our society? Or does it rather reflect the higher salience of conflicting interests between these groups, a salience arising out of their close physical proximity?

The forces at work in our large urban centers are disruptive. No matter what the intentions of the individual citizen, major shifts in the racial composition of neghborhoods affect lives, from the value of homes through the quality of schools to the nature of the play group in the streets. The socioeconomic forces producing these changes are almost beyond the control of the individuals and groups involved. Under such circumstances it is not surprising that both the displacers and those reluctantly being displaced find themselves in situations of confrontation. To assume that such conflicts are the result of natural "ethnic" hostilities rather than the almost inevitable consequence of these forces may be an unfortunate distortion of reality, a confusion of the real issues that cause tension between blacks and ethnics.

The patterns of urban residence and the economics of housing in the United States suggest that each new immigrant group in its search for the cheapest available housing has tended to displace the previous group. In this manner, since World War II blacks have been moving into those neighborhoods occupied by the European ethnic immigrants, neighborhoods that earlier were homes to native Protestants. In short, it is the lives and the neighborhoods of ethnics that are most directly affected by the expanding black population in the large cities.

That ethnics and blacks indeed live in close proximity is suggested by the data in Table 6. The first column presents the proportion of each group in our religio-ethnic classification (see Table 5) that NORC interviewers reported as residing in racially mixed neighborhoods. The second column presents the proportion of each group that lives in census tracts that are 5 or more per cent black.[19]

What does it mean for a white person to live in a neighborhood that also houses blacks? While there are some stable, integrated neighborhoods in the United States, most community racial integration in this country is ephemeral; neighborhoods are likely to be both black and white only in transition, as they turn from virtually all white to virtually all black. These transitions occur quickly. Census tract and interviewer observation data that reflect neighborhood conditions at a single point in time cannot capture, therefore, the experiences of those who have already moved or are about to move away. The point of these data, then, is not to discover which whites have chosen residential racial integration but to provide a clue taken from a single snapshot as to which white Americans are most likely—willingly or unwillingly, temporarily or permanently—to share physical community with blacks.

To the extent, then, that these measures do capture a stable pattern of community life through the unstable phenomenon of racial integration at a certain moment, Table 6 has a clear message: Among whites, it is the ethnics who are most likely to live with blacks. Only 2 per cent of the native Protestants, according to the reports of the NORC interviewers, live in racially mixed neighborhoods; between 10 and 28 per cent of each of the ethnic groups live in such areas. The census data indicate the same pattern. Fewer than 1 in 18 native Protestants living outside the South reside in census tracts that are 5 or more

Table 6. Proportions of Ethnic and Nonethnic Groups Living in Proximity to Blacks

Religio-ethnic Group	Per Cent Living in Racially Mixed Neighborhoods According to NORC Interviewer Designations (in All Regions)	Per Cent Living in Census Tracts 5 Per Cent or More Black (Non-South)
Native Protestants	2 (1346)	6 (903)
Western European Catholics	10 (261)	8 (255)
Southern/Eastern Europeans	20 (184)	18 (220)
Jews	28 (65)	21 (76)

per cent black, while nearly 1 in 5 southern and eastern European ethnics and Jews live in such tracts.[20]

In such circumstances it is not surprising that when blacks and whites clash, the whites are often ethnics. Indeed, western European Catholics and southern and eastern Europeans and Jews particularly seem far more likely to live in racially mixed neighborhoods than do native white Protestants. However, to move from this observation to the conclusion that ethnics are generally more hostile to blacks than native Protestants is to take an unwarranted inferential leap.

The leaders of opinion who interpret events and trends on the basis of information from the society's informal reportorial channels have misinterpreted the facts in this instance. They have viewed the increasingly visible tensions between ethnics and blacks as a consequence of intense racial hostilities on the part of ethnics. We have found no evidence of peculiarly ethnic racial hostilities in these data from several surveys. What we have found is that ethnics tend to live in far closer proximity to blacks than do the native Protestant segments of the population. And it is this proximity, coupled with the tensions that naturally accompany the types of disruptive displacements now occuring in our cities, that account for the apparently great involvement of ethnics in racial confrontations. Yet ethnics report attitudes no less favorable, and those of low income report attitudes more favorable, to blacks than do native Protestants.

The reasons why the racial attitudes of ethnics have been distorted are relatively easy to understand. Racial confrontations tend to bring out the ugliest elements in any community. However, to make generalizations about the underlying attitudes of an entire group on the basis of a few isolated events that provide no built-in control for the representativeness of the "types" of individuals involved violates almost every known principle required to make reasonable generalizations about the causes of social behavior.

While it is relatively easy to understand how events have led to a misconception of the racial attitudes of ethnics, it is harder to explain why ethnics have come to be viewed as a conservative force on other issues. Ethnic opinion on the war in Vietnam appears similar to that of other groups, and in the area of welfare we find them consistently more liberal than native Protestants. If there exists a distinctive ethnic political ethos in our data, here is where it emerges. Whether it is a heritage of ethnic political preferences from the New Deal era or whether it reflects other factors in the ethnic experience, support for government sponsored activity to solve social problems and for government responsibility for helping the poor is notably stronger among ethnics— regardless of level of income—than it is among native Protestants.

We would argue that it is the anti-black image of the ethnics that largely accounts for the view that they are a conservative force in important other areas.

Among opinion leaders and highly politicized individuals in general, attitudes on race are often strongly related to attitudes toward the whole political spectrum—welfare, the war, pollution, foreign policy—because all political and social attitudes are organized into an overarching liberal or conservative ideology.[21] To such individuals evidence of conservatism in one issue area is likely to become evidence of conservatism in the others. The theory of a new ethnic conservatism is thus an exercise in the compounding of errors. First, ethnics have been mistakenly accused of being virulently anti-black. Then, because racial attitudes are for some people highly related to a general liberal philosophy, the image of ethnic racial hostility becomes evidence for ethnic conservatism in other spheres.

Our argument is not that ethnics are the last bastion of liberalism in America today, but rather that it is a misrepresentation of the facts to picture them as a vanguard of conservatism. While the issues we have examined are only a sample from the current political spectrum, we would suggest that they represent some of the most significant issues in the American political arena. The data are clear: In 1967, white ethnic Americans were no less liberal on the war in Vietnam and sometimes more liberal than other Americans. White ethnic Americans were also sometimes more liberal and never less liberal on racial questions, and consistently more liberal on issues of economic and social welfare than other Americans.

We would argue, moreover, that when political and social leaders infer political attitudes among citizen groups from incomplete information or from their own understanding of appropriate ideological linkages, serious distortions with significant consequences may result. Thus Goldwater's stay-at-home conservative voters were either a figment of his unsystematic sample of conservative communications, or they continued to stay at home in 1964. So, too, the ethnic defection (which was not so pronounced as that of other traditionally Democratic groups) from the Democratic standard-bearer in 1972 might better be interpreted as a response to the disparity in image between party leaders and their ethnic constituents than as direct evidence of an increasing ethnic conservatism. Group self-images tend to reflect over time their projected images. If ethnics continue to be understood as an essentially conservative force in American society, perhaps they will soon become one.

NOTES

1. See, for example, Richard M. Scammon and Ben J. Wattenberg, *The Real Majority,* New York: Coward, McCann and Geoghegan, 1971, and Kevin P. Phillips, *The Emerging Republican Majority,* Garden City, N.Y.: Doubleday, 1970.

2. Edward C. Banfield and James Q. Wilson. *City Politics.* Cambridge. Harvard University Press and the M.I.T. Press, 1963. Andrew M. Greeley. *Why Can't They Be Like Us?* New

York: E. P. Dutton and Co., 1971. Edgar Litt. *Ethnic Politics in America.* Glencoe, Ill.: Scott, Foresman and Co. 1970. Brett Hawkins and Robert Lorinskas, eds. *The Ethnic Factor in American Politics.* Columbus, Ohio: Charles E. Merrill, 1969. Michael Parenti, "Ethnic Politics and the Persistence of Ethnic Identification." *American Political Science Review,* **61** (September 1967).

3. Banfield and Wilson, *op. cit.* Also see their article, "Public-Regardingness as a Value Premise in Voting Behavior." *American Political Science Review,* **58** (December 1964) pp. 000–000. For a contrary position see Raymond E. Wolfinger and John Osgood Field, "Political Ethos and the Structure of City Government." *American Political Science Review,* **60** (June 1966).

4. Edgar Litt, *op. cit.,* focuses especially on the noneconomic political conservatism of Irish Catholics in America.

5. Gunnar Myrdal in *An American Dilemma* (New York: Harper & Row, 1969) argues that recent immigrants, in the face of social and economic discrimination directed against them, quickly adopt the dominant white racist ethic. Angus Campbell in *White Attitudes Toward Blacks* (Institute for Social Research, University of Michigan, 1971) traces an historic antipathy between white immigrant groups and blacks to the use of black industrial strikebreakers even before the end of the nineteenth century.

6. Edward Shils. "Primordial, Personal, Sacred, and Civil Ties." *British Journal of Sociology,* (June 1957), pp. 130–145.

7. Clifford Geertz, "The Integrative Revolution," in *Old Societies and New States,* Clifford Geertz, ed. New York: Macmillan and The Free Press, 1963.

8. Few large-scale surveys have included questions on respondents' ethnic or national background. The Louis Harris Organization, conducting a pool on racial attitudes in 1970, developed a typology of its respondents based on information about major nationality background and religious affiliation.

9. This survey, conducted by NORC, was primarily concerned with political participation in the United States. The information on ethnic background and political attitudes was intended to be used in conjunction with measures of participation; the data, however, serve present purposes nicely. Appendix C contains information on the sample; more information on the study is reported in Sidney Verba and Norman H. Nie, *Participation in America: Political Democracy and Social Equality.* New York: Harper & Row, 1972.

10. This survey includes about a thousand more respondents than does the usual national sample survey and, as has been noted above, contains questions about each respondent's national heritage.

11. The general view of the American Jewish political ethos is presented by Lawrence Fuchs in *American Ethnic Politics.* New York: Harper & Row, 1968.

12. Appendix B describes the items used in constructing the ethnic typology.

13. That white "native" Americans are more likely to be hostile to blacks than white ethnic groups is also the finding of a March, 1970 survey conducted by the Louis Harris Organization for the National Urban League. That survey, based on a sample of 1609 people, included Irish, Italian, Polish, and "other" Americans, the last group consisting largely of native Protestants. Respondents were asked if they felt the push for racial equality was too fast; whether they disapproved of the 1954 Supreme Court school desegregation decision; and whether they favored racially separate schools. About half the Anglo-Saxon Americans said the push for equality was too rapid, compared with 37 per cent among the Irish Americans, 42 per cent among the Italian Americans and 44 per cent among the Polish Americans. While 42 per cent of the Anglo-Saxons disapproved the 1954 school ruling, only 31 per cent

of the Irish and Italians and 36 per cent of the Polish opposed it. Among the Anglo-Saxons, 22 per cent favored separate schools, compared with 6 per cent of the Irish, 5 per cent of the Italians and 16 per cent of the Poles. See also data reported in "Attitudes towards Racial Integration: The South 'Catches Up'." Unpublished paper by Andrew M. Greeley and Paul B. Sheatsley, NORC, University of Chicago.

14. The welfare question comes from an American Institute of Public Opinion (Gallup) poll taken in 1968. The race question was asked by Gallup in both 1969 and 1970, and the Vietnam question was asked by Gallup in 1970.

15. Recent demographic data analyzed by Andrew Greeley and presented in Chapter 2 suggests that by 1970 ethnic Americans were moving beyond the lower middle class in terms of income at least.

16. The southern states, whose residents are excluded from this and following tables, include Alabama, Arkansas, Florida, Georgia, Kentucky, Louisiana, Maryland, Mississippi, North Carolina, Oklahoma, South Carolina, Tennessee, Texas, Virginia, West Virginia, and the District of Columbia.

17. Income is used here as the sole measure of status position. Education breakdowns, however, produce substantially the same pattern. Tabulations by occupational status seriously reduce the number of available cases because of missing data and wives who are not employed outside the home.

18. See Sidney Verba et al., "Public Opinion and the War in Vietnam." *American Political Science Review,* **61** (June, 1969). The authors present data that were collected in 1968 and find that attitudes toward the war show little relation to expected demographic and other attitudinal variables.

19. The data in Table 6 are derived from two independent sources. The first column reports interviewer observations as to the racial character of the respondent's neighborhood. The second column is based on 1960 census tract data, coded as to racial composition and matched retrospectively with each respondent. (See Appendix A for interviewer instructions and information on census materials.) The measures are thus obtained by different methods, different people, and at different times: the first by interviewer observation in the field, the second by aggregate data comparison at the point of analysis. Clearly either measure could be expected to provide a general gauge of the extent to which different ethnic groups are likely to live in racially mixed neighborhoods. Equally clearly, however, neither measure could be expected to perform the task perfectly. Interviewer contact with the respondent's neighborhood may be too limited in time and/or too restricted in area to provide the relevant information. Census tracts, on the other hand, are sometimes so large as to include whole towns, and sometimes so small as to include only a few city blocks; they may be either larger or smaller than a neighborhood. In addition the survey was taken in 1967, but the census tract data reports 1960 conditions. Given the limitations of each measure we chose to investigate our respondents' patterns of residence in racially mixed neighborhoods with the help of both. The only place where the measures show as much as a four percentage point variance is among native Protestants, which can probably be explained by the fact that the interviewer data report figures for all regions and include many southerners, who do not appear in the census tract data. The similarity in the results from these two quite different analytic techniques increases our confidence in the validity of each and suggests both the utility and viability of the integration of ecological and survey methods in data analysis.

20. Of this sample, those who live in racially mixed neighborhoods are in fact more likely to report favorable attitudes toward blacks:

	Per Cent Giving Pro-black Responses in Census Tracts Less Than 5 Per Cent Black	Per Cent Giving Pro-black Responses in Census Tracts 5 Per Cent or More Black
Native Protestants	65 (848)	62 (55)
Western Catholics	68 (235)	72 (20)
Southern/Eastern Europeans	64 (181)	77 (39)
Jews	66 (52)	83 (16)

21. Highly organized political belief systems are characteristic of elite populations, but they are usually not found among average citizens. Most researchers who have examined the inter-relation of attitudes in different policy spheres have found such attitudes to be almost totally unrelated. See, for example, Philip E. Converse, "The Nature of Belief Systems in Mass Publics," in *Ideology and Discontent,* David Apter, ed., (New York: The Free Press, 1964) and Herbert McCloskey, "Consensus and Ideology in American Politics," *American Political Science Review,* **58** (June 1964). More recent research suggests, however, a growing ideological consistency in the mass public. (See Norman H. Nie, "Mass Belief Systems Revisted: Political Change and Attitude Structure," forthcoming in the *Journal of Politics.*) In our data it should be clear that ethnic attitudes, whatever their degree of ideological organization, are more rather than less liberal. Work in progress by Norman H. Nie, Sidney Verba, and Andrew M. Greeley indicates, in fact, a considerable degree of at-titude consistency among these ethnic groups and underlines their predominantly liberal orientations.

APPENDIX A

A. **The Race Scale.** The race scale is composed of the following three items:

1. Do you think the government should see to it that white and Negro children go to the same schools or should the government stay out of it?

2. Do you think the government should see to it that Negroes can purchase homes without discrimination or should the government stay out of it?

3. There are many attempts to improve conditions for the Negroes in America. Do you think that those who are trying to improve the Negro's position are trying to do it too quickly, not quickly enough, or about right?

The scale is made up of answers to all three questions. More than a third of the sample said the government should stay out in (1) and (2) and answered "too quickly" to (3). The balance of the responses count as pro-integrationist on our scale.

B. **The Welfare Service Scale.**   This scale is constructed from a battery of 10 items on who has the major responsibility in five areas of welfare. The respondent was first asked which group should have the main responsibility for solving the problem of:

1.   financing medical care
2.   caring for the aged
3.   solving employment problems
4.   providing adequate housing
5.   providing for adequate schooling

The groups listed were:
1.   individual and family
2.   private groups and organizations
3.   local, state, or national government

C. **Helping the Poor.**   This measure is based on answers to the following single question:

Some people say that the government should have the major responsibility for the needs of the poor people in this country. Others say that the poor should themselves have major responsibility to do something about their problems. What do you believe?

Those who said that government should have major responsibility or that both government and the poor should do something are counted as favoring government help for the poor.

D. **The Vietnam Hawk-Dove Scale.**   This is a four item, five step Guttman quasiscale that ranges from 1 ("extreme hawk") to 5 ("extreme dove"). The questions are:

1.   There has been some discussion of the U.S. bombing in North Vietnam. Some say that we ought greatly to increase the bombing; others say that we should stop the bombing; and others say what we are doing is about right. Which do you believe: should we increase the bombing, or stop it, or continue as we are now? (Hand card.)
2.   Would you favor or oppose continuing the fighting in Vietnam if it meant having to have a half million troops in South Vietnam?
3.   A number of different steps have been proposed to end the present fighting in South Vietnam. In order to end the fighting would you approve or

disapprove of forming a new government in which the Vietcong took some part?

4. Suppose you had to choose among continuing the present situation indefinitely, fighting a major war with thousands of American casualties, or a withdrawal of American troops leading to an eventual Communist takeover in Vietnam—which would you choose? (Hand card.)

Hawk responses are: (1) increase bombing, (2) favor additional troops, (3) disapprove coalition government, and (4) continue present situation or fighting a major war. A respondent's score on this scale is obtained by summing the dove responses and adding that number to a minimum value of 1. The cutting point in the table is between 3 and 4. Thus those whose scores were 4 or 5 are here classified as doves.

E. The Gallup Poll Questions. In 1968, the American Institute of Public Opinion asked respondents: "As you may know, there is talk about giving every family an income of at least $3,200 a year, which would be the amount for a family of four. If the family earns less than this, the Government would make up the difference. Would you favor or oppose such a plan?" Table 4 lists respondents who favored such a plan.

The question about voting for a black president comes from a 1969 AIPO poll: "There's always much discussion about the qualifications of presidential candidates—their education, age, race, religion, and the like . . . If your party nominated a generally well-qualified man for President and he happeneed to be a Negro, would you vote for him?" Respondents who said yes are included in Table 4.

The question on school integration also comes from a 1969 poll: "What is your opinion—do you think the racial integration of schools in the United States is going too fast or not fast enough?" The percentage of those responding "too fast" appears in Table 4.

The Vietnam question comes from a 1970 poll: "Here are four different plans the United States could follow in dealing with the war in Vietnam. Which *one* do you prefer?

A. Withdraw all troops from Vietnam immediately.

B. Withdraw all troops by the end of 18 months.

C. Withdraw all troops but take as many years to do this as are needed to turn the war over to the South Vietnamese.

D. Send more troops to Vietnam and step up the fighting."

Respondents who chose alternatives A or B are included in Table 4.

F. Racial Character of Neighborhood Indices

1. INTERVIEWER OBSERVATION. At the end of each interview, the interviewer (not the respondent) was asked to record his description of the racial character of the respondent's neighborhood. The item checked by the interviewer read:

Respondent's neighborhood is:
   1. Predominantly white
   2. Predominantly Negro
   3. Mixed white and Negro
   4. Mixed white, Negro, and other
   5. Other
   6. Don't know

For present purposes a response of 2, 3, or 4 was counted as racially integrated. The table reports observations for the whole sample, including the South.

2. CENSUS TRACT DATA. During the data analysis, racial composition, based on 1960 population figures, was determined for all census tracts in which NORC conducted the 1967 interviews. Each respondent was then matched with his census tract and its racial character. The index in Table 6 reports the percentage of each ethnic group living in census tracts that were 5 or more per cent black. Five per cent is a low cutting point; we chose it not for theoretically interesting reasons but rather because a point any higher left virtually no whites—no matter how ethnic—living in close proximity to blacks.

APPENDIX B: THE ETHNIC CLASSIFICATION

Respondents were asked to identify their country of birth and the country of birth of each parent. If both parents were born in the United States (and only if both parents were born here), respondents were asked the nationality of most of their ancestors. At the time the interviews were coded the decision was made to collapse national distinctions in favor of broad geographical categories (France became western Europe, Russia became eastern Europe, and so forth) for those who responded to the question about ancestors' nationality. Actual countries of origin were specified, however, for those respondents with non-United States parentage. The number of cases among the latter group was small relative to the former. Except for a small proportion of the sample, then, we lacked information on precise national heritage and time of American immigration for the bulk of our sample. We settled for an ethnic typology based on broad geographical groupings, coupled where appropriate with religious af-filiation.

Reclassifying those whose precise national origins were available into the larger geographical designations, we distinguished three major ethnic back-grounds among our respondents—western, southern, and eastern Europe. Among the western Europeans we further divided the sample into Catholic and Protestant groups. Protestants from western Europe came to America in substantial numbers throughout the nineteenth century; Catholic emigration from that area was heaviest after 1850. Southern and eastern European immi-gration were both heavily Catholic and peaked in the early twentieth century. Jews from all three geographic regions are here grouped together. Their number in the total sample was insufficient to distinguish the eastern and western Europeans among them, and it was felt that the historical position of the Jew in Europe and America justified their inclusion as a separate group instead of as members of the broad European categories. The descriptions of each group in the ethnic typology, including proportions of newer immigrants, where available, can be found in the text.

APPENDIX C: DESCRIPTION OF SAMPLES

The Political Participation Study was conducted in March, 1967. It was a multistage area sample based on the standard NORC sampling units. An ad-ditional 1050 interviews were added to the standard 1500 interview NORC Amalgam sample by adding extra interviews in 65 target localities. More detailed information on this sample may be found in Sidney Verba and Norman H. Nie, *Participation in America: Political Democracy and Social Equality*. New York: Harper & Row, 1972.

The NORC Integrated Neighborhood Study sampled white residents in in-tegrated neighborhoods as a self-weighting probability sample of all white residents in such neighborhoods. The sampling procedure is more completely described in Norman Bradburn, Seymour Sudman, and Galen L. Gockel, *Racial Integration in American Neighborhoods, A Comparative Survey*. Chicago: National Opinion Research Center, 1970.

The sample designs for the Gallup Polls are described in Paul K. Perry, "Election Survey Methods." *Gallup Political Index* (now called *Gallup Opinion Index*), Report No. 7, December, 1965.

ADDENDUM

ANDREW M. GREELEY

Two other sets of survey data are available that may be used to confirm the picture presented in this chapter. They are the University of Michigan national election surveys and a study of public attitudes on political matters done by the NORC graduate training program in 1971.

The most obvious thing that can be said about the ethnics is that they are Democrats (Table 7). Irish Catholics were 15 percentage points more likely to vote Democratic in congressional elections during the last 20 years than were most Americans; the Italians were 7 percentage points more likely, and the Poles 21 percentage points more likely. In the 1970 congressional election both the Irish and Poles were 19 percentage points more likely to vote Democratic than the national average. In the presidental elections of 1962 and 1968, the Irish were 17 percentage points more likely to cast their ballots for a Democratic candidate than the national average, the Italians 12 percentage points, and the Poles 18 percentage points. In 1968, the Irish were 21 points ahead of the national average in voting for Hubert Humphrey; the Italians were 15 percentage points ahead of the national average; and the Poles (despite all the talk about their support for George Wallace) were 30 points ahead of the na-

Table 7.   Where Ethnics Stand on Voting Patterns and Party Affiliation

	Irish Catholics	German Catholics	Italian Catholics	Polish Catholics	All Americans
Average per cent voted Democratic Congress, 1952–1970	70	57	62	76	55
Average per cent voted Democratic, 1970	73	45	62	73	54
Average per cent voted Democratic for President, 1952–1968	65	55	60	76	48
Average per cent voted for Humphrey, 1968	65	55	59	80	44
Per cent Democrat or Democrat-leaning, Spring 1972	61	57	63	72	55

tional average in their support of Humphrey. Finally, in the spring of 1972, the Irish, Italians, and Poles ranged from 6 to 17 points ahead of the national average of those describing themselves as "Democrat or Democrat-leaning."

Furthermore, in comparing the Italian and Polish ethnics with the Anglo-Saxon Protestants, one notes that the order of importance of the first five issues listed on Table 8 is precisely the same: war, marijuana, inflation, crime, and pollution. However, the Italians and the Poles were more likely to see each of these as very serious problems than were Anglo-Saxon Protestants. More than half of both groups thought that pollution, inflation, and the war were very serious problems. However, as of spring 1971, three-fifths of the Italians and three-fifths of the Poles thought that marijuana was a very serious problem in the country, putting it in second place on their list of problems, as did Anglo-Saxon Protestants.

Table 9 gives the proportions of respondents in each group who both like and dislike various elements in the society. The overwhelming majority of all the groups is sympathetically disposed to college students, indicating that the younger generation is by no means despised by most Americans. The Irish, Italians, and Poles are somewhat less likely, however, to like college students than are Anglo-Saxon Protestants. Similarly, while the majority of all the groups like college professors, the Irish and the Italians are somewhat less inclined to like them, and only a minority of the Poles (40 per cent) are willing to admit that they like college professors. But while students and professors get good marks from the ethnics, radical students get poor marks; more than four-fifths of each group (and more than four-fifths of the Anglo-Saxon Protestants concur) register dislike of radical students.

Admiration for big business is less among the Catholic ethnics than it is among Anglo-Saxon Protestants, although only the Italians are notably more inclined to like labor unions. Liberals enjoy a better image with the Irish than they do with the other five groups, though only the Italians are less sympathetic to the liberals than are Anglo-Saxon Protestants. Similarly, the German, Italian, and Polish Catholics are somewhat less likely to have a favorable image of conservatives than are Anglo-Saxon Protestants.

There is little difference between the Anglo-Saxons and the Germans, Italians, and Poles in their images of blacks. The Irish, however, are notably more inclined to have a favorable image of blacks. All groups have a most unfavorable image of black militants—indeed blacks themselves are inclined to be slightly more unfavorable than favorable to the militants. The Irish, German, and Italians have about the same image of welfare recipients as do the Anglo-Saxon Protestants, although the Polish image is distinctly unfavorable. Finally, all five groups are favorably disposed to the police.

The ethnics are not "pure" liberals, and indeed a substantial proportion of them seem to dislike "pure" liberalism. Table 10 suggests that there is

Table 8. Where Ethnics Stand on Rank Order of First Six "Very Serious Problems," NORC 1971

Rank of Problem	Anglo-Saxon Protestants		Irish Catholics		German Catholics		Italian Catholics		Polish Catholics	
	Problem	Per Cent	Problem	Per Cent	Problem	Per Cent	Problem	Per Cent	Problem	Per Cent
1.	War	68	War	69	War	62	War	73	War	71
2.	Marijuana	51	Inflation	55	Inflation	49	Marijuana	60	Marijuana	60
3.	Inflation	48	Crime	52	Pollution	46	Inflation	57	Inflation	57
4.	Crime	44	Welfare	42	Marijuana	42	Crime	55	Crime	55
5.	Pollution	42	Unemployment	38	Crime	39	Pollution	54	Pollution	55
6.	Unemployment	30	Pollution	38	Unemployment	30	Welfare	53	Urban unrest	35

Table 9.   Where Ethnics Stand on Their Likes/Dislikes

Object of Likes/Dislikes	Anglo-Saxon Protestants	Irish Catholics	German Catholics	Italian Catholics	Polish Catholics
College students	80/3	67/0	80/2	70/0	72/6
Big business	76/14	42/21	31/26	57/10	33/21
Liberals	27/27	39/28	31/26	15/25	28/21
Blacks	50/12	79/0	49/7	50/2	46/13
Conservatives	46/12	46/18	30/13	38/8	31/13
Hippies	7/77	14/58	3/70	3/66	2/79
Radical students	4/86	7/86	2/81	14/82	0/88
Welfare recipients	30/21	28/17	33/28	28/18	10/35
College professors	63/7	57/10	67/3	57/7	40/2
Police	87/3	86/0	91/5	90/0	78/4
Unions	43/33	43/21	46/30	50/19	45/20
Black militants[a]	2/83	0/96	2/83	5/78	4/86

[a] The black response to this question is 35/37.

nevertheless a strong reserve of potential support among the ethnics for liberalism. The majority of the Irish, for example, favor withdrawal from Vietnam, stiff punishment for pollution, a speeding up of racial progress, government support for family assistance, and a maximum use of resources to eliminate poverty. On each of these issues, the Irish are more "liberal" than Anglo-Saxon Protestants. A surprisingly large minority of the Irish (30 per cent) are also willing to support the legalization of marijuana (perhaps because the Irish romance with John Barleycorn makes them reluctant to deny any kind of narcotic to others). The Irish are also considerably more likely than the Anglo-Saxon Protestants to support government pressure for neighborhood integration and to oppose punishment for student rioters, although in both cases only a minority of the Irish respondents took such a position. On the other hand, 51 per cent of the Irish respondents favored the use of force to end urban unrest. And, finally, the Irish are the most likely of any of the groups under consideration to think that the courts have gone too far in protecting the rights of criminals.

A majority of German Catholics take the "liberal" side only on stiff penalties for pollution, though Germans are more likely to be on the liberal side than Anglo-Saxon Protestants on the war, on solving the underlying problems that cause riots, on family assistance, marijuana, and neighborhood integration.

Table 10. Where Ethnics Stand on Solutions to Issues, NORC 1971

Issue	Anglo-Saxon Protestants	Irish Catholics	German Catholics	Italian Catholics	Polish Catholics
Vietnam: withdrawal/victory	40/36	64/32	46/28	53/32	41/30
Pollution: fines and jail/nothing	71/19	77/23	85/4	83/4	79/11
Riots: solve problems/force	47/38	35/51	58/28	40/52	59/29
Racial progress: speed up/slow down	40/32	57/19	32/27	43/40	22/35
Family assistance: government support/support self	37/40	42/24	42/25	55/30	30/65
Marijuana: allowed/not allowed	8/87	30/52	21/69	12/88	13/79
Rights of criminals: more careful/too far	27/58	13/73	19/64	33/59	17/68
Forced neighborhood integration: government should/should not	22/67	34/49	27/55	28/55	22/23
Student rioters: should not punish/punish severely	11/74	20/67	8/74	23/59	10/75
Government to eliminate poverty: all resources/has done too much	43/37	66/17	45/31	62/31	74/11

Italian Catholics provide majority support for the liberal response on the war, pollution, family assistance, and government efforts to eliminate poverty; and they are also more concerned than any of the other groups for the protection of the rights of criminals and the non-punishment of student rioters.

Finally, even though the Poles are the least likely of the ethnic groups to espouse a "liberal" position, 79 per cent of them favor strong punishment for pollution, and 74 per cent (the highest of any of the five groups) favor the use of all possible government resources to eliminate poverty.

Table 11 presents data gathered in the spring of 1972 on certain other critical issues before the American public. The majority of the ethnics were for gun control, and indeed they were considerably more likely to be in sympathy with such control than Anglo-Saxon Protestants. On the other hand, the majority of them (in the case of the Poles, three-quarters) were also for capital

Table 11.   Attitudes of Ethnics on Issues (Per Cent)

Issue	Anglo-Saxon Protestants	Irish Catholics	German Catholics	Italian Catholics	Polish Catholics
For gun control	65	85	72	81	74
For capital punishment	64	60	63	67	75
Would object to black of same class living on the same block	19	8	13	12	20
For school integration (would send children to half-black school)	80	80	83	73	77
For busing[a]	7	10	11	6	9
Allow Communist to speak	63	69	65	54	38
Allow antireligious person to speak	74	79	82	82	64
Would vote for black president	65	85	78	79	66
For abortion if danger to mother's health	83	68	78	88	89
For abortion if mother wants no more children	38	22	31	34	34

Source: NORC Study #4139, 1972.

[a] 53 per cent of blacks support busing.

punishment. Only a tiny fraction of the ethnic groups would object to a black of the same social class living on their block, and the overwhelming majority (between three-quarters and four-fifths) were willing to send their children to schools where half the students were black. On the other hand, like all other Americans, the overwhelming majority of the ethnics were against busing.

Like most other Americans, a large majority of the ethnics supported the rights of an antireligious person, though barely more than half the Italians and a little under two-fifths of the Poles would concede the same right to a Communist. (The captive nation theme is still important to American Poles.) Eight-five per cent of the Irish, 78 per cent of the Germans, 79 per cent of the Italians, and 66 per cent of the Poles would vote for a qualified black for president (as opposed to 65 per cent of Anglo-Saxon Protestants).

Even though Irish Catholics were less likely to approve of abortion than were Anglo-Saxon Protestants, there are no differences between the other ethnic groups and Protestants on the subject of abortion. A large majority of Americans are apparently willing to approve it if there is a danger to the mother's health, and only a minority support it if the mother simply wants no more children.

Do the ethnics, then, belong to the liberal coalition? How would they do on an ideological test of their purity? On the war, pollution, poverty, gun control, neighborhood and school integration, and civil liberties they are certainly on the "liberal" side. On crime, riots, radicalism, busing, capital punishment, and legalization of marijuana they are not "liberal," although apparently neither are most other Americans. Surprisingly enough, with the exception of the Irish, abortion does not seem to be nearly as serious an issue for the Catholic ethnics as might have been thought.

THE CASE OF THE JEWS AND THE POLES

T HE SO-CALLED "ETHNIC" GROUPS have generally been thought to be politically conservative, racist, and resistant to social change despite their Democratic voting record. Empirical research has indicated that the matter may not be so simple.[1] In many respects the Catholic ethnics may be more "liberal" than their native American counterparts. Thus data gathered from NORC's monitoring of national attitudes on racial integration show that Irish Catholics are the most prointegration of Gentile religio-ethnic groups in the North, and that Italian and German Catholics fall right on the northern mean in their sympathy for racial integration (Table 1). Only the Slavic Catholics (in Table 1, all eastern European Catholics) are below the average for the North, though even they have a somewhat higher prointegration score than do German Protestants. Furthermore, the largest changes on the NORC Integration Scale between 1970 and 1972 was among Italian Catholics, and the second largest was among Irish Catholics. The positive change among Slavic Catholics was about the same as the northern average. Hence as far as NORC's scale is concerned, there was not "white ethnic backlash" between 1970 and 1972.

Table 1, like most research that attempts to analyze diversity among religio-ethnic groups, is seriously deficient in the number of respondents on which the statistics in each cell are based. To generalize about American Slavs on the basis of 49 cases or American Irish Catholics on the basis of 63 cases is a risky enterprise. Unfortunately, the typical national survey sample of 1500 respondents does not provide many respondents for the individual religio-ethnic groups.

However, a study done by the University of Michigan Survey Research Center in 1968 of 15 cities affected by urban unrest does provide a substantial number of respondents for each of the major ethnic groups because it was concerned with cities where much of the "ethnic" population is concentrated.[2] The Michigan survey developed 12 measures of attitudinal response to the 1967 riots, each based on one to four items on their questionnaire.[3] In this chapter we chose 4 of those 12 variables to use as a context for comparing the various white religio-ethnic groups on response to racial unrest. We shall develop a general model to explain such response, and then apply that model to explaining the considerable differences between two urban ethnic groups, the Polish Catholics and the Jews.

The data used in this chapter (except in Table 1) were made available by the ISR Social Science Archive. The data were originally collected by Dr. Angus Campbell and Dr. Howard Schuman of the Survey Research Center, Institute for Social Research, the University of Michigan. Neither the original collectors of the data nor the Archive bear any responsibility for the analyses or interpretations presented here.

Table 1. Prointegration Scale by Ethnicity (Non-South Only)

Religio-ethnic Group	1970	1972	Change, 1970–1972
All Northerners	2.88	3.16	.28
Anglo-Saxons	2.80	3.18	.38
	(220)	(148)	
German Protestants	2.81	2.70	−.11
	(137)	(142)	
Scandinavian Protestants	2.82	2.98	.16
	(29)	(65)	
Irish Catholics	3.06	3.46	.40
	(48)	(63)	
German Catholics	2.97	3.18	.21
	(41)	(44)	
Italian Catholics	2.65	3.14	.49
	(38)	(63)	
Slavic Catholics	2.45	2.76	.31
	(53)	(49)	
Jews	3.79	3.67	−.12
	(24)	(52)	

Source: National Opinion Research Center continuing study of white attitudes toward racial integration, 1963–1972.

Note: Scores on a Guttman Scale based on number of prointegration responses to five items on the NORC questionnaire. See Andrew M. Greeley and Paul B. Sheatsley, "Attitudes toward Racial Integration: the South 'Catches Up'," in *Social Problems and Public Policy: I, Inequality and Justice,* Lee Rainwater, ed. Chicago: Aldine Publishing Company, 1973.

One of the risks of survey analysis is that scales can easily take on meanings from their labels that go above and beyond the items that constitute them. Therefore at the beginning of this chapter we present a list of the four variables (Table 2) that will be used in this analysis and the items that constitute them. All of these scales were constructed by the Michigan research team.

Differences in Racial Attitudes among Ethnic Groups. The scales are presented in the form of "z scores," that is, scores with zero mean and a standard deviation of 1. The z score represents a deviation from the mean. One hundred standardized points would be one standard deviation from the mean.

Table 2. Description of Four Variables in Riot Study

Riot Control by Repression	Interracial Contact	Civil Rights Legislation	Would Vote for Capable Black Mayor
10 point index based on variables 338, 340, 342	Cumulative 5 point index based on variables 268, 274, 282 and 283	4 point index based on variables 266 and 271	
Variable 338 Recode: Most important thing city can do to prevent riots (first mention)	Variable 268 Q. 35(W). Suppose you had a job where your supervisor was a qualified Negro. Would you mind that a lot, a little, or not at all?	Variable 266 Q. 34A(W). Do you favor or oppose laws to prevent discrimination against Negroes in job hiring and promotion?	Variable 0197 Q. 8(W). If a capable Negro of your own party preference was running for mayor of (central city), would you vote for him or not?
Variable 340 Recode: Most important thing city can do to prevent riots (second mention)	Variable 274 Q. 39(W). If a Negro family with about the same income and education	Variable 271 Q. 37A(W). How about laws to prevent discrimination against Negroes in buying or renting houses	
Variable 342 Recode: Most important			

thing city can do to prevent riots (third mention)

0. Other
1. End discrimination
2. Get tough

as you moved next door to you, would you mind it a lot, a little, or not at all?

Variable 282

Q. 43(W). Who do you feel you could more easily become friends with—a Negro with the same education and income as you, or a white person with a different education and income from you?

Variable 283

Q. 44(W). If you had small children, would you rather they had only white friends, or would you like to see them have Negro friends too, or wouldn't you care one way or the other?

and apartments? Do you favor or oppose such laws?

Ten standardized points would be one-tenth of a standard deviation from the mean. In our analysis we follow the convention of commenting only on z scores of 10 points or more.

The first variable we investigate is the one with which the riot study was most directly concerned: the attitudes of the various ethnic groups on what response was appropriate to urban unrest. In Figure 1 we note that two of the Catholic groups, the Germans and the Poles, were more inclined to support a repressive response to the riots (20 standardized points for the Poles and 17 for the Germans), while the Irish Catholics and the Jews were both 10 standardized points below the mean, indicating that they were less likely than the average to support a repressive response to the riots. Jewish liberalism is not surprising, but the liberalism of the Irish Catholics may surprise many readers. While the Poles are indeed substantially above the mean, the Italian Catholics and the Slavic Catholics (here meaning other eastern Europeans) are both close to the mean in their attitudes on riot control.

Figure 2 shows that the Poles are also quite low on support for interracial contact (36 standardized points below the mean), while the Jews are substantially above the mean (28 points). The Irish Protestants are also considerably below the mean (22 points), and the Italian Catholics are somewhat below it (10 points). Scandinavian Protestants are 10 points above the mean. There is far more variation in attitudes toward interracial contact among the religio-ethnic groups than there is toward riot control. In both cases, the Jews are the most "liberal" and the Poles the most "illiberal."

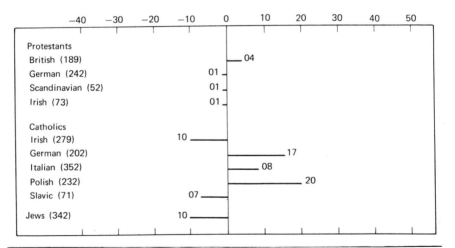

Figure 1. Attitude on riot control of American religio-ethnic groups in 15 cities affected by riots in 1967 (deviation from the mean), high score indicating support for repression of riots.

The same pattern emerges on the issue of support for civil rights legislation (Figure 3). The Jews are very high (50 standardized points), and the Poles are quite low (−19). Slavic and German Catholics are also rather low on this scale, and Irish Protestants are one-tenth of a standard deviation above the mean.

The majority of all the groups would support a tax increase of 10 per cent if such an increase would reduce the danger of riots (Table 3). A majority would also vote for a qualified black candidate for mayor, or at least say they would. The most enthusiastic supporters for a black mayoral candidate are Jews, of whom four-fifths indicate a willingness to support a black mayor. The Poles along with the Irish Protestants are the least likely to support a black mayor (58 per cent), while the Irish Catholics are the strongest supporters of a black mayor among the Gentiles (72 per cent). Italian Catholics match the 15-city average; 66 per cent are willing to support a black mayor.

In Figure 4, willingness to support a black mayor is transformed into a z score. Jews and Irish Catholics are above the mean; British Protestants, Scandinavian Protestants, Irish Protestants, and Polish Catholics are all below the mean. Thus there seems to be greater diversity among the American religio-ethnic groups in their willingness to support a black mayor than there is in the other three issues under investigation.

In summary, among respondents in the 15 cities affected by the 1967 riots, the Jews are clearly the group most favorably disposed to the blacks, and the Poles are the group least favorably disposed. Of the Gentile groups, the Irish Catholics are the most supportive, Italian Catholics differ little from the 15-

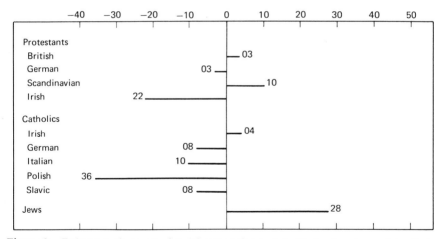

Figure 2. Estimation of amount of racial contact that is desirable for American religio-ethnic groups in 15 cities affected by riots in 1967 (deviation from the mean), high score indicating support for interracial contact.

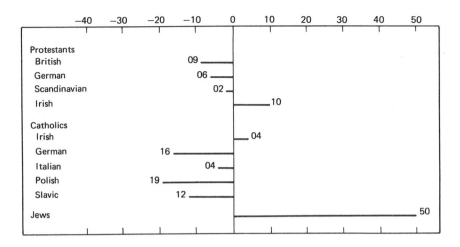

Figure 3. Support for civil rights legislation among American religio-ethnic groups in 15 cities affected by riots in 1967 (deviation from the mean), high score indicating support for legislation.

Table 3. Support for 10 Per Cent Increase in Taxes to Ease Causes of Riots and Would Vote for Black Mayor (Per Cent)

Religio-ethnic Group	Would Support Tax Increase	Would Vote for Black Mayor
Protestants		
British	83	62
German	80	64
Scandinavian	85	63
Irish	84	58
Catholics		
Irish	81	72
German	78	61
Italian	78	66
Polish	67	58
Slavic	55	69
Jews	56	80
National average	79	66

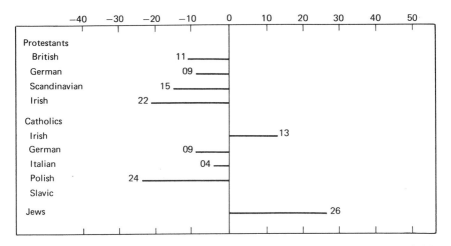

Figure 4. Willingness to vote for black mayor among American religio-ethnic groups in 15 cities affected by riots in 1967 (deviation from the mean), high score indicating willingness to vote for black mayor.

city mean, and German Catholics and Irish Protestants and Slavic Catholics are sometimes supportive and sometimes not.

A Model to Explain Response to Urban Unrest. Having discovered substantial differences between Polish Catholics and Jews on the four major racial issues we are investigating, one might be content to conclude that Poles are "racist" and that the Jews are not, or that in comparison with the Jews and the Irish Catholics the Poles are more likely to be "racist." While much analysis, both popular and serious, of American racial problems appears content with such conclusions, it does seem appropriate for serious researchers to try to explain the reasons for such differences among major population categories. An explanation of such diversity might be of some use to those social policy-makers who must deal with urban situations in which ethnic heterogeneity is a given.

As social research moves gingerly toward causal explanations rather than mere correlational analysis, it becomes clear that longitudinal research is in most cases indispensable for the creation of causal models. In the absence of longitudinal research, the models one can produce are at best tentative and speculative. There seems to be justification, however, for constructing such models, if only because they may force us to look at a phenomenon analytically and to make explicit causal assumptions that in correlational analysis frequently hide between the lines. The model-construction exercise in this chapter, then, is carried on with full awareness of all the weaknesses inherent in such an approach.

Why would some people be more inclined to support the black protest movement than others? There are a number of explanations that might be derived from both the social science and humanistic literature on the subject. Those who are "enlightened" on the race question may be better educated, they may have more frequent contact with blacks, they may have a greater perception of the amount of racial injustice in the country, and greater sympathy for its victims. Those who are threatened by racial progress may have more intolerant personalities and may be frightened by "real" threats to what they perceive as their own welfare[4]—for example, the increase of crime and the deterioration of property values in their neighborhoods with the coming of racial integration. The riot study data provide good measurements for five of these six variables: education, "black friends," "sympathy for protest," "perception of discrimination," and "intolerant" personality.[5] Unfortunately, there was no good item to tap the dimension of "real" fear. Hence, as a surrogate for that dimension, a variable was chosen that indicated whether a respondent thought that there ought to be some sort of limitation on the percentage of blacks who might live in a given neighborhood. *One* of the reasons for having such an attitude might be that the respondent realized that after a certain "tipping point," an entire neighborhood would turn black and racial integration would become impossible. After the "tipping point" is reached it might be said that the threat to property values and the possibility of violence in the school and neighborhood would be such that all white residents would flee. The "fear for neighborhood" item, admittedly, is not the best possible surrogate for "real" fear, but it was the only one available to us.

Since there was a moderate level of intercorrelation (Table 4) among five of the items (excluding education, for the moment), an oblique factor analysis was done. Two significant factors emerged after rotation (Table 5). The heaviest loadings on the first factor were sympathy for black protest and perception of discrimination. There was a somewhat smaller loading on the in-

Table 4. Intercorrelations among Variables Predicting Racial Attitudes

Black friends				
Fear for neighborhood (quota)	.25			
Sympathy for black protest	.18	.33		
Perception of discrimination	.09	.29	.45	
Intolerance	.14	.21	.34	.26

Table 5. Factor Loadings among Predictor Variables

A. Rotated Factors

	I	II
Intolerance	.155	.115
Sympathy for black protest	.523	.236
Perception of discrimination	.302	.002
Black friends	.030	.296
Fear for neighborhood	.112	.383

B. Separate Factors

I		II	
Intolerance	.173	Fear for neighborhood	.497
Sympathy for black protest	.274	Black friends	.497
Perception of discrimination	.586		

tolerance scale. The "black friends" and "fear for neighborhood" items loaded more heavily on the second factor. Two separate scales were then constructed (Table 5, section B) based on separate factor analyses for the first three variables and for the last two. The first factor, with heavy loadings on sympathy and perception of discrimination and a less heavy loading on the intolerance scale, has been labeled the "support" factor, because tolerance for diversity, perception of discrimination, and sympathy for black protest indicate a disposition of positive support for blacks. The second factor has been called the "avoidance" factor, because fear for neighborhood (represented by the desire to impose a quota on the number of blacks that could live in one's neighborhood) and absence of black friends seem to indicate both past avoidance and desire for future avoidance. It should be noted, however, that both the labels are nominalistic and have no more content than the items that constitute the factors.

As can be seen in Table 6, the three predictor variables—education, "support," and "avoidance"—correlate quite well with the four dependent variables—support for a black mayor, support for civil rights laws, attitudes toward riot control, and support for interracial contact. Education is the least strong of the three predictors, correlating .21 with black mayor and .19 with interracial contact, .17 with civil rights laws support, and only .06 with riot control. It is interesting to note how little impact education seems to have had on people's feelings about how riots should be handled.

Table 6. Intercorrelations of Predictor and Dependent Variables

Education						
"Support" factor	.34					
"Avoidance" factor	.27	.34				
Would vote for black mayor	.21	.32	.38			
Support for civil rights legislation	.17	.41	.35	.31		
Riot control	.06	.28	.15	.13	.16	
Interracial contact	.19	.39	.34	.42	.47	.16

Both the avoidance and support variables correlated at reasonably high levels with the four independent variables. Only one of the coefficients is under .20 (.15 between the avoidance factor and riot control). Another of the coefficients is .28 (between the support factor and riot control), but all the other coefficients are above .3. Thus the hypothesis implicit in the previous paragraphs seems to have been supported: education, sympathy, perception of discrimination, intolerant personality, and interaction with black friends all seem to have some impact on one's response to urban unrest.

It would be most helpful for both theoretical and social policy reasons if there were some way to establish a causal relationship between the avoidance factor and the support factor (they correlate .34). However, there is simply no way in which this can be done with the present data base available to us. Thus in the simplified path diagrams presented in Figure 5, we assume that education has a causal impact on both support and avoidance.[6] These in turn have causal impacts on the dependent variable, but we place the two factors in paired rather than causal relationships in our model.

It may well be that security in one's neighborhood situation and interaction with blacks on a friendship basis leads one to be more tolerant, more perceptive, and more sympathetic. But it may equally well be that tolerance, perception, and sympathy generate greater security in one's neighborhood and greater propensity to have black friends. In all likelihood, however, a relationship between the two sets of variables is so complex that even with far better data than is presently available to us we would be hard put to sort them out. Hence, placing them at the same stage in the path diagram may not be just a compromise but a recognition of the complexity of reality.

The explanatory model of education-support-avoidance is moderately successful in explaining the variance in support for a black mayor, for civil rights legislation, interracial contact, and liberal positions on riot control. Eighteen per cent, 22 per cent, 30 per cent, and 9 per cent of the variance respectively are explained. The avoidance factor is stronger than the support factor in explaining sympathy for interracial contact and for a black mayor. On the other hand, the support factor is the only one directly influencing riot control attitudes, and is stronger than the avoidance factor in the model explaining variation in attitudes on civil rights laws.

The absence of avoidance attitudes, then, seems to be stronger in explaining acceptability of interracial contact and a black mayor, while the presence of support factors is more important in explaining sympathy for liberal riot con-

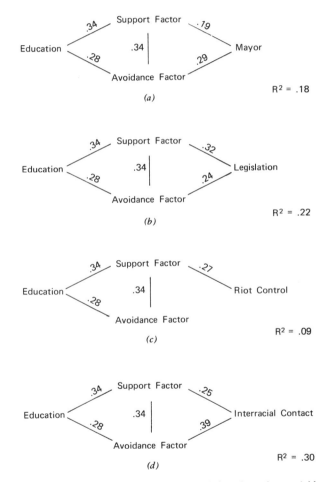

Figure 5. Causal model for explaining racial attitudes with four dependent variables.
(a) Path diagram explaining support for black mayor.
(b) Path diagram explaining support for civil rights legislation.
(c) Path diagram explaining support for stringent riot control.
(d) Path diagram explaining support for interracial contact.

trol and for civil rights laws. People are against interracial contact and a black mayor because they are afraid of or wish to avoid blacks; they are for civil rights laws and permissive riot control because they sympathetically support blacks. It is also worth noting that there is no direct path between education and any of the dependent variables. The explanatory model is far less powerful in explaining variation on the riot control scale than it is in coping with variation in the other three dependent variables. The reason may be that civil rights laws, election of black mayors, and sympathy for interracial contacts were less urgent questions at the time of the 15-city study in 1968 than how a riot should have been handled.

The Case of the Jews and the Poles.   Having constructed an explanatory model that does a reasonably presentable job of explaining variation, as social science models go, we now ask whether this model will assist us in reducing the differences between Jews and Poles on the four interracial scales we are investigating. Can the differences between Jews and Poles—two proper nouns—be reduced to differences in education, avoidance, and support—three common nouns? In Table 7, we present the differences in standard deviations (or in standardized points) between the Poles and the Jews and, for comparison purposes, between the Poles and the most liberal of the Gentile group, the Irish Catholics. In the first row of each section, the raw differences between the two groups are shown. In the second, third, and fourth rows, there are listed the differences with the influence of education taken into account, then of education and avoidance, and, finally, of education, avoidance, and support.

One can see at a glance that if the explanatory model does not convert the differences from proper nouns to common nouns completely, it does make substantial headway in that direction. Thus the difference between Poles and Jews in support for a black mayor goes from one-half of a standard deviation to one-tenth of a standard deviation. The difference between Poles and Irish Catholics on the same scale declines from 37 standardized points to 10. The difference between Poles and Jews in support for civil rights legislation is cut in half, from 69 points to 34 points. And between Poles and Irish Catholics, it declines from 29 points to zero. Differences in attitudes on riot control between Poles and Jews go from 30 points to 8, and between Poles and Irish Catholics, from 30 to 16. Finally, differences between Poles and Jews on interracial contact go from 64 points to 26, and between Irish Catholics and Poles from 40 to 15. In other words, in all cases the differences between the Poles and the other two groups are cut in half at least, and in most cases they are cut to a third or one-fourth or one-fifth. Poles are more likely to be opposed to blacks than are Jews because the Poles have less education and have higher scores on the avoidance

Table 7. Reduction of Differences Between Jews and Poles and Poles and Irish Catholics by Explanatory Model (Standard Deviations)

	Poles and Jews	Poles and Irish Catholics
A. Support for Black Mayor		
Raw difference	.50	.37
Standardized for education	.37	.32
Standardized for education and external factor	.55	.21
Standardized for education and both factors	.11	.10
B. Support for Civil Rights Legislation		
Raw difference	.69	.29
Standardized for education	.59	.19
Standardized for education and external factor	.53	.14
Standardized for education and both factors	.34	.00
C. Support for Repressive Riot Control		
Raw difference	.30	.30
Standardized for education	.26	.27
Standardized for education and external factor	.14	.23
Standardized for education and both factors	.08	.16
D. Support for Interracial Contact		
Raw difference	.64	.40
Standardized for education	.51	.34
Standardized for education and external factor	.47	.26
Standardized for education and both factors	.26	.15

scale and lower scores on the support scale. To put the matter differently, Jews are more favorable to blacks than are Poles because they have better education, have less avoidance of blacks, and show higher support predispositions.

In the comparison between the Poles and the Jews, the greatest decline in difference occurs between the third and fourth rows in Table 7 (with the exception of the riot control item in section C). That is, even when the effect of education and the avoidance factor are taken into account, the most powerful explanation of differences between Poles and Jews has to do with the support factor. Poles are less likely to have perception of black problems and sympathy for the black cause.

The explanatory model eliminates most of the diversity among American ethnic groups on the four scales we are studying (Table 8). The Jews continue to be the strongest supporters of civil rights laws and interracial contact. The

Table 8. Z Scores for Certain Ethnic Groups on Racial Attitudes after the Effect of the Explanatory Model Has Been Taken into Account

Religio-ethnic Group	Vote for Black Mayor	Civil Rights Laws	Riot Control[a]	Interracial Contact
British Protestants	−17	−04	00	03
Irish Catholics	07	04	−07	00
Italian Catholics	04	01	07	−02
Polish Catholics	03	03	10	−09
Slavic Catholics	25	−06	00	07
Jews	08	31	02	16

[a] High score indicates support for repression.

Slavic Catholics emerge as the strongest supporters for a black mayor, and the Irish Catholics as those most opposed (though not by very much) to oppressive riot control. Only two scores exceed 10: the 17 point English Protestant opposition to a black mayor and the 10 point Polish support for repressive riot control.

Causal Models for Three Ethnic Groups. In this section we apply the causal model developed previously to variation in racial attitudes within each of the three ethnic groups—the Poles, the Jews, and the Irish. We shall determine whether there might be not only differences in racial attitudes but also differences in the causes of variation in these attitudes within each ethnic group (Figure 6).

There is relatively little difference between the Poles and the Jews in the first step in the model. Education correlates with the avoidance and support factors at approximately the same level, and the correlation between the two factors is .42 for the Poles and .34 for the Jews. However, the Irish model seems substantially "looser." The correlation between education and the two factors is lower than it is for Jews and Poles, indeed only .1 for the correlation between education and avoidance. Furthermore, the correlation between the two factors (.22) is substantially lower than it is for the Jews and the Poles. In other words, education has relatively slight impact on avoidance for the Irish, and avoidance and support have lower impact on each other for the Irish than is to be found among either the Poles or the Jews. It may be that the political pragmatism of the Irish inclines them to be less consistent than the other two groups.

For both the Jews and the Poles, only the avoidance factor has a direct path to support for a black mayor, a pattern that is very different from that of the model for the total population presented in Figure 5. Jews are more inclined to support a black mayor because they do not fear blacks and they have black friends. Poles are less inclined to support a black mayor because they are afraid of blacks and do not have black friends. In both cases support for the black cause is less important than it is in the general population.

As for the Irish, the strongest beta is a .28 on a direct path between education and support for a black mayor, which makes them different from the model in Figure 5 also. Approximately half the explained variance, then, in Irish support for a black mayor is channeled outside the two factors and is a result of direct influence of education. Again, it may be that for a politically

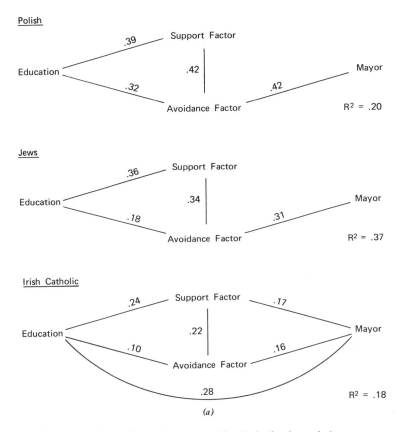

Figure 6. Causal model to explain variation in racial attitudes for three ethnic groups. (a) For support of black mayor.

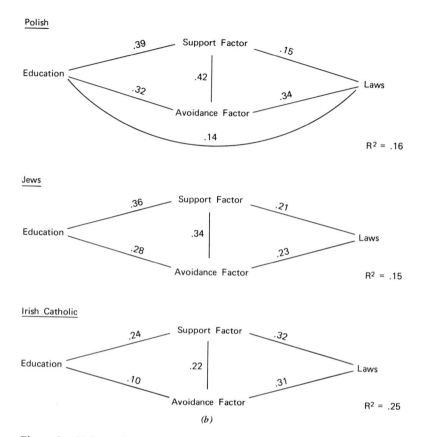

Figure 6. (b) For civil rights legislation.

pragmatic group, such things as support and avoidance are not nearly as important as they are for other groups.

On the question of civil rights legislation (Figure 6, section B), the Poles are different from the Jews and indeed from the general population (Figure 5B) in that there is a direct path between education and sympathy for civil rights laws, and the beta between avoidance and sympathy for laws is larger than the beta between support and sympathy for civil rights legislation. The Irish and the Jews, then, are basically similar to one another and similar to the national population in the causes of sympathy for civil rights legislation. And they all differ from the Polish Catholics.

There are three different models, however, explaining variance in riot control attitudes. Both the Poles and the Jews have no direct path between avoidance and riot response—in which respect they are like the national model in

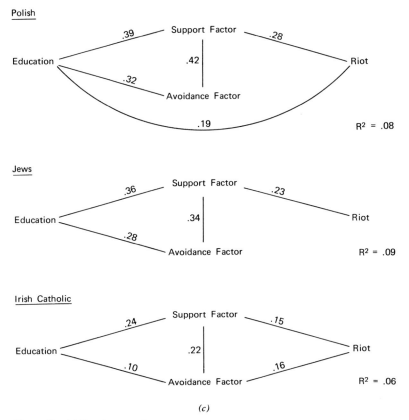

Figure 6. (c) For riot control.

Figure 5. On the other hand, there is a .19 direct path between education and riot control attitudes for the Poles and no such path for the Jews. The Irish, unlike the other two groups and the total population, have a direct path between the avoidance factor and riot control response.

Finally, as might be expected, there are strong betas between avoidance of blacks and sympathy for future interracial contact (Figure 6D) in all three groups. However, among the Poles there is no path between support and desire for future interracial contact. For the Jews there is a moderate coefficient (.15), and for the Irish Catholics a somewhat larger coefficient (.24). In addition, there is also a direct path between education and support for racial contact among the Irish.

What is one to make of the intricacies and complexities of the diagrams presented in Figure 6? In most respects the Polish and Jewish diagrams are

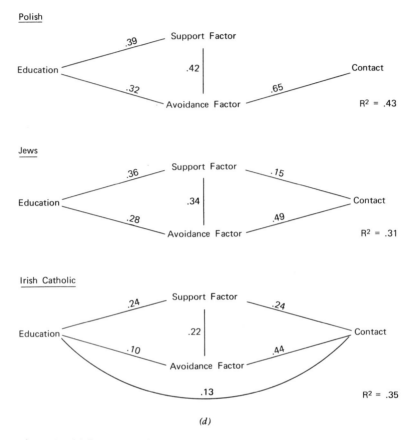

Figure 6.   (d) For interracial contact.

more similar to each other than either are to the Irish Catholics. Indeed, if it were not for the direct paths between education and the dependent variable in sections B and C for Poles, one might conclude that the explanatory model for Polish racial attitudes and Jewish racial attitudes were virtually the same. The Irish Catholics—the most "enlightened" of the Gentile groups on matters of race—seem to respond to racial issues for a different mix of reasons. More secure in their Americanism than the Poles but less committed to ideological liberalism than the Jews, the Irish seem to have developed a pattern of resonating to racial issues that is distinctly their own and unlike both the two extreme groups and the model operating for the general 15-city population.

But there is diversity, not merely in response to racial issues but in the causes for these responses. No one who must deal with the complexity of ethnic diversity in the urban milieu can afford to act as though all population groups were alike. The implications of our data are that the groups differ from each other not only in their responses, but that they may also differ in the reasons for those responses.

The Alienation of the Poles?   Our explanatory model does not "solve" the problem of why the Poles and the Jews respond differently to black militancy. Even after the model is applied, differences remain (though they are far smaller). A more important point is that education provides only a limited explanation of why Poles are high on avoidance and low in support and Jews are high on support and low on avoidance. We have moved the problem back one step in our explanatory model from the dependent variable to the intervening variable. The challenge for further research is to discover why, when education is held constant, these two groups have such different sets of predispositions on the subject of racial diversity.

There are two sets of explanations one might fall back on. It may be that there is something in the heritage with which a group comes to the United States that predisposes it to certain responses when faced with racial diversity. Or it may be something that has happened in the group's experience since it arrived here that has made it suspicious of other groups in the society. And of course it most probably is a complex interaction of the two. There is a long Polish history of oppression and betrayal by strangers; but there is nothing in Jewish history that would dispose that group to be very trusting either. Furthermore, the family structures of the two groups seem to differ. The Jews have a much stronger maternal figure in their family life than the Poles. It remains to be seen whether or how these two different family structures produce different responses to racial problems.

It is worth noting that the ancestors of most American Jews came from the same areas of eastern Europe as did the ancestors of most American Poles. Furthermore, recent research indicates that until the middle of the last century, Polish and Jewish elites worked together for the liberation of Poland from foreign rule. But Polish immigrants did not come to the United States with a radical or socialist tradition like that held by many Jewish immigrants, perhaps because many Polish immigrants came from the farms and fields of southern Poland, while many of the Jewish immigrants were from more urban backgrounds. The differences between the Poles and the Jews in their attitudes toward race may have their roots in the peasant origins of one group and the more urban origins of the other. However, both the Irish and Italian Catholics also have peasant origins and they react very differently to racial questions.

The Jews have met with more success in the United States than have the Poles. Indeed, recent demographic research indicates that the Poles are lagging behind other Catholic ethnic groups in the pursuit of affluence. It may well be that as a group, Poles do not feel accepted in American society. They do not feel as upwardly mobile as others, and hence are more disposed to be suspicious of those beneath them than are groups like the Italians and the Irish who are moving upward rapidly. Even a control for education would not eliminate such feelings; one may be educated and still feel one's group is not being given an equal chance. It is worth noting, incidentally, that the Slavic group (non-Polish eastern European Catholics) is very different from the Poles in its response to racial questions. But then Slovaks, Slovenes, Czechs, and Lithuanians do not have reserved for them a special joke category.

It may be that the Poles are alienated. It may be that somehow they have been left out of the American dream, or at least placed under severe limitations in achieving that dream. There were three measures in the riot study that might enable us to tap such alienation. They are measures of "efficacy," "competence," and "trust" of government.[7] On all three of the items, the Poles score substantially below the mean (Table 9). The Irish Catholics are somewhat low on efficacy and competence but high on trust in government (perhaps because in some cities, they are the government). Italians are low on feelings of efficacy but above the mean on competence and trust. Jewish scores are close to the mean on all three items. Hence one can make a fairly persuasive case that there is an alienation syndrome among American Polish Catholics. But unfortunately for our purposes, there does not seem to be much correlation between the efficacy, competence, and trust measures and the four independent variables we are investigating (Table 10).

The question still remains whether these alienation measures will correlate with racial attitudes for the Poles despite no such correlation in the larger population (Table 11). Lack of trust in government correlates above .2 in the Polish subsample with attitudes on a black mayor and riot control; and

Table 9. Measures of "Alienation" for Certain Ethnic Groups

Religio-ethnic Group	Efficacy	Competence	Trust of Government
British Protestants	11	16	−12
Irish Catholics	−08	−15	26
Italian Catholics	−22	06	09
Polish Catholics	−11	−21	−14
Slavic Catholics	−04	−07	02
Jews	02	07	00

Table 10. Correlations Between "Alienation" Variables and Racial Response Variables for Entire Sample

Racial Attitudes	Trust	Efficacy	Competence
Vote for black mayor	.04	.04	.08
Civil rights legislation	.04	.05	.01
Riot control	.02	.01	.01
Racial contact	.02	.01	.02

feelings of competence correlate above .2, with the attitudes on civil rights laws and riot control. Thus it can safely be said that for the Poles there is some relationship between "alienation" and racial attitudes. We should note that the relatively small correlations between the alienation variables and the avoidance and support factors would suggest that the influences of "alienation" on Polish attitudes are not "channeled" through the paths in our model. "Alienation" would not much improve our capacity to explain why Poles are high on avoidance and low on support. Clearly, Polish racial response in the 15 cities under consideration is a fascinating and socially important question that merits further research.

Conclusion. The effort reported in this chapter is both tenuous and tentative. It attempts to offer some preliminary suggestions as to why different ethnic groups respond differently to urban unrest. Such explanations are not absent in ordinary conversation about the cities of the United States. If the speculations in this chapter have any merit at all, it is that they have been submitted

Table 11. Correlations Between "Alienation" Variables and Racial Response of Polish Catholic Religio-ethnic Group Only

Racial Attitudes	Trust	Efficacy	Competence
Vote for black mayor	.20	.15	.16
Civil rights legislation	.08	.00	.21
Riot control	.31	.12	.23
Racial contact	.08	.02	.00
Support	.17	.07	−.06
Avoidance	.12	.12	−.12

to a more precise social science analysis than is the case in ordinary conversational speculation. Unfortunately, the tools for this analysis, while they are the best currently available, are far from adequate.

There is a strong tendency in contemporary social policy and even in social research to assume that once the magic word "racism" is uttered all need for further understanding—to say nothing of compassion—has been eliminated. There may be every reason to suspect that bigotry lurks in every human personality (although the object of bigotry may vary); it may be that some of the fears of certain segments of the population have a basis in reality; it may be, indeed, that the very word "racism" has become so wide in its meaning that it has lost any precise meaning. But if one deals with certain ethnic groups, one must attempt to understand the causes of the responses of those groups to racial issues. To write entire groups off as "racist" and so be done with them may well be socially and politically counterproductive.

NOTES

1. See Andrew M. Greeley, "Political Attitudes among American White Ethnics," *Public Opinion Quarterly,* **36** (Summer 1972), pp. 270–277; and Andrew M. Greeley and Paul B. Sheatsley, "Attitudes Towards Desegregation," *Scientific American,* (December 1971); and Norman Nie, Barbara Currie, and Andrew M. Greeley, "Ethnics and the Coalition," *Ethnicity* I (April 1974).

2. For a description of the Michigan study, see Appendix A.

3. See Appendix B for a list of all 12 variables and the questions on which they were based.

4. I use the word "real" in this chapter to describe threats and fears that are a response to something that exists in the external environment and are not the result of prejudice and bigotry. The issue is complex, and as far as I know none of the psychologists of prejudice have addressed themselves to it. A given white person living, let us say, in the Gage Park district of Chicago may well be a racist bigot; he also may be frightened for the safety of his children in the high school that has become predominantly black, afraid to walk the streets of his neighborhood at night, and afraid of the collapse of the resale value of his home. His prejudices do not create the conditions of his social and physical environment that make his fears valid. Neither can his fears be airily dismissed on the grounds that he is a racist, for he has something to be afraid of. Liberal intellectuals who think they have solved the Gage Park Problem when they write its white inhabitants off as racists may have salved their own consciences and dismissed them from their own minds as deserving respect or compassion. They have not, of course, solved any problem at all. It is possible that there may be a substantial number of Gage Parkers who would score low on any scale measuring racism, but who are still frightened. It is also possible (likely, in fact) that the response of most people (including Hyde Park, University of Chicago intellectuals) to a racially changing neighborhood is a mixture of prejudice and valid fear that is terribly difficult to untangle. The appropriate response of both Gage Parkers and Hyde Parkers might be to minimize the occasions that cause fear so that the residue of racism might be dealt with directly. Such a strategy, of course, is far more difficult than to dismiss the ethnic hard hats and their valid fears as racist.

5. See Appendix B for items determining these variables.
6. As is customary in most path analysis, all coefficients with a beta less than .10 are eliminated from the diagrams in the figure.
7. See Appendix B for an explanation of the items constituting these variables.

APPENDIX A

Following is part of the official description of the study from the Survey Research Center of the University of Michigan :

The study of racial attitudes in fifteen American cities was conducted by Dr. Angus Campbell and Dr. Howard Schuman of the Survey Research Center, Institute for Social Research, The University of Michigan. It was undertaken at the request of the National Advisory Commission on Civil Disorders. All respondents were interviewed during the first four months of 1968.

The study . . . seeks to define the social and psychological characteristics and aspirations of the black and white urban populations.

A black and a white sample were obtained in each of the fifteen cities in the study (Baltimore, Boston, Brooklyn, Chicago, Cincinnati, Cleveland, Detroit, Gary, Milwaukee, Newark, Philadelphia, Pittsburgh, St. Louis, San Francisco, and Washington, D.C.). Approximately 175 black and 175 white respondents were interviewed in each of the cities. In addition, 366 whites were interviewed in two suburban areas. The study, taken as a whole, consists of 2809 black respondents and 2950 white respondents (including the suburban whites).

The study used two questionnaire forms—one for whites and one for blacks. Questions dealing with personal data information were nearly identical in the two forms, with minor exceptions resulting from the presence (or absence) of approximately eight questions in one or the other of the forms. Identical questions were also present in the remaining attitudinal questions of both interview forms, but there were a greater number of questions addressed exclusively to one racial group or to the other. Both interview schedules contained open and closed-ended questions.

The personal data section gathered information about the occupational and educational background of the respondent, of the respondent's family head, and of the respondent's father. The respondent's family income and the amount of that income earned by the head of the family were obtained, and it was determined if any of the family income came from welfare, social security or veteran's benefits. This section of the questionnaire also ascertained the place of birth of the respondent, his mother, and his father, in order to measure the degree of southern influence. Other questions investigated the military background of the respondent, his religious preference, his marital status and his family composition. Attitudinal questions probed the respondent's satisfaction with his home and neighborhood, in addition to his financial expectations and feelings of personal efficacy. Information from the coversheets is also contained in the personal data section. Included are the sex and age of the respondent, and the age and relationship to the respondent of each person in the household, as well as information about the number of persons in the household, their race and the type of structure in which they live.

Both the black and white questionnaire forms contained attitudinal questions probing the respondent's satisfaction with neighborhood services, his feelings about the effectiveness of the government in solving urban problems and his experience with police abuse. Questions about the respondent's familiarity with and participation in antipoverty programs were included. Additional questions centered around the respondent's opinions about the 1967 riots: the main causes, the purpose, the major participating classes, and the effect of the riots on the black cause. The respondent's interracial relationships, his attitude toward integration and his perception of the hostility between the races were also investigated.

The white questionnaire surveyed opinions on the use of governmental intervention as a solution for various problems of the blacks, such as substandard schools, unemployment, and unfair housing practices. The respondent's reaction to non-violent and violent protests by blacks, his acceptance of counter-rioting by whites and his ideas concerning possible governmental action to prevent further rioting were elicited. Inquiries were made as to whether or not the respondent had given money to support or hinder the black cause. Other items investigated the respondent's perception of racial discrimination in jobs, education, and housing, and his reaction to working under or living next door to a black.

The user should consult *White Attitudes Towards Black People*, by Angus Campbell (Ann Arbor: Institute for Social Research, 1971) for a discussion on the methodology, sampling design, and substantive results of the survey. Additional information may be found in the following sources:

CAMPBELL, ANGUS and SCHUMAN, HOWARD. "Racial Attitudes in Fifteen American Cities," in *Supplemental Studies for the National Advisory Commission on Civil Disorder*. Washington, D.C.: U.S. Government Printing Office, July 1968, pp. 1–67; New York, Washington, London: Frederick A. Praeger, Publishers, 1968, pp. 1–67. The article has been reprinted as a monograph by the Survey Research Center, Institute for Social Research, The University of Michigan, Ann Arbor, 1968.

DANIEL, JOHNNIE. "Social Class Identification among Blacks and Whites." Unpublished Ph.D. dissertation, Department of Sociology, The University of Michigan, 1972.

EDWARDS, OZZIE. "Intergeneration Variation in Racial Attitudes." *Sociology and Social Research* (October 1972).

EDWARDS, OZZIE. "Skin Color as a Variable in Racial Attitudes of Black Urbanites." To appear in *Journal of Black Studies*, (June 1973).

GRUENBERG, BARRY. "Characteristics of Negro Non-Respondents." *Methodological Report #2,* June 3, 1968. Available upon request from the Social Science Archive.

MOORE, VERNON. "Evaluation of the Questionnaire by Interviewers." *Methodological Report #1,* June 1, 1968. Available upon request from the Social Science Archive.

SCHUMAN, HOWARD. "Free Will and Determinism in Public Beliefs about Race." *Trans-Action* (December 1969), pp. 44–48; *New Society,* (June 4, 1970), pp. 959–962; in *Majority and Minority: The Dynamics of Racial and Ethnic Relations,* Norman R. Yetman, ed. Rockleigh, N.J.: Allyn and Bacon, 1971, pp. 382–390.

——and GRUENBERG, BARRY. "The Impact of City on Racial Attitudes." *American Journal of Sociology* **76** (September 1970), pp. 213–261. Reprinted as a monograph by the Survey Research Center, Institute for Social Research, the University of Michigan, Ann Arbor, 1970.

——and GRUENBURG, BARRY. "Dissatisfaction with City Services: Is Race an Important Factor?" in *People and Politics in Urban Society,* Harlan Hahn, ed. Beverly Hills and London: Sage Publications, 1972, pp.369–392.

APPENDIX B: DESCRIPTION OF VARIABLES IN RIOT STUDY

BLKMAYR1—WD VOTE CAPABLE BLK FOR MAYOR

Variable 0197

Q. 8(W) If a capable negro of your own party preference was running for mayor of (central city), would you vote for him or not?

EFFICACY—PERSONAL EFFICACY

Based on Variables 175–178

Variable 175

Q. 71(W), 95(B). Have you usually felt pretty sure your life would work out the way you want it to, or have there been times when you haven't been sure about it?

Variable 176

Q. 72(W), 96(B). Do you think it's better to plan your life a good way ahead, or would you say life is too much a matter of luck to plan ahead very far?

NEWFSCAL—NEW F SCALE[a]

Based on Variables 180–182

Variable 180

Q. 76. When you read about the long-haired hippies and people like that, do you feel some curiosity about their ideas, or do you feel mostly distaste for such people?

Variable 181

Q. 77. In schools do you think it's more important for children to learn about many different countries of the world or to concentrate on our own country's history and geography?

Variable 177

Q. 73(W)., 97(B). When you do make plans ahead, do you usually get to carry out things the way you expected, or do things usually come up to make you change your plans?

Variable 0178

Q. 74(W)., 98(B). Some people feel they can run their lives pretty much the way they want to; others feel the problems of life are something too big for them. Which one are you most like?

Variable 182

Q. 78. Do you favor trying out new ways of teaching subjects like arithmetic in schools, or do you think it's better to stick with the well-tried methods of the past?

[a] Intolerance scale.

COMPTNC—CITIZEN COMPETENCE

Variable 0326, Based on Variables 190,191

Variable 190
Q. 3(W). If you have a serious complaint about poor service by the city, do you think you can get city officials to do something about it if you call them?

Variable 191
Q. 3A(W). Have you ever called a city official with a complaint about poor service?

DISTRUST—GOVERNMENT DISTRUST

Variable 0327, Based on Variables 192-194

Variable 192
Q. 4(W). Do you think the mayor of (central city) is trying as hard as he can to solve the main problems of the city, or that he is not doing all he could to solve these problems?

Q. 4A(W). (If not doing all he could) Do you think he is trying farily hard to solve these problems, or not hard at all?

Variable 193
Q. 5(W). How about the state government? Do you think they are trying as hard as they can to solve the main problems of cities like (central

BLKQUOTA—NEIGHBORHOOD RACIAL QUOTA

Variable 0284
Q. 45(W). Suppose there are 100 white families living in a neighborhood. One white family moves out and a Negro family moves in. Do you think it would be a good idea to have some limit on the number of Negro families that move there, or to let as many move there as want to?

city), or that they are not doing all they could to solve these problems?

Q. 5A(W). (If not doing all they could) Do you think they are trying fairly hard to solve these problems, or not hard at all?

Variable 194
Q. 6(W). How about the federal government in Washington? Do you think they are trying as hard as they can to solve the main problems of cities like (central city) or that they are not doing all they could to solve such problems?

Q. 6A(W). (If not doing all they could) Do you think they are trying fairly hard to solve these problems, or not hard at all?

BLKSYMP—SYMPATHY
WITH BLACK PROTESTS

Variable 0344, Cumulative 6 Point Index Based on Variables 238, 239, 254, 256, and 262

Variable 238

Q. 23(W). Some people say these disturbances which occurred in Newark and Detroit (in the summer of 1967) are mainly a protest by Negroes against unfair conditions. Others say they are mainly a way of looting and things like that. Which of these seems more correct to you?

Variable 239

Q. 24(W). Do you think the large disturbances like those in Detroit and Newark were planned in advance, or that there was some planning but not much, or weren't they planned at all?

RIOTCON—RIOT CONTROL
BY REPRESN

Variable 0343, 10 Point Index Based on Variables 338, 340, 342

Variable 338

Recode: Most important thing city can do to prevent riots (first mention)

Variable 340

Recode: Most important thing city can do to prevent riots (second mention)

Variable 342

Recode: Most important thing city can do to prevent riots (third mention):

0. Other
1. End discrimination
2. Get tough

DISCRIM—R'S PERCEPTION
OF RACIAL DISCRIMINATION
IN HIS CITY

Variable 345, 5 Point Cumulative Index Based on Variables 230, 257, 269, and 273

Variable 230

Q. 19(W). It is sometimes said that the things we have just been talking about, such as unnecessary roughness and disrespect by the police, happen more to Negroes in (central city) than to white people. Do you think this is definitely so, probably so, probably not so, or definitely not so?

Variable 257

Q. 32(W). On the average, Negroes in (central city) have worse jobs, education, and housing than white people. Do you think this is due mainly to Negroes having been dis-

Variable 254

Q. 30A(W). If that (orderly marches to protest racial discrimination) doesn't help, do you think Negroes are justified in protesting through sit-ins?

Variable 256

Q. 31(W). Some Negro leaders are talking about having non-violent marches and demonstrations in several cities in 1968 to protest lack of opportunity for Negroes. Do you think some demonstrations are different from riots, or that there is no real difference?

Variable 262

Q. 33(W). Some say that Negroes have been pushing too fast for what they want. Others feel they haven't pushed fast enough. How about you—do you think Negroes are trying to push too fast, are going too slowly, or are moving at about the right speed?

criminated against, or mainly due to something about Negroes themselves?

Variable 269

Q. 36(W). Do you think that in (central city) many, some, or only a few Negroes miss out on jobs and promotions because of racial discrimination?

Variable 273

Q. 38(W). Do you think that in (central city) many, some, or only a few Negroes miss out on good housing because white owners won't rent or sell to them?

CIVLEGIS—ATTD CIVIL RTS LEGISLATION

Variable 347, 4 Point Index Based on Variables 266 and 271

Variable 266
Q. 34A(W). (Unless first preference given to white people in Q. 34) Do you favor or oppose laws to prevent discrimination against Negroes in job hiring and promotion?

Variable 271
Q. 37A(W). How about laws to prevent discrimination against Negroes in buying or renting houses and apartments? Do you favor or oppose such laws?

RACECON—ATTD INTER-RACIAL CONTACT

Variable 348, Cumulative 5 Point Index Based on Variables 268, 274, 282, and 283

Variable 268
Q. 35(W). Suppose you had a job where your supervisor was a qualified Negro. Would you mind that a lot, a little, or not at all?

Variable 274
Q. 39(W). If a Negro family with about the same income and education as you moved next door to you, would you mind it a lot, a little, or not at all?

BLKFRNDS—DOES R HAVE NEGRO FRIENDS

Variable 351, 2 Point Index Based on Variables 278 and 280

Variable 278
Q. 40B(W). Are you friends with any of them (Negroes who live around)?

Variable 280
Q. 42(W). Have you ever known Negroes outside this neighborhood with whom you were friends?

Variable 282

Q. 43(W). Who do you feel you could more easily become friends with—a Negro with the same education and income as you, or a white person with a different education and income from you?

Variable 283

Q. 44(W). If you had small children, would you rather they had only white friends, or would you like to see them have Negro friends too, or wouldn't you care one way or the other?

11.   ETHNICITY AMONG "WASPS"?

Amerrican social science has paid scant attention to the possibility of regional diversity in the country's population. Historians, of course, have scarcely been able to overlook the South, and the tradition of research represented by C. Vann Woodward has recently been favorably reappraised from the improbable perspective of Marxism by the brilliant historian Eugene Genovese. Influenced by V. O. Key, political scientists have not been completely immune to regional questions. But psychologists, psychiatrists, and sociologists have virtually ignored the possibility that regional differences might be important, save for an occasional cross-tabulation that compares "South" with "non-South."[1]

Furthermore, sociologists of religion have not been particularly concerned with the denominational diversity within American Protestantism. Many writers have simply lumped all non-Catholic Christian denominations into the general category "Protestant" when preparing their tables. Those who have looked at denominational differences are more interested either in the correlations between social class and denominational membership or in the question of which denomination was progressing more rapidly down the road to "secularization."

But anyone who takes seriously the comment of Fredrik Barth quoted at the beginning of this book must ask what are the culture-bearing, boundary-creating differentiations that are to be found in the white Protestant population of the country. No one can travel across America and fail to note the substantial differences in different regions of the country. That sociologists have ignored these differences suggests how powerful the homogenization ideology is. That sociologists of religion have ignored the equally obvious differences among American Protestant denominations suggests how powerful the secularization ideology really is.

We have asked repeatedly at the Center for the Study of American Pluralism in the last two years whether we could find any forms of differentiation among American Protestants that might be the functional equivalent of Catholic ethnic groups. Are there subcultures within the Protestant population, which if they do not necessarily provide explicit self-definition are nonetheless are bearers of distinctive culture?

All that we can do in the present chapter is to raise the question and explore tentatively some data that may provide the beginnings of answers. In particular, our regional categories may very well be too large. It is unlikely that anyone in the country thinks of himself as being from the "west south central" region, but it is probable that certain people within that region would define themselves as Texan. If, however, we are able to establish that there are some differences to be found among the large regions that the census uses to divide the United States, we may be justified in suggesting that more regional research is appropriate.

In this chapter we inspect data from two of the studies used in this book—the Verba-Nie political participation study and the ongoing NORC study of June 1961 college graduates. Only white Protestants of English, Irish, and "other" background will be considered. There are virtually no hypotheses to test other than the implicit hypothesis garnered from Killian and Reed, that southerners may be an ethnic group distinct from the rest of the country.

There are, first of all, considerable differences in voting behavior among American Protestant denominations. Fundamentalists are 35 standardized points beneath the mean and Baptists are 16 points beneath the mean. Congregationalists and Presbyterians are 24 points above the mean, and Episcopalians and Lutherans are 15 points above the mean. Similarly, Baptists and fundamentalists are the least likely to engage in political campaigning, while Episcopalians and Presbyterians are the most likely to be political activists. Methodists and Episcopalians are the most devoted to civic activity, and fundamentalists and Baptists are again the least likely to be engaged in such activity. As for political participation, there is prima facie evidence of considerable variation among American Protestant denominations. The differences between Congregationalists and fundamentalists, for example, on voting is in excess of a half of a standard deviation, and the difference between Episcopalians and Baptists in campaigning is .4 of a standard deviation. The difference between them on civic activity exceeds one-third of a standard deviation. We notice in the second panel of Table 1 that these differences diminish somewhat when the influence of education is taken into account, although the Congregationalists are still more likely to vote, and the Baptists and fundamentalists are less

Table 1. Political Participation by Denomination for American Protestants (Standardized Points)

Denomination	Voting	Campaigning	Civic Activity	Controlled for Education		
				Voting	Campaigning	Civic Activity
Baptist (375)	−16	−20	−20	−13	−12	−08
Methodist (332)	07	08	16	05	03	14
Lutheran (205)	15	00	−09	10	04	−02
Congregational (112)	24	08	07	24	09	07
Presbyterian (162)	24	17	10	00	08	−10
Episcopalian (62)	15	20	15	−08	00	−09
Fundamentalist (136)	−35	−27	−15	−35	−08	01

likely to vote. The Methodists are still more likely to engage in civic activity, and the Baptists less likely. Nevertheless, the differences among American Protestant denominations in their political participation can be more easily explained by social class than can the differences among Catholic ethnic groups on the same participation variables. The differences do not go away, but they are diminished by taking educational background into account.

If one uses the convention of only commenting on deviations from the mean of 10 points or higher, there are only two regions where the voting behavior is worth noting (Table 2). The citizens of the Northwest and Mountain regions seem somewhat more likely to vote than those who live in other parts of the country. Those in the west north central are somewhat more likely to campaign, while those in the Mountain region score rather low on political campaigning. The most activist of American Protestants live in the West Coast region, a finding that ought not to be altogether surprising given what we know of politics in Washington, Oregon, and California. The West Coast Protestants are also the most likely to participate in civic activity, while those in the east south central (the so-called Deep South) are the least likely to be concerned about civic affairs. There are, then, some interesting variations in political participation among American regions. The northeast is somewhat more likely to vote; the west north central is more likely to engage in civic activity; the Mountain region is high on voting and low on campaigning; the Pacific region is high on both campaigning and civic activity.

But what about the possibility of regional variation within Protestant denominations? Might not the real subcultures among white American Protestants be created by a combination of denomination and region? Ob-

Table 2. Political Participation by Region for American Protestants (Standardized Points)

Region	Voting	Campaigning	Civic Activity
Northeast (74)	14	−02	06
Middle Atlantic (340)	03	−05	02
East north central (284)	05	04	04
West north central (207)	07	10	19
South Atlantic (183)	−06	−03	08
East south central (63)	05	04	−12
West south central (165)	04	−05	−09
Mountain (53)	16	−18	00
Pacific (237)	05	14	19

viously there are not enough respondents in our sample to enable us to make a judgment about the regional diversity in all the denominations, but there are enough Methodists and Baptists in most of the regions to allow some tentative comparisons to be made between them (Table 3).

Methodists are more likely to vote than Baptists in all the regions of the country except the west north central, where exactly the opposite is the case. There are however considerable variations within both denominations. Baptists in the west south central (or the Southwest) are half a standard deviation lower than those in the west north central (the Plains states) in their score on the voting scale. Methodists in the north Atlantic states are more than a third of a standard deviation higher in their voting than are Methodists in the west north central. We are not able to even guess why these differences exist, but in fact they do exist. A much closer look at regional differences among American Protestant denominations may well be in order.

Similarly, Methodists are consistently more likely to be campaign activists than Baptists, with a third of a standard deviation separating the two groups in both the Pacific and south Atlantic regions. But among Methodists almost two-fifths of a standard deviation separates the high participators in the Pacific region from the low participators in the east north central (or Middle West).

Table 3. Political Participation by Region for American Baptists and Methodists (Standardized Points)

Region	Voting		Campaigning		Civic Activity	
	Bap-tist	Meth-odist	Bap-tist	Meth-odist	Bap-tist	Meth-odist
Middle Atlantic	−24 (95)	24 (59)	−21	−02	−08	29
East north central	00 (76)	20 (65)	−20	−09	−03	12
West north central	12 (41)	−11 (44)	−12	08	−11	21
South Atlantic	−29 (33)	06 (46)	−27	05	−11	27
West south central	−39 (43)	04 (35)	−08	07	−28	09
Pacific	−07 (50)	02 (43)	−03	30	−05	31

Why California Methodists, for example, should be more likely to campaign than Illinois Methodists is very difficult to say, though the finding does not run contrary to the impressions one might pick up from the American press and television during presidential primary campaigns.

Finally, Methodists in all regions are notably more inclined to civic activity than are Baptists, but West Coast and Middle Atlantic Methodists are far more oriented to civic activity than are Methodists in the west south central, and there are differences between Baptists in the east north central and the west south central. One would have to know far more than we do now about the history and development of these regional varieties of American Protestantism to understand the differences recorded in Table 3.

To some extent—but only to some extent—the differences can be explained by differences in education (Table 4). Even with education taken into account, Methodists are more inclined to political participation than are Baptists, but there remain considerable regional variations within both denominations. Variations decline somewhat, especially in campaign activism, but they do persist. The highest positive score in Table 4 is the 26 standardized points for Methodists on civic activity in the south Atlantic regions. The score is 21 points higher than that of Methodists in the east north central region. Why Methodists in the Carolinas and Georgia would be more devoted to civic activity than those in Illinois and Indiana even when educational differences are held constant must remain a mystery for the present. Similarly, the lowest score in Table 4 is the −38 in civic activity for Baptists in the west south central region. These Texas, Arkansas, Oklahoma, and Louisiana Baptists are almost half a standard deviation below their fellow Baptists in the Midwest and Far West, and more than half a standard deviation lower than their fellow

Table 4.   Political Participation by Region for American Baptists and Methodists Controlled for Education (Standardized Points)

Region	Voting		Campaigning		Civic Activity	
	Bap-tist	Meth-odist	Bap-tist	Meth-odist	Bap-tist	Meth-odist
Middle Atlantic	−19	18	−11	−02	02	27
East north central	05	08	−07	04	08	05
West north central	14	−23	−07	03	−06	15
South Atlantic	−26	−04	−19	−13	02	26
West south central	−31	−04	−02	02	−38	25
Pacific	−10	−11	01	22	08	19

southwesterners who are Methodists—even when educational differences are held constant.

We conclude our commentary on the first four tables with the observation that regional and denominational, and especially the combination of these differences in American Protestantism are well worth more intensive investigation, at least as far as political participation is concerned.

In the next tables we turn to differences in family attitudes and behavior among American Protestants. Table 5 shows that Lutheran young women clearly have a different pattern of response from other American Protestant denominations. They are more likely to report early romantic experience and satisfactory sexual adjustment, and more likely to report stronger affectionate relationships with the mother than with the father. They also score rather low on the scale measuring the traditional role of women. Baptists also deviate somewhat from the Protestant mean. They are more mother oriented than father oriented, and have a far more traditional view of the role of women; but unlike their Lutheran counterparts they are far more unlikely to report early romantic experience. Both Baptists and fundamentalists score low on early romantic experience and high on the traditional role of women, but the fundamentalists seem to come from strongly father-oriented families, at least as far as achievement and support are concerned. Episcopalians are low on the mother saliency scales and somewhat high on romantic experience. The Congregationalists, like the Episcopalians, are somewhat low on the mother scales, but they are lower still on both romantic experience and sexual adjustment. Neither Presbyterians nor Methodists deviate in any important way from the national mean.

Most of the difference in the first four scales (mother saliency scales) disappears when father's education is taken into account (Table 6). There are no differences in excess of 10 on the importance of mother scale, but the Baptists are somewhat more likely to report mother support as opposed to father support, and the fundamentalists continue to score low on the achievement and support scales.

Differences in romantic experience, sexual adjustment, and attitudes on the traditional role of women are far much durable when father's education is taken into account. Baptists are the most conservative on the role of women, Lutherans the most progressive. Lutherans are the most likely to report a high level of sexual adjustment, Congregationalists the most likely to report a low level. The Lutherans are also the most likely to report early romantic experience, and the fundamentalists the least likely. We can conclude that the separate Lutheran cultural pattern reported in Table 5 is enhanced by a control for education. There is, it would appear, a separate Lutheran culture that affects relationships between young women and their parents, and that persists into adolescence and young adulthood in areas of romantic experience, satisfac-

Table 5. Family Attitudes and Behavior for Protestant Women (Standardized Points)

Denomination	Importance of Mother	Mother Affection	Mother Achievement	Mother Support	Romantic Experience	Sexual Adjustment	Traditional Role of Women
Baptist (99)	11	06	12	13	−13	−06	24
Methodist (188)	03	00	07	02	05	06	02
Lutheran (40)	08	25	−07	−09	20	25	−13
Congregational (63)	−08	−05	−14	00	−24	−14	−07
Presbyterian (160)	−05	−10	−01	−02	08	04	02
Episcopalian (101)	−13	−06	−20	−06	15	03	05
Fundamentalist (24)	−03	05	−24	−19	−33	02	17

Table 6. Family Attitudes and Behavior for Protestant Women with Fathers' Education Controlled (Standardized Points)

Denomination	Importance of Mother	Mother Affection	Mother Achievement	Mother Support	Romantic Experience	Sexual Adjustment	Traditional Role of Women
Baptist	07	06	04	14	-08	00	20
Methodist	03	05	10	04	02	02	00
Lutheran	04	24	-13	-02	23	16	-18
Congregational	02	00	-10	05	-29	-30	-09
Presbyterian	00	04	06	03	-24	00	-04
Episcopalian	00	04	-05	01	04	-08	-07
Fundamentalist	-09	03	-35	-12	-30	-08	13

tory sexual adjustment, and "liberal" notions about the role of women. These differences are not notably affected by taking social class into account.

There also seems to be a fundamentalist culture system in which fathers play a considerably stronger role in family life for young women than they do in other groups. Fundamentalist patterns include less early romantic experience, less likelihood of sexual adjustment, and a more traditional version of the role of women—even when paternal education is held constant.

Finally, there may also be a separate Congregationalist subculture in which romantic experience and sexual adjustment are quite low, even when the traditional role of women is less likely to be endorsed than it is among some other Protestant groups. The fundamentalist culture may simply be a form of rigid American puritanism. The Lutheran culture may result from a traditionally relaxed approach to sexuality (which Martin Luther himself manifested in his later years). But why young women college graduates from a Congregationalist background would be low on both romantic experience and sexual adjustment is not altogether clear, unless there may be residues of seventeenth- and eighteenth-century puritanism in American society.

In Table 7 we attempt to determine whether there may be distinctive regional subcultures in family attitudes and behavior. The most obvious pattern in Table 7 is of the Rocky Mountain region in which mothers are more salient than they are in other parts of the country; romance and sexual adjustment are lower, and the response on the scale measuring the traditional role of women is a half standard deviation above the mean. As there are only 36 young women from the Mountain region in our sample, we must be cautious about interpreting the finding; but it is nonetheless worth noting that the control for father's education applied in Table 8 does not appreciably change this pattern of Rocky Mountain distinctiveness. If our data are reliable, there is a separate family subculture among those who came from the Mountain region.

Those from the New England states are slightly lower on the mother scales and romantic experience. Those from the north central are the least likely to endorse the traditional role of women, and those from the South are generally higher on the mother saliency scales than other American Protestants.

Taking father's education into account virtually eliminates the differences from the mean of Protestants in the Northeast and Middle Atlantic regions—though the low score on romantic experience becomes even lower in the Northeast when social class is taken into account. Young women from the west north central continue to be the least likely to endorse the traditional role of women. One is hard put to say why girls from the Plains region would be more likely to be "feminists," unless there is some lingering female independence from the frontier days. Young women from the South continue to be higher on the mother saliency scales, and young women from the West Coast lower on the scale measuring traditional role for women.

Table 7. Family Attitudes and Behavior for Protestant Women by Region (Standardized Points)

Region	Mother Importance	Mother Affection	Mother Achievement	Mother Support	Romantic Experience	Sexual Adjustment	Traditional Role of Women
Northeast (34)	−10	−12	00	−15	−12	−03	00
Middle Atlantic (136)	−14	−11	−17	−11	−03	−03	−08
East north central (173)	03	06	01	01	11	05	03
West north central (62)	−05	−10	00	02	−06	04	−22
South (138)	15	07	14	15	04	06	05
South central (60)	00	−03	08	05	02	00	00
Mountain (36)	18	16	02	30	−10	−09	51
West (123)	−01	−01	01	02	06	00	−14

Table 8. Family Attitudes and Behavior for Protestant Women by Region with Fathers' Education Controlled (Standardized Points)

Region	Mother Importance	Mother Affection	Mother Achievement	Mother Support	Romantic Experience	Sexual Adjustment	Traditional Role of Women
Northeast	-01	-04	09	-09	-20	-06	-02
Middle Atlantic	-09	-05	-11	-06	-08	-07	-10
East north central	07	11	02	05	07	02	00
West north central	-02	-06	01	03	-09	00	01
South	14	10	11	16	04	00	01
South central	00	02	07	02	02	04	-02
Mountain	13	14	09	30	-04	-13	47
West	03	03	02	00	-12	03	-15

Are there regional differences in family structure among American Protestants even when social class is taken into account? There are surely some, particularly among those from the Rocky Mountain areas, but also there are apparently some differences between the South and the rest of the country (which would hardly surprise John Shelton Reed) on the importance of mother in the family. There are differences between the east north central and the West in attitudes on the role of women.

It is more difficult to consider the differences between Methodists and Baptists in our sample of college women than in the national sample, because there are fewer Baptists in the college sample. We must make do with six Baptist respondents from both the Middle West and east north central regions. Hence our findings are even more speculative and tentative than those in the previous tables in this chapter. Nevertheless, there are a number of interesting phenomena to be observed in Table 9. Among the Baptists, for example, there are striking differences between respondents from the south central region. Mother saliency is higher in the south central than it is in the South for Baptists, and the mother achievement factor is substantially lower in the south central and in the South on the mother affection and mother support factors. Indeed, there is almost nine-tenths of a standard deviation separating south central from southern Baptists on that scale. Similarly, south central Baptists are lower than southern Baptists on romance and sexual adjustment and higher on the traditional role of women. It would appear, then, that rather different family cultures exist among Baptists in the South when they are compared with their Baptist neighbors in the south central region. Furthermore, Methodists in all regions are higher than Baptists in all regions in reporting romantic experience. They are also higher in the Middle Atlantic, the South, and the south central regions on sexual adjustment, and more likely to hold feminist positions on the role of women except for those in the east north central region. Finally, there also seems to be a pattern among Methodists from the east north central. Compared to other Methodists they score higher on three of the four mother saliency scales, lower on sexual adjustment, and higher on traditional role of women. They also have a high score on early romantic experiences. It is interesting to note, incidentally, that both Baptists and Methodists in the South have higher scores on sexual adjustment than their counterparts in the south central. They have lower scores on the traditional role of women measure.

A control for paternal education (Table 10) does not modify the pattern of differences reported in previous paragraphs between those who live in the South and the Southwest. Nor does it eliminate the high mother saliency of Methodists in the east north central region.

To summarize Tables 8, 9, and 10, differences between Methodists and Baptists in family behavior and attitudes can be found in all regions of the

Table 9. Family Variables for American Baptist and Methodist Women by Region (Standardized Points)

Region	Mother Importance		Mother Affection		Mother Achievement		Mother Support		Romantic Experience		Sexual Adjustment		Traditional Role of Women	
	Meth-odist	Bap-tist	Meth-odist	Bap-tist	Meth-odist	Bap-tist	Meth-odist	Bap-tist	Meth-odist	Bap-tist	Meth-odist	Bap-tist	Meth-odist	Bap-tist
Middle Atlantic	-23 (31)	13 (6)	05	-98	18	-66	00	-13	03	-38	00	-33	-23	13
East north central	32 (47)	12 (6)	17	20	16	06	26	17	27	07	-09	17	32	12
South	-03 (32)	19 (43)	01	16	25	28	-09	57	15	09	24	13	-03	19
South central	-09 (22)	29 (19)	-20	-06	-08	13	-01	-29	41	-16	15	-14	09	29
Pacific	-13 (28)	30 (10)	-09	26	-04	-06	-04	-42	09	-09	05	03	-13	30

Table 10. Family Variables for American Baptist and Methodist Women by Region with Fathers' Education Controlled (Standardized Points)

Region	Mother Importance		Mother Affection		Mother Achievement		Mother Support		Romantic Experience		Sexual Adjustment		Traditional Role of Women	
	Meth-odist	Bap-tist	Meth-odist	Bap-tist	Meth-odist	Bap-tist	Meth-odist	Bap-tist	Meth-odist	Bap-tist	Meth-odist	Bap-tist	Meth-odist	Bap-tist
Middle Atlantic	14	-10	22	-40	07	-83	02	12	-11	-55	-01	-55	-26	11
East north central	26	06	21	-04	20	14	28	13	12	03	-11	45	29	08
South	07	34	22	23	01	17	-10	58	06	00	22	14	-07	14
South central	-06	-26	01	-08	-16	-18	02	-36	23	-16	16	-17	07	25
Pacific	00	-07	04	-15	-05	21	-01	-45	-10	-15	04	-05	-15	26

country. Methodists in the east north central seem to have a special pattern of family behavior, and there also seem to be considerable differences in both denominations between the South and the south central regions—the latter are substantially more "conservative."

What has our search for diversity among white Protestants, English, Irish, and "other" revealed? The following assertions can be made:

1.   Fundamentalists are different from other American Protestants in both familial and political matters.
2.   Lutherans have distinctive patterns of family behavior.
3.   There is some distinctiveness in political and familial matters among Baptists.
4.   There are also some political and familial differences characteristic of American Congregationalists.
5.   There is political and family distinctiveness in the Mountain region.
6.   There are less systematic political and familial differences characteristic of Protestants in the Pacific coast region.
7.   Protestants in the west north central region (the Plains states) are high on civic activism and in their rejection of the traditional role of women.
8.   Finally, Methodists and Baptists are consistently different from one another in each region, but there are notable regional differences within each of the two denominations.

To summarize the substance of our findings in a brief and oversimplified form: The Pacific coast tends to be more liberal, the Mountain states more conservative, the Plains states more liberal and more activist in certain respects. In familial matters, the Lutherans are liberal, the Baptists and the fundamentalists more conservative, and the Congregationalists surprisingly less adjusted sexually.

This analysis labors under severe handicaps. We have no theory to guide us, the regional categories are probably too large, the number of respondents in many of the cells in our tables is far too small, and many of the differences reported are not great. Nevertheless, there is some retrospective plausibility in many of the findings reported in this chapter. That Baptists and fundamentalists might be more conservative in family matters is consonant with their religious tradition. The Congregationalists' problem with sexual adjustment may well be a residue of puritanism, while the apparent Lutheran ease in matters sexual may also be compatible with their heritage. The civic activism of the Methodists is certainly in keeping with the Wesleyan tradition, and the relatively high level of political participation for Congregationalists may be characteristic of a democratic church that has become socially respectable. Activism and liberalism on the West Coast fits popular impressions, and conservatism combined with high voting and low campaigning is not all that surprising in the sparsely populated Mountain region. Finally, the civic activism combined with an untraditional view of the role of women does not seem inappropriate in the old frontier states of the Great Plains.

It is a little more difficult to cope with the regional variety within the Baptist and Methodist denominations. If the Southwest is thought of as the "New South" as opposed to the "Old South," however, it may not be surprising to find greater flexibility in family matters among both Methodists and Baptists in the Southwest.

We then can fit most of our findings into a reasonable explanatory framework and tentatively conclude that it is at least an open question whether region and denomination and combinations of the two may not play a quasi-ethnic role for white Anglo-Saxon American Protestants. Such regional and denominational differentiation may not provide self-definition within the white Protestant community (although it may), but apparently it does serve in some fashion as the bearer of culture, as Fredrik Barth has used the term. In any case, there is no evidence for the notion that in white American Protestantism heterogeneity has been eliminated except for that attributed to social class.

The question then arises as to whether there might be important regional variation among American Catholic ethnic groups. There is only one data set available to us that contains a sufficient number of Catholic ethnics to explore the possibility of regional diversity. We therefore turn to the study of the cities affected by the 1967 urban riots to see whether the responses of Catholic ethnics to racial questions vary from region to region.

The differences turn out to be surprisingly large (Table 11). Thus the Midwestern[2] Irish are far more conservative on both civil rights legislation and interracial contact than are the Irish from the Northeast[3] or the mid-East.[4] The difference is in excess of a half standard deviation when one compares those from the Northeast and Middle West. Similarly, on all items the Midwestern Poles are also the most likely to take an anti-black stand. The pattern is less evident for the Italians; those from the Middle West are actually more favorably disposed to interracial contact and to a black mayor than those from the Northeast.

It is obvious that on all four items the most anti-black response comes from the Middle West—indeed Midwestern Jews are below the national score on interracial contact. To some extent the low scores of the Poles are a function of their Midwestern location. With the exception of civil rights laws support, Poles are still lower than all other Midwestern groups. To compound the complexities, however, the Midwestern Irish, lower than other Irish on both civil rights legislation and interracial contact, are above the national mean on support for a black mayor, though they are not so high as Italians who live outside the Northeast.

Table 11. Racial Attitudes for Catholic Religio-ethnic Groups by Regions (Deviation from the Mean)

Region	Irish	German	Italian	Polish	British	Jewish	All
A. Black Mayor							
Northeast[a]	13	-05	-05	-02	21	27	11
	(116)	(29)	(178)	(33)	(746)	(202)	
Middle East[b]	-13	10	33	-12	-19	49	03
	(17)	(53)	(22)	(62)	(49)	(30)	
Middle West[c]	11	-32	12	-43	-30	03	-16
	(74)	(71)	(84)	(88)	(744)	(51)	
B. Civil Rights Laws							
Northeast	28	-29	08	00	54	55	27
Middle East	15	-05	-28	-15	-14	34	-13
Middle West	-42	-20	-25	-27	-37	32	-20
C. Riot Control							
Northeast	09	-40	-09	-05	15	10	05
Middle East	23	08	-09	-12	-34	22	00
Middle West	08	-39	-08	-32	-09	09	-10
D. Interracial Contact							
Northeast	19	-01	-15	-26	13	13	09
Middle East	09	02	-17	-22	-03	-03	-08
Middle West	-35	-17	-02	-53	-23	-23	-12

[a] Boston, New York, Philadelphia, Newark.
[b] Detroit, Cleveland, Pittsburgh, Cincinnati.
[c] Chicago, Gary, Milwaukee, St. Louis.

There are considerable regional differences within the Catholic ethnic collectivities. While there is some pattern of the Midwestern groups being less supportive of blacks, this pattern does not hold for the Italians and the Germans. It may be that the various groups had different historical experiences in the different regions, and hence respond differently to certain social issues.

We conclude with two observations. First, regional and denominational diversity among American Protestants may play a quasi-ethnic role. And second, there is considerable internal variety among Catholic ethnic groups, some of it linked to region.

We might add that further research on regional diversity seems very much in order.

NOTES

1. Two books by sociologists have appeared recently on the subject of the South: *White Southerners*, by Lewis M. Killian (New York: Random House, 1973), and John Shelton Reed's *The Enduring South* (Lexington, Mass.: Heath, 1973). Reed's book in particular advances the suggestion that Southerners might indeed be an "ethnic group."

2. Chicago, Gary, Milwaukee, St. Louis.

3. Boston, New York, Philadelphia, Newark.

4. Detroit, Cleveland, Pittsburgh, Cincinnati.

12.   IS THERE A WHITE ETHNIC MOVEMENT?

THE 1960s AND THE EARLY 1970s were a time of social movements. As is common among American Catholics, the white ethnics have jumped aboard the bandwagon just when everybody else seems to be getting off of it. But to understand and evaluate the white ethnic movement, one must view it in the context of the movement phenomenon of recent years.

I suggest in this chapter that social forces that produce movements are more important than the movements themselves. A movement may diverge from the thrust of those forces because of the personalities of its leaders or through a misunderstanding of forces and their thrust. The roots of pervasive and lasting change may be found in the social forces, not the movement. A movement, in other words, is an epiphenomenon, the tip of an iceberg. I am not suggesting that movements can or should be ignored or dismissed, but they may be one type of lens for looking at the social reality that has generated them.

Many types of social movements can and should be distinguished. Some, like the trade union and temperance movements, have been successful. Others, like the early twentieth-century socialist movement, have been failures, even though many of its programs were taken over in later years by established political parties. Some, like the Irish Republican Army, become fixated at one stage of development; others simply cease to exist. Some movements begin as social movements and end up political parties, structured organizations, or veto groups within the larger society. Some leaders are geniuses, some are mediocre, some are poor, and some may be half-mad. Some social movements are benign influences in both the larger society and the group they claim to represent, while others bring little positive benefit to anyone. Because of this diversity, it is impossible to say whether one is in favor of or against social movements on principle. They are an inevitable part of the social process of a relatively free society. The purpose of this chapter is not to level value judgments on social movements in general or on the social movements with which we are presently concerned. An attempt to understand why these movements have come to be and what their life histories have been is not to pass judgment on their contributions to either the groups they claim to represent or to the larger society.

A social movement is itself the result of massive social changes that have already occurred. It may impel some further social change, but the forces that lead to further germination will in many cases be far more important and far more lasting than the changes the movement itself produces. Movements result from a more or less temporary incapacity of the society's conflict mechanisms. Every human society has a series of procedures, protocols, processes, and institutions that enable social conflict to surface, to articulate itself, to run its course, and to be resolved. These mechanisms are designed to take note of and to adjust to social, cultural, and economic changes and the

272

resulting discontents, dissatisfactions, and pressures in a society. Social movements arise when conflict mechanisms do not take sufficient note of change and the resulting pressures, or at least they do not take note of them quickly and effectively enough.

I would submit that there are two ways of coping with social change and the resulting conflict. Adjustments and changes are made within the existing social structure so that the critical majority of those who are dissatisfied become relatively more satisfied without creating intolerable costs for the rest of the society, or, alternately, the society tears itself apart and starts over from scratch. Which of these responses occurs is not a function of which one is more "moral" or "better," more "radical" or more "correct." Whether social change is evolutionary or revolutionary is almost solely the result of whether society's conflict mechanisms are adequate to the challenge that a particular crisis poses. Lacking real economic security for the most part, the majority of ordinary people want no part of revolution if there is any conceivable evolutionary way to create a tolerable position for themselves within the society. The average citizen perceives that in revolutionary situations many people will suffer serious losses, and he suspects, with good reason, that he will be one of the losers. He therefore strongly resists the pressures of some militant radicals to make society so intolerable that revolutionary restructuring will become imperative.

A social movement results when the conflict mechanisms have not proved responsive enough to changes and their resulting pressures, but before they are perceived as having failed completely. The radical component of a movement may announce that the "system" has failed, but the movement will not turn to revolution until a substantial proportion of its constituency is also persuaded of that failure.

The Social Movements of the 1960s. What, then, are the underlying causes of the social movements of the 1960s? Why did blacks, young people, women, Chicanos, Puerto Ricans, American Indians become militant? At the risk of oversimplification, I would suggest that the underlying cause of current social unrest is the economic affluence that the United States has experienced since the end of World War II. Coupled with this is the tremendous expansion of higher education, which is probably both the result and the cause of the affluence (more result than cause, I suspect). Virtually all the leaders of the movements emerged through the higher educational process. They developed in that process the personally and socially healthy ability to articulate their own frustrations and dissatisfactions. As long as most young people began working at age 18, as long as most women assumed that housewifery was their only legitimate role, and as long as most blacks were lucky to get out of high school, there was little if any social unrest in these three population groups. But with the advent of universal higher education and the leisure time available during and after the educational experience for college-educated professionals, the movements appeared on the scene. It was no accident that the black movement was born in the lunch counter sit-ins by students at black colleges. The time to think about their problems, the vocabulary to articulate them, and the organizational skills and philosophical justifications to respond to them only became available when a substantial segment of that population group became upper middle class. Movements arise, in other words, not when a group is effectively oppressed but when it begins to produce its own college-educated elite. It is no accident, then, that the campus was the center for all the social movements of the sixties. If American society wanted to keep blacks, young people, women, and white ethnics content, it should have kept them off the college campuses.

It seems to me likely that the black movement and the women's movement would have emerged in the 1960s no matter what happened in the larger society. But as it happened, two phenomena combined to aggravate existing social pressures and to create new and powerful pressures. The baby boom that followed World War II increased the proportion of youth in the population, and this gigantic age cohort came of age and reached political maturity at a time when the country was involved in an unpopular war. American society was "unlucky"—mass higher education, an outsized large youth cohort, and an unpopular foreign war occurred at the same point in time. Any one of the three could create difficult social imbalances and might have given rise to social movements. The intersection of these three sets of social pressures guaranteed a considerable amount of unrest and disturbance in the society during the 1960s. To use an analogy, one might suggest that each of the separate sources of social pressure had a multiplier effect on one another. The capacity of American society to more or less absorb all these pressures may seem impressive to historians of the future.

In this perspective, the great progress that has been made in the social and economic conditions of American blacks since 1960 (a progress that Wattenberg and Scammon have recently pointed out as having been obscured by a conspiracy of silence) is probably more a cause of the black movement than a result of it. As a college-educated black upper middle class began to emerge in substantial numbers, it became conscious that it lacked respect and power in American society and began to demand both. It also became conscious that a substantial number of its brothers and sisters were not enjoying the benefits of American affluence and vigorously identified itself with the cause of the black poor. Paradoxically, the burden of the evidence is that the condition of the black middle class continues to improve dramatically, while the condition of the black poor apparently changes very little if at all.

A fascinating historical and sociological question is whether social change has been in any way accelerated by the black movement.[1] Wattenberg and Scammon raise the related question of whether the upward mobility of blacks under age 35 is a result of the Great Society legislation of the mid-1960s. It seems to me, however, to be naïve to think that dramatic changes of the sort described by Wattenberg and Scammon can be caused in a brief period of time either by a social movement or by legislation. The dynamics of black upward mobility were no doubt already at work in the late 1950s. Increased educational levels of blacks, the opening up of job opportunities, and the generally high level of affluence in the society would probably have produced a rapidly growing middle and upper middle class regardless of what happened politically in the 1960s. The black movement and the Great Society legislation have accelerated and legitimated the process and may have provided benefits to some blacks—particularly those who earned their livings off the Great Society or the black movement—but it is dubious whether either have yet contributed substantial benefits to the black poor. I must emphasize that I am not critical of the movement when I point out that a given movement did not benefit all the members of its constituency. Many blacks did not benefit from the black movement, many students did not benefit from the student movement, and many women are not benefiting from the women's movement. All that follows is that movements deal with complex and difficult social problems and that movement leaderships do not work miracles. When I argue that the movements' successes are finite, I am not attacking them; I observe merely that the world is an imperfect and frequently intractable place.

Also, I doubt the self-evident causal analysis that would argue that since the dramatic social and economic progress of the blacks was recorded in 1970 after the black movement began and after Great Society legislation was passed, it must have been caused by that movement and that legislation. Social changes among American blacks produced the movement and, to some extent, produced the Great Society legislation.

Similarly, the women's movement is an epiphenomenon that resulted from a dramatic increase in college education for women, smaller families, more effective means of birth control, and the slow opening up of professional careers for women. These factors produced a group of American women who had reached the upper middle class on their own performance, and not merely by marriage. The women's movement facilitated and accelerated major changes in sexual role definitions, but these changes were already well under way, or the women's movement would not have begun in the first place.

Finally, mass higher education (of the sort so well described by Clark Kerr) inevitably produced a substantial number of young people with acute (if shallow) critical faculties. These students were also intensely restless and dissatisfied with the impersonal nature of their educational experience. Like the black upper middle class and the female upper middle class, the student upper middle class demanded that it be given power and respect in keeping with the new position it felt itself to be assuming in society. But restlessness, discontent, and criticism among the children of affluence scarcely needed the SDS or Abbie Hoffman to exist. On the contrary, Tom Hayden, Rennie Davis, Abbie Hoffman, and Jerry Rubin became the celebrities they were precisely because they articulated discontent and dissatisfaction that was already powerfully latent in the youthful population.

All three of these movements and the comparable movements among Spanish-speaking and American Indians would have come into being without the war in Vietnam. But the war did give considerable impetus to the dissatisfaction that the newly educated groups in the society were feeling, and it provided a rallying point around which all the movements could agree.

American society provided two and one-half decades of uninterrupted affluence for most of its population and college educations for large numbers of young people, including women and nonwhites, and unleashed for itself a series of social changes and social pressures that created dramatic and powerful strains in its culture and structure. Under such circumstances, social movements were inevitable.

But social movements are tricky. If they are to appeal to more than tiny, unimportant factions they must articulate to large constituencies the problems that they feel and cannot articulate themselves, and they must simultaneously communicate these problems to the rest of the society. As long as a substantial number of those for whom the movement leaders purport to speak are prepared to say in effect, "Yes, that's how we feel," the movement will flourish. If the movement leaders lose their capacity to sense what is inchoately and inarticulately going on in their consitutency, the movement will lose its thrust. This is not just a moral prerequisite. It is gratifying, of course, to know that leaders really speak for those whom they claim to represent; but quite apart from the ethical satisfaction to be found in such a situation, a spokesman without a constituency is a voice crying in the wilderness.

To sustain momentum, movement leadership must be able to do four things:

1. It must be sensitively tuned in to what is going on in its contituency and adroit enough to push it a little further than it would like to go but not further than it is ready or willing to go.

2. It must be able to deliver to a broad constituency at least some of the things it has promised, things that that constituency perceives as valuable.

3. It must be able to call upon a substantial proportion of that consituency for support, whether it be financial, organizational, or conflict support.

4. It must persuade the rest of society that it indeed does have the power to "deliver the votes" of its constituency.

A classic example of a social movement that was more or less successful in these four prerequisites was the labor movement of the 1930s and 1940s. It did resonate to the demands of its membership; it was able to deliver substantial improvements in wages and working conditions; it was able to collect dues and to produce organizational support on the picket lines when strikes were required; and it could deliver the votes by both calling the workers out of the plants and by bringing political and financial muscle to bear in election campaigns.

While the labor movement is now anathema to most of its successors on the movement scene, I would submit that if any social movement is going to be more than an epiphenomenon or more than a reflection of general cultural trends, it must develop the capacity to do much the same thing that the labor movement did. The labor movement of the 1930s had many of the same sorts of problems that the more recent movements have had—internal conflict, extremist spokesmen, difficulty in communicating with potential allies, rhetoric that offended potential supporters. The difference between the labor movement on the one hand and the black movement and the women's movement on the other may simply be that the first completed its life cycle from social outburst to organization structure and the second two have yet to complete a similar cycle—though the black movement seems to be well on its way. The most that can be said of the black movement today is that it seems to be moving rapidly in a direction toward traditional political involvement; the women's movement does not seem to be moving so rapidly, and the student radical movement appears to be moribund.

Admirers of social movements often lament the fact that they eventually become "institutionalized." There is something raw and primal about a social movement in its early stages. Spontaneity, outrage, vigor, courage, and high principled refusal to compromise are heightened by a sense of beleaguered community. As time goes on and the movement becomes organized and structured, the problems of administration, coalition formation, and inevitable compromise seem to deprive it of its admirable primitive energy.

But social movements do not come into being to provide community or entertainment but to impel social changes. Institutionalization may eventually inhibit creativity within a movement. The late Gustave Weigel remarked that all human enterprises given sufficient time go badly, but is Bobby Seale less admirable when he runs a responsible campaign to be mayor of Oakland than he was when he toted a rifle in the California state legislature? Which tactic is likely to have more effect on the society and is more likely to improve the condition of Seale's constituency?

In any case, as Peter Berger remarked, even revolutionaries have to sleep, and permanent revolution is simply not a tolerable situation for most human beings.

The element most critical for sustaining a social movement is the continuation of the movement's leadership capacity to articulate dissatisfactions and frustrations that social change has produced in its membership. A movement leader who has lost his ability to speak to and for his constituency, or one who never had that ability, will lose effective social and political power.

But in contemporary American society two phenomena have emerged that enable movement leaders to sustain power and influence and prestige long after they have lost mass constituency support. First, mass media and particularly television emphasis on movement spokesmen makes it possible for a person to become a nationally known, politically influential, and economically successful social movement spokesman without ever having extensive grass roots support. One can be "important" so long as one is clever enough and adroit enough to maintain one's position as a media spokesman. An example was seen in the conviction of George McGovern's staff that Jesse Jackson was a charismatic political leader with massive support in the black community. Surely it was an image that the Reverend Jackson had worked mightily to build, and one that he very successfully portrayed. In fact, as the black politician Penn Kimball is said to have remarked, "Jesse couldn't lead vampires to a blood bank." Eventually, of course, social reality catches up with television commentators, and a spokesman without a constituency or without the capacity to "deliver the votes" becomes as out of date as yesterday's headlines.

Second, techniques of moral and psychological blackmail have been developed against organizations with substantial components of college-educated elites in their work forces. Universities, publishing companies, and broadcast networks are prime examples. A handful of people capable of throwing up a picket line, seizing control of an office, summoning a collection of fellow travelers, and attracting a TV camera crew can have immense power against a corporate or government bureaucracy with a delicately balanced structure that cannot afford too much disruption and that is peculiarly vulnerable to cries of outraged morality. The protest demonstration, the takeover, the sit-in are not effective ways of winning consensus on major issues from the larger society, but they are most effective techniques for gaining short run (though important) concessions from certain easy targets within the society. A serious problem can arise when a disruption tactic is successful in one context and is transferred by unintelligent leadership to a context where it is bound to fail or be counterproductive. Of course, after a while one runs out of targets where psychological and moral blackmail provide quick and easy payoffs.

But while these two techniques can postpone the day of reckoning, there still comes a time when movement leadership must face the fact that it may have lost its ability to articulate to and for its constituency, or at least to sufficient numbers of it to be an important political factor in the society. Indeed, by relying on the media instead of grass roots support for power, some leaders create a situation in which the loudest and most obnoxious spokesmen and the most extreme and counterproductive tactics invariably dominate the movement. The media are not interested in moderate spokesmen, and the easy victims of disruption will feel most guilt ridden in the face of only the most extreme onslaughts. And since most women, most blacks, and most young people, including those who are in sympathy with the goals of the movements, are not revolutionaries and are, indeed, as conservative as the rest of society, they will quickly lose confidence in and withdraw support from the radical spokesmen and the violent tactics.

As should have been clear before the 1968 election and was certainly clear after it, the SDS and the less radical liberal activist student leadership were simply incapable of delivering the votes of the youthful population. On occasion, and particularly during spring, young people may have rallied to the causes of radical protest, but the protest leaders, the media, the intellectual elites, and the McGovern staff were all wrong when they thought that such activity meant that youth—even college youth—was more revolutionary now than its parents or its peers of two and three decades ago.

The black movement probably has not had an effective national leader since the death of Martin Luther King, and some question if in his last months King was able to speak to and for the black population the way he had in previous years. Black leadership in the country is passing from the long line of bizarre characters who have cavorted across the television screen to the far more sedate, respectable, and representative black elected political leadership, a leadership that is perfectly willing to admit off the record that it deeply resented the power white society ceded to those self-anointed spokesmen. As one black politician pointed out to me, "I don't see why white people prefer leadership that hasn't been elected by anyone to those who have been duly elected by black people. If I behaved the way some of those guys do, I would be turned out of office by the black voters at the next election."

Black political leadership, like any social movement leadership that requires the sustained support of its constituency, simply cannot afford to lose its capacity to communicate to and for its rank and file. Leaders who resent the fact that the media spokesmen swept them aside when they were riding high and treated them with comtempt may have reasons for their resentment. Black political leadership is not yet ready to put down publicly the media spokesmen because of the need to maintain the facade of black unity. But the facade is beginning to crack. Power, real power, is passing from the movement leaders to the black politicians, and, except for rhetoric and nostalgia and the possibility of government errors in strategy, the black movement may quickly follow the student movement into oblivion.

One of the interesting aspects of the black movement is that black political activity antedated the movement and has coexisted alongside it. Thus it was altogether possible for some of the black movement leaders to switch easily from agitation and demonstration to more traditional political strategies and tactics. One of the important contributions of the black movement may well be that it imparted greater vigor and dynamism to black politics, while bringing certain new leaders into the black political arena. The real "action" for blacks will probably be in politics of the more traditional variety—an "action," be it noted, that follows the path laid down by other urban ethnic immigrant groups.

Finally, one may well wonder how long the group of seeming man haters, children haters, family haters, and lesbians who have constituted themselves a substantial part of the women's movement will be taken seriously as spokesmen (or spokespersons) for the constituency of American women, even college-educated women. The law of the dominance of extremist spokesmen is working as effectively on the women's movement as it did on the black and student movements. Kate Millett, Jill Johnston, Gloria Steinem, Bella Abzug simply do not, cannot, and will never speak for any more than a tiny fraction of American women. This does not mean that they and their allies will not win important gains for their factions or accomplish some important changes in the society; it simply means that when the chips are down, they have very little organizational support and cannot deliver the votes.

The social, cultural, and economic changes of the last quarter-century have not come to a halt. Dramatic modifications in the places of young people, non-whites, and women in American society continue to take place. New organizations will emrge to act as lobbies and pressure groups for specific segments within those population groups. But we will soon lose completely the illusion that there are mass social movements that comprise the overwhelmiag majority of their own constituencies and for which the self-appointed spokesman can always legitimately speak. In this sense there never was a youth movement or a women's movement, and there has not been a black movement since the death of Martin Luther King. It is only a polite fiction, but television hungers for images to keep illusions alive.

Illusion can be a self-defeating prophecy. The 1972 Democratic convention was in part a convocation of movement leadership, a leadership that was supremely confident that for once, nonwhites, the young, and women were adequately represented. George McGovern would be elected by the enthusiastic vote of the New Coalition. The nonwhites did vote for McGovern (which they would have done in any case), though with little enthusiasm, and women and young people voted for Nixon.

A number of fallacies can deceive a movement leadership into thinking that it has grass roots support and can at the same time deceive social and cultural elites as to how important the self-appointed spokesmen really are.

1. *The eschatological fallacy.* According to this viewpoint, large numbers of people are getting ready to "rise up." Blacks or women or young people (or, more recently, white ethnics) are angry, restless, discontented, and ready to tear the society apart. The demographic and economic forces of the society are such that those things the movement leadership stand for are inevitably going to happen. They are the wave of the future. Germaine Greer, Eldridge Cleaver, and Mark Rudd speak for that group within their constituency who are going to shape the society of the future. Since their victory is inevitable, we may as well go along so that we too will ride the crest of the wave. It is precisely this sort of argument that enabled Frederick Dutton to persuade George McGovern that McGovern would be elected President of the United States.

2. *The "radical" fallacy.* According to this line of reasoning, it is morally necessary that society be completely remade according to a new and more "correct" design. Because of his superior intelligence, his greater rectitude, and his more perceptive vision, the radical has the moral right to rule. Instead of engaging with the "system" and contaminating himself with the social pressures and social conflicts that are inevitable in "system" politics, the radical would rather begin by wiping the slate clean and building an entirely new society. He will happily draw up its constitution for us. The social psychologist Howard Ehrlich contended in the conclusion of his recent book on the psychology of prejudice that for prejudice to be eliminated from American society, "pluralistic" democracy must be replaced by "participatory" democracy. Ehrlich is not too clear about what he means by this, but I can imagine only two possible situations. Either in this new participatory democracy the majority will rule (and Ehrlich and his supporters, stripped of the constitutional safeguards of American pluralism, will be promptly tossed into jail), or the minority elite will govern the society on the basis of their superior dignity and worth (and this includes Ehrlich and his supporters, no doubt). Such a social science version of Plato's Republic may be admirable, but it is scarcely either freedom or democracy as most Americans understand these terms. It can come into being only as a result of an inconceivable surrender of political power by the American public. Radicals either win coalition support and thus stop being radical, or they don't win coalition support and never acquire political power. Indeed, one definition for a radical could be that he is someone who does not have the votes necessary to implement his policy and is searching for some other means of imposing his policy on the people whether they want it or not.

3. *The consciousness-raising fallacy.* In this perspective the self-annointed spokesman who has lost the support of his constituency (if he ever had it) argues to the social and cultural elites that he ought to have power because he represents the only "authentic" vision of the needs and aspirations of his

constituency. He is the black, or the student, or she is the woman who speaks the way all blacks, or all students, or all women would speak if they didn't have "false consciousness." Until enough of the constituency can go through the consciousness-raising experience (that is to say, until they are "converted"), they will not have earned the right to be taken seriously. The person who accuses others of having a false consciousness may appear arrogant and patronizing, but then missionaries and convert-makers are rarely considered attractive or open-minded people. When you possess the truth and others are ignorant you can hardly be expected to treat them with respect. A missionary who has a capacity to listen and learn may be respected and will have a good chance of being effective. But those missionaries caught in rigid ideological visions rarely have the humility, the patience, or the personal security that are prerequisites for listening.[2] Society should be wary of those who accuse others of false consciousness; most murderous religious wars have been fought by just such people.

4. *Finally, there is the "victim" fallacy, or at least identification with the "victim."* Franz Fannon and the Brazilian Catholic educator Pauolo Friere have both insisted on the moral necessity of identifying with the victim. It is difficult to see how this is psychologically possible or how it is politically feasible, at least in a society where the victims are anything but the majority. Identifying with the victim presumably means unidentifying with your own groups, your own class, your own heritage, a process that in other contexts is known as alienation. Those most inclined to identify with the victim are probably those who are most likely to be alienated to begin with. Identifying with the victim provides some people with a justification for spewing hatred on their own families and friends, and of course on themselves. But if one is to identify with the victim it cannot be just with any victim. The upper middle class suburban housewife who is trying to finish her college degree and at the same time assuming the family role she both wants and thinks she ought to assume is not considered an appropriate "victim," for example. Nor is one to identify with the hard-working lower middle class black who is saving money to send his children to a private school, or with the Polish student in a commuter college who is the first of his family to go beyond high school. Such "victims" have false consciousnesses, and one must identify with "victims" who have "true" or "authentic" consciousness. When one successfully identifies with a true victim, one has acquired human and moral worth just as the victim himself, ipso facto, has such worth. Both the victim and one identifying with him can then legitimately make demands on the rest of the society, and of course they can engage in aggressive behavior toward their moral inferiors.

This sort of romanticism may well provide interesting conversations; people who agree with this stance will applaud you and reinforce your moral superiority. But in the United States at the present time it is no way to build an effective social movement, much less an effective political organization.

In summary, then, it seems to me that the social movements of the 1960s were only marginally successful, largely because they did not produce (with the exception of Dr. King) a leadership that was able to articulate to and for their constituencies over a sustained period their deeply felt needs and problems. The movements called public attention to serious social pressures, had marginal impact on some institutions, stirred up some opposition (but not as much as the backlash myth would have led us to believe), and accelerated somewhat the pace of social change. But the social and cultural dynamics that produced the movements will continue to operate after the movements have run out of steam. One may have to conclude on balance that now the movements must be judged as having lost important opportunities, principally because their leadership was seduced by media publicity and because of a propensity of some members of the society's elite to substitute for serious social analysis their own personal abasement to movement spokesmen.

Before turning to the specific case of the white ethnic movement I want to make one further comment about the movements of the 1960s. To a considerable extent they were more concerned about issues of symbol and respect than they were about issues of economics. Few of the movement leaders were themselves poor, and while they claimed to speak in the name of the poor and the oppressed, in fact more of the goals they struggled for and achieved were unlikely to improve the conditions of their constituents, be they bored suburban housewives, dehumanized students, or unemployed blacks.

Historians of the future may find it paradoxical that while the black movement talked about the poor it devoted much of its energies to finding better jobs for the black college-educated; while the women's movement talked about the oppressed suburban housewife it devoted much of its energy to obtaining better jobs for women professionals; and while the student movement talked about dehumanized students it put much of its time and energy into obtaining political power for student leadership. Desegregating lunch rooms, schools, and public transportation were important indeed for reasons of human dignity and respect, but they provided little economic payoff. Obtaining symbolic victories, such as the use of the term "Ms.," the use of "black" instead of "Negro," and student participation in faculty committees somehow assumed more importance than obtaining jobs for the black underclass, opportunities for part-time employment and education for upper middle class wives and mothers, and an improvement of the quality of the classroom instruction for the student masses.

A cynical interpretation would be to suggest that the movement leadership used the alleged oppression of its constituency as a pretext for enhancing its own social prestige, prerequisites, and payoffs. But it is not necessary to be cynical. In a country where the majority of the population is at least moderately comfortable, issues of respect and power can become very important. The student wishes to be treated with respect by his university, the college-educated woman wants respect from her family and the professional world, and the black college graduate wants respect from the white society. All three experience disrespect not so much from individuals as from a culture and a social structure that have not thought it important in the past to show them respect.

A passion for respect, then, is widespread in contemporary American society, and if the movements represent a search for it and for the political power that can guarantee it, they are indeed demanding something that large numbers of their constituents want too. The movement leaders may simply have made the fatal mistake of concluding that respect was so important that people would go to the barricades to obtain it. Those potential members of the movements whose physical situations were close to intolerable might have been ready to fight for an issue more basic than one of respect, and those who were attracted by that emphasis were not ready to fight. They had too much to lose. As the first social movements in history where respect was an important part of the agenda, the movements of the 1960s had a unique set of problems. Perhaps it can even be said of the women's movement and the black movement that at least they succeeded in increasing the amount of respect that women and blacks enjoy in American society. That is progress of a sort, probably more than the basic social and economic dynamics could have produced by themselves. Such an accomplishment is not unimportant, but a revolution it is surely not.

The "White Ethnic Movement". What then can one say about the "white ethnic movement" that seems to be creating so much concern among those American elites who seemed to have nothing but applause for the other movements? It would be simple to say that there is no such thing as a white ethnic movement. The white ethnic groups in the United States are not socially, economically, or politically oppressed. They are not dissatisfied with American society; on the contrary, they are pleased by it and loyal to it. The Irish, the Germans, and the Italians have prospered in the United States and have moved above the national average in income and education. They are above the average for those areas of the country in which they live. Eastern Europeans are lagging behind somewhat, but they cannot be considered among the economically disadvantaged. Nor is there any persuasive evidence that there has been a notable move to the political right by the ethnics, despite the mythology of the backlash. Almost half the Catholic population (48 per cent), for example, voted for George McGovern, which was substantially above the national average. Support for racial integration is no lower among the ethnics than it is for comparable non-Catholic white groups in northern cities. Irish and Italian support for integration is higher than the average. The alienated, angry, hostile hard hat ethnic is a fiction of liberal journalists and intellectuals. All existing research shows that from its beginning the Catholic ethnic was more likely to be opposed to the war in Vietnam than his native American counterpart. The image of the militant ethnic ready to rally to some devisive fascist movement is false. As Professor Thaddeus Radzialowksi remarks:

> During the first hundred years that the Polish community in Detroit has existed, the American view of the immigrant and his progeny has changed considerably. The brutish, antidemocratic ignoramus; the strikebreaking supplanter of honest American labor; the advance guard of anarchism and bolshevism; the mindless tool of the papal conspiracy was transformed by the 1940s into the kindly, gentle, slightly comic fellow who, waving his citizenship papers proudly, burbled heartwarming patriotic clichés in his broken, nightschool English. Now, he is again transformed into the racist hard-hat. These racial stereotypes, many of them conflicting, reveal much more about the projected hopes and fears of American society than they do about the immigrant.[3]

But what of the "ethnic revival" or the "resurgence of ethnicity" or the "new ethnic consciousness"? For one thing, it seems to me that ethnicity is not new; neither is it reviving nor resurging. But certain social and economic dynamics at work in American society have highlighted the ethnics in ways that are far more important than the emergence of any white ethnic movement.

1. First, certain American elites needed some explanation why their crusade to eliminate the effects of poverty and racism was not an immediate success. Blacks could not be blamed; that would by definition be blaming the victims. These elites could not be blamed, because they had already acknowledged and confessed their guilt and were busy identifying with the victims. Nor could they concede that some problems are solved only very slowly because that would be immoral "gradualism." Thus a scapegoat became necessary. The scapegoat could not come either from the top (where the elites were), or from the bottom of society. Only middle America remained—and that was where a substantial segment of the "blue collar ethnics" lived. Despite evidence that ethnics are now no more likely to be blue collar than anyone else, the label stuck. In order for this scapegoat group to be visible it had to be "rediscovered," studied, analyzed, and then converted to the cause of social justice. The ethnics had to be won away from their sins of racism and narrow self-interest. The elites, in other words, rediscovered the ethnic as enemy, or at least as sinner-to-be-converted.

2. By legitimating black cultural diversity, America legitimated other kinds of cultural diversity. Rather than discovering their own uniqueness, the ethnic groups now simply felt free to talk about it. In other words, ethnics have been permitted to rediscover themselves, and scholars have been permitted to do research on ethnics. In fact, however, the ethnics always knew that they were there and so did some scholars.

3. The ethnics want to be respected. To be Polish, Italian, Slovak, Slovene, Lithuanian, or even Irish is to be the object of greater or lesser amounts of disrespect and contempt among America's intellectual and cultural elites. As the man from Yale remarked, "If there is an inferior race, it has to be the Italians." Just as blacks, women, and Spanish-speaking are climbing into the upper middleclass professional and intellectual world, so are the Catholic ethnics. And they are becoming more and more conscious that they have been cast in the role of scapegoat for certain social ills. There is no evidence that the ethnics are any more angry at black militancy than anyone else in the society, but there is substantial evidence that they are angry at being typecast as society's worst racists, of being stereotyped as having stereotypes, of being treated with contempt on the grounds that they are more likely to have contempt for others. As Professor Joseph Schwab once remarked, "Students who are told that they should try to sympathize with Polish people as well as with black people turn up their noses in contempt. 'How could anyone sympathize with them?'"

It is in this context that ethnic spokesmen like Michael Novak must be understood. His anger at the Jewish and Anglo-Saxon dominated cultural world of New York City is not the same anger that the Slovak coal miners in Pennsylvania may feel about being stereotyped as racists and hard hats and pigs. Novak found that in the world of the intellectual elite he had to stop being a Slovak. For a while he was willing to go along with it, but then abruptly he changed his mind and protested vigorously the sacrifice demanded of him. The words may be different, but the sentiment is the same, whether it is the Slovak intellectual or the Slovak coal miner: "Goddamn it, treat us with respect!"

The cry is not dissimilar from that of the northern black, or the militant woman, or the militant Chicano. That the ethnics would make it too indicates that the cry need not be rooted in serious economic adversity.

It is interesting to note that Novak's most severe critics come from the Catholic intellectuals of somewhat older than his generation who have been accepted in the New York-Cambridge intellectual establishment. For all practical purposes they had to stop being Irish Catholics (whatever devotional affiliations they may have maintained with the Church). An Irish Catholic, in other words, could "make it" so long as he was not too obviously Irish or too blatantly Catholic. Novak's protest was in fact a severe judgment on those who had "sold out." It is small wonder that they reacted angrily. As an increasing number of ethnics make it into the intelligentsia, protests like Novak's may become more and more frequent.

In reading the literature of the white ethnic movement carefully,[4] one discovers how often the theme of respect is emphasized. To some extent the leaders of the white ethnic movement accept the elite stereotype that ethnic spokesmen like Novak and Barone clearly have more to do with respect than with economic improvement. (Barone, however, insists that one of the goals of his ethnic activities is an eventual coalition between blacks and ethnics that will create considerable social and economic change, benefiting both blacks and white ethnics.) One might even say that the leaders of the ethnic movement have somewhat more legitimate reasons for stressing symbolic goals than do leaders of the black movement—there are far fewer poor ethnics than poor blacks.

There are criticisms that can be leveled at some aspects of the ethnic movement. There is a tendency toward every one of the four fallacies discussed previously. That the ethnics comprise a "movement" at all reflects to some extent the fact that in American society today it seems that everybody has to have one to get any attention at all. Whether the ethnic spokesmen will articulate to, for, and with their potential constituency any better than leaders of the other movements have remains to be seen. One thing seems clear: The white ethnic movement does not and cannot represent a political, economic, or social backlash. The social dynamic of economic deprivation and suffering among the white ethnics to make such a thrust possible simply does not exist. I am not saying that there are no poor ethnics, but rather that the economic disadvantages experienced in the ethnic communities are not likely to produce violent or even militant political responses.

I can imagine two situations in which the white ethnic movement could become militant to the point of violence. Both cases would lead to the sweeping away of the present rather gentle movement leadership. First, the efforts to impose quotas on every dimension of American life imply a polarization of American society ("affirmative action" is a euphemism for quotas). If these efforts are successful, the ethnics may demand *their* quotas, and if they don't get them they may become inflamed.

Second, it is also possible that a serious attempt to redistribute income in American society might lead to a violent outburst of the ethnics. To what extent opposition to Senator McGovern was based on fear of income redistribution is not clear. Rightly or wrongly, those ethnics who are either just above or just below the line separating blue from white collar worker seem to be convinced that any major attempt to redistribute income will be done especially at their expense. They perceive that the minimun income level for those who do not or will not work will be pegged only slightly below what they earn through hard work. Those favoring redistribution will find it difficult to persuade the middle class ethnics of the justice of such a policy. The principal reason for this attitude is the widespread feeling among the ethnics that they are the ones who have had to pick up the tab for most of the social and economic changes of the last decade. They may be wrong, but the very fact that they feel that way is an important social reality that must be dealt with.

But short of polarization or leveling, neither of which seems imminent, the white ethnic movement will continue to be as moderate and gentle as Michael Novak and Geno Barone are. At the present time I do not think the ethnic movement has a very wide base of popular support. Indeed, it can scarcely be said to exist at all. But the thought that it is racist or fascist or a threat to American democracy is absurd.[5]

Should ethnicity be "encouraged" in its broader social and cultural and academic forms or in its movement manifestations? This is a question that is often asked of those who have chosen to articulate the ethnics' demand for respect and of those who are fascinated by ethnicity as an intellectual question with important social policy ramifications. It is, of course, an arrogant and patronizing question. Catholic ethnics scarcely need to be encouraged by anyone. They have struggled to economic and educational success in American society with precious little help from any of the society's professional do-gooders. If ethnics are able to earn greater respect for their own heritages by their political and organizational skills and power, then so be it. If the funding agencies can be persuaded to support cultural programs for the ethnic communities by plausible arguments from the leaders of those communities, fine. Such activities hardly need to be evaluated in terms of higher ethical questions. In other words, if in our pluralistic society, ethnic movements and ethnic organizations are able by the ordinary processes of conflict, competition, cooperation, and consensus to earn support and acceptance, then more power to them— literally as well as figuratively. If they are unable to do so, then society need not concern itself greatly about their failure.

There are few things more harmless in American society than the white ethnic movement. It is harmless in its leadership, its goals, and in the issues for which it is likely to mobilize support. Those who see in it the grim spectre of danger are, to paraphrase Professor Radzialowski, telling us more about themselves than they are about the white ethnic movement.

The problems of poverty are not solved in American society. Despite the evidence that great progress is being made, we still are either unwilling or unable to cope with the poverty of the old, the rural, and the father-absent family. And linked to the problem of poverty, though separable from it, is the problem of respect. In the short run, poverty is a more acute problem for American society, but in the long run, when our society can approach poverty-free levels, the problem of respect may assume greater importance and may actually threaten the pluralistic society. Can we really tolerate the diversity that we have brought to our shores? Can we really legitimate it by our political and cultural systems? Can we really live in trust and peace and even enjoyment with those who are not "our kind of people"? More important, can we solve the problems of poverty unless we learn how to respect those who are different from us? If the movement leadership that captured control of the Democratic party in 1972 had been able to respect the ethnic, the labor union leader, the blue collar worker, and even Richard J. Daley, might the country now be run by a very different coalition? Was the judgment of the Italians in Newark (as reported by Joseph Kraft) that "McGovern and his friends don't respect us" an indictment not only of McGovern but of a substantial segment of America's cultural elite?

Does one have to respect everyone—not only blacks, hippies, and women, but also Slovak philosophers, Italian monsignors, and shanty-Irish sociologists—to govern America? Since when were they victims?

NOTES

1. Black father-present families under age 35 in the North now earn about the same income as do comparable white families.

2. Some youthful activists have displayed impressive abilities at listening and learning when they work in the political precincts. Indeed, I suspect that a good deal of the political future of the country may well be shaped by those who have gone into the precincts with enthusiasm and open minds.

3. Thaddeus Radzialowski, "The View from the Polish Ghetto: Some Observations on the First Hundred Years in Detroit." Unpublished paper, Department of History, Southwestern Minnesota State College, Marshall, Minnesota, 1972.

4. See, for example, the works of Michael Wenk, F. M. Tomasi, and, particularly, Geno Barone, *Pieces of a Dream: The Ethnic Worker's Crisis with America.* New York; Center for Migration Studies, 1972.

5. Some of those involved in ethnic movements are of course not as moderate as Barone and Novak. One thinks of the Jewish Defense League, the Italian American Civil Rights League, and the followers of Anthony Imperiale in Jersey. I would contend that these are miniscule factions that have a certain capacity for nuisance value but ought not to be taken seriously either in themselves or as representatives of major components of American ethnic communities.

13.   AN ALTERNATIVE PERSPECTIVE FOR STUDYING AMERICAN ETHNICITY

IT IS THE INTENT of this chapter to suggest an alternative perspective for the study of those forms of differentiation in American society that are not attributable to social class (as this concept is normally understood), age, or sex. The most immediate concern of our inquiry will be the study of the descendants of those western European immigrant groups that have become the focus of much social science interest in recent years. However, the perspective (or "model," a word I would prefer to apply only to a perspective that can be stated in mathematical terms) can also be used to study differences based on race, religion, and geography.

"Ethnicity" in the narrow sense refers to the descendants of the European immigrants. "Ethnicity" in the wider sense refers to any differentiation based on nationality, race, religion, or language. Part of the problem in thinking clearly about ethnicity in the American context is that some groups that Americans think of as "ethnic" are constituted by religion (Jews), some by nationality (Poles), some by religion and nationality (Irish Catholics), some by race (blacks), some by language (Spanish-speaking—if indeed such an ethnic group exists), and one by region (Southerners—see Reed 1972). This chapter focuses mainly on ethnicity in the relatively narrow sense as constituted by religion and nationality; such a focus seems to me strategically the best place to begin.

Definitions of ethnicity abound. To a considerable extent the definition one chooses is a function of the "picture" or perspective from which one is making one's analysis or the point one wishes to make. For our present purpose an elaborate but sufficiently general definition of Schermerhorn (1969, p. 123) will be adequate:

> A collectivity within a larger society having real or putative common ancestry, memories of a shared historical past, and a cultural focus on one or more symbolic elements defined as the epitome of their peoplehood. Examples of such symbolic elements are: kinship patterns, physical contiguity (as in localism or sectionalism), religious affiliation, languages or dialect forms, tribal affiliation, nationality, phenotypical features, or any combination of these. A necessary accompaniment is some consciousness of kind among members of the group. This would place it in Bierstedt's category of "societal group."

Any comment on human society, whether it results from common sense analysis or rigorous scholarly research, inevitably utilizes perspectives or pictures or paradigms. Such tools are indispensable for the beginnings of analysis, and though they may be refined in the analytic process, they are rarely discarded. David Matza (1964, pp. 1–2) comments on the functions of such "pictures":

> Pictures are intimately related to the explanation of social systems. Systems of action may usually be typified in ideal fashion. Indeed, this simplification is almost mandatory if the analyst wishes to proceed to the task of explanation. A system, whether it be capitalism or delinquency, has exemplars, basic figures who perpetrate the system. The accurate characterizing of exemplars is a crucial step in the development of explanatory theory. Given the present state of knowledge, pictures are not true or false, but rather plausible or implausible. They more or less remind us of the many discrete individuals who make up a social category.
>
> Systems of action have exemplars, and a portrayal of them is a crucial step in the elaboration of causal theory. Thus, for example, a plausible picture of the capitalist was implicit in the various theories explaining the rise of capitalism. This hardly means that a system may be reduced to the character of exemplars; rather, an exemplar is a personification or microcosm of the system. A crucial step from a Marxian to a Weberian theory of the origins of capitalism consisted of a basic shift in the portrait of the exemplary capitalist. Somewhere in the dialectic between competing scholars the pirate capitalist of Marx was transformed to the bookkeeper capitalist of Weber. The more authentic ring of Weber's portrait is largely responsible for the more widespread acceptance of his rather than Marx's theory of the emergence of capitalism. Whatever the other virtues of Marx's theory, it suffers from an initial implausibility. It seems conceived on a false note. How, we ask, can we believe in a theory that apparently falsifies the character of the exemplars? Whatever the failings of Weber's theory, it seems more plausible because it is more reminiscent of the early capitalists we have studied or read about.

The assumptions contained in such pictures are both absolutely essential for social research and also dangerous for its goals: "they tend to remain beyond the reach of such intellectual correctives as argument, criticism and scrutiny. . . . Left unattended, they return to haunt us by shaping or bending theories that purport to explain major social phenomena" (Matza 1964, p. 1).

Two "pictures" shape most analyses of the ethnicity phenomenon: the domination (or oppression) picture, and the assimilation (or, in its more popular form, the "melting pot") picture.

The domination image (Mason 1970) is most frequently used in the study of colonialism. It is basically a conflict picture in which one group (white or mixed blood) is perceived as controlling and usually oppressing another

(usually nonwhite or native) group. The assimilation image is more accommo-
dationist in its assumptions and focuses on the adjustment of two cultures to
each other after encounter and interspersion. Its concerns are "culture
contact," in which the culture of the host society is threatened by the culture of
a numerically inferior but politically dominant group (Europeans on natives),
or "acculturation," in which the culture of the immigrant group is threatened
by that of a numerically and politically dominant host society. Both pictures
assume a strain toward homogenization—political and structural in the domination picture and social and cultural in the assimilation picture.

Both pictures or images are used to study American society, with the
domination perspective applying mostly to relationships between white and
nonwhite and the assimilation perspective applying mostly to relationships
among the various white groups, particularly between the so-called Anglo-
Saxon[1] and later immigrant groups. It is the inadequacy of the latter picture
that is the principal concern of this chapter.

The literature on assimilation in America is immense.[2] Some authors see the
process as rapid, others see it as slow. Some think it desirable that ethnic differentiation be eliminated so that a "common culture" may emerge, others
think that assimilation ought to be decelerated so that many different cultures
may flourish under the American umbrella. Gordon (1964) has distinguished
between "structural assimilation," in which ethnicity is no longer pertinent
even to primary group formation, and "cultural assimilation" (or acculturation), in which cultural differences diminish but the propensity to choose
primary group relationships from within one's own group persists. Gordon
argues that the latter process is far along in American society, while the former
proceeds much more slowly.

What all the assimilationist literature, popular and serious, sophisticated or
simplistic, assumes is that the strain toward homogenization in a modern industrial society is so great as to be virtually irresistible. The influences of the
common school, the mass media, common political and social norms, and
ethnic and religious intermarriage work toward the elimination of diversity in
a society. Basic beliefs, socialization styles, personality characteristics, political
participation, social attitudes, expectations of intimate role opposites, all tend
toward a similarity that is differentiated only by social class. Social class is
generally assumed to be a "rational" basis for differentiation as opposed to differentiation based on religion and national origin, which are "irrational."
Race was formerly an irrational focus for differentiation but is now rational.

The picture of American society as stated in the abstract categories of social
science or the concrete categories of popular journalism is one of many different cultures merging into one common "American" culture. Only minor differences (such as special foods) persist. It may be debated whether this merging
produces either a totally new culture that is a combination of its various

inputs, or whether in fact it is rather a matter of the various immigrant cultures adapting themselves to the host culture, which I shall term "Anglo conformity." Whatever theoretical position one may take, in practice, Anglo conformity is what is assumed to occur, even though a few immigrant items, such as Jewish humor and Italian food, may be taken over by the host culture. Once one assumes, as most of the literature does, that the immigrant culture is the dependent variable and the host culture the independent variable, Anglo conformity has entered one's model.

The assimilation picture is pervasive in American society. It is part of our popular folk wisdom as well as an important component of the repertory of pictures available to social science theorists. Politicians, TV commentators, movie critics, social planners, and reform political candidates all take it for granted. The picture has been wedged into our individual and collective unconscious, and has achieved the status not merely of conventional wisdom but of common sense.

There are two things that happen almost inevitably when such a picture becomes common sense. It becomes, as Matza suggested, undiscussed and undiscussable; it begins to become normative. It is now no longer a description of the way things are, it is a description of the way things ought to be. Data that do not fit the picture are ignored or discarded or subjected to the sorts of paralyzing questions against which no data can stand. Instead of being viewed as new and potentially very informative findings, such data are written off as irrelevant or even as potentially dangerous.

It is but a short step from being undiscussably *descriptive* for a picture to become *prescriptive*. The picture becomes not merely an ideal type, it becomes a norm. To untangle the strands of nativism, liberal optimism, vulgar Marxism, secular rationalism, and immigrant self-rejection that underpin the "melting pot" norm is a challenge to which practitioners of the sociology of knowledge might wish to respond. Sociology is supposed to involve questioning assumptions (even criticizing them, if we are to believe the younger members of the profession). That few have asked whether there might be other pictures for looking at the phenomenon of ethnic differentiation in American society besides the "official" assimilationist one, or the moderately revisionist version of it advanced by Gordon, seems to have been a major failure of the profession.

The most basic and fundamental assumption of the assimilationist picture is that in a modern society the forces working for homogenization—at least within broad social class groupings—are so powerful as to be irresistible. With the exception of research by Wilensky (1964), this assumption has been so deeply embedded in the collective unconscious that it is almost never questioned. But one need only look up from one's computer output or one's mathematical model or the latest issue of the *New York Review of Books* to realize that differentiation runs rampant in American society. Processes of homogenization and differentiation are going on simultaneously. We are, to put the matter in popular terms, becoming more like one another and more different from one another. A repertory of pictures of social reality that does not have room for paradoxical models may be neat, clean, and simple. Whether it is helpful for understanding human behavior is another matter.

The assimilationist perspective is indispensable for coping with the social reality of America. The Irish ethnic and the Polish ethnic who live next door to one another have far more in common than their great grandparents did—common language, common citizenship, and a common set of television channels. But in some ways they may be more dissimilar. Their grandparents were in all likelihood peasant farmers, but the two American ethnics may have totally different occupational perspectives. Certain differences rooted in historical heritages may persist between the two Americans with no signs of diminution. For example, more than a member of any other ethnic group, the Irishman is likely to be a political activist; the Pole is less likely. It is at least a researchable question as to whether in some respects the two neighbors are becoming increasingly different from one another. The Irishman may be defecting to the Republican party, while the Pole is much less likely to be doing so, for example. A whole set of pictures, or perhaps one extraordinarily elegant paradoxical picture, is required to do justice to this complex reality. The assimilation picture by itself simply won't do.

Certain limitations of the assimilation picture must be considered. It frequently turns out to be not particularly helpful in generating hypotheses or in ordering data. It is difficult to determine, for example, whether a set of findings we reported in Chapter 3 on the transmission of cultural heritage among the Irish and Italians shows a high rate of "acculturation" or a low rate. The assimilation perspective provided no clue as to why "acculturation" occurred more rapidly for the Italians on some items (attitudes toward the role of women, for example) and on others more rapidly for the Irish (importance of sustaining relationships with one's parents, for example). In other words, when we limit ourselves to the assimilation perspective many research findings on the differentiation among ethnic groups in the United States can neither be predicted nor interpreted.[3]

Glazer has observed that the ethnic groups came into existence in the United States;[11] but no one has seriously investigated the possibilities latent in such an assertion. As Fabian remarked, "It is often overlooked that immigrants when they arrive in a new country do not constitute a group or a community—they *may* become one over time" (Fabian 1972, p. 7).

The acculturation picture offers no insight into why there are presently some self-conscious attempts to create ethnic groups. In the Northeast, for example, there is a deliberate and self-conscious attempt to create a "Spanish-speaking" ethnic group (an attempt that is not supported, incidentally, in the

Southwest). An American Indian group is struggling to emerge, with some success; and in Chicago there is even an effort, as yet rather ineffective, to create an Appalachian white ethnic group. Cruse (1971) has also suggested that the black power movement is essentially an attempt to create a black ethnic group, a suggestion that Metzger (1971) has echoed from a very different perspective. The political and social leaderships concerned with the creation of ethnic groups must have insights into how power is exercised in the United States that are quite foreign to the acculturation picture.[4]

Similarly, the acculturation perspective does not take into account the fact noted by many historians that ethnicity was perceived by the immigrants as a way of becoming American. The hypen in the hyphenate American was a symbol of equality, not of inequality. In an urban environment where everyone including the native American was something else besides "American," one had to be an ethnic to find one's place on the map. Furthermore, Brown (1966) notes that the principal argument of the nineteenth and early twentieth-century Irish American nationalists who favored freedom for Ireland was that only when Ireland was a free and independent member of the family of nations would Irish Americans be accepted by the native Americans as being worthy of full-fledged American citizenship. And Greene (1968) has demonstrated that support among Polish Americans and Czech Americans for the nationalist movements in their native countries during World War I came only after the United States entered that war. Such support for free Poland and the new Czech republic was, paradoxically, an exercise in American patriotism more than an expression of Polish or Czech patriotism.

More historical research is obviously required, but there is sufficient reason to state, at least as a tentative hypothesis, that the creation of ethnic groups in the United States was a way for the immigrant population to look at its present and future in America rather than at its past in the Old World. In a complex society of an "unstable pluralism" (Kammen 1972) you had to be "something" if you were going to be "anybody." Such a view of social reality is obviously completely foreign to the acculturation picture.

The acculturationist assumes that "unstable pluralism" is a socially dangerous situation.[5] He expects social harmony to emerge out of the creation and reinforcement of a "common culture." In such a perspective the question becomes, How does a common culture emerge and how does it survive the assaults of periodic regressions to a rational differentiation?

One who operates in the acculturation perspective has no way of addressing himself to the question of how American society manages to keep from tearing itself apart despite its condition of unstable pluralism. During the last quarter of a century, when ethnic, racial, and religious violence has erupted all over the world, the United States has been relatively free from serious violence. The urban riots of the late 1960s were minor in comparison with those of Indonesia, Bangladesh, the Sudan, Burundi, and Ulster. Despite the unstable pluralism, which Kammen tells us worried Americans in 1700, there has been only one civil war, and that was mostly between two British American groups. The pertinent question ought to be not how one protects the "common culture" and propagates it, but rather what there is in the national culture that has legitimated considerable diversity while creating at the same time implicit protocols by which violent social conflict has been avoided in the main. The assimilationist perspective marvels at how homogenous American society is becoming, and hence sees no real need for striving to understand the nation's capacity for observing and coping with our complex racial, religious, nationality, geographic, and social differentiation, a differentiation that came into being in a relatively short period of time as the histories of human societies go.

Another problem with the acculturation picture is that is does not account for the self-conscious manipulation of ethnic symbols in American society, a manipulation which in the acculturation picture ought to be increasingly difficult and infrequent, but which in the social reality around us does not seem to be difficult at all and seems, if anything, to be more frequent in recent years. Polish and Italian self-consciousness, for example, can easily be written off as a response to black militancy. Yet it could also be argued that ethnic consciousness is merely a result of the fact that by accepting black self-consciousness the larger society legitimated the public manipulation of ethnic symbols, which in prior years had been manipulated privately. A particularly interesting example is the appearance of tricolor bumper stickers on the cars of many Italian Americans in the eastern United States. It is safe to assume that most of these self-conscious Italians came from southern Italy and Sicily where until fairly recently the tricolor represented the "foreign" domination of the Piedmontese. The Sicilians came to the United States and discovered that they were Italian Americans. Now they have discovered that they are Italian, a process exactly the reverse of that suggested by using only the acculturation picture. It is of course a research question as to how widespread the response is to such symbol manipulation. One would presume that sociologists would abstain from dismissing it as an irrelevant and unimportant phenomenon until they have studied it in detail.

As an alternative and complementary perspective, I would suggest the picture of "ethnicization" (Fabian's term) or "ethnogenesis" (a term used by David Greenstone in an NORC seminar) or "the creation of an ethnic group." Ethnic groups come into being in the United States and have a "natural history." The study of their genesis and history, free of the dogmatic assumption that their destiny is obliteration, can be useful in approaching both the history and the sociology of ethnic differentiation in the United States.

One need not subscribe to Lévi-Strauss's view of the binary differentiating propensities of the structure of the human mind[6] to be aware that humans code reality by differentiation. As Suttles (1972) has remarked, one creates neighborhoods so that one may have a chart of the city and know where one is going to encounter role-opposites whom one can reasonably trust. But the mental chart that divides the city into many different neighborhoods is only one of a considerable number of such charts that we carry around in our minds. There are microstructure charts that divide the family into parents and children, children into boys and girls or "big kids" and "little kids," for example. And there are macrostructure charts that divide the world or the human race or the population of the nation into various categories. Such categories enable us to engage in preliminary "coding operations" that help us to move in a tentative fashion through the maze of potential relationships that constitute human society. Even academics, proudly aloof from the prejudices and biases of ordinary men, still code their own departments, if not by cliques or factions, then at least by specializations and/or interaction networks. The pertinent question is not whether such charts exist but rather which chart is going to be imposed on what social phenomenon.[7] It is much like using overlays that drop down over the blank figure of the human body to show first the arterial system, then the venous, nervous, and musculature systems, until finally the picture is complete, though incredibly complex.

For purposes of preliminary coding, such differentiation is not necessarily binary, although there may be a basic binary division of potential role relationships—those in which you can be reasonably trusting and those in which you must be cautious about extending trust, for example. Nor need the differentiation be conflict-producing. While it is certainly true that most conflict flows from some form of differentiation, it is not true that differentiation necessarily leads to conflict. Indeed, Harris (1972) has pointed out that even in Ulster most Catholics and most Protestants are not in active conflict with each other, but rather live in a condition running anywhere from suspicious coexistence to reserved friendship.[8]

The pertinent question about American ethnicity, then, is not why there is differentiation in American society, but why the ethnic coding system becomes a relevant chart of differentiation for many Americans under certain sets of circumstances. Why, in other words, is ethnic identity important and useful for some Americans? In the present state of our knowledge, the most one can do is to hazard guesses that might be converted into research hypotheses.

First of all, while it is a truism that there are no native Americans, that everyone immigrated to the country at some time or other, it is frequently overlooked how recent this immigration was for many American families. Indeed, in the middle 1960s, half the American Catholic adult population was either first or second generation. If one believes in the power of the mass media and the common school to wipe the cultural and psychological slates clean in the space of a few decades, the persistence of ethnicity will come as a surprise.

But if one believes in a certain inertial strength of cultural traits and family memories, it is not at all surprising that collectivities which took their origin in a very recent immigration experience persist.

Secondly, as historians like Kammen, Mann, and Wood have made clear, American society was structured in its formative years by men who had a remarkably high degree of self-consciousness about the problems of cultural diversity, or, as Kammen (1972, pp. 73–74) calls it, "unstable pluralism."

> And so it was that American colonial history, which had begun with a quest for purity and homogeneity, ended with a sophisticated rationale for pluralism and heterogeneity. What had happened was not really so paradoxical as it may seem, for the so-called melting pot had been a boiling cauldron all along, from Jamestown to James Madison. There is a very real sense in which the American nation emerged, not in response to new-found national unity, but rather in response to provincial disunity, in response to a historical problem of long duration: how best to control unstable pluralism, how best to balance the areas of compulsion and freedom in American life.

Mann has pointed out in remarks made in NORC seminars that the early naturalization laws were remarkably tolerant about what it took to be an American. One merely had to accept the political principles of the Constitution and the Declaration of Independence. One was not required to give up one's religion or nationality, or even one's language (in fact, English as a requirement for citizenship was a twentieth-century innovation). Mann argues that the political philosophers who created the American republic were aware that they needed some sort of cultural cement to hold the republic together. They fell back on allegiance to eighteenth-century political theory, because they realized that the religious, geographic, and ethnic diversities that already existed made it impossible to use any other kind of cement. They were not easy with this device. As George Washington remarked, "The more homogeneous our citizens can be made . . . the greater will be our prospect of permanent union" (Kammen 1972, p. 74). Tyack (1966) observes that Benjamin Rush may have been the first to have introduced the idea of "melting," although he was concerned about the diversity of the states. He advocated a federal university where "the youth of all the states may be melted (as it were) together into one mass of citizens" (Tyack 1966, pp. 31–32).

However much they may have lamented "unstable pluralism," those who created the structure of federalism had no choice but to build a political apparatus that could deal with it, and by the very fact that the structure was so tolerant of differentiation (although many American citizens were less tolerant) there was considerable opportunity for later immigrants to create their own interest groups that would correspond to those they already saw existing in the society (and not all of them were by any means social class groups). Madisonian federalism was designed, as Wood (1969) and Levine (1972) have suggested, to absorb the dynamisms of unstable pluralism by a process of government through compromise and coalition formation. The immigrants soon discovered, unconsciously and unexplicitly perhaps, that to be part of the coalition formation game required having a collectivity of one's own. Since the rest of society categorized people on the basis of nation of origin, it seemed sensible to go along with the process and use it for one's own political, economic, and social advantage.

Ethnicity reveals itself as a relatively safe form of differentiation. While there may be conflict and competition among the various ethnic groups, the conflict is rarely violent. Society has implicitly legitimated ethnic differentiation (if not required it) and has provided protocols and processes whereby the potential conflict that could arise from such differentiation is minimized. The immigrants never saw their claim to be hyphenated Americans as involving any danger of tearing apart the new society, which on the whole was relatively benign to them. While they may have been charged with being un-American on occasion and, more often, suspected of not being American enough, they never realistically perceived themselves as being a threat to the relative peace and harmony in the society. Despite the fears of the advocates of a "common culture" and assimilation, ethnic differentiation was never a serious threat to the social order.

Furthermore, it provided the immigrants and their children and grandchildren with considerable political, social, economic, and psychological advantages. The ethnic group became one of the avenues to political power for immigrants. It provided a special market in which the emerging business and professional class within the immigrant community could build its own economic base. It offered a social mobility pyramid that the more ambitious immigrants could ascend; if the social pyramid of the host culture was inaccessible, they could at least move to the social apex within their own collectivity. And psychologically, it provded continuity between the Old World and the New and made possible the preservation of a minimum of family values that were thought to be essential. To say that any of these functions has diminished importance for the children and the granchildren of the immigrants is to make a dogmatic assertion and to advance a hypothesis that has not been supported by research evidence.

The ethnic collectivity served as a context in which certain skills, traits, and characteristics brought from the Old World and proven advantageous in the New could be preserved and strengthened. Did hard work and intellectual ambition prove extremely helpful in American society? Such work and ambition could be reinforced by telling children that it was an especially Jewish trait, and to be good Jews they must develop it. Did a certain kind of informal political skill open up avenues to power and prestige? Then such political skills could be legitimated and reinforced on the grounds that they were Irish. Even more than this may be said. The conviction that a particular trait or style of behavior is characteristic of one's "own kind" legitimates that behavior style or trait. at least in one's own mind.

No differentiation is without costs, but the costs of ethnic differentiation in American society are modest—if one is white. There are certain clubs and certain buildings and certain companies from which Jews are excluded. There are similar, if more subtle, biases against Catholics (particularly southern and eastern Europeans, along with occasional Irish victims). All the white ethnic groups, however, have managed to achieve moderate economic success in American society (and the Irish and the Jews, major success) despite nativist bigotry. As we reported in Chapter 2, members of eastern and southern European groups under age 40 have achieved something better than parity with their British American neighbors (even holding region and city' size constant to eliminate the advantage the immigrants have from living in the North and in the cities). There were and are, of course, certain severe psychological costs, and the emphasis on "respect" among some of the current militant ethnic groups indicates how heavy these costs may have been for some people. Many ancestral memories had to be repressed (the Irish have been particularly successful at this repression) for one to become thoroughly American. But given the situations the immigrants left behind, the costs of ethnic differentiation seemed relatively minor compared to the benefits the new society was capable of bestowing on them, or, more precisely, benefits that could be wrested from the host society if one was prepared to join with one's own kind to create a more equal match.

Ethnic differentiation, then, turns out to be safe, to involve a number of important payoffs, and to be relatively inexpensive. Under such circumstances, it would be surprising if ethnic groups did not emerge. Implicit in this perspective is the notion that ethnicity is not a residual social force that is slowly and gradually disappearing; it is, rather, a dynamic, flexible social mechanism that can be called into being rather quickly and transformed and transmuted to meet changing situations and circumstances. The coming-into-being and the transformation and transmutation of the ethnic collectivity constitute extremely useful foci for social research. Fabian (1972, p. 16) argues that ethnicization is the "process by which immigrants from one society become ethnic in another." She describes the process as follows:

> People, while living in their own society, take their culture and identity to a great extent for granted. When, due to some historical circumstances, they leave, this unproblematical nature of reality

> disappears. But questions of cultural identity arise only when immi-
> grants are asked by the host society, "Who are you?" Significantly,
> the question, the context within which self-identification is
> requested, and the evaluation placed upon it are in terms of another
> culture which in some sense predetermines the answers. Hence the
> self-identification of the immigrant is not merely a reflection upon
> the old culture, [it is] also a response to a question posed by the
> host society in terms of its own categories.

But if we grant that the process Fabian describes seems to be a reasonable account of what has happened, we are still faced with the question of why the boundaries of the ethnic collectivity are not more rigid, and why ethnic identification is not even more important in American society than it seems in fact to be. Surely it is not nearly as decisive in the United States as it is, let us say, in the north of Ireland or Belgium—to say nothing of Cyprus or Nigeria. On the contrary, the chart of differentiation provided by the ethnic overlay may be useful in American society, but even for the relatively recent immigrant it is by no means the only chart he has at his disposal. He quickly discovers that while there are ethnic boundaries in the United States the boundaries are permeable, especially for someone who has made or is in the process of making a great deal of money. But whence comes this permeability?

It might be argued that the most striking aspect of American ethnic differentiation is that by definition ethnic boundaries are *supposed* to be permeable. In other countries (one thinks again of Ulster, Belgium, and Nigeria) ethnicity is considered a way of finding oneself in a systematic way as being "over against" the rest of society. Under such circumstances, ethnic differentiation by definition implies ethnic separation. But among white groups (and the theory becomes a dilemma on the subject of nonwhite groups) in the United States ethnicity has never been primarily a means of separation, much less isolation. As we remarked earlier, the hyphen denotes equality; it is not a way of withdrawing from the rest of society so much as an institution for dealing oneself into the society. The ethnic collectivity does indeed provide a rationale for self-definition, and in all self-definitions there is implicit some sort of separation from those who do not have the same self-definition. But even the ethnic self-definition in the United States is more concerned with defining oneself as part of the American society and not separate from it. Under such circumstances ethnic group boundaries are permeable, because the political and social culture has decreed that they ought to be permeable and because they have been so structured.

It is also required, both by the national, political, and social culture and by the implicit constitutional structure, that membership in an ethnic collectivity be optional. One has the right, American society assumes, to be an ethnic if one wants to be, but one is under no obligation to be an ethnic. In practice, of course, it is easier for some individuals to dispense with their ethnic identification than it is for others. Blacks, Chinese, Japanese, American Indians, to some extent Chicanos and perhaps to a lesser extent Puerto Ricans and Cubans would find it difficult indeed to persuade other members of society that they are not part of the ethnic group to which they have been assigned. But in theory and to a considerable extent in practice the ethnic collectivity is a community of "limited liability" (to lift a phrase from a different but related discussion), one of the many such communities of limited liability that are available to an American. Whether and when a person chooses to so identify himself in his own thinking is completely up to him, and in theory, though scarcely yet in practice, such decisions ought to be accepted by others. To return to the image of the overlay, the ethnic chart is available to be used or not, frequently or rarely, whenever one wishes to code the possible relationships that are available. The pertinent research question is, who uses this chart and when? As the distinguished political philosopher, Martin Dooley, put it (Dunne 1898, pp. 54–56):

> An Anglo-Saxon, Hinnissy, is a German that's forgot who was his parents. . . . I'm an Anglo-Saxon. . . . Th' name iv Dooley has been th' proudest Anglo-Saxon name in th' County Roscommon f'r many years. . . . Pether Bowbeen down be th' Frinch church is formin' th' Circle Francaize Anglo-Saxon club, an' me ol' frind Dominigo. . . . will march at th' head iv th' Dago Anglo-Saxons whin th' time comes. There ar're twenty thousan' Rooshian Jews at a quarther a vote in th' Sivinth Ward; an', ar-rmed with rag hoods, they'd be a tur-r-ble thing f'r anny inimy iv th' Anglo-Saxon 'lieance to face. Th' Bohemians an' Pole Anglo-Saxons may be a little slow in wakin' up to what th' pa-apers calls our common hurtage, but ye may be sure they'll be all r-right whin they're called on . . . I tell ye, whin th' Clan an' th' Sons iv Sweden an' th' Banana Club an' th' Circle Francaize an' th' Pollacky Benivolent Society an' th' Rooshian Sons of Dinnymite an' th' Benny Brith an' th' Coffee Clutch that Schwartzmeister r-runs an' th' Tur-rnd' yemind an' th' Holland society an' th' Afro-Americans an' th' other Anglo-Saxons begin f'r to raise their Anglo-Saxon battle cry, it'll be all day with th' eight or nin people in th' wurruld that has th' misfortune iv not bein' brought up Anglo-Saxons.[9]

I shall recapitulate here by proposing four schematic charts. The nonsociological reader must realize that we sociologists are fond of such charts, and that we cheerfully concede that they are bare bones oversimplifications of reality. Nonetheless, as Otis Dudley Duncan has remarked, the most obvious use of such charts is that they force us to make clear and explicit exactly what implicit causal explanations underlie our prose. For the sociological reader I must note that my charts are not path analyses in any technical sense. It might be possible to use path analytic techniques to suggest some of the assumptions implicit in the causal diagrams here, but these particular charts are not recursive models. They are designed to show the direction of influence on the culture systems of the immigrants through time and an increasing number of generations since immigration and experience with the common school. Each chart represents one of the perspectives on ethnicity discussed earlier.

Figure 1 presents the Anglo conformity perspective. Host and immigrant culture systems are separate. Through time, as the immigrants extend their generations in the United States and experience the influence of the common school (and one might wish to include the mass media as "educational"), they become more and more like the hosts. Finally, at a certain moment either in the present or yet to come, host and immigrant are part of one common American culture, which remains the Anglo-American host culture.

Each box is a collection of myriad cultural variables. The chart suggests that on each of these cultural variables the immigrants become more and more like the host as generation and education increase. The most obvious test of the validity of this perspective is whether when generation and education are controlled the differences between the hosts and the immigrants disappear. Since there is a strong correlation between education and generation, controlling for one is for all practical purposes the same as controlling for the other. Nonetheless, whenever possible we will take into consideration the impact of both education and generation. Unfortunately, many of the data sets available to us lack generational information. To the extent that one finds cultural variables on which the immigrants still differ from the hosts when education and generation are held constant, the Anglo conformity perspective loses some

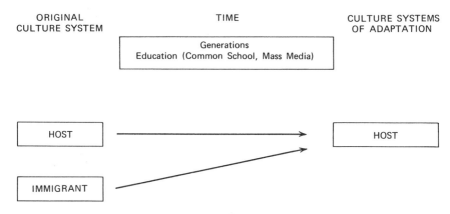

Figure 1. Anglo conformity perspective.

of its utility. But the defenders of this perspective could argue that the amount of time necessary to effect assimilation is not sufficient. It is still taking place, they might contend, and will be accomplished in the future. One might respond, however, that if those groups who are well into their fourth generation continue to be different, the Anglo conformity perspective leaves much to be desired.

The "melting pot" usually means Anglo conformity. However, in its more romantic statements, such as in Israel Zangwill's famous play, the concept has a slightly different meaning. In Figure 2 the movement is not completely of immigrant toward host, but of host and immigrant toward each other, so that the common American culture that emerges is a combination of two cultures, though it is never clear how much and what the host culture absorbs from the immigrant. Such a model is difficult to test since we do not have measures on the host culture at the time of specific immigrant group arrivals. Certain limited tests might be made, however. One could, with enough patience and resourcefulness, measure the diffusion of Italian food on menus in American restaurants in the past 70 years, or the diffusion of black slang expressions among those who speak white English, or perhaps the diffusion of the celebration of St. Patrick's Day. Clearly the creation of a common culture in which each group shares some of the culture traits of the others does occur in American society, but whether the melting pot is an important process in American society in this sense must be considered problematic.

A third perspective (Figure 3) is that of the classical cultural pluralism position as enunciated by Kallen. The immigrant does become like the host to some extent; hence the line jogs upward. He becomes an American citizen, he commits himself to American political values, he learns the English language and enjoys the common mass media as well as the media of his own group. This is cultural pluralism as it exists in countries like Switzerland, Holland, Ulster, Ceylon, and perhaps some African countries.[10] However, few observers think that this kind of cultural pluralism exists in the United States, although certain black and Chicano groups advocate such a pluralism for their own communities. There are unquestionably small groups in the society, mostly

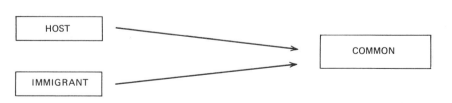

Figure 2.   Melting pot perspective.

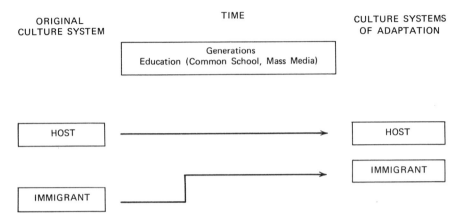

Figure 3. Cultural pluralism perspective.

rural (though the Hassidic Jews in Williamsburg are certainly urban), that have been able to sustain something very much like the classical picture of cultural pluralism.

However, when most contemporary defenders of ethnic diversity speak of cultural pluralism they mean something like the perspective that is presented in Figure 4. Milton Gordon has labeled this perspective "acculturation but not assimilation."[11] This position sees the immigrant absorbing large numbers of cultural traits from the host, and the host picking up a few traits from the immigrant. What emerges is a common culture that both immigrant and host share. But because "acculturation" occurs it does not follow that "assimilation" does too. Some cultural traits still distinguish host from immigrant; in particular, the two groups maintain some distance from one another in the private spheres of their lives. Intermarriage does occur, of course, but at a substantially lower rate than if the choice of marriage partner occurred in-

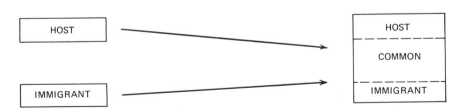

Figure 4. Acculturation but not assimilation perspective.

dependent of ethnic background. Similarly, close friends, recreation partners, and informal associates are far more likely to be chosen from one's own ethnic community than from the common pool of society. Put quite simply, when people are free to choose they tend to choose from their own kind—even though they share large numbers of cultural traits with other groups in the society.

In a limited sense the fourth perspective is simplicity itself to test. One attempts to determine whether marriage is independent of religio-ethnic background. As Harold Abramson has demonstrated,[12] the ethnic factor is still pertinent in a choice of spouse, though less than it used to be. One also might ask whether the immigrant and the host continue to be different on a certain number of cultural traits, and whether these differences persist within educational and generational groups. Those who doubt the utility of the acculturation-assimilation perspective might respond to such a test by saying that the differences that persist are declining, and in any event the variables being measured are not "important." Usually those who argue in such fashion find the Anglo conformity perspective more to their taste. The acculturation-assimilation perspective was close to my own at the time I began the research for this volume. Much of the analysis in this book would support the contention that the assimilation-acculturation perspective is still useful, although I would be hard put to refute an assertion from those who favor the Anglo conformity perspective that its utility is declining. But this is only because neither they nor I have much in the way of data from the past from which trend lines could be projected through the present measurements into the future.

My choice of language in these pages has been deliberate. I have spoken of "perspectives" and "utility." I believe that we are dealing with different ways of looking at American society. If all four perspectives described in this chapter have their utilities and limitations, if this book is an argument that ethnic pluralism persists in American society, it is also implicitly an argument that there must be a pluralism of perspectives for considering the phenomena of unity and diversity within that society. In the final chapter I suggest a new perspective that attempts to combine and supplement the other four. Suffice it for the present to say that I think Anglo conformity, cultural pluralism, mixing of cultures, and "cultural but not structural" assimilation (to use Gordon's words) are all going on, have gone on since the beginning of ethnic immigration in the United States, and are likely to continue for at least as long as any of us are concerned about such matters.

The reader will have noted, of course, that I assume only two groups of cultural system, host and immigrant. Obviously, there have been many immigrant groups, depending on time and place of arrival, and probably many host groups too. There is no reason to assume that each immigrant group has moved its way along the lines of my charts at the same pace and in the same fashion. Their numerical size, education upon arrival, internal cohesion, resources provided them by their religion, skills and sophistication of their religious and political leaders—all of these factors and a host of others too affect the process of merging with and adjusting to the host cultures. In an ideal world the four perspectives would be applied to each of the immigrant groups, and even then we would still have the problem of the interaction of the immigrant groups one with another. For example, it is quite reasonable to suppose on the basis of the historical evidence available to us that German Catholics, Polish Catholics, and Italian Catholics experienced encounters not only with the dominant Protestant Anglo-American group but also, and perhaps more importantly, with the Irish Catholic group, which ran (and to a considerable extent still does) the Roman Catholic church.[13]

These charts, then, may be a somewhat pathetic attempt to schematize a reality of extraordinary variety and complexity, but they are a beginning.

What we are suggesting, then, is a picture of American ethnic differentiation that sees immigrants forming collectivities of limited liability based on presumed common origin, because these collectivities are tolerated and even encouraged by the larger society, provide substantial payoff with marginal risks, and incur only limited costs. In addition to studying the acculturation of immigrants we should also be studying their ethnicization, that is to say, the genesis and natural history of such collectivities. And we should be studying them fully conscious that they are dynamic flexible mechanisms that can grow and change, whose disappearance ought not to be assumed on a priori grounds.

The fifth figure is a development of the four perspectives on ethnicity I presented earlier. It schematizes the "ethnicization" perspective, and is in some measure an extension of the acculturation-assimilation perspective shown in Figure 4. There are a number of important differences, however.

Figure 5 shows that the host and immigrants may have had something in common to begin with. Some of the Irish, for example, spoke the English language and understood something of the English political style of the eighteenth and nineteenth centuries. The other European groups were part of the broad Western cultural inheritance. Under the influence of education, generation, and the experiences in American society both at the time of immigration and subsequently, the common culture grows larger. Immigrants become more like the host, and the host may become somewhat more like the immigrants. Certain immigrant characteristics persist, but in addition, under the impact of the experience of American life, some traits become more rather than less distinctive. Certain aspects of the immigrant heritage are emphasized and developed in response to the challenge of American society. What appears at the end (the right-hand portion of the figure) is that the ethnic group has a

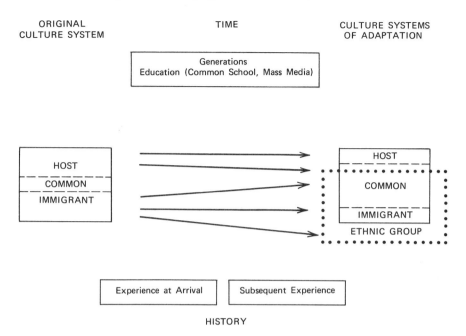

ORIGINAL
CULTURE SYSTEM

TIME

CULTURE SYSTEMS
OF ADAPTATION

Generations
Education (Common School, Mass Media)

HOST

COMMON

IMMIGRANT

HOST

COMMON

IMMIGRANT

ETHNIC GROUP

Experience at Arrival

Subsequent Experience

HISTORY

Figure 5. Ethnogenesis perspective.

cultural system that is a combination of traits shared with other groups and traits that are distinctive to its own group. For the ethnics, then, the mix of traits and the emphasis within the cultural system are different from those of their immigrant predecessors. They share more with the common culture than they did to begin with, but in some respects they also may be more different from the descendants of the hosts than their ancestors were from their hosts. In principle there is nothing to prevent testing of the various components of my perspective. In practice, however, an immense amount of social and historical research will be required. It is worth noting, incidentally, that while all the lines in Figure 5 are straight, in the reality this chart attempts to schematize the lines might well be jagged. For example, if one considers the variable of ethnic consciousness as part of the original immigrant system of traits, that consciousness may well have waxed and waned through the years, moving away from the common culture, then toward it, and away again in zigzag fashion.

In Figure 5 I have tried to combine the four previous perspectives on American ethnic diversity within a rather more broad and precise framework. I may have only complicated something already too complex. But the influence of the immigrant groups' experiential history in this country and in the country of origin toward the creation of distinct cultural systems is too important to ignore.

There are two knotty problems to which our picture can at best provide only partial solutions. The first is the question of ethnic origin versus ethnic identification. Approximately three-quarters of the American public can give an ethnic identification, and approximately two-thirds have little trouble specifying one such identification. But identification may not indicate that one's origins are not mixed. Thus one professional colleague, when asked the nationalities of his four grandparents, claimed French, Dutch, Scots, Irish, and Sioux Indian ancestry. But when he was asked his ethnic identification he replied "Irish." Such responses raise two questions. First, How do those of mixed ethnic origins determine which identification they are going to choose? And second, To what extent does such a choice lead to attitudes and behavior that the chooser defines as being pertinent to the identification he has given himself? Would a "mixed ethnic" with Indian and Irish "blood" in him be more inclined, for example, to political activism because he has defined himself as Irish, and political activism is an "Irish thing"?

The solution to the problem of identification versus origin is in principle relatively easy. One simply asks both sets of questions and analyzes the interactions between definition and origin—at least one does so if one has a mammoth sample base that permits the vast variety of cross-tabulations that would be necessary.

But a far more complex problem is the question of the relationship between ethnic identification and ethnic culture. Three terms must be briefly defined. By "ethnic identification" we mean the place in which one puts oneself in the ethnic chart. By "ethnic heritage" we mean the explicit and conscious recollection of one's past history, either in the Old World or in the United States. By "ethnic culture" we mean attitudes, personality styles, and behaviors that correlate with ethnic identification (or ethnic origin, as the case may be). Thus when an American asserts that he is Polish, he has given his ethnic identification. When he becomes interested in the pro-Jewish legislation of King Casimir the Great and King Stefan Bartori or the Polish involvement in the Little Steel Strike of 1937, he is concerned about his ethnic heritage. When he and his fellow Poles prove more likely on election day to vote than Americans of any other ethnic group and also more likely to vote Democratic, they are manifesting a Polish ethnic culture trait, which probably has far more to do with the experience of the Polish American collectivity than anything in the Polish ancestral past. Ethnic culture, then, is composed of those attitudinal and behavioral traits that correlate with the specific sort of ethnic identification.

Identification, heritage, and culture apparently interrelate in different ways at different times in the natural history of an ethnic group. Thus the American

Irish whose ethnic identification may be somewhat weak and whose consciousness of ethnic heritage is weak indeed nonetheless display cultural traits that make them considerably different from other Americans, whether the others be Protestants or their fellow Catholics.

The sorting out of the interrelations of heritage, culture, and identification is a task not even begun. But if one sees the interaction of these three variables as being a part of the natural history of the ethnic group—indeed perhaps the most important part of that natural history—one at least has perspectives from which to begin. Furthermore, one will be fully prepared for the increase in explicit concern about ethnic heritage and the increasingly explicit use of the ethnic identification chart that seems to be occurring among some American ethnic groups at the present time.

To put the matter somewhat differently, one can only begin to explain the considerable cultural diversity that still exists among American ethnic groups if one begins to investigate the natural history of such groups. There seems to be no way in which sociologists and historians can avoid cooperating with each other on this project. One must first of all know something about the land of origin at the time of migration. One must know which stratum or strata of the society migrated and under what sets of circumstances migration occurred— were they poor, impoverished, half-starving illiterate peasants, as were the Famine Irish, or well-educated middle class professionals, as were many of the post-World War II "DPs"? What was the economic, political, and social situation in the United States when they arrived? In which parts of the country did they tend to settle? Were Swedes more welcome than Italians, and what impact did this have on both the natural history and the culture of those immigrant groups, for example? What kinds of occupational choices did the immigrants make and in what directions did these choices point for the second, third, and fourth generations? (Young Irish Catholics are more than three times as likely to choose law as a career than the national average—and apparently quite independently of whether they think of themselves as Irish. Is this the result of family career patterns that their grandparents and great grandparents set by taking the jobs provided by the political machines in the late nineteenth and early twentieth centuries?) Where did the collectivity of immigrants fit in the ethnic stratification system that emerged during the immigrant years? Were the Italians, for example, at a particular disadvantage because the Irish had already preempted the best political positions in both the civil and ecclesiastical structures, and showed no signs of giving them up? What cultural characteristics, perhaps reinforced by simplistic references to ethnic heritage, were especially functional or especially dysfunctional in the early and later years of ethnic group history? What geographic differences exist in ethnic groups? (The Chicago Irish claim to be appalled at the parochialism of the Irish in Boston and New York.) Does it make a difference if a group's immigration to the United States was spread rather evenly over a long period of time, as was the German, or happened relatively quickly, in the space of two or three decades, as was the case with the Poles and the Italians? What is the impact of internal conflicts within the ethnic collectivities— between Catholics and agnostics in the Czech community or Catholics and Lutherans in the Slovak community, for example? In particular, what is the impact of the conflict between different "waves" of immigrants within the same collectivity? Most of the eastern European groups are split into pre-1920 and post-1945 segments, for example. Hungarians and Czechs have a third group made up of those who emigrated after the Hungarian revolution of 1956 and the ill-fated Dubcek spring in Czechoslovakia in 1968. The old immigrants tend to regard the more recent arrivals as foreigners and the more recent immigrants tend to dismiss their predecessors as peasants. There is of course a considerable amount of truth in both labels.

Perhaps the single most important issue to be faced both by the historian and the sociologist is the question of family structure and childhood socialization practices, for these two phenomena represent the basic mechanisms by which ethnic culture and implicit ethnic heritage are transmitted. They are also likely to play a fairly important part in determining how important and how self-conscious ethnic identification is likely to be.

It is well to remember, incidentally, that to the extent that they were shaped by Old World culture, ethnic heritage and ethnic culture antedated the existence of the ethnic group. The Irish, for example, had a strong propensity for drink and political activism long before an Irish American ethnic group came into existence. In this perspective, then, it is not surprising to find that neither political activism nor excessive drinking correlates with strength of Irish identification or explicit concern about Irish heritage. Glazer and Moynihan (1970) address themselves to the question whether the ethnic group is a bearer of cultural heritages or perspectives. I might suggest the following answer: Those who belong to ethnic groups apparently transmit certain culture patterns to their offspring, but these culture patterns may have existed before the ethnic group came into being and can be transmitted with little explicit reference to the ethnic group. Culture transmission, in other words, does go on within the group but, at least up to a point, not necessarily because of the group.

Viewing American ethnicity from the perspective taken in this chapter, a number of specific kinds of research activities are appropriate:

1. Detailed studies should be made of different ethnic collectivities in American society. Zeman (1973), in work still under way, contends that the "path" to acculturation for some groups (most notably the Irish) is different from that of other groups (most notably, eastern Europeans). It is not merely that the Irish learned American ways more quickly. Different factors seem to facilitate this learning for the Irish than facilitate similar learning for eastern

Europeans (parochial schools, for example). Thus it becomes necessary to do comparative studies of the emergence and development of different ethnic collectivities. Some groups might be chosen for their inherent interest. The Greeks, for example, have met great success in the United States, yet maintain tight communal boundaries (Chock 1969). Other groups might be chosen because they are large but little is known about them. The Poles and the Irish Protestants are a mystery to almost everyone. Still others might be studied because their culture survives despite a low level of self-conscious ethnic identification. The Irish Catholics would be the most obvious example of this phenomenon.

2. Within groups, the various "waves" of immigrants might be studied. In the eastern European communities the interaction between pre-1945 and post-1945 immigrants might reveal much about the internal dynamics of ethnic group creation.

3. Far more careful and detailed research is required on the subject of diversity of family role definition and structures in the various ethnic collectivities. In work in progress, McCready and Greeley (1973) have uncovered considerable variety in the relationships between husband and wife, children and parents, mother and son, and father and daughter in the different ethnic groups. Indeed, family structure differences are apparently greater than differences in political attitudes and behavior, differences that are considerable. Given the possibility that there might be a relationship between differences in childhood experiences and differences in adult political behavior, it would make sense to study these two phenomena simultaneously. Research on family structures is also of high priority, because it seems reasonable to assume that the basic cultural values, which differ among the various groups, are transmitted in a familial context and especially during the early years of life.

4. While very large samples will be required, it is important to determine what ethnic identification (if any) and what ethnically linked cultural traits may be transmitted to the children of ethnically mixed marriages. Does a young person assume the identity and/or the cultural propensities of his father or those of his mother, the parent of the same sex or of the opposite sex, the better educated parent or the parent who exercises the most influences in the family? Those who are interested in studying American ethnic groups often say that the ethnic groups vanish after intermarriage, but there is no evidence to support such an assertion. The child of a Polish mother and an Italian father may choose to define himself as Polish or Italian or Italian-Polish or even only as American, but he is not likely to think of himself as Anglo-Saxon. His personality may show traits that are more frequent in Poles or Italians, but he is not likely to display a constellation of Yankee or Jewish traits.

5. While cross-national research is now being written off in some quarters as a passing fashion, there is reason to think that on the subject of ethnic diversification cross-national research would provide a rich intellectual payoff. One

strategy would be to include in a sample of nations as much variety as possible. One could study ethnicity in India, Kenya, Ceylon, and the United States, for example. If one's goal (and I confess it to be mine) is to understand American ethnicity, the most effective kind of study would concentrate on countries that are rather like the United States. Thus one would study nations with an English heritage, a racial problem, and a continental European immigration. Canada, Australia, New Zealand, and the United States are good examples. What differences and similarities are there in their problems of racial, religious, and nationality diversity? All that exists at present is the most sketchy of impressionistic data. If comparable national surveys were to be done in these countries, the most appropriate foci of such surveys would appear to be political behavior and family structure and role differences.

6. Another variety of the cross-national strategy would be to study the emigrants from those nations that have gone to different receiving nations. Germany, Italy, and Ireland, for example, have sent large populations to many different countries. What are the differences and similarities of adaptations to the various countries? What survives from the culture and heritage in different contexts and what does not? What is the developmental process of an ethnic group in one country as opposed to the development of its cousin group in another country? Are there contexts that are more conducive and others that are less conducive to "ethnogenesis"? (Our impression is that the context in Canada is more conducive to ethnogenesis than is the context in the United States, while in Australia the context is less conducive than in the United States.) The Irish might well be the most interesting and the most feasible of the European groups to study. They migrated in considerable numbers to all the English-speaking countries (including Great Britain), they came in most cases with a command of the language and with a religious institution and faith to hold them together, and proved reasonably successful in every country they entered. One would need to add only Great Britain and the Republic of Ireland to the list of former British colonies suggested as subjects for cross-national research in the previous paragraph.

Such a listing of needed research projects, while hardly exhaustive, shows that the perspective advocated in this chapter does have the power to produce questions that can be answered by specific empirical research activities.

Finally, are there any social policy implications to the alternative perspective suggested in this chapter? Does the ethnogenesis picture have anything to say about the agonized question that is frequently raised not only by policy-makers but also by researchers? Is ethnicity a "good thing"? Our picture seems to suggest that the issue is not whether ethnicity is a good thing but whether the question itself is a good question. Indeed, there has been considerable social dysfunction in the "unstable pluralism" that has characterized America since at least 1700. But it may well be that the structures and institutions of the political and social culture that were devised to cope with this unstable pluralism greatly facilitated the absorption of 50 million immigrants in little more than a half-century. The existence of ethnic collectivities undoubtedly put some strain on the American body, politic and social; but such collectivities also facilitated the relatively smooth and harmonious integration of immigrants into American life. It may also have enriched the national life. The right question might rather be, Under what circumstances is the use of the ethnic differentiation chart functional for American society and under what circumstances is it dysfunctional? To leave aside sociological terms, whether ethnicity is good or bad "depends." On what it depends is a question that we find extremely difficult to answer at present. A serious study of the natural history and the social structure and culture collectivities must be made, and we must proceed with all due speed before any answer can be assayed with confidence.

NOTES

1. I prefer the term "British-American," which was used in pre-Revolutionary days and resurrected before World War I as a response to Irish pressure on the American government.

2. See, for example, Gordon (1964), Lieberson (1963), Zangwill (1917), Kallen (1956), Berkson (1920), and Drachsler (1920).

3. It is true, of course, that a given well-to-do Irishman and well-to-do Pole may have far more in common with each other than they do with less affluent members of their own ethnic group. I do not want to give the impression here that because I think ethnic differences are important I do not believe that social class differences are important too. Obviously they are.

4. It might be a mistake to conclude that the self-conscious formation of an ethnic group is a new development in American society. One wonders what reason there is to think that the leaders of previous efforts at ethnic group construction were acting unself-consciously.

5. See, for example, the recent writings of Robert Alter, Norman Podhoretz, and Harold Isaacs in *Commentary*.

6. I am not inclined to subscribe to Lévi-Strauss's view.

7. One of our colleagues observed that when she was growing up in Florida she thought of herself as an American; when she went to Washington, D.C., she discovered that she was Cuban; and when she came to Chicago, she was told that she was "Spanish-speaking."

8. Might I suggest that trying to end conflict and oppression by eliminating diversity is like trying to dry up the ocean in order to abolish hurricanes? It probably won't work; if it did, it might do more harm than good.

9. Reprinted by permission.

10. James Duran suggests that in cities in Kenya the ethnic diversity that emerges may be more like the American variety than the European. See "The Ecology of Ethnic Groups from a Kenyan Perspective," *Ethnicity* 1 (April 1974), pp. 000–000.

11. Figure 4 is a simplification of Gordon's position in his book, *Assimilation in American Life*. New York: Oxford University Press, 1964. Gordon's position has become more refined and subtle through the years, and was presented in its most recent form in a paper at the

American Academy Conference of Ethnicity, Boston, October 26–28, 1972. The forthcoming collection of the papers from this conference, *Ethnicity in Our Time*, edited by Daniel P. Moynihan and Nathan Glazer, will contain the Gordon essay.

12.   See his book, *Ethnic Diversity in Catholic America.* New York: John Wiley & Sons, 1973.

13.   The archbishop of Boston is Portuguese, the archbishop of Philadelphia and president of the American hierarchy is Polish, the bishop of Brooklyn is Italian, the archbishop of Cincinnati is Italian, the archbishop of Washington is German, the bishop of Manchester is French; but the Irish still run the American Church. They constitute 15 per cent of the Catholic population, 30 per cent of the clergy, and over half of the hierarchy. See Andrew M. Greeley, *American Priests: A Report of the National Opinion Research Center.* Chicago, 1971.

REFERENCES

Berkson, Isaac B. *Theories of Americanization: Critical Study.* American Education: Its Men, Institutions and Ideas Series. New York: Arno Press, 1920. Reprinted in 1969.

Brown, Thomas N. *Irish-American Nationalism: Eighteen Seventy to Eighteen Ninety.* Philadelphia: J. B. Lippincott Company, 1966.

Chock, Phyllis Pease. "Greeks in the United States." Unpublished Ph.D. dissertation, University of Chicago, 1969.

Cruse, Harold. *Crisis of the Negro Intellectual.* New York: William Morrow and Company, Inc., 1971.

Drachsler, Julius. *Democracy and Assimilation: The Blending of Immigrant Heritages in America.* Westport, Conn.: Negro University Press, 1920. Reprinted in 1971.

Dunne, Finley, P. *Mr. Dooley in Peace and War.* Boston: Scholarly, 1898.

Fabian, Ilona. "The Transformation of Culture Knowledge and the Emergence of Ethnicity Among Czech Immigrants in Chicago." Unpublished research proposal, Department of Anthropology, University of Chicago, 1972.

Glazer, Nathan. "Ethnic Groups in America," in *Freedom and Control in Modern Society*, Monroe Berger, Theodore Abel, and Charles H. Page, eds. New York: D. Van Nostrand Company, 1954.

Glazer, Nathan and Daniel P. Moynihan. *Beyond the Melting Pot*, 2nd ed. Cambridge: MIT Press, 1970.

Gordon, Milton. *Assimilation in American Life.* New York: Oxford University Press, 1964.

Greeley, Andrew M. "The Demography of Ethnic Identification." Unpublished paper, 1972.

Greeley, Andrew M. and William C. McCready. "The Transmission of Cultural Heritages: The Case of the Irish and the Italians." Paper presented at the Seminar on Ethnicity of the American Academy of Arts and Sciences, Boston, Oct. 26–28, 1972.

Greene, Victor R. *The Slavic Community on Strike.* Notre Dame, Ind.: Notre Dame Press, 1968.

Harris, Rosemary. *Prejudice and Tolerance in Ulster: A Study of Neighbors and Strangers on a Border Community.* New York: Rowman, 1972.

Kallen, Horace M. *Cultural Pluralism and the American Idea.* Philadelphia: University of Pennsylvania Press, 1956.

Kammen, Michael. *People of Paradox.* New York: Alfred A. Knopf, 1972.

Levine, Erwin L. "The Ghost of John C. Calhoun and American Politics." Skidmore College Faculty Research Lecture reprint, 1972.

Lieberson, Stanley. *Ethnic Patterns in American Cities*. New York: The Free Press, 1963.

Mason, Philip. *Patterns of Dominance*. New York: Oxford University Press, 1970.

Matza, David. *Delinquency and Drift*. New York: John Wiley and Sons, Inc., 1964.

McCready, William C. and Andrew M. Greeley. "Fundamental Belief Systems of the American Population." A study in progress at NORC, sponsored by the Henry Luce Foundation, 1973.

Metzger, L. Paul. "American Sociology and Black Assimilation: Conflicting Perspectives." *American Journal of Sociology,* **76,** 4 (January 1971), pp. 644–647.

Reed, John Shelton. "The Cardinal Test of a Southerner: White Southerners as an Ethnic Group." Unpublished paper, University of North Carolina, 1972.

Schermerhorn, Richard A. *Comparative Ethnic Relations: A Framework for Theory and Research*. New York: Random House, 1969.

Suttles, Gerald D. *The Social Construction of Communities*. Chicago: University of Chicago Press, 1972.

Tyack, David. "Forming the National Character: Paradox in the Educational Thought of the Revolutionary Generation." *Harvard Educational Review,* **36** (1966), pp. 31–32.

Wilensky, Harold L. "Mass Society and Mass Culture." *American Sociological Review,* **29,** 2 (April 1964), pp. 173–197.

Wood, Gordon. *Creation of the American Republic 1776–1787*. Chapel Hill: University of North Carolina Press, 1969.

Zangwill, Israel. *The Melting Pot*, 2nd revised ed. New York: Macmillan, 1917.

Zeman, Douglas. "*E Pluribus Unum?*: Factors in Ethnic Assimilation." Unpublished Ph.D. dissertation, University of Chicago, 1973.

14.   CONCLUSION

ANDREW M. GREELEY AND WILLIAM C. McCREADY

THIS PRELIMINARY RECONNAISSANCE has been an investigation of diversity in American society. It is a reaction to the assumption that diversity that is not related to age, social class, and race (and more recently, sex) is disappearing in American society. This assumption of homogenization is hard to contend with. It rarely becomes explicit, and when one adduces evidence, as we have in this book, that it is in error, many social scientists assert that they never held the assumption in the first place.

Some sociologists we know will comment in great detail and marvel about the differences between the Czech tradesmen who work in their summer resort areas and their Jewish university faculty colleagues. They will also tell anecdotes about their grandmothers from the old country, yet they will conclude by wondering if ethnicity is not a dangerous thing. They will not ask nationality or denomination questions (other than the general categories, Protestant, Catholic, Jew) in their survey questionnaires and rarely look at regional differences other than South and non-South. One must not permit the impressions of everyday life to interfere with the dogmatic assumptions that guide our research.

Diversity, we are told, is disappearing. But such an assertion is a slippery proposition. Diversity is disappearing relative to what? Is the differentiation with which we have been occupied in this volume less than it was 25 years ago? If so, how do we know? A heroic act of faith is not enough. Furthermore, even if it is disappearing, is there not still enough of it around to justify studying it, if only because the disappearance of so much diversity ought to be interesting to watch?

We began this book with certain relatively simple questions:

1. *Are the Catholic ethnics in fact more "blue collar" than anyone else?* We discovered that with the possible exception of Poles (who are moving up the mobility ladder), the ethnics are no more blue collar than any other group in the society. And some of them, most particularly the Irish and to an increasing extent the Italians, are becoming predominantly upper middle class.

2. *Do ethnic cultures survive even after sustained periods in the United States?* The answer was that to some extent some dimensions of the ethnic culture do indeed survive and enable us to predict some aspects of the behavior of the children, grandchildren, and great grandchildren of immigrants.

3. *Do ethnically linked cultures diminish with generation and education?* We found indications that many ethnically linked cultural traits do indeed survive. The Irish, for example, are a highly political group even into the third and fourth generations. Even young college-educated Irish women have a very traditional view of the role of women.

4. *Is the "ethnic factor" the same as the religious factor?* Our evidence is that it is not; indeed, ethnicity is a more powerful predictor of attitudes and behavior than religion.

5. *Is ethnicity merely another way of looking at social class?* Are differences that are apparently ethnic in fact social class (as measured by education) differences? Our evidence is that some of the ethnic diversity we have uncovered is independent of social class differentiation. It is not explained by differences in social class.

6. *How does ethnicity compare to social class as a predictor of attitudes and behavior?* Using the technique of multiple classification analysis, we discovered that on some variables ethnicity net of social class had about the same impact on attitudes and behavior as did social class net of ethnicity. We concluded that it made as much sense to drop an ethnic question from a questionnaire as it did to drop an occupational question.

7. *How are ethnic cultures and heritages transmitted?* It seems at least plausible at the present time to suggest that they may be transmitted in the very early years of life in a context of the different family structures that seem to exist in different ethnic groups.

8. *Is ethnic consciousness required for the transmission of ethnic culture?* Our evidence would indicate that there are surprisingly low correlations between ethnic consciousness and the persistence of ethnic traits.

9. *Is ethnic diversity socially dysfunctional?* We could find little evidence that most of the so-called white ethnic groups were any less liberal politically, socially, or racially than the rest of society. There was evidence that on some issues they were more liberal. Only Polish Catholics seemed to fit the stereotype of the "white ethnic backlash," and even here we were able to explain a good deal of this so-called backlash phenomenon.

10. *Are the white ethnics alienated?* On the contrary, most of them seem to be quite successful in American society and anything but alienated. The one possible exception to this is the Polish group.

11. *Is there denominational and regional differentiation in American Protestants that may constitute the Protestant equivalent of nationality for the Catholic ethnic groups?* We found fascinating diversity among American Protestants both in regional and denominational categories. The Southwest and Mountain regions, the Lutherans and the Congregationalists, as well as the Baptists and the fundamentalists, seemed to represent different subcultures somewhat similar to the Catholic ethnic groups. Furthermore, there were notable regional differences within the Protestant denominations. Finally, we also discovered striking regional diversity among the Catholic ethnic groups.

12. *Is there an "alternative perspective" to the "melting pot" and "cultural pluralism" dilemmas that emerge in a consideration of ethnic differentiation?* We suggested that the the ethnogenesis model, stressing the complex interaction between heritage, culture, and identification, may be a useful complement to the assimilation-acculturation model. American ethnic groups may be dynamic and flexible institutions for becoming a part of American society.

In Chapter 13 we suggested a number of areas for further research, a set of new questions to be asked within the context provided by out tentative answers to those questions we began with. To recapitulate these suggestions briefly, we think six areas need further investigation:

1. How was new ethnic consciousness created among the immigrants to American cities? Research on currently developing ethnic consciousness may give us some insights as to how the consciousness for the ethnic groups of western European origin was developed between a half century and a century ago.

2. How are the implicit and "less than conscious" ethnic traits transmitted from generation to generation? Why is it, for example, that fourth generation Irish are both more politicized and more inclined to drink than other groups in the society, quite independently of whether they are conscious of being Irish or not?

3. Are there different processes of socialization into meaning systems in the various communities of meaning in American society? Is socialization different, for example, among Poles, Jews, blacks, and Irish?

4. What happens to the children of ethnically mixed marriages? With which group, if either, do they choose to identify? Which ethnically linked traits, if any, are transmitted? Is the mother's or the father's group more powerful? Or is it the parent of the same sex or the parent of the opposite sex who has the dominant ethnic influence? Do some ethnic groups have higher status than others? Such questions are obviously of considerable importance given the fact that exogamy rates among American ethnic groups increase rather rapidly, at least up to a point. Unfortunately, none of the sample currently available to us provides us with a sufficient number of respondents to enable us to answer these questions.[1]

5. What happens to the "cultural baggage" brought by the first generation? Some of it disappears, some of it does not, some of what remains "mutates" in the history of the ethnic group in this country. What survives, what disappears, and what mutates? How?

6. What are the different styles of "intimate" behavior among ethnic groups? How do the various groups "do" family, marriage, friendship, birth, death? Is it possible in the United States to divide the population into "communities of consciousness"? Can we map these communities within the social matrix while remembering that their tracings may be only one of many acetate overlays of that matrix?

If one of the principal measures of the success of a research enterprise is its capacity to generate more questions than answers, it may well be that we can claim some success. We have provided some answers, but in the process we have raised questions that seem even more difficult than those we posed originally.

There have been times during the past two years when we have wondered about the vitality of the new interest in ethnicity. It is a subject that a small but distinguished band of political scientists and sociologists (Gordon, Glazer, Lieberson, Moynihan, Wolfinger, Wilson, Banfield, Parenti) have labored on for many years. Suddenly it seems to have become popular—although our colleagues in history tell us that it is about time. Historians never had to "rediscover" ethnicity because they have known about it all along. The mass media suddenly became conscious of the ethnic and the religious diversity of the country. The popular and not so popular national journals began to write about it. Ethnicity was a fad, and fads have a way of dissipating quickly in American society. (Martin Marty of the University of Chicago Divinity School has said that one publishing season is a fashion, two a trend, three a movement, and four is an epoch.) A small amount of impressive work had been done on American ethnicity, and it began to look as if more were beginning; but the debate rages as to whether or not this "more" was a serious scholarly thrust or merely a passing fashion.

Ethnicity remains a sensitive subject. We think that those who write it off as a fad are wrong. We began our research with the knowledge that relatively little was known about American ethnic groups, and we are witnessing the birth of a new journal, *Ethnicity,* which has in its files 800 pages of manuscript. If we are raising more questions than we can answer, then we do so with the consoling thought that many others are now asking questions too.

This leaves the question raised by many observers of American society. Is ethnicity a positive force, or should we work to eliminate it from our consciousness? Few sociologists would argue that sex, age, socioeconomic, and racial differentiation are peripheral forms of human diversity that could and should be ignored when they design social research. However, many of these same scholars consider religious, linguistic, ethnic, and regional diversity to be so peripheral to our understanding of social processes that they seldom consider these forms of diversity worthy of serious investigation.

Does the region, the clan, the neighborhood, the "local," have a right to its existence in a rational, contractual, universalistic society? Are these forces not ultimately dangerous to the common good? Are they not divisive and polarizing influences that militate against the "let's all pull together" spirit that forms the mythical base for social progress? Does one have the right to speak, as the radical political scientist John Schaar does, of the "noble tension between love of your own place and respect for someone else's"?

Implicit in this questioning of the right of the particular in society to exist is the assumption that it can be eliminated. Also implied even more subtly is the judgment that it would be a good thing to eliminate it.

Universalists seem to be every bit as good at making war and ravaging the environment as particularists. Indeed, there is strong logic in the position that a man firmly rooted in his own homeland is far less likely to take steps to endanger either the peace or the natural purity of that land than one who finds his values diffused across all lands. Particularism is capable of small steps taken one at a time, and that is the way ideals become realized.

Even if it were possible to eliminate particularism, if it were true that Dante's passionate love for his native city of Florence would not have been tolerated in a more rational, "civilized" era, should we attempt its elimination? Perhaps the alternative to a society tearing itself apart through excessive polarization is not homogenization but harmonization. The lasting achievement of American society has not been its ability to eliminate diversity and particularism but rather the development of ways of being able to harness the powers of flexible expression contained in a system of diverse cultural heritages. The appropriate research question does not involve a judgment of whether pluralism is right or wrong; it is, rather, How does it work?

This is an appropriate if difficult question for social scientists to ask. It is difficult because it runs counter to the universalistic style of thought inherent in any elite segment of a population. "Seeing the larger picture," "long-range planning," and "humanitarian ideals" all make it difficult for a liberal intellectual elite to avoid implying that everyone should ultimately share these ideals and goals. Homogenization, in other words, means that everyone should agree with the elite view of social reality even though not all would be permitted to shape it.

We confess to thinking that such a society would be a pretty dull place.

NOTE

1. Research currently being undertaken in conjunction with Alexander Astin, Director of Research for the American Council of Education, on a very large sample of college freshman is beginning to shape some answers to these questions.

AMERICAN ETHNICITY:
A SELECTED BIBLIOGRAPHY

General

Abramson, Harold J. "Ethnic Diversity within Catholicism: A Comparative Analysis of Contemporary and Historical Religion." *Journal of Social History*, 4 (Summer 1971), pp. 359–388.

———. *Ethnic Diversity in Catholic America*. New York: John Wiley & Sons, 1973.

Allswang, John M. *A House for All People*. Lexington: University Press of Kentucky, 1971.

American Immigration Collection Series 1. Separately titled volumes. Edited by Oscar Handlin *et al*. Reprinted in 41 volumes. New York: Arno Press, 1969.

American Immigration Collection Series 2. Separately titled volumes. Edited by Victor Green *et al*. Reprinted in 33 volumes. New York: Arno Press, 1970.

American Jewish Committee. *The Reacting Americans: An Interim Look at the White Ethnic Lower Middle Class*. New York: The American Jewish Committee, 1968.

Anderson, Charles H. *White Protestant Americans: From National Origins to Religious Group*. Englewood Cliffs, N.J.: Prentice-Hall, 1970.

Bailey, Harry A., and Katz, Ellis, eds. *Ethnic Group Politics*. Columbus, Ohio: Charles E. Merrill Publishing Co., 1969.

Baltzell, E. Digby. *An American Business Aristocracy*. New York: Macmillan, 1962.

———. *The Protestant Establishment*. New York: Random House, 1964.

Banfield, Edward C., and Banfield, L. F. *The Moral Basis of a Backward Society*. Glencoe, Ill.: The Free Press, 1958.

———, and Wilson, James Q. *City Politics*. Cambridge: Harvard University Press, 1963.

———, and Wilson, James Q. "Public-Regardingness as a Value Premise in Voting Behavior." *American Political Science Review*, **58** (December 1964), pp. 876–887.

Barron, Milton L. *The Blending American: Patterns of Intermarriage*. Chicago: Quadrangle Books, 1972.

Barth, Frederik, ed. *Ethnic Groups and Boundaries: The Social Organization of Culture Differences*. Boston: Little, Brown and Company, 1969.

Bellush, Jewel, and David, Stephen M., eds. *Race and Politics in New York City: Five Studies in Policy-Making*. New York: Praeger Publishers, 1971. Paperback.

Berger, Bennett M. *Working-Class Suburb: A Study of Auto Workers in Suburbia*. Berkeley: University of California Press, 1968.

Berger, Peter. "The Blueing of America." *New Republic*, April 3, 1971.

Berghe, Pierre L. van den. *Race and Racism: A Comparative Perspective*. New York: John Wiley & Sons, 1967.

Berkson, Isaac B. *Theories of Americanization: A Critical Study*. New York: Arno Press, 1969. (Reprinted from 1920 edition.)

Bernard, William S. *American Immigration Policy*. New York: Harper, 1950.

Billington, Ray Allen. *The Protestant Crusade, 1800–1860: A Study of the Origins of American Nativism*. New York: Macmillan, 1938.

Bradburn, Norman M., Sudman, Seymour, and Gockel, Galen L. *Racial Integration in American Neighborhoods*. Chicago: Quadrangle Books, 1970.

Note: Material preceded by two asterisks may be requested from the Center for the Study of American Pluralism, National Opinion Research Center, University of Chicago, Chicago, Illinois 60637.

Brown, Francis J., and Reucek, Joseph S., eds. *Our Racial and National Minorities: Their History, Contributions and Present Problems.* New York: Prentice-Hall, 1952.

———. *One America: The History, Contributions, and Present Problems of Our Racial and National Minorities.* 3rd. rev. ed. New York: Prentice-Hall, 1952.

Brown, Lawrence. *Immigration.* New York: Langman, Green and Co., 1933.

Campbell, Angus. *White Attitudes Toward Black People.* Ann Arbor: Institute of Survey Research, University of Michigan, 1971.

Cavan, Ruth Shonle, and Cavan, Jordan T. "Cultural Patterns, Functions and Dysfunctions of Endogamy and Intermarriage." *International Journal of Society and the Family,* **1** (May 1971), special issue.

Clark, Terry N. "Citizens, Values, Power and Policy Outputs: A Model of Decision-Making." *Journal of Comparative Administration,* **4** (February 1973) pp. 385–427.

Cohen, David K. "Immigrants and the Schools." *Review of Educational Research,* **40** (February 1970), pp. 13–27.

Coles, Robert, and Erikson, Jon. *Middle Americans: Proud and Uncertain.* Boston: Little, Brown and Company, 1972.

Davis, James. *Great Aspirations.* Chicago: Aldine Publishing Company, 1964.

Dissent. "The World of the Blue-Collar Worker." Special issue (Winter 1972).

Drachsler, Julius. *Democracy and Assimilation: The Blending of Immigrant Heritages in America.* Westport, Conn.: Negro University Press, 1971. (Reprinted from 1920 edition.)

Duncan, Otis Dudley, and Featherman, David L. "Psychological and Cultural Factors in the Process of Occupational Achievement." *Social Science Research,* **1** (June 1972) pp. 121–146.

Edwards, David L. *Religion and Change.* New York: Harper & Row, 1970.

Ehrlich, Howard. *The Social Psychology of Prejudice.* New York: John Wiley & Sons, 1973.

Eisenstadt, S. N. *The Absorption of Immigrants.* Glencoe, Ill.: The Free Press, 1955.

———. *Essays on Comparative Social Change.* New York: John Wiley & Sons, 1965.

Enloe, Cynthia H. *Ethnic Conflict and Political Development.* Boston: Little, Brown and Company, 1973.

Ernst, Robert. *Immigrant Life in New York City, 1825–1863.* Empire State Publications Series No. 37. New York: Friedman, 1949.

Feagin, Joe R., ed. *The Urban Scene: Myths and Realities.* New York: Random House, 1973.

Featherman, David L. "The Socio-Economic Achievement of White Religio-Ethnic Subgroups." *American Sociological Review,* **36** (April 1971).

Feinstein, Otto. *Ethnic Groups in the City.* Lexington, Mass.: Heath Lexington Books, 1971.

Fellows, Donald K. *A Mosaic of America's Ethnic Minorities.* New York: John Wiley & Sons, 1972.

Ferkiss, Victor. *Technological Man: The Myth and the Reality.* New York: George Braziller, 1969.

Fishman, Joshua, A., ed. *Language Loyalty in the United States.* London and The Hague: Mouton, 1966.

Francis, E. K. "The Nature of the Ethnic Group." *American Journal of Sociology,* **52** (March 1945) pp. 393–400.

Friedman, Murray, ed. *Overcoming Middle Class Rage.* Philadelphia: Westminister Press, 1971.

Fuchs, Lawrence H. ed. *American Ethnic Politics.* New York: Harper Torchbooks, 1968.

Gans, Herbert. *The Urban Villagers*. Glencoe, Ill.: The Free Press, 1962.

———. *The Levittowners*. New York: Pantheon, 1967.

Geertz, Clifford. "The Concept of Culture and the Concept of Man." *Social Education*, **32**, 2 (February 1968).

———. *Islam Observed*. New Haven: Yale University Press, 1969.

Gelfand, Donald E., and Lee, Russell D. *Ethnic Conflicts and Power: A Cross-National Perspective*. New York: John Wiley & Sons, 1973.

Gilkey, Langdon. *Naming the Whirlwind*. Indianapolis: Bobbs-Merrill, 1969.

Gill, James. "Why We See It in Priests." *Medical Insight* (December 1969).

Glazer, Nathan. "Ethnic Groups in America." Part of the symposium *Freedom and Control in Modern Society* by Monroe Berger, Theodore Abel, and Charles H. Page. New York: Van Nostrand, 1954.

———. "The Integration of American Immigrants." *Law and Contemporary Problems* **21** (Spring 1956), pp. 256–269.

———. "Dynamics of Ethnic Identification." *American Sociological Review*, **23**, 1 (1958), pp. 31–40.

———. "The Immigrant Groups in American Culture." *The Yale Review,* **48** (March 1959), pp. 382–397.

———. "Blacks and Ethnic Groups: The Difference and the Political Difference, it Makes." *Social Problems*, **18** (Spring 1971), pp. 444–461.

———. "Slums and Ethnicity," in *Social Welfare and Urban Problems,* Thomas D. Sherrard, ed. New York: University of Columbia Press, 1971.

———, and Moynihan, Daniel Patrick. *Beyond the Melting Pot*, 2nd ed. Cambridge: MIT Press, 1970.

Gleason, Phillip. "The Melting Pot: Symbol of Fusion or Confusion?" *American Quarterly,* **16** (Spring 1964), pp. 20–46.

Goering, John M. "The Emergence of Ethnic Interests: A Case of Serendipity." *Social Forces,* **49** (March 1971), pp. 379–84.

Gordon, Albert I. *Intermarriage: Interfaith, Interracial, Interethnic*. Boston: Beacon Press, 1966. Paperback.

Gordon, Milton. *Assimilation in American Life*. New York: Oxford University Press, 1964.

Gosnell, Harold. *Machine Politics: Chicago Model*. Chicago: University of Chicago Press, 1937.

Gottfried, Alex. *Boss Cermak of Chicago: A Study of Political Leadership*. Seattle: University of Washington Press, 1962.

Greeley, Andrew M.

Books

———. *The Catholic Experience: A Sociologist's Interpretation of the History of American Catholicism*. New York: Doubleday, 1967.

———. *Why Can't They Be Like Us?* New York: E. P. Dutton, 1971.

———. *The Denominational Society*. Glenview, Ill.: Scott, Foresman, 1972.

———. *Unsecular Man: The Persistence of Religion*. New York: Schocken Books, 1972.

————. *Building Coalitions: American Politics in the 1970s.* New York: New Viewpoints, 1974.

————, Marty, Martin E., and Rosenberg, Stuart E. *What Do We Believe?* New York: Meredith Press, 1968.

**Articles

————. "A Note on Political and Social Differences Among Ethnic College Graduates." *Society of Education,* **42,** 1 (Winter 1969), pp. 98–103.

————. "Intellectuals as an Ethnic Group." *New York Times Magazine,* July 12, 1970, p. 22.

————. "Religious Intermarriage in a Denominational Society." *American Journal of Sociology,* **75,** 6 (May 1970), pp. 949–951.

————. "Ethnic Politics and the Liberal Heartland." Published as "Take Heart from the Heartland." *New Republic,* December 12, 1970, pp. 16–19.

————. "The Rediscovery of Diversity." *Antioch Review,* **31,** 3 (Fall 1971), pp. 343–366.

————. "The New Ethnicity." Published as "The New Ethnicity and Blue Collars." *Dissent,* (Winter 1972), pp. 270–277 (Special Edition).

————. "Political Attitudes Among American White Ethnics." *Public Opinion Quarterly,* **36** (Summer 1972), pp. 213–220.

————. "Civic Religion and Ethnic Americans." *World View,* **16** (February 1973), pp. 21–27.

————. "The 'Religious Factor' and Academic Careers—A Final Continuity." *American Journal of Sociology,* **78** (March 1973), pp. 1247–1255.

————. "Making It in America: Ethnic Groups and Social Status." *Social Policy,* (September/October 1973), pp. 21–29.

————. "Political Participation Among Ethnic Groups in the United States: A Preliminary Reconnaissance." *American Journal of Sociology,* forthcoming.

————, and Sheatsley, Paul B. "Attitudes Toward Desegregation." *Scientific American,* (December 1971), pp. 13–19.

————, and Sheatsley, Paul B. "Attitudes Toward Racial Integration: The South Catches Up," in *Social Problems and Public Policy: I. Inequality and Justice.* Lee Rainwater, ed. Chicago: Aldine Publishing Company, 1973.

**Papers

————. "The Alienation of White Ethnic Groups." Paper presented at the Conference on National Unity. Sterling Forest Gardens, N.Y., November 19–20, 1969.

————. "The Positive Contribution of Ethnic Groups in American Society." Paper presented at a meeting sponsored by the American Jewish Committee, May, 1970.

————. "State of the Union, Black and White." Paper presented at the Chicago Conference, Institute of Public Affairs, Mundelein, Ill., November 4–7, 1970.

————. "The Ethnic and Religious Origins of Young American Scientists and Engineers: A Research Note." Unpublished. October, 1971.

————. "Religion, Ethnicity, and the Scientific Enterprise." Paper presented at the California Institute of Technology Symposium on Women and Minority Groups in American Science and Engineering. Pasadena, California, December 8, 1971.

————. "The Importance of a Neighborhood." Paper presented to the Beverly Community Relations Council. Chicago, January 17, 1972.

————. "Report to the Ford Foundation of the Center for the Study of American Pluralism of NORC." Unpublished. 1972.

————. "The Future of the Ethnic Revival." Paper presented at the National Conference on Ethnicity. Cleveland State University, May 12, 1972.

————. "Towards Understanding America." Paper presented to the Rockefeller Foundation, New York, N.Y., November 22, 1972.

————. "An Alternative Perspective for Studying American Ethnicity. Unpublished. 1973.

————. "The Demography of Ethnic Identification." Unpublished. March 1973.

————. "The Socioeconomic Status of American Ethnic Groups." Unpublished. March 1973.

————, and McCready, William C. "The Transmission of Cultural Heritages: The Case of the Irish and the Italians." Paper presented at the Seminar on Ethnicity of the American Academy of Arts and Sciences, Boston, October 26–28, 1972.

**Greenstone, J. David. "Ethnicity, Race, and Urban Transformation." Paper presented at the meeting of the American Political Science Association. Chicago, September, 1971.

Greer, Colin. *The Great School Legend: A Revisionist Interpretation of American Public Education.* New York: Basic Books, 1972.

Handlin, Oscar. *The Uprooted.* Boston: Little, Brown and Company, 1951.

————. *The American People in the Twentieth Century.* Cambridge: Harvard University Press, 1954.

————. *Race and Nationality in American Life.* Garden City, N.Y.: Anchor Doubleday Books, 1957.

————. *Children of the Uprooted.* New York: Grosset & Dunlop, 1968.

————. *Boston's Immigrants: A Study in Acculturation.* Cambridge: Harvard University Press, 1941. Revised and enlarged edition. New York: Atheneum, 1970.

————. "Historical Perspectives on the American Ethnic Group." *Ethnic Groups in American Life. Daedalus,* (Spring 1961), pp. 202–232. Special Issue.

Hansen, Marcus Lee. *The Immigrant in American History.* Cambridge: Harvard University Press, 1940. Reprinted, Harper Torchbooks, New York: Harper & Row, 1964.

Herberg, Will. *Catholic-Protestant-Jew.* New York: Doubleday, 1955.

Herskovits, Melville J. *Acculturation: The Study of Culture Contact.* Gloucester: Peter Smith, 1971.

Highham, John. *Strangers in the Land: Patterns of American Nativism, 1860–1925.* New Brunswick, N.J.: Rutgers University Press, 1955.

Isaacs, Harold. "Group Identity and Political Change: The Role of Color and Physical Characteristics." *Daedalus,* **96** (1967), pp. 353–375.

Jones, Maldwyn Alan. *American Immigration.* Chicago: University of Chicago Press, 1960.

Kallen, Horace M. *Cultural Pluralism and the American Idea.* Philadelphia: University of Pennsylvania Press, 1956.

————. *People of Paradox.* New York: Alfred A. Knopf, 1972.

Kantrowitz, Nathan. *Ethnic and Racial Segregation in the New York Metropolis: Residential Patterns Among White Ethnic Groups, Blacks, and Puerto Ricans.* New York: Praeger Publishers, 1973.

Kennedy, John F. *A Nation of Immigrants*. Revised and enlarged. New York: Harper & Row, 1964.

Kennedy, Ruby Jo Reeves. "Single or Triple Melting Pot? Intermarriage Trends in New Haven." *American Journal of Sociology*, (January 1944), pp. 56–59.

Killian, Lewis M. *White Southerners*. New York: Random House, 1970.

Kinzer, Donald L. *An Episode in Anti-Catholicism: The American Protective Association*. Seattle: University of Washington Press, 1964.

Kolm, Richard. *Bibliography of Ethnicity and Ethnic Groups*. Washington, D.C.: National Institute of Mental Health, 1973.

Komarovsky, Mirra. *Blue-Collar Marriage*. New York: Random House, 1964.

Ladd, Everett Carl, Jr., and Hadley, Charles D. "The American Party Coalitions: Patterns in Differentiation by Issues, 1940–1970." Paper presented at the meeting of the American Political Science Association, Washington D.C., September 5–8, 1972.

Lane, Robert E., and Lerner, Michael. "Why Hard-Hats Hate Hairs." *Psychology Today*, (November 1970).

Laumann, Edward O. "The Social Structure of Religious and Ethno-Religious Groups in the Metropolitan Community." *American Sociological Review*, 34 (April 1969), pp. 182–197.

Leggett, John. *Class, Race, and Labor: Working-Class Consciousness in Detroit*. New York: Oxford University Press, 1968.

Lerner, Michael. "Respectable Bigotry." *American Scholar*, 38 (August 1969), pp. 606–617.

Levy, Mark R., and Kramer, Michael S. *The Ethnic Factor: How America's Minorities Decide Elections*. New York: Simon & Schuster, 1972.

Lieberson, Stanley. *Ethnic Patterns in American Cities*. Glencoe, Ill.: The Free Press, 1963.

Light, Ivan H. *Ethnic Enterprise in America*. New York: World, 1972.

Litt, Edgar. *Beyond Pluralism: Ethnic Politics in America*. Glenview, Ill.: Scott, Foresman and Company, 1970.

Luebke, Frederick C. *Ethnic Voters and the Election of Lincoln*. Lincoln: University of Nebraska Press, 1971.

Lynn, Otto. *Personality and National Character*. London: Pergamon Press, 1971.

**McCourt, Kathleen. "Politics and the Working-Class Woman: The Case on Chicago's Southwest Side." Unpublished paper. March 1972.

———. "Women and Politics: An Investigation into the Political Consciousness and Participation of Working-Class Women in Chicago." Unpublished Ph.D. dissertation, University of Chicago, 1974.

McCready, William. "Faith of our Fathers: A Study of the Process of Religious Socialization." Unpublished Ph.D. dissertation, University of Illinois Circle Campus, 1972.

McDermott, John. "Laying on of Culture." *The Nation*, 208 (March 10, 1969), pp. 458–462.

McKenna, Marian C. "The Melting Pot: Comparative Observations in the United States and Canada." *Sociology and Social Research*, 53 (July 1969), pp. 433–447.

Mann, Arthur. "A Historical Overview: Education, the Lumpen-Proletariat, and Compensatory Action." Charles V. Daley, ed. *The Quality of Inequality: Urban and Suburban Public Schools*. Chicago: University of Chicago Center for Policy Study, 1968.

Mason, Philip. *Patterns of Dominance*. New York: Oxford University Press, 1970.

Matza, David. *Delinquency and Drift*. New York: John Wiley & Sons, 1964.

Newman, Katherine D. *The American Equation: Literature in a Multi-Ethnic Culture*. Boston: Allyn & Bacon, 1970.

Newman, William M. *American Pluralism: A Study of Minority Groups and Social Theory.* New York: Harper & Row, 1973. Paperback.

Nie, Norman H. "Mass Belief Systems Revisited: Political Change and Attitudinal Structure." *Journal of Politics*, forthcoming.

————, Powell, B., and Prewitt, Kenneth. "Social Structure and Political Participation: Developmental Relationships, Parts I and II." *American Political Science Review*, 2 (June 1969), pp. 361–378 and 3 (September 1969), pp. 808–832.

————, and Verba, Sidney. *Class, Party, and Participation, a Multinational Perspective.* Forthcoming.

**————, and Currie, Barbara. "Political Beliefs among American Ethnics." Unpublished paper, 1972.

Novak, Michael. "White Ethnic." *Harper's*, September 1971, pp. 44–50.

————. *The Rise of the Unmeltable Ethnic.* New York: Macmillan, 1972.

O'Grady, Joseph P., ed. *The Immigrants' Influence on Wilson's Peace Policies.* Lexington: University of Kentucky Press, 1967.

Parenti, Michael. "Ethnic Politics and the Persistence of Ethnic Identification." *American Political Science Review*, 61 (September 1967), pp. 717–726.

Parsons, Ann. *Belief, Magic and Anomie.* Glencoe, Ill.: The Free Press, 1969.

Plax, Martin. "On Studying Ethnicity." *Public Opinion Quarterly*, 36 (Spring 1972), pp. 653–674.

Raab, Earl, ed. *American Race Relations Today: Studies of the Problems beyond Desegregation.* Garden City, N.Y.: Doubleday Anchor Book, 1962.

Rainwater, Lee, ed. *Social Problems and Public Policy I: Inequality and Justice.* Chicago: Aldine Publishing Company, 1973.

Reed, John Shelton. *The Enduring South: Subculture Persistence in Mass Society.* Lexington, Mass: D. C. Heath & Company, 1972.

Reports of the Immigration Commission: Abstracts of the Reports of the Immigration Commission, Vol. 1. Washington, D.C.: U.S. Government Printing Office, 1911.

Reports of the Immigration Commission: The Children of Immigrants in Schools, Vol. 1. Washington, D.C.: U.S. Government Printing Office, 1911.

Rose, Peter I., ed. *Nation of Nations: The Ethnic Experience and the Racial Crisis.* New York: Random House, 1972. Paperback.

Rose, Richard. *Governing without Consensus.* Boston: Beacon Press, 1971.

Rosenberg, Milton J., Verba, Sidney, and Converse, Philip E. *Vietnam and the Silent Majority: A Dove's Guide.* New York: Harper and Row, 1970.

Rosenthal, Erich. "Acculturation without Assimilation?" *American Journal of Sociology*, 66(November 1960), pp. 275–288.

Scammon, Richard M. and Wattenberg, Ben J. *The Real Majority.* New York: Berkeley Publishing Corp., 1972.

Schaar, John. "Reflections on Authority. " *New American Review 8*, 1970.

Schermerhorn, Richard A. *These Our People.* Boston: D. C. Heath & Company, 1949.

————. *Comparative Ethnic Relations: A Framework for Theory and Research.* New York: Random House, 1969.

Schrag, Peter. "The Forgotten American." *Harper's*, August 1969, pp. 27–34.

Segal, Bernard E., ed. *Racial and Ethnic Relations.* New York: Thomas Y. Crowell Company, 1966.

Shannon, James P. *Catholic Colonization on the Western Frontier*. New Haven: Yale University Press, 1957.

Sheir, Carl. "Black and White—Unite or Fight." *Dissent,* **16** (January, February 1969), pp. 22–24.

Shils, Edward. "Primordial, Personal, Sacred, and Civil Ties." *British Journal of Sociology,* **8** (June 1957), pp. 130–145.

Shostak, Arthur, and Gomberg, William, eds. *New Perspectives on Poverty*. Englewood Cliffs, N.J.: Prentice-Hall, 1965.

Smith, Timothy L. "Immigrant Social Aspirations and American Education, 1880–1930." *American Quarterly, 21* (Fall 1964), pp. 523–543.

———. "Religious Denominations as Ethnic Communities: A Regional Case Study." *Church History, 35* (June 1966), pp. 207–226.

———. "Lay Initiative in the Religious Life of American Immigrants 1880–1950," in *Anonymous Americans: Explorations in Nineteenth-Century Social History,* Harven, Tamara K., ed. Englewood Cliffs, N.J.: Prentice-Hall, 1971.

Stein, Rita K. *Disturbed Youth and Ethnic Family Patterns*. Albany: State University of New York, 1972.

Steinfield, Melvin. *Cracks in the Melting Pot: Racism and Discrimination in American History*. Beverly Hills: Glencoe Press, 1970.

Stinchcombe, Arthur L. "Environment: The Cumulation of Events." *Harvard Educational Review, 39* (Summer, 1969), pp. 511–522.

Suchman, Edward A. "Sociomedical Variation Among Ethnic Groups." *American Journal of Sociology, 70* (November 1964), pp. 319–331.

Suttles, Gerald D. *The Social Order of the Slum: Ethnicity and Territory in the Inner City*. Chicago: University of Chicago Press, 1968.

———. *The Social Construction of Communities*. Chicago: University of Chicago Press, 1972.

Swierenga, Robert P. "Ethnocultural Political Analysis: A New Approach to American Ethnic Studies." *Journal of American Studies, 5* (April 1971), pp. 59–79.

Tavuchis, Nicholas. *Pastors and Immigrants*. The Hague: Nijhoff, 1963.

Taylor, Philip. *The Distant Magnet: European Emigration to the U.S.A.* New York: Harper & Row, 1971.

Vecoli, Rudolph J. "Ethnicity: A Neglected Dimension of American History," in *The State of American History,* Herbert J. Bass, Ed. Chicago: Quadrangle Books, 1970, pp. 70–88.

Verba, Sidney, Ahmed, Bashiruddin, and Bhatt, Anil. *Caste, Race and Politics: A Comparison of India and the United States*. Comparative Politics Series. Beverly Hills: Sage Publications, 1971.

———, Nie, Norman H., and Kim, Jae-On. *The Modes of Democratic Participation: A Cross-National Comparison*. Comparative Politics Series. Beverly Hills: Sage Publications, 1971.

———, and Nie, Norman H. *Participation in America: Political Democracy and Social Equality*. New York: Harper & Row, 1972.

Vrga, Djuro J. "Differential Associational Involvement of Successive Factionalism and Alienation of Immigrants." *Social Forces, 50* (December 1971), pp. 239–248.

———, and Fahey, Frank J. "Status Loss as a Source of Ethno-Religious Factionalism." *Journal for the Scientific Study of Religion, 10* (Summer 1971), pp. 101–110.

Warner, W. Lloyd. *Yankee City Series Vol. III*. New Haven: Yale University Press, 1945.

———, and Srole, Leo. *The Social Systems of American Ethnic Groups*. New Haven: Yale University Press, 1945.

Weber, Max. "The Ethnic Group." in *Theories of Society, Vol. I*, Talcott Parsons, Ed. Glencoe, Ill.: The Free Press, 1961.

Weed, Perry L. *Ethnicity and American Group Life: A Bibliography*. National Project on Ethnic America of the American Jewish Committee. New York: Institute of Human Relationships, 1971.

———. *The White Ethnic Movement and Ethnic Politics*. New York: Praeger Publishers, 1973.

Wenk, Michael, Tomasi, S. M., Baroni, Geno, eds. *Pieces of a Dream: The Ethnic Worker's Crisis with America*. New York: Center for Migration Studies, 1972.

Wilensky, Harold L. "Mass Society and Mass Culture." *American Sociological Review,* **29** (April 1964), pp. 173–197.

Wilson, James Q. "Generational and Ethnic Differences Among Career Police Officers." *American Journal of Sociology,* **69** (March 1964), pp. 522–528.

Winch, Robert F., Greer, Scott, and Blumberg, Rae L. "Ethnicity and Extended Familism in an Upper Middle-Class Suburb." *American Sociological Review,* **32** (April 1967), pp. 265–272.

Wittke, Carl. *We Who Built America: The Saga of the Immigrant*. New York: Prentice-Hall, 1939.

Wolfinger, Raymond and Gield, John Osgood. "Political Ethos and the Structure of City Government." *American Political Science Review,* **60** (June 1966), pp. 306–326.

Wood, Gordon. *Creation of the American Republic 1776–1787*. Chapel Hill: University of North Carolina Press, 1969.

Wright, James E. "The Ethnocultural Model of Voting: A Behavioral and Historical Critique." *American Behavioral Scientist,* **16** (May/June 1973), pp. 653–674.

**Zeman, Douglas J. "Three Neighborhood Study." Unpublished paper, 1971.

———. "Political Ethos: A Criticism." Unpublished paper, 1972.

———. "E Pluribus Unam? Factors in Assimilation among Chicago Catholics." Unpublished Ph.D. dissertation. University of Chicago, 1973.

Zangwill, Israel. *The Melting Pot*. 2nd rev. ed. New York: Macmillan, 1917.

Asia

Light, Ivan H. *Ethnic Enterprise in America: Business and Welfare among Chinese, Japanese and Blacks*. Berkeley: The University of California Press, 1972.

Petersen, William. *Japanese Americans: Oppression and Success*. New York: Random House, 1971.

Black

Cruse, Harold. *Crisis of the Negro Intellectual*. New York: William Morrow & Co., 1971.

Frazier, E. Franklin. *The Negro Family in the United States*. New York: Macmillan Co., 1957.

Gutman, Herbert. "Family Structure in American Ethnic Groups." Paper presented at a seminar sponsored by the Center for the Study of American Pluralism, NORC. Chicago, May 10, 1971.

Liebow, Elliot. *Tally's Corner: A Study of Black Streetcorner Men*. Boston: Little, Brown and Company, 1967.

Lincoln, Eric C. *The Negro Pilgrimage in America*. New York: Bantam, 1972.

Metzger, L. Paul. "American Sociology and Black Assimilation: Conflicting Perspectives." *American Journal of Sociology*, **76** (January 1971), pp. 644–647.

The Negro American. Special edition of *Daedalus*, The Journal of the American Academy of Arts and Sciences, **94** (Fall 1965).

Pettigrew, Thomas F. *A Profile of the Negro American*. Princeton: D. Van Nostrand Co., 1964.

Williams, Robin M. *Strangers Next Door*. Englewood Cliffs, N.J.: Prentice-Hall, 1964.

Woodward, C. Vann. *The Strange Career of Jim Crow*. 2nd rev. ed. A Galaxy Book. New York: Oxford University Press, 1966.

British Isles

Erickson, Charlotte. *Invisible Immigrants: The Adaptation of English and Scottish Immigrants in 19th Century America*. Coral Gables: University of Miami Press, 1972.

England

Berthoff, Rolant T. *British Immigrants in Industrial America*. Cambridge: Harvard University Press, 1953.

Schrag, Peter. *The Decline of the WASP*. New York: Simon & Schuster, 1973.

Ireland

Birmingham, Stephen. *Real Lace: America's Irish Rich*. New York: Harper & Row, 1973.

Brown, Thomas N. *Irish-American Nationalism, 1870–1890*. Philadelphia: J. B. Lippincott Company, 1966.

Chubb, Basil. *The Government and Politics of Ireland*. Palo Alto: Stanford University Press, 1970.

Duff, John B. "The Versailles Treaty and the Irish-Americans." *Journal of American History*, **55** (December 1968), pp. 582–598.

**Greeley, Andrew M. "The South Side Irish Since the Death of Studs." Published as "The American Irish Since the Death of Studs Lonigan." *The Critic*, (May/June 1971), pp. 27–33.

———. "Portrait of the Neighborhood Changing." *The Critic*, **30 (September-October 1971), pp. 14–23.

———. "A Most Distressful Nation: The American Irish." Published as "The Irish, 'A Most Distressful Nation!'" *Dissent*, **18 (October 1971), pp. 450–459.

———. "Occupational Choice Among the American Irish." *Eire-Ireland*, **7 (Spring 1972), pp. 3–9.

———. *That Most Distressful Nation: The American Irish*. New York: Quadrangle Books, 1972.

———, and McCready, William C. "An Ethnic Group Which Vanished—The Strange Case of the American Irish." *Social Studies: Irish Journal of Sociology*, (January 1972), pp. 78–79.

Jackson, John A. *The Irish in Britain*. Cleveland: Press of Case Western Reserve, 1963.

Jenkins, Brian. *Fenians and Anglo-American Relations During Reconstruction*. Ithaca, N.Y.: Cornell University Press, 1969.

Larkin, Emmet. "A Devotional Revolution in Ireland—1850 to 1875." *The American Historical Revue*, **77** (June 1972), pp. 625–652.

Leary, William M. "Woodrow Wilson, Irish Americans, and the Election of 1916." *Journal of American History*, **54** (June 1967), pp. 54–72.

Levine, Edwin M. *The Irish and Irish Politicians*. Notre Dame: University of Notre Dame Press, 1966.

Schrier, Arnold. *Ireland and the American Emigration, 1850–1900*. Minneapolis: University of Minnesota Press, 1958.

Wittke, Carl. *The Irish in America*. New York: Russell & Russell, 1970.

Woodham-Smith, Cecil. *The Great Hunger, Ireland 1845–1849*. New York: Harper & Row, 1962.

Scotch-Irish

Dunaway, Wayland F. *The Scotch-Irish of Colonial Pennsylvania*. Chapel Hill: University of North Carolina Press, 1944.

Ford, Henry Jones. *The Scotch-Irish in America. American Immigration Collection Series 1*. New York: Arno Press, 1969.

Wales

Conway, Alan. *The Welsh in America*. Minneapolis: University of Minnesota Press, 1961.

Ellis, David Maldwyn. "The Assimilation of the Welsh in Central New York." *New York History*, **53** (July 1972), pp. 299–333.

Hartmann, Edward George. *Americans from Wales*. Boston: The Christopher Publishing House, 1967.

Rowse, A. L. *The Cornish in America*. London: Macmillan, 1969.

Eastern European

General

Greene, Victor R. "For God and Country: The Origins of Slavic Catholic Self-Consciousness in America." *Church History*, **35** (December 1966), pp. 446–460.

———. *The Slavic Community on Strike: Immigrant Labor in Pennsylvania Anthracite*. Notre Dame: University of Notre Dame Press, 1968.

Portal, Roger. *The Slavs*. New York: Harper & Row, 1969.

Czechoslovakia

Capek, Thomas. *The Czechs in America. American Immigration Collection Series 1.* New York: Arno Press, 1969.

Fabian, Ilona. "The Transformation of Culture Knowledge and the Emergence of Ethnicity among Czech Immigrants in Chicago." Unpublished research proposal, University of Chicago, Department of Anthropology, 1972.

Poland

Fox, Paul. *The Poles in America. American Immigration Collection Series 2.* New York: Arno Press, 1970.

Greenstone, J. David. "Ethnicity, Class and Discontent: The Case of the Polish Peasant Immigrants." Unpublished paper. University of Chicago, 1972.

Radzialowski, Thaddeus. "The View from the Polish Ghetto: Some Observations on the First Hundred Years in Detroit." Unpublished paper. Southwestern State College, 1972.

Thomas, William I., and Znaniecki, Florjan. *The Polish Peasant in Europe and America.* Chicago: University of Chicago Press, 1918.

Wytrwal, Joseph A. *America's Polish Heritage: A Social History of the Poles in America.* Detroit: Endurance Press, 1961.

———. *Poles in American History and Tradition.* Detroit: Endurance Press, 1969.

Wood, Arthur Evans. *Hamtramck: A Sociological Study of a Polish-American Community.* New Haven: College and University Press, 1955.

Zand, H. S. "Polish-American Childways." *Polish American Studies,* **16** (July/December 1959), pp. 78–79.

Russia, Baltics, Ukraine

Davis, Jerome. *The Russians and Rhuthenians in America.* New York: George H. Doran Co., 1922.

———. *The Russian Immigrant. American Immigration Collection Series 1.* New York: Arno Press, 1969.

Halich, Wasyl. *Ukrainians in the United States.* Chicago: University of Chicago Press, 1937.

Parming, Tonu. "Selected Bibliography of Baltic-Americans, Including Materials in Estonian." Unpublished. Yale University, 1973.

Roucek, Joseph S. *Baltic Countries.* Torun, Poland, V 2 (nr. 2, 1936).

———, and Brown, F. J., eds. *One America.* Rev. ed. New York: Prentice-Hall, 1949.

Yugoslavia, Croatia

Govorchin, Gerold G. *Americans from Yugoslavia.* Gainesville: University of Florida Press, 1961.

Prpic, George J. *The Croatian Immigrants in America.* New York: Philosophical Library, 1971.

———. "Croatia and Croatians: An Annotated and Selected Bibliography in English." Institute for Soviet and East European Studies, John Carroll University, 1972.

Germany and the Netherlands

Barry, Coleman J. *The Catholic Church and the German-Americans*. Milwaukee: Bruce Books, 1953.

Child, Clifton J. *The German-American in Politics, 1914–1917. American Immigration Collection Series 2*. New York: Arno Press, 1970.

Cunz, Dieter. *The Maryland Germans: A History*. Port Washington, N.Y.: Kennikat, 1971.

Faust, Albert R. *The German Element in the United States. American Immigration Collection Series 1*. 2 volumes. New York: Arno Press, 1969.

Gleason, Phillip. *The Conservative Reformers: German-American Catholics in the Social Order*. Notre Dame: University of Notre Dame Press, 1968.

Hagedorn, Hermann. *The Hyphenated Family: An American Saga*. New York: Macmillan, 1960.

Hawgood, John A. *The Tragedy of German-America: The Germans in the United States of America During the Nineteenth Century and After*. New York: Arno Press, 1970.

Knittle, Walter A. *Early 18th Century Palatine Immigration*. Baltimore: Genealog Publications, 1965.

Lucas, Henry S. *Netherlanders in America: Dutch Immigration to the United States and Canada 1789–1950*. Ann Arbor: University of Michigan Press, 1955.

Rothan, Emmett H. *The German Catholic Immigrant in the United States, 1830–1860*. Washington, D.C.: Catholic University of America Press, 1946.

Schalk, Adolph. *The Germans*. Englewood Cliffs, N.J.: Prentice-Hall, 1971.

Stoudt, J. J. *The Pennsylvania Dutch*. Allentown, Pa.: Schlecter, 1951.

Walker, Mack. *Germany and the Emigration: 1816–1885*. The Historical Monograph Series 56. Cambridge: Harvard University Press, 1964.

Wittke, Carl. *Refugees of Revolution: The German '48ers in America*. Westport, Conn.: Greenwood Press, 1952.

Zucker, A. E. *The '48ers*. New York: Columbia University Press, 1950.

Jewish

Landes, Ruth, and Zborowski, Mark. "Hypotheses Concerning the Eastern European Jewish Family," in *Social Perspectives on Behavior,* Herman D. Stein and Richard A. Cloward, eds. Glenview, Ill.: The Free Press, 1958.

Lipset, Seymour Martin, and Ladd, Everett C. "Jewish Academics in the United States: Their Achievements, Culture and Politics," in *Jewish Year Book,* Michail Wallace, ed. Hartford, Conn.: Prayer Book, 1971.

Rosenthal, Erich. "Studies of Jewish Intermarriage in the United States." *American Jewish Year Book,* **64** (1963), p. 51.

Sklare, Marshall. *America's Jews*. New York: Random House, 1971.

———. "Intermarriage and Jewish Survival." *Commentary,* **49** (March 1970), pp. 51–58.

Wolfenstein, Martha. "Two Types of Jewish Mothers," in *Childhood in Contemporary Cultures*, Margaret Mead and Martha Wolfenstein, eds. Chicago: University of Chicago Press, 1955.

Mediterranean

Armenia, Syria

Hitti, Philip K. *The Syrians in America*. New York: George H. Doran, 1924.

Malcolm, M. Vartan. *The Armenians in America*. Boston and Chicago: The Pilgrim Press, 1919.

Wolf, Grace Daniels. "The Political Acculturation of Armenian-Americans." Unpublished M.S. thesis, University of Chicago, 1966.

Greece

Chock, Phyllis Pease. "Greeks in the United States." Unpublished Ph.D. dissertation, University of Chicago, 1966.

Fairchild, Henry P. *Greek Immigration to the United States*. New Haven: Yale University Press, 1911.

Kourvetaris, George A. *First and Second Generation Greeks in Chicago*. Athens: National Centre of Social Research, 1971.

Saloutos, Theodore. *They Remember America: The Story of the Repatriated Greek-Americans*. Berkeley and Los Angeles: University of California Press, 1956.

———. *The Greeks in the United States*. Cambridge: Harvard University Press, 1964.

Tavuchis, Nicolaos. *Family and Mobility among Second Generation Greek-Americans*. Athens: National Centre of Social Research, 1972.

Vlachos, Evangelos C. *The Assimilation of Greeks in the United States*. Athens: National Centre of Social Research, 1968.

Xenides, J. P. *The Greeks in America*. New York: George H. Doran Company, 1922.

Italy

Brandfon, Robert L. *Cotton Kingdom of the New South: A History of the Yazoo Mississippi Delta from Reconstruction to the Twentieth Century*. Cambridge: Harvard University Press, 1967.

Campisi, Paul. "Ethnic Family Patterns: The Italian Family in the United States." *American Journal of Sociology*, **53** (May 1948), pp. 443–449.

Child, Irvin L. *Italian or American: The Second Generation in Conflict*. New Haven: Yale University Press, 1943.

Cottle, Thomas J. *Time's Children*. Boston: Little, Brown and Company, 1967.

Covello, Leonard. *The Social Background of the Italo-American Schoolchild*. Leiden: E. J. Brill, 1967.

Cronin, Constance. *The Sting of Change: Sicilians in Sicily and Australia*. Chicago: University of Chicago Press, 1970.

DeConde, Alexander. *Half Bitter Half Sweet: An Excursion into Italian American History*. New York: Charles Scribner's Sons, 1971.

Ianni, Francis A. *A Family Business: Kinship and Social Control in Organized Crime*. Beverly Hills: Sage Publications, 1972.

Iorizzo, Luciano J., and Mondello, Salvatore. *The Italian-Americans*. New York: Twayne, 1971.

Lopreato, Joseph. *Present No More*. San Francisco: Chandler, 1967.

———. "Upward Social Mobility in Political Orientation." *American Sociological Review,* **32** (August 1967), pp. 586–592.

———. *Italian Americans*. New York: Random House, 1970.

McLaughlin, Yans. "Patterns of Work and Family Organization: Buffalo's Italians." *Journal of Social History,* **5** (Fall 1971), pp. 299–314.

Mann, Arthur. *LaGuardia: A Fighter Against His Times 1882–1933*. Philadelphia: J. B. Lippincott Company, 1959.

———. *LaGuardia Comes to Power: 1933*. Philadelphia: J. B. Lippincott Company, 1965.

Musmanno, Michael A. *The Story of Italians in America*. Garden City, N.Y.: Doubleday, 1965.

Nelli, Humbert S. *The Italians in Chicago 1880–1930: A Study in Ethnic Mobility*. New York: Oxford University Press, 1970.

———. "Italians and Crime in Chicago." *American Journal of Sociology,* **74** (January 1969), pp. 373–391.

Pisani, Laurence F. *The Italian in America: A Social Study and History*. New York: Exposition Press, 1957.

Rolle, Andrew G. *The Immigrant Upraised: Italian Adventurers and Colonists in an Expanding America*. Norman: University of Oklahoma Press, 1968.

Tomasi, Lydio. *The Ethnic Factor in the Future of Inequality*. New York: Center for Migration Studies, 1973.

Tomasi, Silvano M., and Engle, Madeline H., eds. *The Italian Experience in the United States*. Staten Island, N.Y.: Center for Migration Studies, 1970.

Vecoli, Rudolph J. "*Contadini* in Chicago: A Critique of the Uprooted." *Journal of American History,* **51** (December 1964), pp. 404–417.

———. "Prelates and Peasants: Italian Immigrants and the Catholic Church." *Journal of Social History,* **2** (Spring 1969), pp. 217–268.

Ware, Carolyn F. *Greenwich Village, 1920–1930*. New York: Houghton Mifflin Company, 1935.

Whyte, William F. *Street Corner Society: Social Structure of an Italian Slum*. Chicago: University of Chicago Press, 1943.

Scandinavian

Bergmann, Leola. *Americans from Norway*. Philadelphia: J. B. Lippincott Company, 1950.

Bjork, Kenneth G. *Saga in Steel and Concrete: Norwegian Engineers in America*. Northfield, Minn.: Norwegian American Historical Association, 1947.

Blegen, Theodore C. *Norwegian Migration to America, 1825–1860*. 2 Volumes. Americana Series, No. 37. New York: Haskell House Publishers, 1969.

Dowie, James I., and Espelie, Ernest M. *The Swedish Immigrant Community in Transition: Essays in Honor of Dr. Conrad Bergendoff*. Rock Island, Ill.: Augustan Historical Society, 1963.

Hoglund, William A. *Finnish Immigrants in America, 1880–1920*. Madison: University of Wisconsin Press, 1960.

Janson, Florence E. *The Background of Swedish Immigration, 1840–1930. American Immigration Collection Series 2*. New York: Arno Press, 1970.

Kolehmainen, John I., and Hill, George W. *Haven in the Woods: The Story of the Finns in Wisconsin.* Madison: State Historical Society of Wisconsin, 1965.

Lindmark, Sture. *Swedish America 1914–1932: Studies in Ethnicity with Emphasis on Illinois and Minnesota.* Studia Historica Upsaliensia XXXVII. Uppsala, Sweden: Scandinavian University Books, 1971.

Stephenson, George M. *The Religious Aspects of Swedish Migration: A Study of Immigrant Churches. American Immigration Collection Series 1.* New York: Arno Press, 1969.

Qualey, Carlton C. *Norwegian Settlement in the United States.* Northfield, Minn.: Norwegian American Historical Association, 1938.

Spanish-Speaking

Borman, Leonard. "Melting Pot: Spanish-Americans and Other Myths." *Library Trends,* **20,** 2 (October 1971), pp. 210–222.

Fitzpatrick, Joseph. "Intermarriage of Puerto Ricans in New York." *American Journal of Sociology,* **71** (November 1966), pp. 395–406.

———. *Puerto Rican Americans.* Englewood Cliffs, N.J.: Prentice-Hall, 1971.

Index